Allis[...]

thank y[...] supp[...] !

FASTEN YOUR
SEAT BELTS

AND EAT YOUR FUCKING NUTS

JOE THOMAS

XOXO

Joe

I dedicate this book to my husband, Matt.

Without you, I'd be single!

This book is filled with a lot of inappropriate shit.
You have been disclaimed.

TABLE OF CONTENTS

Welcome Aboard Letter!

Dear Ladies and Gentlemen, welcome aboard.

If you are reading this, I have successfully finished this book. Thank Madonna, the Material Girl. Writing this book has been the hardest thing I have ever done and I am pleased that it is finally over.

Let me confess something before I say another word. You are bound to find out sooner or later in the pages that follow; I am an atheist. Which means I don't believe in God. I also don't believe in: Satan, cockrings, angels, The Tooth Fairy, Voldemort, cilantro, anal without lube, The Easter Bunny, and finally—make sure the kids have left the room—Santa Claus. A few of you probably just slammed this book shut or threw your iPad against the wall. Things only get worse from this point forward so man up. If I was writing a children's book I would have called it, *Fasten Your Car Seats & Stop Fucking Crying!* With that said, I am not a soulless monster who believes in nothing. Oh, I believe. I believe in Madonna Louise Veronica Ciccone. And that's why I referred to her as The Material Girl. I don't want to confuse anyone into thinking I was talking about Jesus' mom. I refuse to thank a woman who goes around lying to everyone about being a virgin and then pops out a kid nine months later in a manger. Seriously? A manger? Get a fucking hotel room. It's Bethlehem in the year 0, not Gaza in 2015. Personally, I feel way more comfortable thanking a woman who rolls around on the floor singing about being a virgin than one who knocks on stranger's doors in the middle of the night demanding a place to stay professing to be a virgin.

The fact that you are reading this book means more to me than you can ever imagine. My nipples are rock solid. I'm seriously that fucking happy. Unless you downloaded it illegally. In that case I will hunt you down and demand $30.00. That shouldn't be the actual price of this book. I hate to say it but if you paid that much you obviously know nothing about the value of money.

I never set out to write a book. The idea that it's actually happened makes me laugh. Why? Because I can barely speak without stumbling over every other word. And I hate to admit it but I am easily distracted. A Catholic priest at an all-boy's summer camp has an easier time focusing than I do. My husband is notorious for stopping me mid-sentence as I attempt to recant a story and politely remind me, "Use your words, Joe." It's true. Vocabulary and sentence structure are about as foreign to me as dicks are to lesbians.

Then why write a book? Why put myself out there for the world to judge? The answer is quite simple: I am an extrovert who loves to make people laugh. I enjoy telling stories and putting on stand up comedy routines for all my friends. If you've ever experienced one of my storytellings, you understand. I seek applause and approval at every turn. I'm the definition of a true attention whore. And let's be honest, I am a gay man. If there's one thing I'm more comfortable with than discrimination, it's being judged. Gay men are judged every single time they place a dick in their mouth. Sadly, I am not judged as often as some of my gay friends. I thank marriage equality for that cockblock.

When I became a flight attendant I gave up my deepest passion, acting in community theatre. Did you think I was going to say something dirty? I bet you did. No worries. There's enough cock and ball talk in this book to last you a few weeks. Community theatre was the equivalent to a drug addiction. The praise. The cheering. The behind the stage shenanigans. The drunken after parties at the local Chili's. The articles written up in the newspaper in regards to my fabulous acting skills. The Best Lead Actor award I received for my portrayal of George Hay in *Moon Over Buffalo*. The thrill intoxicated me each time the curtain lifted. Unfortunately, taking on the role of full time flight attendant forced me to retire from acting on stage. Lucky for me, I still had the opportunity to stretch my acting muscle daily. The flight attendant role is truly the most challenging role I have ever encountered. Each and every time we step onto the airplane we are depicting a character. Seriously, I hate to disappoint you but we act the fuck out of that role. Enough dramatics that the Academy of Motion Picture Arts and Sciences would struggle producing enough golden statuettes for all of us, and that's even without nominating any black flight attendants. We are constantly acting through a rollercoaster of emotions. Bad mood? Still required to smile. Going through a divorce? Nobody cares. Your cat got squashed under a car 10 minutes before you left for the airport? Who gives a fuck? The fat bitch in 5C wants her third Diet Coke. You know, because she's on a diet.

It never ends.

Becoming a flight attendant preoccupied me enough that I almost forgot how elated acting made me feel. I'd simply stand up in the airplane during each flight and imagine I was performing. The airline even provided us with a handy announcement script to follow verbatim. This tricked me into believing I was in front of an audience who actually paid to see me perform instead of an audience filled with rude motherfuckers who only paid to see how fast I could pour a cup of coffee during turbulence. As days turned into weeks, and eventually months, I noticed my creative muscle begin to wilt.

I fell into a depression. My husband Matt picked up on it quickly. A few months after I started the job we were eating dinner at the dining room table when he asked, "What's wrong? Are you okay?"

"I miss the theatre. I didn't realize how important it was to me."

He responded before I took my next bite, "Why don't you start blogging? You could write and be creative that way."

"A blog? Really? I barely read any books, I don't think I could write."

"Of course you can. You can do anything you set your mind to. You do love to express yourself."

"This is true. I love to Madonna myself." I took a bite and finished it, "I wouldn't even know where to begin."

He grabbed my arm from across the table, "Let me help you," he smiled, "this will be good for you."

And that's how it all began.

It wasn't all TMZ and Huffington Post popularity for my blog. Quite the opposite; it was tragic. Nobody read my shit. Nobody! During the early years, my blog was lucky enough to see 200 other human beings visit in a year. It got to the point where I'd place the laptop on the sofa next to the cats and open it up to a blog page just so another living creature looked at the site instead of me. Sad? Pathetic? I agree. But is it pathetic enough to get you to buy this book again? My bank account hopes so.

My blog, at that time given the name The Joe Show, was more of an online journal. I had no ads, no connections, no audience. Correction: I had an audience that consisted of Matt, his mother, and me. The three of us... and the cats. That was it, and I wrote my fucking ass off. I wrote every single day. I wrote about boring layovers in Milwaukee. I wrote about religion. I wrote about politics. I wrote about topics that I should have left to the professionals. I even wrote about roast beast.

I'm just making sure you were paying attention.

Why not give up? Why continue torturing my soul this way? All I had to do was quit social media and my life would get easier. Right? Wrong. Although I did think about giving it up on a weekly basis, I didn't quit. I questioned myself as to why I continued this charade. What the hell was wrong with people? They'd watch drunk assholes on MTV but wouldn't give my shit a second glance over. The bitterness struck me like spending an afternoon sucking on a big fat lemon.

I even bitched to Matt about it, "Why the hell won't people visit my blog? This post about the DoubleTree beds is fucking hilarious. I don't get it. And the cookies. Don't people care about the warm fucking cookies?"

"Why did you start blogging? Who do you write for?"

He made me think for a brief second. He always does that, "I write for myself."

"Then why are you getting upset? Just continue what you are doing. You love to write. You do it all the time. Just write for yourself."

The best advice anyone has ever passed along to me. I'll say this about my husband, he may not know how to drive but he sure can steer me in the right direction. Side note—when he reads that I will have hell to pay.

My readership drought lasted until I happened to write a blog post instructing passengers how to order a drink on the airplane. It was on that day that The Joe Show was reborn as Flight Attendant Joe. Once I straddled the flight attendant wave of writing, I rode it like a long, hard surfboard.

You thought I was going to say cock? You dirty bitches. This actually pleases me. You will do just fine for the remainder of this book.

After the post about ordering drinks went viral—it really did, I still can't believe it—I wrote one on tips for carry on luggage and another one about flying standby on buddy passes. I created a section in the blog where I shared situations that occurred on my flights and called it Flight Attendant Stories. Once I collected enough flight attendant stories I decided it was time to write a book. Which brings us to this exact moment where I'm ready to share it with the world. If you end up loving this book, I love you for having a sense of humor. If you end up hating this book, you most likely have a redwood tree branch stuck up your ass so, honestly, I'm not too concerned about your opinion.

For legal reasons, most names, years, flight attendant bases, flight destinations, and some sexes have been altered to protect the privacy of all individuals involved in this book. These are true accounts of a flight attendant's life and I have attempted to retell these stories to the best of my ability and memory. With that said, some may also be wine induced fantasies and/or dreams. At this point—who fucking knows.

Now please, place your tray tables and seat backs in the up and locked position. Stow all your carry on items under the seat in front of you and for the sake of every flight attendant on this insane planet... fasten your seat belts and eat your fucking nuts!

P.S. One more important thing before I forget. Anyone reading this book who happens to find themselves on a train with Amy Poehler or Tina Fey PLEASE drop this book in their lap. I don't care which one you give it to first. I'm not picky. I worship them both equally. Here's a tip: if they are traveling together, just throw it in the air and let them fight over it. Thanks in advance!

Sincerely,
Flight Attendant Joe

THE FLIGHT ATTENDANT PERSONALITY GUIDE

The Passive-Aggressive: Doesn't like the flight attendants, pilots, or passengers they are flying with but lies about their feelings. "I'm fine. Nothing's wrong," while hurling bags of nuts through the air at the lady sitting in the window seat.

The Whore: Has three kids with three different fathers and brags about it on the jumpseat. Lives for hook ups while on layovers and thinks it's an honor to be grabbed like a six pack by random strangers at the local biker bar.

The Straight Guy: Really?

The Old Bitch: This lady worked the inaugural Pan Am Clipper flight in 1934 and requires a wheelchair to complete her security checks. Sadly, the bitch won't fucking retire and allow anyone to move up a spot in seniority.

The Sweet Guy: Always willing to lend a hand—and a mouth—when a passenger or pilot requires his service.

The Cougar: You might fuck her but not without copious amounts of alcohol. She likes hanging out at the hotel bar with the young first officers and refuses to buy her own drinks. Rumor has it that having sex with her is like throwing a suitcase in the cargo hold of an airplane.

The Ex-Cop: Starts all conversations with, "I got this. I was a cop." Unfortunately, nobody gives a damn.

The Fattie: Can't fasten their jumpseat harness during take offs and landings but has no problem stuffing their face silly with leftover first class meals.

The Wimp: Is afraid of any type of confrontation. A toddler strapped in a car seat would win a boxing match with this guy.

The Unkept One: Ring around the collar is the last thing this guy should worry about. His shirt's wrinkled, hair disheveled, and has stained pants but stands in the back galley complaining that the material the airline uses for the flight attendant uniforms makes him look "messy".

The Slightly By The Book: She walks throughout the airplane correcting everyone else. Where they should put this, when they should do that, and all while explaining to anyone who will listen why she's the best flight attendant in the Milky Way. Then she turns around and does whatever the fuck she wants.

The Pilot's Wife: She's hot, skinny, sexy, and you want to stab her in the labia with a hot poker.

The Anti-Airline: Hates everything about the airline. The airline gave him a $1,000 bonus and he complained about paying the taxes on it.

The Christian: Preaches about God to you, the other flight attendants, and the pilots—but that's never enough. Once the safety demonstration is completed, this Christian psycho is on the interphone preaching to the passengers like she's Mike Huckabee.

The Biological Clock: This chick demands to hold every newborn on the flight, even if the mother or gay dad doesn't require assistance. TSA checks her bags upon leaving the airport for undead babies and/or fertilized eggs harvested from a sleeping passenger's uterus. She's been known to pump air from her breast into bottles for the hell of it.

The Cat Lady: She's got more pictures of pussy on her phone than a butch lesbian.

The Blogger: Reminds you in the crew briefing that they have a blog and if you act stupid—you'll surely end up a guest star on it.

The Transgender: Wears the female flight attendant uniform but has an Adam's apple the size of a lemon. When she sits down on the jumpseat you don't know if she's got big balls or if she's smuggling prepackaged sandwiches off the flight.

The Flaming Homosexual: This queen's fire could light up the night sky. The planet Jupiter can see him from 365 million miles away. He prances around the airplane to the point where passengers hit their call bells questioning why they smell smoke.

The Reporter: Reminds you constantly about the other flight attendants they have reported throughout the years. The first time they say, "I had to report her..." you jot down their flight attendant number and avoid them for the rest of your career.

The Drama Queen: This flight attendant wants to divert for any possible reason, no matter how ridiculous. The passenger in 11A has a headache and she starts prepping the airplane for an emergency landing.

The Bisexual Nuyorican: During the flight he talks to you about his wife and beautiful children. He even shows you pictures. When you land at JFK he offers you a ride home and then—SURPRISE—he pulls out his uncut dick and offers it up to you like a cheese blintz in the airport food court.

The Couple: Not always love at 38,000 feet. These two met at the airline and they do everything together. They live together, fly together, and constantly fight on the airplane together. You pray they get terminated together.

The Future Pilot: This guy is training to become a pilot and wants everyone to know about it. He tells his fellow flight attendants, the gate agents, the pilots, the passengers, the van driver, the hotel front desk clerk, and even wakes up the sleeping homeless guy outside the hotel to tell him. That's all fine. The annoying part is when he tries explaining to you a play-by-play of what he thinks the pilots are doing in the flight deck during the entire flight.

The Alcoholic: This flight attendant has gone through drug rehab more times than Lindsey Lohan. While working a flight they get randomly tested for alcohol and it comes back positive. The last thing you hear them yelling as security walks them out is, "No! I'm sober. I had ribs last night. It was the Jim Beam Barbecue Sauce."

The Thief: Carries two suitcases when they fly. One for their clothes—one for stolen goods to sell on Craigslist.

The New Hire: This newbie has been with the airline for 20 minutes and is already complaining about their schedule. TWENTY FUCKING MINUTES!

The Ex-Management: Follows all the rules perfectly for the first week they are back on the airplane—after that that they don't give two fucks what happens.

The Comedian: Patiently awaits the day that an employee from human resources meets their flight and removes them from duty for telling one too many dick jokes on the airplane.

The Announcer: You can't keep this flight attendant off the interphone. They have confused the front galley of the airplane for a *Saturday Night Live* stage. Sadly, they are not funny and you wish you could eject them down the emergency evacuation slide into shark infested waters.

The Rule Breaker: This select group knows all the airline rules but refuses to follow them. If the airline requires beverage service to start at the front of the airplane, these folks will start from the back. Flight attendant suitcases go over row 10—these assholes put them over row 20. Report time to the airplane is an hour before departure, these cocky bastards show up whenever they want... with their take-out coffee in hand.

The Celebrity: Actor. Writer. Singer. Wheel of Fortune winner. Server of fucking nuts.

The Slam Clicker: It doesn't matter if they have a 10 hour layover or a 40 hour layover, this flight attendant enters their hotel room and doesn't leave until airport van time.

The Pregnant Breastfeeding One: She pumps herself dry more often than an airplane full of high school rugby players. After she's done, she enjoys showing you her breast milk and adding, "Would you like to try it?"

The Lavatory Napper: A quick bathroom break on a red-eye flight lasts over an hour for this guy. When he comes out—face red, eyes crusty, and hair a mess—he states, "I must have fallen asleep."

The Work Out King: Turns the entire back galley into his own personal 24 Hour Fitness and transforms the airplane door into a Bowflex, but still looks weak.

The Non-Revenue Flight Attendant: They walk on the airplane like you are old friends but you've never met this person in your entire life. Dressed like they just stepped out of a threesome—hair a mess, ripped jeans—and asks you, "Can you buy me a drink? Do you have some headphones? What food options do you have?"

The Book Reader: This person only cares about one thing and one thing only and that's how their book ends. You could be standing in the middle of the airplane screaming for medical assistance while a passenger is having heart attack and this flight attendant waits until they finished the chapter to assist.

The Sex Offender: Has the highest record of complaints from female passengers about inappropriate touching. This is the guy who "accidently" drops a cup of Diet Coke in your lap and then demands he rinses out your vagina with seltzer water.

The Almost Terminated: Brags throughout the entire flight about being on final disciplinary action but insists the airline will never terminate them. The following week your seniority number goes up by one and you never see or hear from that person again.

The Mental Illness: You believe things are going well during boarding and the second after you sit on the jumpseat the other flight attendant looks at you and says, "I'm bipolar and I've stopped taking my medication. Be prepared for anything."

The Celebrator: Keeps so busy celebrating passengers' birthdays, anniversaries, engagements, bar mitzvahs, first time periods, and sex reassignment surgeries that she has no time to do the job she's actually paid to fucking do.

The Drug Smuggler: There's no question about it—this girl swallows... bags of cocaine. Single, works as a part time flight attendant, and lives on the Upper East Side. If you ask her how she does it she'll tell you her guy friend helps out, when he can. When she does work a flight it's usually to Bogota or Mexico City and it's always with an empty suitcase and some Ex Lax.

The Overly Excited Union Supporter: If the union pins, bag tags, and stickers don't give this guy away—the hours of him sitting on the jumpseat explaining the pros and cons of having the union will. He eats, sleeps, and breaths the union. He's so obsessed he made his new girlfriend sign a five year contract and then promoted his mother to union steward.

FEAR IS NOT AN OPTION

In the winter of 1997, I realized I was nothing more than a chicken shit. A 25 year old chicken shit, sleeping on his friend's sofa and working as a male nurse at a medium-sized hospital in Kissimmee, Florida. I trained myself to add the word *male* to my title early in my career. On more than one occasion, I walked into a patient's room to introduce myself and they'd stare at me deadpan, "Oh, you're a male nurse."

It wasn't a question. It was a statement. Like I had no fucking idea who, or what, I was.

I'd write my name on the whiteboard across from the patient's bed and refrain from correcting them with a witty, "Actually, I am a nurse with balls. Now take your medication and go back to sleep."

During this time I was single. Let me just state that being single, gay, and 25 was devastating. To make matters worse I was a virgin. A gay virgin. A 25 year-old gay virgin chicken shit. Teenagers had more sex before they turned 18 than I did in my entire twenties. Don't get me wrong, the last thing I wanted was to be a virgin. Sex was on my mind constantly and I had the cum-filled white tube socks to prove it—a tradition I had kept since I was 13 years old and living at home with my mother, Irene.

Irene found more tube socks under my bed than in the hamper. When she unearthed them she did nothing to help with my embarrassment, "What the fuck is in this sock?"

Looking up and removing my headphones, "What?"

"What's in this sock?"

"Glue." I'd immediately go back to my Walkman.

She quized me again,"Glue? Are you telling me glue is cementing this sock together?"

"Yes."

"Well," she started out of my room, "Please put your glue in a tissue or towel next time."

It was humiliating, but it didn't keep me from filling up my socks well past my mid-twenties.

I had no sexual companionship. There were nights I contemplated turning a bar stool over and humping one of the rusty metal legs. I may have been desperate for sex, but I was not crazy enough to destroy my chances of ever having another healthy bowel movement. Being single was equivalent to being diagnosed with cancer. With cancer there were options: chemotherapy, radiation, smoking copious amounts of weed. My only option was my right hand, or my left when I wanted to feel the touch of a stranger. I spent hours searching for the love of my life in the AOL Instant Messenger "M4M" chat rooms. I even visited chat rooms of other countries: M4M Mexico, M4M Canada, M4M England. I visited so many of these rooms I needed a new passport. The single life hung over my head like storm clouds over someone without an umbrella.

When was I going to meet the man of my dreams? Was he out there? What was I doing wrong? I couldn't see through the thick fog that surrounded my life. When we put our energy into focusing on what we *don't* have we forget everything we *do* have. I forgot what I had while spending countless nights working the graveyard shift concocting a plan to escape my dreadful single life. I was blind to the rich opportunity laid out in front of me. My checking account was overdrawn but what I lacked in dollar bills, I made up for in a different kind of fortune: freedom.

I had the freedom to do anything I wanted and go anywhere I deemed acceptable. I was single, which was something my coupled friends envied and never let me forget. They reassured me how lucky I was to be single but I refused to believe them. I took their words as pity for my situation. I knew a change was on the horizon but I was afraid of what that meant. After months of dread and feeling sorry for myself I concluded it was time to revise my life in a drastic way. That revision included a one way ticket out of Central Florida.

During countless hours working the night shift at the hospital, I created a plan and set it into motion. I looked after my patients but every free second was centered on this project. I picked up extra shifts so I'd be forced to sit at the nursing station and plan my relocation. I was so preoccupied that one night I gave a patient too much insulin and spent the rest of the night vomiting and praying to Madonna that this old lady made it out alive. She did. Don't judge.

I was easily distracted at home but during the late hours at the hospital, when sleep wasn't an option, I found my creative side on how to plan an ambitious move. I did this while eating Filipino food and shooting up patients with too much insulin. It was challenging but I managed. Whenever I had doubts, or fear crept in, I reminded myself I had planned a large move like this before. It was actually an escape.

When I was 15 years old I worked part time at The Grocery Barn, a small grocery store in East Hartford, Connecticut. After months of saving, I collected $400 to secretly purchase two one-way tickets on a Greyhound bus so Irene and I could liberate ourselves from my alcoholic and abusive father. If I had devised a plan then, when my life depended on it, certainly I could do it when I was 25, had a career, and owned my own car.

On a warm early morning in April, right before my shift, I completed the first draft of my plan: a fresh start in a new city. It had to be the perfect city, with a lively gay scene and lots of activities. After laboring over my decision for weeks, I narrowed it down to four cities: Denver, Boston, Phoenix, and Seattle.

Denver offered the Rocky Mountains. I could take up skiing, find the love of my life, and enjoy romantic evenings with him beside the fire. Boston was familiar because I was from New England. I spoke the language and it would be like returning home. Phoenix had beautiful desert landscapes and my relatives lived in nearby Mesa. And then there was Seattle. I had never been to Seattle. I hadn't been to Denver or Boston either, but every time I uttered "Seattle," it rolled off my tongue like I was meant to say it often. I imagined myself telling people, "Hi. I live in Seattle. Where do you live?"

For four months I studied everything I could about these four cities. I spent hours researching online, talking to anyone who had ever visited these cities, and flipped through travel books at the local library deciding which city would welcome me with open arms. I knew the answer. My soul had already moved there even though my body was thousands of miles away.

I had fallen in love with Seattle without ever stepping foot in the state of Washington. Denver was too cold, Phoenix was too hot, and Boston was way too expensive. Seattle, the furthest city of the four, was just right. Seattle had the perfect location between the sea and mountains, but I quickly forgot how far it was from everyone I knew.

When I announced in mid-August that I'd be moving to Seattle, the rest was easy. During the next few months I found myself hired on at Seattle Children's Hospital without ever visiting the hospital for a face-to-face interview. I rented an apartment via fax machine and registered my new Seattle phone number with the telephone company. It was official: I was moving to Seattle. All I had to do was pack my car and drive.

The night before I started my drive to Seattle, I loaded up my black 1997 Kia Sportage, leaving barely enough room to shift gears. I spent my last night on a friend's sofa and told Irene I'd stop at her house before I left so we could have breakfast and say our goodbyes.

Irene was not happy with my decision to move so far away. She confessed later that she spent many nights crying herself to sleep over it. Even though she shed a few tears over my decision, she never stood in my way. I give her credit for that type of control. She encouraged me the entire time even though she never fully understood why I wanted to leave.

That last night I was struck with insomnia. I lay on the sofa and my mind raced faster than a car around a track. Nothing brought down the checkered flag. I gazed at the clock underneath the living room television for hours, watching the minutes creep closer and closer to my departure time.

I finally fell asleep, because the alarm woke me at 5 a.m. After taking a quick shower and packing up the few items I brought into the house, I snuck out unnoticed. When I arrived at Irene's house I honked the horn but found the kitchen windows were devoid of light with zero movement in the house. She always sat at the kitchen table drinking her coffee and enjoying her morning cigarette, so I figured she was still sleeping. I shut off the engine and walked up the sidewalk to the front door. I knocked. Nothing. I wouldn't put it past her to throw a wrench into my plans 20 minutes before my scheduled departure. She had been so cooperative and understanding; this made perfect sense. Her method of destroying my happiness came when I least expected it—the moment I was leaving. I considered turning around, getting in my car, and driving off without saying goodbye. Fuck her and her games. As my mind ran through all the devious things she was doing to me, the door unlocked from the inside and she opened it. Standing in the doorway in her robe she said, "I'm sorry, Joe. I just woke up."

I am such a dick. "That's ok," I walked passed her into the living room, "We don't have to go to breakfast if you don't want," she closed the door and walked over to me, "I'm kinda running late anyway."

She wrapped her arms around me, "I'd really like to go. Let me get dressed," and hurried off to her bedroom.

I meandered around the living room. After a few moments staring at a picture of my grandparents from their wedding day, I moved over and sat on the golden sofa that was once white. The feel of my grandmother's crocheted afghan blanket against my hand soothed me. It made me feel loved, made me feel warm inside. Warm inside? Why was I warm? Did I have to pee? The discomfort came on stronger and stronger until a heavy pain camped out in my stomach. Anxiety had to be normal during a time like this, right? I attributed the feeling to my lack of sleep and that I was already past the time I had allotted myself for breakfast. When I heard Irene's bedroom door open I let go of the afghan and stood up to walk to the back of the house. While she sat on the edge of her bed putting on her shoes I plopped myself down on the other side.

"Are you excited?" She asked cheerfully even though I knew she was miserable that her only child was moving across the country. To her, another planet.

"I don't know. I guess." What was happening to me? Sweat started collecting on my brow and the first drop made its way down the bridge of my nose. The pounding in my chest beat with the force of fifty drums while I fought back the urge to empty the contents of my stomach on her bedspread. A feeling of loneliness took hold of me.

Standing up from the bed she walked around to face me, "Are you ok?"

"I can't go."

"Excuse me?"

"I'm afraid." I looked up at her. I wanted her to smile and be excited but she looked confused and ready to attack—like a burglar broke in to steal her cigarettes and beer. I quickly looked back down to the floor.

"What do you mean you're afraid?" Her agitation rose which made the volume of her voice increase, which ignited her smoker's cough like a raging forest fire. "You've been planning this all year!"

"I can't do it. Something is telling me not to go." I avoided making eye contact again. My own disappointment was too difficult to face, and seeing my reflection in her eyes would have destroyed me.

Always the master at making everything about her, she became enraged, "How dare you put me through this shit for months, and now you don't wanna go?"

"I'm sorry. I don't know what's wrong with me. I was ready to go this morning but now I'm scared." I stood up from the bed and slowly moved to the full length mirror draped in front of her closet door like a starched housecoat. "Maybe I'm not ready to be so far from home."

"Joe, I'm pleased you don't want to go but I'm shocked." She grabbed one of her Winston 100's—pausing for a moment to light it and inhale smoke into her lungs. She looked over at me, "Look at me."

I did as I was told.

"Did your friends put you up to this?"

"They have nothing to do with it," I responded, "I don't know why you always have to bring them up in my shit." My fear of looking at her directly in the eyes faded. I stepped away from the mirror and walked back to the bed and sat down.

Irene took one last drag of her cigarette and choked out, "They are always involved in your shit. That's why I fucking bring them up. You moved out of my house to live with them." Hacking on her last puff, "Now see what you've done. Goddamnit. You've worked me up and I've smoked my cigarette too fast!" She moved to her bedside table and extinguished her cancer stick in the ashtray.

"I gotta go. I'll see you later." I started towards her bedroom door making my way by the nicotine-yellow walls and stained carpet that matched the sofa. The smoke-filled haze lingered for days and attached itself to every stitch of clothing and follicle of hair that entered the house. It was disgusting. I felt bad for her cat, Maggie.

"Run to your friends. You always do," she spit out. I thought she might have been pleased that I chickened out of moving to Seattle, but instead she turned the morning into a war that I was not ready to fight. Irene was always ready to battle with me and I hardly ever backed down. Emotionally drained, I decided to postpone our argument for a later date. There were more important things going on at that moment. I had whiplash from my life doing a complete hundred and eighty degree turn in the past fifteen minutes. I needed Advil and a neck brace—not a knock-down, drag-out fight with Irene.

I walked out the front door and never looked back, but I knew she was behind me. I felt defeated and she wanted me to feel even worse. I climbed in my car and quickly shut the door. Without looking up I turned the key to ignite the engine and backed out of her driveway. Irene was standing in the door yelling something but I already drowned her out with the stereo. After driving a few blocks down the palm tree-lined street with the cookie cutter houses, I pulled over to the side of the road and turned off the engine.

Tears flowed down my chin. As soon as I wiped them off, more followed. My first instinct was to go back to her house and finish the battle. I may not have been prepared to win but I was ready to tell her the fuck off. That was the exact reason I always went running back to my friends, because she was a lunatic. She was a manipulator who made me feel horrible about myself. Irene was never there for me and she never could be. Irene didn't know how to truly love me because she couldn't even love herself. I wanted to turn my Kia around and go back and share all this with her but I chickened out.

The next morning I couldn't shake the pain that crushed my heart with the force of a hundred pound weight. The emotional dam had broken, flooding my entire body with disappointment and regret. My perfect new life was only a three day drive away, but here I was, right back on my friend's lumpy sofa with way too much dog hair. By lunchtime I had reclaimed my old job at the hospital and my familiar life was restored. Seattle was already a memory. Irene ignored my phone calls, which was probably for the best. We both needed time to heal from our dramatic outburst.

I let the fear of loneliness blind me and my goal. What was I actually afraid of? All the hard work was done. All I needed to do was pull out my poster-sized atlas, hit the gas pedal, and enjoy the scenery. I couldn't even do that. I vowed to never let fear dictate my life again but I have learned that vows are easily broken, even ones we make to ourselves.

Fear lay dormant inside me for years until it broke out again like a painful case of shingles. It controlled my every decision and experience. I was hungry for a boyfriend but afraid to go on dates. I craved a new job but barely worked the nursing agency shifts that I picked up. I refused to face Irene because, even though I never admitted it, she was right about my friends. Fear forced me to do things that I would have never done if I had known how to stand up to it. I employed fear as my personal assistant. It stunted my growth as a person, scheduled my life, and managed my experiences. Fear was a parasite, invading the deepest parts of my brain, through my bloodstream, and feeding off the horrors I kept sequestered from my friends, loved ones, and most often myself. Fear delayed me from maturing into a healthy adult who could maintain a loving relationship, prevented me from traveling to exotic locations to lands I never set foot on, and from taking risks.

It kept me in unhealthy relationships when all I really wanted to do was run screaming to escape for the betterment of both individuals involved. I ignored opportunities because fear worked me over like a drunken puppeteer with a marionette. Drinking made these feelings worse.

I've struggled with fear everyday of my life, and even though it has had a strong hold on me, it's not something that defines me anymore. It should never be an obstacle but the wick that lights the fire under our asses to make our dreams come true. Fear should propel us forward to live life and gain knowledge from things we felt too afraid to accomplish. Whether it's going after a job we never thought we were qualified for, winking at the handsome guy across the bar and buying him a drink, or—if you are like me— traveling on an airplane without having a nervous breakdown.

I don't remember the exact moment I wanted to become a flight attendant. It could have been under the influence of drugs, but I don't think the occasional Ibuprofen mixed with a few Bud Lights has the same effect as say, downing four Vicodin. Being hired as a flight attendant was as foreign to me as owning a dog, two things that were not on my to-do list. Dogs are not my pet of choice, and flying was something that I dreaded every time I packed my suitcase. I haven't always been afraid to fly but I have always been afraid to die. In my mind that was the only possible outcome when I boarded a flight. I couldn't control myself. My husband couldn't control me. The seatbelt couldn't contain me. The sweat, tears, and thoughts invading my mind were overwhelming with every noise the airplane made.

"What was that?

"I think they're loading on the bags." Matt said trying to get his thighs into the economy seat.

"What if the cargo door snaps off during the flight and we get sucked out?"

"Does that happen? Why are you thinking of these things?"

"You know it's happened before."

"What?" He asked fighting to get his large frame in a comfortable position.

"The cargo door broke off during a flight and a row of people were sucked out into the engine."

"Jesus Christ! You are so grim. Read your book and relax!"

All that while the airplane was still parked at the gate with the jet bridge attached. Once the pilot released the brake, the tug pushed the airplane away from the gate, and we taxied to the runway; I needed another seat belt extension to make sure I didn't run around screaming.

The charming pilot's voice over the public address system (PA) did nothing to sooth me. Hearing "Ladies and gentlemen, we will be underway shortly. Flight attendants, prepare the cabin and take your seats for departure…" was equivalent to a judge sentencing me to death. Not a peaceful death like lethal injection or falling into a coma. I prayed for that. I'm talking seriously fucked up death by fireball in the sky. The kind of death that melts the skin of your face and results in a member of the NTSB slipping on your entrails in a burnt out corn field in the middle of South Dakota.

That kind of death. The kind that comes from flying on Malaysia Airlines.

The airplane rolled to the end of the runway and I became inconsolable. While Matt rolled his head wondering what to do with me, I fantasized about wringing his neck for getting me on a metal deathtrap.

"What's wrong with you?" He whispered carefully placing his hand on top of my knee. A calming gesture lost to my hysteria.

"Don't touch me. Just leave me alone." I refused to look at him or out the window that I demanded to sit next to.

Irritated his voice rose, "You need to order a bloody mary. You are a mess." After realizing how loud he was his voice lowered, "Calm down. I am only trying to help."

Nothing helped. Matt's calmness intensified my jitters, but explaining that made no sense. Igniting an argument with my husband moments before I was sure to die at the end of the runway was not how I wanted to remember our time together. I wanted to remember the laughs and fun times, not the screams and terrors. The only way to solve the problem was to get me off the airplane and onto a fast moving train. Or my car. I would have ridden a tricycle with training wheels and rainbow tassels to my destination if it were plausible. Anything was better than mustering up the courage it took to sit prisoner on an airplane. None of these were options. I sat in my window seat, suspended in fear, reliving every movement the airplane made until its final right turn to face the long runway.

The roar and pressure from the engines dissolved the glue that held me together. If only I had the option of turning on my cell phone and making a quick call to my therapist, who I was sure could get me through this torture. Unfortunately for me, the electronic device policy was cock blocking my sanity.

What would I even say to her? "Hi Melinda. I'm about to die in a plane crash so I won't make my next appointment. Thank you for everything. Oh yeah, one last thing, what was that breathing technique you taught me?" I really should have paid attention the first time.

Matt observed me like a scientist watching a monkey put together a puzzle. It was moments like this when he questioned my stability and considered never flying with me again. I couldn't blame him. As the airplane sped down the runway, slamming into what seemed like large speed bumps every few feet on, I was seconds away from a mental decompression. Were they fucking kidding me with this? Speed bumps on the runway? Why not just hang me from my belt in the lavatory during take off. This was more of a mental breakdown than a mental decompression although a mental decompression might actually have worked in my favor. Think about it. My mental decompression would cause the oxygen masks to release leading us back to the gate where I'd tell the airline, its flight attendants, pilots, and ground employees to refund my money, keep my airline points, and shove them up their ass. Airline points wouldn't matter because I never planned on flying again. My new best friends instantly became Amtrak, Greyhound, and Budget Rent-a-Car.

While the airplane and its magazine-reading, television-watching, music-listening passengers eased into their freakishly tight coach seats, removing their sneakers for a comfortable flight, I was wishing I had hair to pull out of my head. I'd just pull out Matt's. It was his fault I was here. It wasn't really his fault but someone needed to take the blame. The anticipation of blowing a tire, swerving off the runway, and cartwheeling like a high school cheerleader during football season infected my brain like syphilis. I wanted to shout, "Does anyone have any cocaine? I'll need a dollar bill, too"

Instead of screaming out for drugs, I took cleansing breaths, placed my right index finger and thumb to the bridge of my nose, and rocked back and forth in my window seat. This soothed me into a state of calm. In my warped delusional mind my rocking was assisting the airplane with lift so that we wouldn't return to the Earth and explode into a million pieces.

"Are you alright?" Matt asked as the airplane broke through the dark clouds. I did not respond right away. My life was flashing before my eyes on what looked like an IMAX screen. It was a dull life controlled by fear. Sad. My first thought was that I should have masturbated more often when I was a teenager instead of worrying about getting caught in the restroom stall at Kmart. I also wished I had eaten more chocolate chip cookies for breakfast.

"I'll be alright," I reassured myself aloud as the airplane banked aggressively to the left. I forgot where I was and blurted out, "Oh my god! What's that? Why are we turning?"

Flustered from my outburst and the passengers now craning their necks to see the crazy person, Matt cooley smiled, "We have to turn, babe. If we don't we'll just fly straight and eventually run out of gas and crash into the ocean."

Is that what you tell someone who believes they are about to become shark food?

The five minutes it took for us to go from screaming down the runway until 10,000 feet was an eternity.

The double ding chime was equivalent to the snap of a hypnotist's finger. Once I heard the flight attendant pleasantly reciting our beverage options over the PA I became a different passenger. I was calm, cool—almost human. Matt sensed my bipolar mood shift and relaxed knowing that Dr. Jekyll had returned and Mr. Hyde would reemerge later when we departed from our final destination.

Taking off flared up my fear. My angst wasn't flying at cruising altitude but the time it took to get there. From the moment we reached 10,000 feet until we were safely taxing to the gate at our destination, I was a seasoned airline passenger. Nothing to fear while cruising along at 38,000 feet except for the unexpected turbulence which sent me back to rocking in my seat. When the airplane finally landed and I was able to undo my seatbelt I wanted nothing more than to get off the airplane. We shuffled behind all the slow-ass people and I really wanted to start kicking them and their children down the aisle.

Walking behind me Matt asked, "That wasn't so bad, was it?" His attempt at being encouraging came off as condescending.

"It wasn't bad. I just don't like taking off." I stepped off the airplane and smiled at the gate agent who was waiting with paperwork in her hand.

"Hope you had a nice flight." She smiled.

Did she really want to know the truth? Probably not. I nodded walking passed her towards the terminal. Once inside, I walked alongside Matt embarrassed at how I acted on the airplane even though I had no control over it. "I hate acting like that."

"Why are you so afraid? Have you always been afraid to fly?"

"No. I haven't."

It was never my favorite thing to do but I tolerated it because the reward was landing in a new and exciting destination. It fascinated me that I could leave a city and be thousands of miles away in two hours. Incredible. I knew airplanes crashed but I never thought much about it. I traveled by air from Orlando, Florida to Hartford, Connecticut on numerous occasions and only had a minor meltdown when I flew a few days after ValuJet Flight 592 crashed into the Everglades. I traveled by myself and never once felt panicked or that my life was threatened. It wasn't life threatening. It was flying in an airplane, not sharing needles with a prostitute or having unsafe sex outside a gay bar in Ft. Lauderdale. My fear came from the actions of the terrorist on September 11 when they used airplanes as weapons of destruction.

9/11 pushed me over the edge. The fear of crashing during take off haunted me. That and flying into a building while I watched it approach out my window. That fucked me up too. The fear switched off the moment we reached 10,000 feet. In my mind I was finally safe. I didn't worry about being blown out of the sky, which sounds odd to me now. It was normal for me to panic and prepare to die each time I got on an airplane.

That all changed a few years later. On a whim, Matt and I decided on traveling across the pond to visit Manchester, UK. We booked an overnight nonstop flight direct from Orlando because I figured it was best to go nonstop and keep the takeoffs to a minimum. I was eager but deathly afraid of the Boeing 747. If I went into hysterics on a 737 how would I react on this giant? Bigger airplanes make bigger explosions.

We arrived at Orlando International Airport and after walking up to the boarding gate area I glanced out of the window to take in all her beauty. The 747 may have been frightening, but she was majestic. She really was the Queen of the Skies. I know a lot of queens so I took a few deep breaths and felt confident that we'd get along just fine.

Matt wasn't so sure. "Are you hungry? Do you want to get something to eat and a few drinks at Outback?"

"Sounds great. I probably need a drink."

"That's why I suggested it."

Boarding wasn't scheduled for another hour and after flying with me for years, Matt knew what to expect. He was risking jail time for purchasing a seat next to mine. The 747 was the largest airplane I had ever flown on and like anything that big— you gotta take it with great ease—and alcohol. Ingesting four beers put me in the right state of mind to walk down the jet bridge, put my bag in the overhead bin, and find my aisle seat without running away screaming. When boarding had completed, one of the lovely blonde flight attendants made her way down the aisle stopping at each row to talk to the passengers.

"Hello sir," She said with an intense smile. She had wonderful teeth which answered my question about all British having horrendous teeth, "We have over 200 open seats available on this flight. You are more than welcome to move once we reach cruising altitude."

"Thank you. Anywhere?"

Her smile almost blinded me this time, "Yes. Anywhere except first class."

I looked over at Matt. He was seated next to the window with the seat between us empty. He grinned at me. I grinned back. Then my grin turned into a frown. Through that entire interaction I hadn't realized we already moved away from the gate and were taxiing to the end of the runway.

I panicked. "Are they going to do a safety demonstration?"

"Yes, honey. Everything is going to be alright."

That was easier said than done. The moment he finished his sentence the television screens in the seatbacks flickered to life and a friendly British man proceeded to tell us how to evacuate the airplane in an emergency.

"You're right again, Schmoopie." I said putting my hand out to grasp onto his.

The safety demonstration video ended and the pilot came on, "Crew, take your seats. We are about to depart."

I released Matt's hand and gripped the armrest so tight I could have snapped it like a twig. He placed his hand over mine to calm my nerves. It did not work. This impressive aircraft lurched forward, I let out a squeak, and after a few white knuckle moments we were airborne. It was such a gentle lift that I couldn't even tell we were moving.

"You can open your eyes now."

"We are in the air already? Wow." It was like skating across untouched ice.

When we leveled off, the flight attendants sprung from their jumpseats and pranced around preparing for service.

The seatbelt sign went off and Matt and I grabbed our small bags and moved into our own rows toward the front of the airplane. I unpacked my headphones and book and settled in. It was pure airline travel bliss. I couldn't believe I was actually flying and not sitting on the end of the runway awaiting clearance to depart. The flight was that smooth.

I was plugged in channel surfing when the overly-friendly British flight attendant, with a less than stellar smile, stopped the cart next to my row, "May I offer you a glass of wine with dinner?"

"How much is that?"

"It's complimentary."

Complimentary? I found my happy place and it was on an international carrier. "Yes, please."

She placed my dinner on the tray table with a crisp white napkin, "White or red?"

"White."

"Will there be anything else?"

"No. This is wonderful."

"Enjoy your dinner." She unlocked the cart and moved up to Matt's row.

I was all smiles. I wanted to pinch myself but was afraid I'd wake up from this amazing dream. While flying along the east coast and enjoying my meal, I switched from the map channel back to searching for a movie to watch. Nothing interested me so I clicked on the button leading to the preprogrammed offerings available on the flight. That was when I saw it hiding among the travel and cooking shows.

Are You Afraid To Fly? Such a simple title that screamed out at me and grabbed me by the collar. I choked on my shepherd's pie. I answered out loud as if the television was talking to me, "Yes."

I sipped on my complimentary white wine enthralled with this 30 minute broadcast like a toddler watching *Sesame Street*. The same British man who informed me how to get out of the burning airplane was now teaching me the ins and outs of airplanes. Why don't all airlines with a television have this option?

For each questioned I conjured up in my brain, he had an answer. How do airplanes stay in the sky? Magic. How do the wings stay attached during the flight? Magic. How do pilots know how to navigate through the clouds? You guessed it—magic. In all honestly, he never once said magic but that's what my brain processed. Maybe it was that second glass of wine I asked for when the flight attendant came back through the cabin. No, it was definitely the British dude sucking the fear right out of me and into the television screen. My first British sucking and—I won't lie—it was damn good. Nothing like a good sucking at 38,000 feet over the Atlantic Ocean to take away your fears of flying.

By the time the credits rolled I felt different. Maybe it really was the wine. The flight attendant came by smiling and picking up trays, "Coffee?"

"I'm good. Can I have another glass of wine?"

"Coming right up."

When she pushed the cart passed my row I got up from my seat to use the lavatory. Confidence ran through my veins while wine ran through my bladder. The release of the fear was thrilling. If knowledge was power than this knowledge made me Wonder Woman. The only outcome to ruin my euphoria would be to end up like the FedEx airplane in *Castaway*. I quickly flushed that thought down the toilet. I came out of the lavatory and stopped at Matt's row and sat down in the aisle seat. My excitement was electrifying, "Hey Schmoopie. What's up?" I didn't let him answer, "I just watched this awesome show about airplanes. The guy talked about all these different sounds and what they mean. I feel great." The flight attendant found me and handed me my glass of wine. "I'm not afraid to fly anymore."

Matt took a sip of beer, "Really? That's great babe." He probably thought I was on my seventh glass of white instead of my third. He took another sip, "Good for you."

"I'm serious, Schmoopie. I'm over my fear." The freedom to fly was an added bonus I never expected to receive with my purchased ticket. Death, that's what I expected.

A week later, on our flight back home, the airplane was full with no option to move and stretch out in our own rows. Matt noticed I was calmer during take off. No screaming. No crying out for help from the flight attendants. No rocking back and forth.

He looked over at me after the wheels went up, "You did great. Are you scared?"

Flipping through the onboard magazine I smiled. "Not really. I'm good." No sooner did I say that did we hit slight turbulence and I grabbed his leg. He smiled.

Laughing out loud I added, "I said I'm good. I didn't say I was cured."

Eight months later I started training to become a flight attendant.

FAT BOY | SKINNY AIRPLANE

If you have ever questioned your weight and wondered about curbing your calories, my suggestion is to apply, interview, and get hired as a flight attendant, then report for training. Your excitement over being hired and making it through the strenuous interview process will quickly vanish the moment you arrive at the training center. I know that female flight attendants from the 1960's and 1970's followed strict guidelines when they took jobs as flight attendants. They had to weigh in, be a certain height, were not allowed to get married, and hell—if they got pregnant—they better have an extra hanger in their suitcase.

I figured things had changed. As long as my hips didn't get stuck between the row of seats while I walked down the aisle everything would work out. My size wouldn't matter with my fellow trainees as long as I was friendly. I was incorrect. After watching all the skinny, anorexic, gay flight attendants sashay into the auditorium on the first day of training I prayed ipecac was one of my required items. And fen-phen.

In my defense, I wasn't a sea cow when I started training. I had a decent sized gut and tits big enough for toddlers to grab onto as flotation devices, but I wasn't fat. I was a husky bear—loved by many. In this group of queens it was different. I was the iceberg that sunk the Titanic. This was nothing new to me. Keeping my weight down has always been challenging. Up. Down. Up. Down. Like a boy scout in the backseat of his pack leader's pre-owned minivan. When I was growing up in Hartford, Connecticut, in a middle class neighborhood, my classmates tormented me with every kind of name. After these assholes ran out of names, they created new ones. Their favorite, which happened to be my least favorite, was Joebosity.

The moment a bully uttered that insult, usually in front of a large group in the lunchroom, it sent me into a tearful frenzy.

"Joebosity. Joebosity."

"Leave me alone!" I'd yell while eating my tasteless school lunch, "Why do you call me that? I'm not fat."

"You are too, Joebosity. You're a fat fuck." They all started in at the circular lunch table across from me, "Joebosity. Joebosity. Joebosity!" These bullies chanted and laughed until I ran out of the cafeteria and straight to the nurse's office to fake an illness.

The nurse was no help, "You don't have a fever. I can't send you home."

"I feel terrible. Just call my mom, she'll come get me. Please."

Wiping my saliva off the thermometer and placing it back in her desk, "Why don't you just lay down in the back room on one of the cots for 15 minutes and see how you feel."

I hated her. I doubt she was a real nurse anyway. To me she was just a bitch who was in cahoots with the bullies. The moment I lay down on the cot I knew what to do. My fingers were down my throat quicker than Karen Carpenter. It was rare anything erupted out of me and most of the time the nurse sent me back to class to finish the day being taunted. Somedays I found myself hiding in the restroom sobbing in a stall until one of the teachers discovered me. During my entire junior high experience I probably finished three lunches. I had no idea their bullying and ridicule was an early phase of Jenny Craig.

These asshole kids were brutal and had no qualms about telling me that I was fat, ugly, and should go outside in the school yard and kill myself. When I was in the eighth grade my friend Lacy enjoyed drawing whales on the blackboard and writing my name next to it. With friends like that you can imagine my enemies. After being found and thrown out of the restroom, I'd walk back into the classroom with my head hung low while my classmates pointed at the outline of Moby Dick on the blackboard while bursting into uncontrollable laughter. It was a wonder I never hung myself in the closet. Probably because it had low ceilings and wasn't a walk-in. I also never wanted to give them the satisfaction of knowing they were upsetting me. I'd try and ignore their words because, as we all know, words are simply that—words—and they only hurt us if we allow them to. I handled all words flung at me. I was strong and tough. These childhood bullies are the reason I dislike children today. Kids are assholes and have been ever since I was one of them. If you can't trust your own kind, you are really shit out of luck.

Flight attendant training was no different. It was like junior high school but with alcoholic adults. I was quickly transported back to 1985, but instead of parachute pants and big hair, I was surrounded by skinny jeans and dirty looks. I fought back the urge to run home to Matt, eat a bag of Doritos, and damn them all to gay hell—which is just like normal hell but with no PrEP and endless football on Logo.

I knew I had to slim down but it was a struggle. I will not put all the blame on my husband but he did make it difficult whenever I decided to lose weight. When I hinted the need to drop a few pounds he instantly whipped up a batch of homemade chocolate chip cookies that would put Great American Cookies out of business. This happened at least once a day.

Determined to go for a run, I'd be ready to leave the house until I stepped into the kitchen to find Matt standing there with freshly baked cookies,"When did you make cookies?"

"Last night while you were sleeping."

"You made cookies while I was sleeping?" I asked.

"I wanted to surprise you."

Who had time for a run when there were moist chewy chocolate chip cookies the size of your hand waiting to be devoured. "I'm gonna have one for breakfast."

"Enjoy."

It worked in his favor almost every time. I know what you are thinking and you can stop right there—Matt is not a feeder. He enjoys feeding himself before anyone else. This sly chocolate cookie move was his way of keeping me stocky enough so he could continue rubbing my belly like his personal stuffed teddy bear. I gave in easily. That's love. I am no gainer. I am just a chubby bitch who enjoys the occasional chocolate chip cookie for breakfast over running three miles in the Florida heat.

During our first day orientation the instructors scheduled mini breaks throughout the day so we could stretch our legs. Most of us ran to the lobby to make phone calls or use the restroom. The smokers made a mad dash outside to inhale cancer. I scanned the auditorium for body types equivalent to mine. There had to be someone in the group my size, or if I was *really* lucky, bigger. My first scan proved successful as my eyes settled on Paul Foley leaning against the wall talking to a fellow new hire. Paul was put together and carried himself well. He projected a confidence that I wished was sold on a shelf at Target. You could tell from across the room that Paul did not give a damn what people thought of him. Paul was hefty and accepted it. He owned his weight, something I could never see myself doing. I put all my weight on credit, with the expectation to eventually pay it off in full. Paul and I had to be friends, but what was the best way to approach him without hurting his feelings? I decided honesty was the best way to see this through— break the ice the way I normally do with strangers—rip off the Band-Aid and see how it goes.

I scooted down the row, squeezing passed a few of people, and popped out at the other end. Paul continued chatting with this skinny nerdy trainee when I interrupted, "Hey. My name is Joe."

"Hey brother, I'm Paul. This is Victor."

I shook Victor's hand and went right back to Paul. "I think we are the biggest guys in this group. What do you think?"

"I think you may be right."

Victor bowed out at that time. Honestly, it was for the best. He was hired to work ground operations and any future friendship between the two of them was doomed from the start. Stick with your own kind, Victor, and let me establish friendships with the large future flight attendants of this airline. These were not proud moments but desperate times called for desperate measures.

I swayed from side to side, "These skinny bitches. I don't like any of them." Paul let out a thunderous laugh. He got me, better yet—he got my humor. "You know, Paul, I think we need to be friends."

"Really? Why?"

This was the moment of truth. Did I lie or just rip the Band-Aid off? "You're bigger than me and make me look skinny."

Another thunderous laugh, "Is that how you make new friends?"

"No. But these are some skinny bitches."

Another round of rowdy laughter from both of us and I noticed break time was coming to an end. The new hires sauntered into the auditorium returning to their seats. "Sweet. We can be friends. I'm cool with gay guys."

"How do you know I'm gay?" I asked while walking down the aisle towards my row.

"You keep staring at me like I'm a piece of meat."

We erupted into laughter, again. I squeezed back down my row and found my seat, happy with how easy it was to make a friend. Paul had a cuteness about him that reminded me of an adult Dennis the Menace.

That night I called Matt to update him on my first day of orientation, "We haven't even started flight attendant training yet and I made a new friend. His name is Paul. He's a straight bear."

"Is he cute?"

"He's alright. Chubby and cute. You'd like him."

"Nice. Can you invite him over?"

"Goodnight Matthew. I have to study."

On the third day of orientation we started flight attendant training. There were over 90 of us in our class, the biggest class the airline ever had. The only space large enough to accommodate us for three weeks of training was the auditorium. After new hire orientation wrapped up we remained seated while the other departments filed out and began their own journey as airline employees. It was the beginning of January and we were the first flight attendent class of the new year. Every flight attendant hired after our class would be junior to us. In a world where seniority rules everything, this was huge. I was thrilled to be there; I was also thrilled that I didn't send the Unknown Caller call to voicemail when the airline called to offer me the job.

The auditorium was large enough for everyone to spread out comfortably. It also allowed for everyone to break into cliques. We were overrun with cliques. We had the geeks, the busty blonds, the smokers, the borderline bisexual male Puerto Ricans, the English as a second language female Puerto Ricans, the former flight attendants, the skinny gay guys, and my clique—the guy who drove his Jeep to training and drives people around.

There were only four people in my clique: Tasia, Richard, Derek, and me. I drove the four of us back and forth between the hotel and training center on a daily basis. It was almost like *Driving Miss Daisy*. It was more like Driving Miss Tasia and the Queens.

The four of us sat on the left hand side of the auditorium and stuck together like glue. Paul sat with the geeks on the other side of the room a few rows down from the skinny gay guys; the clique I should have been part of but at no time felt welcomed. Occasionally I made conversation with a few of the cliquey gays but never strayed far from my clique. I received most of my attention from my outrageously loud laugh that bounced off the walls at the most inappropriate times. I think I am still known for that laugh when people see me in the crew lounge.

At the end of our first week it was time to hand in our travel benefit documents. Living in Florida, I didn't know how to differentiate between significant other and domestic partner. I was legally married in the state of Connecticut but in Florida, where bigots and evangelic Christians hunker down, I was as single as a knocked up teenager. Was Matt my domestic partner? Was he my significant other? Confused and stressed about filling out the forms correctly I searched for answers from my fellow classmates. My first instinct was to go straight to Paul but I abandoned that thought quick. He didn't know the first thing about gay problems. I asked Richard, Derek, and Tasia but they just stared at me like I told them my Jeep broke down. Assistance was needed before the end of the day and I knew where to find it. The answers to my questions came directly from the skinny gay clique. I required one of those skinny queens with perfect hair, a chiseled face that belonged on the cover of *Instinct* magazine, and pants so tight you could make out his joystick. I found that gay in Evan.

Evan never paid much attention to me during the first week of training. He split his time between fixing his hair and making googly eyes at Sean Larson—the biggest smoker in our class. When I approached Evan he was standing by the double door entry into the auditorium, "Do you know if I should put my partner on as a domestic partner or significant other?"

He stared blankly at me processing my question. I asked again, "Should I put my partner Matt on as a significant other or domestic partner?"

Smiling he answered, "I don't know. Probably domestic partner, right?"

"Do you think?" I took the form out of the folder tucked underneath my armpit, "I want to make sure I choose the right one so I don't fuck up my benefits."

"If you have the documents to prove he's your domestic partner then do that."

"Yeah. I got them. Sounds good to me." I put the form back into the folder, "Thanks." I turned to walk back to my seat.

"Sure thing. You should come hang out at Chili's with us tonight."

How nice I thought, "I'll try."

That was as far as our conversations went for the next few weeks. I found out months later he was thrown off by my question. In his own words he confessed, "I thought you were a straight Christian Republican who was married with three kids."

When this revelation came to light it brought me back to that exact moment standing in the auditorium entryway. I concluded he was calling me fat. Every crazy Christian Republican straight family man I had ever seen on television was fat. That was his way of politely telling me I was fat. Whether or not that was the message he was delivering—I will never know—but that was my interpretation. When we believe something deeply enough, nobody can change our minds.

I slowly let my guard down and became friendlier with a few more classmates. Some of them appreciated my distasteful humor and contagious laugh. We continued to sit in our secluded groups but the feeling of separation had vanished. All any of us wanted was to make it through training in one piece, and by one piece I meant hired and not handed a one-way ticket back home as a failure. On average we were losing two trainees per day. We walked around on eggshells. Our numbers were dropping like a case of chlamydia overtook the auditorium. One by one we were being taken out with no Z-pack prescription in sight. Now that I think about it there was a pilot initial class going on at the same time, so it was highly possible it really was chlamydia. We'll never really know thanks to HIPAA.

Every time we stepped out of the testing room with a passing score we'd remind ourselves there was another test tomorrow. We were never off the hook and never had the opportunity to feel confident. We were all one failed test away from being sent home. In junior high school, unless you really fucked up, you were guaranteed to move on to high school. In flight attendant training, one failed test meant your wings were ripped away before you had a chance to try them on. There were not many second chances, but when a trainee did get a second chance, they usually failed that too. The fear of failure kept the cliquish attitudes grounded. This brought us together as a group and stopped us from worrying about what other people looked like or what clique they were initiated into.

With each passing week training became slightly easier to manage… socially. The knowledge checks and tests gave us a constant headache that Tylenol could not cure. There were still moments when I felt completely out of place and questioned if I could survive in a world filled with skinny gay flight attendants.

My lowest point was on our third day of training. I reviewed our schedule of events and read that the last two hours of the day was dedicated to flight attendant uniform fittings. Everyone was getting to know each other and new friendships were forming like an evolutionary video on fast forward. I got nervous when the uniform ladies came into the auditorium and started lining us up for fittings.

"Are they going to do this behind a curtain?" I asked Derek while we inched our way up the line towards the racks of uniforms against the wall. Quitting was more of an option than taking off my shirt. I refused to take my shirt off at the beach so I damn sure wasn't prepared to let my man tits hang out in an auditorium filled with other future flight attendants. I'd literally have the shortest flight attendant career ever.

Derek turned to me, "They're only measuring us right now. We will try on pieces later."

"Ok. Then why do they have all the uniform pieces here?"

"I don't know," he turned back to look at me, "Calm down."

"Alright," now I was talking outloud to myself, "You'll be alright."

"What's wrong with you? Why are you rocking back and forth like a serial killer?"

Derek was completely fucking wrong! The Puerto Ricans and skinny gay guys were dropping their pants, taking off their shirts, and showing off more ribs than served during lunch at Sonny's BBQ. Sweat permeated through my shirt and my eyeglasses began slipping off my nose. Damn being bald and not having hair to collect the waterfall of sweat cascading down my forehead.

I was snapped out of my trance. "Next."

I didn't move.

"Wake up over there." The seamstress yelled from the front of the line that I was not standing in.

"Oh, sorry. Are you talking to me?"

"Yes," she summoned me with her finger, "Come over to this lane and get your fitting done."

I made my way over to her while everyone buzzed around the auditorium chatting about their fittings. I was positive nobody paid attention to me. I called this the binge-and-purge portion of the day because that's what I felt like doing once the seamstress started yelling out my measurements.

She flung the yellow measuring tape around my waist like she was roping cattle, "42 waist"

"42? Are you sure?," I questioned while looking down at her as she moved to measure my pant length, "I'm a 38."

"It's 42. Trust me. Did you get that Mary? Joe Thomas is a 42 inch waist"

"Do you really have to say all this out loud?"

She ignored me, "19 and a half inch neck. Jacket size is a three extra large." Mary jotted down my thickness on a sheet of paper. She was lucky this was America because if we were in Britain I might have thrown my weight in stones at her head. I was confused as to why she carelessly announced my weight and size loud enough for everyone to hear; she was no Calista Flockhart.

Pedro Malo was behind me in line and sarcastically announced, "Do they even make jackets that big?"

He didn't whisper which led me to believe his plan was to humiliate and embarrass me. It worked. I never liked Pedro after that. He might as well have jabbed me with a hot poker while I tanned on the beach. I wanted to cry; I probably did. It was junior high school all over again. The only thing missing was a whale drawing projected on the screen so the entire room could join in on the laugh. I was thirty five years old, had credit cards, a husband, two cats, and a house. I was a fucking adult but here I was being bullied by some Latino asshole who found it funny to pick on the fat kid in the group.

When I heard Pedro and his amigo, Carlos Sereno, laughing about my jacket size I wanted to take my fist and pound Pedro on the top of his heads like a Pez dispenser. Trying to ignore him I stood in the auditorium fully clothed but feeling completely naked. The uniform nazi worked quickly around my stomach like it was going to explode, spraying everyone with the ham and cheese sandwich I had for lunch. Would I be able to walk down the aisle of the airplane without knocking all the passengers out? I could walk sideways but that might lead to scoliosis. Fat with a new diagnosis of scoliosis—this was turning out to be a fucking nightmare.

A few years later I became Pedro's flight attendant supervisor. I cringed every time I saw his name on the report sheet. I hated him more than Jehovah's Witness knocking on my door during one of my many jerking off sessions. I wished bad things on him. Nothing too dramatic; just something like enough passenger complaint letters so I could fire him… or AIDS. These evil thoughts consumed me but I was professional and always helped him whenever he needed assistance. It was difficult. When he reported to the airport for a flight he'd stroll into the office greeting me like one of his long lost best friends. That always pissed me off. His conversations usually began with, "Hey Joe…" and my brain stopped processing. The rest of his babble came out as, "Do they even make jackets that big? Do they even make jackets that big? DO THEY EVEN MAKE JACKETS THAT BIG?" on a continuous loop like a broken record.

Pedro had forgotten how powerful his words were that day in the auditorium during our uniform fittings. Maybe he did remember but figured I had forgotten. I didn't. Bullies tend to overlook their actions or their victims feelings. Victims never forget. We carry it around like an additional carry on. It's true. We even have no problem paying the extra fee for it.

I never let go of my anger for Pedro. I try to live life with no regrets but I allowed him to poison my thoughts and confidence for years to come. I regret that but I am only human. My anger crushed my chest making it hard to breathe, kind of like my heavy man boobs. Within my first year as a flight attendant I lost enough weight to give the jacket away. I kept it. It hung in my closet as a reminder that even though the fitting was embarrassing, I was able to get through it. Like every difficult obstacle thrown at me. Eventually, Pedro was terminated. Not at my hands, unfortunately. I wanted to fire him more than I wanted to win Supervisor of the Year—but I never had the opportunity. I had gone back to the skies as a flight attendant long before he was sent packing.

Even though I eventually lost all the extra weight, I initially carried it around with me all through training, on my first flight to New York City after graduation, and right into my crash pad where I was challenged to sleep on bunk beds made for children, or people who weigh under 200 pounds.

THE BUNK BED LIFE

I was 16 years old the first time I slept in a bunk bed. Irene purchased a set of wooden bunk beds when we moved from East Hartford, Connecticut to Orlando, Florida. There was nothing wrong with buying bunk beds except that I was an only child. I could understand purchasing bunk beds if I had a brother, sister, foster brother, or large dog who lived with us, but it was just me in my room. Who did she expect me to share my bunk bed with, Casper the Friendly Ghost? That was insane. I hadn't talked to Casper since I was eight years old.

Irene gave me no say in the matter; she just went out and bought these bunk beds. For the first few weeks we fought about where I'd sleep and she practically had to tie me down to the bottom bunk so I wouldn't flee to the living room. It freaked me out sleeping in a bunk bed with nobody else in the room. Just rolling over and having the bed creak sent me running like the top half was on fire. I figured when I was 17 years old and moved out of Irene's house, I would have said goodbye to bunk beds for the rest of my life. I was mistaken.

During our initial flight attendant training we had no knowledge of what base we'd be flown off to. This was an added stressor that none of us needed. A flight attendant's base is the airport where we report, start, and end all our flights. It's a hub for flight attendants and pilots. Our mothership. Flying for free gives us the opportunity to live thousands of miles from our base. That sounds wonderful, right? It is, but if we choose to live away from base we are still responsible for being at our assigned base, on time, and ready to fly as per our schedule. No excuses.

When I meet people with no knowledge of the airline industry this question always comes up, "How does this work? You can live in Orlando and be based in New York?"

"Yes. That's how it works."

"I don't get it."

"We can live anywhere we want. We just have to make sure we get to work on time."

It boggles their mind. I carry around paper towels in case their heads explode so I can clean off my shirt. We are like traveling salesman but instead of vacuums and insurance we sell duty free goods and pillows.

Before we started digging into our flight attendant manuals, our instructors informed us which bases were taking new flight attendants: New York, Cleveland, and Jacksonville. Those were our three options. No more. No less. The instructors came right out and reminded everyone that if that didn't work for us then maybe, "This isn't the job for you."

The thought of disagreeing never crossed our minds because for most of us this was our dream job. We dreamed of becoming flight attendants more than Sarah Palin did about becoming vice president. Thankfully, our dream became a reality. During interviews and training we agreed to everything. If the airline demanded us to work 23 hours a day, sleep on the floor in the airport, and pay them to fly (instead of the other way around) we would have concurred. For every space we occupied in that auditorium there were thousands of others waiting for us to fuck up so they could step in.

On the fifth day of training we bid for our desired base airport. At that time, my airline had only four bases. Even though our Los Angeles base was not accepting new flight attendants, we still had the opportunity to request it as a base. It was a tease that gave some trainees false hope, like my friend Richard who lived in Los Angeles. He was determined to be based there, "I'm still going to bid for LA. Do you think I'll get it?"

Looking up from my sheet of paper with the list of bases, "They said nobody is getting Los Angeles."

"Then why are they allowing us to bid it?"

"Because they want to fuck with you? I don't know."

I really had no clue. After making it clear there were only three bases taking flight attendants it seemed absurd to even offer Los Angeles.

We were encouraged to list our base preference in order of most important. The chance of being awarded our first choice was slim but if there was a chance of getting my first choice, I didn't want to lose it.

My preferences were as follows:

- John F. Kennedy International Airport (JFK)
- Cleveland Hopkins International Airport (CLE)
- Jacksonville International Airport (JAX)

It felt like graduating college. Having the opportunity to pick a new city to start our exciting careers had us buzzing around the auditorium like trapped mosquitoes. As the excitement went viral throughout the auditorium, we were quickly sprayed with Off! and reminded that all base assignments were awarded in seniority order. No matter how badly we wanted a certain base it depended on when we were born. It was a great time to be old in a class full of young wannabe flight attendants. The older trainees would most likely be granted their first choice. Their insolence shined through as they walked past younger trainees who were already crying over what to do if their first choice was not awarded. Not 15 minutes after our instructors informed us how it would all play out, people were already complaining. Typical flight attendants: complaining before they knew the outcome.

One week before graduation our instructors lined up military style in the front of the auditorium to read off the base assignments. Most of us were a nervous wreck, except for the senior citizens in class.

I wanted the list to be posted on a bulletin board. I imagined running and pushing my way to the front of the group to catch a glimpse of what everyone was given like in an episode of *Glee*. Instead, our instructors decided to read off the list in front of the entire class.

They should have had therapists set up at tables outside the auditorium before they started rattling off names, "Attention everyone." The entire room stopped what they were doing, including the blond chick who was putting her hair up in a pony tail. "Please listen for your name to be called: Bigby, Gienapp, Hillion, Alence, Raviola,

Thomas, Malo, Sereno, Yates…" The list seemed to go on forever. "You are all going to JFK." There was a moment of deafening silence before, "Aaaaaaand the rest of you will be going to Cleveland."

What happened next looked like a scene from the movie *Airplane*. The cheers echoed off the high walls surrounding the auditorium. Some gave powerful high-fives to each other while others quickly started discussing options on where to live. The youngest in our class were caterwauling in their seats. Most of them lived in New York City but were assigned Cleveland. I couldn't blame them. I might have cried too. My friend Richard was stressed because he was assigned Cleveland and had no intentions on moving from Los Angeles.

I had no time to worry about other people. I was sad Paul, who lived outside of New York City, and the other members of my clique wouldn't be joining me on this adventure but I had to focus on me. The moment I heard my last name called I knew my life had officially changed. I'd be commuting from Orlando to New York City.

What had I gotten myself into?

Being 35 years old worked out well, it gave me a spot in the seniority bracket where I was awarded my first choice. I fantasized about living in New York City my entire life and now I was being handed my chance and with a paycheck. Fuck Willy Wonka—this was the true golden ticket.

When you live in Orlando and believe New York City is the prize at the end of the yellow brick road, you want to click your ruby slippers together faster than Dorothy did to get out of Oz. Instead of listening to lectures or interacting in group assignments, I caught myself daydreaming about strolling through Times Square, buying tickets to every Broadway show, and living a glamorous big city life. The life I was meant to live.

Then I found out JFK was in Queens and I wanted to throw my ruby slippers at the instructor and go home. My journey from Park Avenue to Skid Row happened before lunch. This realization was equivalent to finding a dirty diaper in a seatback pocket and being bitch slapped with it. I am not saying that Queens was horrible but when you are a reserve flight attendant, waiting for Crew Scheduling to call, missing your family, and practically chained to your luggage—it was soul crushing.

After graduating from flight attendant training I had a few days to find a crash pad in New York. I should take a moment to define crash pad because even I was thrown off the first time I heard the term. To anyone not in the airline industry the word *crash* may be taboo. I don't know how or why the term crash pad has stuck all these years but it has. A more realistic term would be 'adults sleeping in bunk beds' pad, but who am I to change tradition? Crash pads are homes, apartments, or any dwelling that is set up for airline employees to use as temporary housing while in their base. These crash pads are owned by all sorts of people and they have one main goal: to squeeze as many people into them as humanly possible. This allows the landlord to make the most money. Great for the owner, terrible for the occupants. If a landlord charges $200 a month and they have 20 residents in the house you can see how quickly that money adds up. That's where the bunk beds come into play; the more bodies the more money. While you sleep in a bunk bed and share a room the size of a walk in closet with 10 other people, your landlord drives around town in his brand new black Mercedes.

The easiest way to find crash pads was through word of mouth. After getting a few tips from some classmates, Matt and I flew to JFK to lock down a crash pad. We had no sense of where we were going but found the Airtran, rode that to Jamaica Avenue, and then boarded the J train. We stepped off at 121 Street and after taking the stairs down from the platform, we found ourselves in the neighborhood of Richmond Hill.

"I'm nervous, Schmoopie. I don't think I can live here."

"Sure you can. It's not so bad," Matt cheerfully responded as we walked passed two homeless guys fighting over a slice of pizza. I was going to die on this street. Maybe not today, but I was convinced no later than spring.

Excitement was replaced with fear regarding my move to New York. Fear entered me with a vengeance and popped up like a cold sore before a first date. I needed to quit. I would never make it to my first flight. How was I going to survive living here without my husband and my cats? I had no social connection with anyone in New York City and the few people I did know were from my initial training class—and I barely liked them. Evan was coming to JFK, which was a silver lining, but the rest of my friends were younger and went to Cleveland.

Who says age is just a number? In the flight attendant world it can ruin your social life.

It was the beginning of February and I forgot to check the weather for our day trip to New York City. No jackets.

No gloves. No scarves. It was disgusting. The rain, wind, and dirty streets of Richmond Hill made me want to cry. I was experiencing an internal panic attack and Matt was with me. What was I going to do when I had to come here alone? We walked down Jamaica Avenue and then kept to the right and followed Myrtle Avenue until we reached 116th Street and made another right. I was relieved to see the apartment building that would be my future home away from home.

The four-story brick building loomed above us and, compared to the other properties in the surrounding area, had to be the newest on the block if not the entire borough. Each rowhouse had its own staircase. We quickly walked by two staircases and found the address for the first floor apartment where I hoped to be moving. The rain was hitting us hard so we found shelter underneath one of the staircases and waited for the landlord to arrive.

Kader Aziz pulled up and double parked his brand new black Mercedes in front of the apartment building. We had never met so I had no way of knowing it was him until he briskly walked towards us. I made eye contact with him and smiled, he did not. With his jet black hair and chiseled face he could easily make any woman or gay man swoon. I did not swoon; I barely blinked.

When he walked up he was all business, "Hello. Joe?"

"Hi," I stepped out into the rain to shake his hand and it was as cold as I expected his heart to be.

He shook Matt's hand and then opened the apartment door on the first floor, "The cost of the crash pad is two hundred and fifty dollars per month. I will need first and last month as a deposit. That will be five hundred dollars."

At least he could do math, "That seems reasonable. I'd like to move in on Friday. Is that ok?"

"Yes. That will be fine." We walked over the threshold and out of the cold. The heat was welcoming. "You will be in this apartment."

My future part time home was on a single floor and completely renovated inside. We were the first tenants. While Kader led us through the sparsely furnished living room he added, "I will be purchasing a flat screen television and new chairs for the living room next week."

"Cool." I was glad he acknowledged that because even though the new flooring and crown molding were impressive none of that mattered if there was no television to watch.

We passed the stainless steel refrigerator at the end of the open kitchen, went down a small hallway, and passed the bathroom. My eyes scanned the entire floorplan and besides a missing television I could not find one single thing wrong with the apartment. It was beautiful and made my own house look like an abandoned shack.

At the end of the hallway there were two doors side by side. Kader opened the door to the left and he walked in stepping to the side to allow me to enter, "You'll be in this room."

There were two sets of wooden bunk beds in the small room. I did not expect bunk beds, "I'd like to be on the bottom because I don't think I can sleep on the top bunk."

"That's fine, that shouldn't be a problem. There's only one other person moving in this week."

I wrote out the check and had a place to live in Queens for only $250 a month. It was that easy. Why are there homeless people in New York City? Everyone should live in crash pads where 16 people cohabitate in a four bedroom apartment.

After our meeting with Kader, Matt and I went into Manhattan to explore the city for a few hours. We bought rain gear and I contacted Paul begging him to pick us up and drop us off at JFK. He did, which was wonderful because we were waterlogged. The entire flight home I sat with my eyes closed trying to absorb everything that was about to happen. It was almost too much.

The next day I packed my essentials and felt like I was moving out. I had to fight back the tears. Even though I was excited about this new adventure, I feared not coming back. Our brains are very powerful and sometimes, no matter how much we grow, learn, and spend time on a therapist's couch, our old brains kick in and erase everything new we have learned.

When Matt dropped me off at Orlando International Airport the next afternoon I was a mess. I had more suitcases than I would eventually allow other passengers to carry on and I had a box stuffed with a comforter, pillows, and random bathroom supplies. I knew I wasn't being kicked out, but it felt like it.

Sitting outside the departure terminal I could barely hide my fear, "I don't want to do this."

"This is your job now. This is what you wanted, right?"

"I guess."

He was confused. So was I. "Do you still want to be a flight attendant? You've gone through so much to get to this point."

"Yeah. I want to be a flight attendant. I'm just scared."
I raised my voice, "Can you cut me some slack?"

"I'm not yelling at you, babe. I just want to understand. What are you scared of?"

"I don't know."

I was lying to Matt. I knew exactly why I was afraid. I do that all the time to him, to everyone actually. If I am upset or bothered by something I immediately shut down. Close the door, shut off the lights, put up the closed sign. Done. That was the simplest way to deal with the crazy stories swimming around in my head. Stories I created because I was afraid that my life as a flight attendant might force me away from home so much that Matt would forgot about me. Worse than that, I feared being replaced by someone new. These thoughts never crossed my mind during training. Probably because I was too engrossed in learning airport codes and how to manually inflate a 36-man raft, but the moment I was back home and had time to clear my head these concerns invaded me like parasites. My irrational brain didn't consider the fact that we had been together for four years and already had a strong history together. We weren't trying to build a new relationship, just create new boundaries for our current one.

Try telling that to an unreasonable guy like me.

I cried the entire way to JFK from my window seat. The passenger sitting next to me was concerned, "Are you alright?"

I was in my flight attendant uniform crying like the airplane was going down off the coast of North Carolina. Pulling myself together was the only option, "Yes. I'm alright. Thank you." I put my head against the fuselage and zoned out for the rest of the flight. This was going to be harder than attending catechism classes at Our Lady of Sorrows.

I paid $40 for a cab ride from the airport to the crash pad because I didn't feel safe taking the train alone at night. Stupid move on my part. I'd realize soon enough how much I needed that $40 for food. Within my first month of living in New York City I became an expert at riding the train at night. When the cab pulled up in front of the apartment building I stumbled out of the taxi and dragged my belongings to the front door. Thank the universe I was on the first floor.

I opened the front door and Carlos Serrano greeted me while he put away groceries in the refrigerator. Remember Carlos? The friend of Pedro Malo? The—DO THEY EVEN MAKE JACKETS THAT BIG—asshole. He was the other tenant? Fuuuuck! I still hadn't forgiven him for joining in on the laughter during my fitting.

"Hola, Joe. How are ya buddy?"

"I'm great, Carlos." I fibbed while pulling my belongings into the apartment. He walked over to help but I waved him off. The last thing I needed was help from someone I considered a bully. "Is there anybody else here?

"Nope. Just us. Two other people moved in today but they aren't here."

That was curious; Kader told me there were only two people moving in this week, not four. Leaving my stuff at the front door, I walked passed Carlos and made my way to the back part of the apartment. I walked into the bedroom and noticed the two bottom beds were already made up with other people's effects strewn across them. This was not starting out well. "Carlos, can you come here?"

He was there quick, "Yeah. What's up?"

Leaning with my hand against the bunk bed frame, "Did you take a bottom bunk?"

"No," he walked across the small room to his bunk and slapped his hand down on his mattress, "I took this top bunk."

"Who's down in these two?"

He started back out of the room, "I guess the guys that moved in today. I wasn't here. I think they're with another airline."

Panic set in, "Fuck! I can't sleep on the top bunk."

"Why not?" He asked stopping at the door and looking back.

He was fucking with me. It was obvious. These bunk beds were completely wooden and not made to support the weight of a full grown husky man like myself. Shit, they would probably buckle under the weight of a Mississippi toddler.

"That's the only bed available. Just take it."

"No. I can't sleep on the top bunk." I refused to confirm my fatness; Carlos was well aware. "I need to call Kader."

It was late but I knew Kader would answer. He was probably on his iPhone spending my $500 as I dialed in his cell phone number. After our quick conversation he suggested I move into the upstairs apartment where there was one bottom bunk left. It was on the third floor. Kader's concern was not where I slept but that my check cleared.

As long as it was a bottom bunk, I did not care. It was already 9:30 p.m. and I had to be up at 4 a.m. to work my first flight, a transcon turn to San Diego and back, which I quickly learned I did not like.

After collecting all my shit and leaving the downstairs apartment, I went back outside and climbed up the set of concrete stairs. When I entered the other apartment I was greeted by another set of stairs. This was going to be a bitch to climb with all my luggage. I walked up another level and was in the main landing of the apartment which was the same layout as the one downstairs.

Sheila from my initial class was laying on the sofa, "Hey Joe," she got up and walked towards me, "I didn't know you were moving up here."

I put my box down and wrapped my arms around her, "I didn't either until about five minutes ago."

"You must be upstairs with Evan," she went to the kitchen to grab a glass, "the door left of the bathroom. Oh…" she continued, "there's like six of us taking the Q10 bus at four-forty tomorrow morning so be ready."

"Oh cool. Thanks." I shuffled up another flight of stairs and finally made it to the third floor. I would be skinny in no time. Maybe this move was for the best.

I entered the bedroom and found my three new crashmates lounging in their bunk beds. Evan, Sean, and Mark had arrived earlier that day and staked claim on their bunks. Their stuff crowded every corner of the room. It was like being an adult foster kid in a group home. This did not make the experience any better. I smiled at them dragging my suitcases behind me with the box under my arm.

Evan jumped off the top bunk bed to help me out. "Hey queen. Oh my god! I'm super excited you're gonna be in here with us." Evan was the only face that I was excited to see. Maybe this wasn't as bad as I thought. My mind was consumed with being at home with Matt and the cats. Sean camped out in the bunk underneath Evan and Mark was in the bed above mine. Sean nodded up at me from inside his bunk cave while Mark sipped red wine from a bottle nestled between his legs.

I placed my stuff against the wall, "How many people live in this apartment?" and immediately opened my box.

Evan swiped his finger through the air counting, "It's a five bedroom," he thought silently for a moment, "And I think there are a total of 16 beds. Is that right?"

Mark answered while flipping through his flight attendant manual, "Sounds about right. I thought you were moving in downstairs?

My mind tried processing that 16 people lived in one apartment. Was that legal? Sounded overcrowded even for a five bedroom apartment. Made me realize Anne Frank didn't have it as bad as she portrayed in her book.

Pulling the twin sheets out of the box to make my bed I answered, "I was gonna but they only have a top bunk and I'm too fat for the top bunk."

Evan chimed in while moving the ironing board out of the way, "You aren't fat. Don't be silly."

"Thanks. But I'm not sleeping on no top bunk and killing someone."

The room erupted into laughter. That made me feel better. Evan slammed the door behind me and became giddy with excitement, "This is going to be so much fun. I can feel it."

I smiled but did not feel his excitement. With four full grown adult men, four bunk beds, all our luggage, and a full size dresser this was the smallest room I had ever attempted to live in.

I innocently asked, "Are you guys going home after our trip tomorrow?"

The three of them stared at me. Did I say something wrong? I had barely finished making my bed and already pissed off my new foster brothers. I could kiss getting adopted out goodbye with this kind of attitude. Evan jumped up onto his top bunk with one swooping motion which verified my claims that I would ultimately kill someone if I was on the top bunk. He weighed no more than 170 pounds and the way that bunk bed swayed to and fro when he jumped up there, I knew my 260 pound ass would collapse it like a handful of pick up sticks.

"No. We live here." Sean said from his cave. I noticed that while I made my bed and unpacked a few items he spent the entire time making homemade cigarettes like my relatives from Canada. This was going to be a seriously poor group of people if Sean was already rolling his own cigarettes. If things were this grim, I soon expected to be standing in line at the Kew Garden's CTown cashing in my food stamps and WIC checks.

Then I felt guilty for being careless with my words. Here I was feeling sorry for myself because I'd have to spend a few nights a week here and they moved in. This was their new home. A cramped bedroom with three other adults in a crash pad with 13 other full grown adults. I knew it was cheap but goddamn, even child laborers in China have better living conditions. "Oh. I was just wondering." I placed my clothes on the bed and took my pajamas into the bathroom to change. The bathroom that the eight people living on the third floor shared. It reminded me of a sorority powder room with countless bottles of gels, creams, and cans of hairspray lining the windowsill. The amount of masturbating to occur in this crash pad bathroom would put an Equinox gym locker room to shame.

In a situation like this you might think the four of us instantly bonded, but that was not the case. I barely knew these three guys. The person I connected with the most was Evan and our friendship had only blossomed the last week of training. I couldn't care less about the other residents in our overstuffed townhouse. It was nothing personal; I just wanted to be home. All I focused on was going home.

I spent countless hours on my laptop hibernating in the bunk bed waiting to be assigned a trip. Whenever Crew Scheduling called I crossed my fingers, toes, and balls in hopes to be assigned an Orlando layover. It was usually Pittsburgh.

Evan was the polar opposite. He loved hanging out in the crash pad and interacting with the other crashmates. It was a constant party for him, a party that I refused to attend. He'd text me from the sofa while I hid in my bunk bed: *"Queen! Come down and hang out."*

My response was always the same: *"I'm good. I'm on my laptop."*

He never gave up: *"You're always on your laptop, Hel-looooooooo! Get down here."* When I stopped responding he would add: *"We are going to the Kew Club for some drinks. You wanna go?"*

That was the one thing that motivated me to socialize. I had no problems going out and getting wasted. It dulled the pain of being away from home; to sit in the living room and interact with my crashmates, that was rare.

I lived for being home and not in Queens. All my excitement of living in the Big Apple faded when it became clear I'd rarely make it into Manhattan. I was destined to spend my days slumming it along Jamaica Avenue waiting to take the shitty Q10 bus to JFK and spend the night somewhere glamorous—like Grand Rapids or Omaha. Most of my crash pad crashmates adjusted well to living in Queens. Evan made friends with other airline employees and some non-airline people. Mike found himself a boyfriend who happened to have an addiction to masturbating. An addiction so out of control he actually rubbed the skin off his dick. Why Mike shared this with me, I will never know. It could have been the fact that I spent the most time in the crash pad rubbing one out in the shower. Thankfully, not enough to watch my skin go down the drain. That was just disgusting. Sean moved into a smaller room on the main floor of the apartment. The room was an add-on with no windows and reminded me of a cell. He spent all his spare time in that room with the door opened, rolling those fucking cigarettes. With the number of cigarettes he produced he could have opened a bodega on the front porch. That might have helped him with his financial problems.

After a few months of this bullshit, Matt was itching to come to New York. He sold it to me like I knew nothing about mileage and distance, "It's easier for me to fly to New York to see you then for you to fly to home."

"Really? I thought it was the same distance because—*it's the same distance.*"

No arguing with that man. I had a few days off between reserve days and discussed with my crashmates the idea of Matt spending the night at the crash pad. A delicate subject when living with so many people. It was frowned upon to have guests in the crash pad over night. Especially when it was a co-ed apartment and most female crashmates were uncomfortable seeing strangers in the apartment. Evan was on a trip so he didn't care; he wouldn't have cared anyway. I asked Mike even though he'd most likely be masturbating with his boyfriend or in a wine-induced coma by 6 p.m. I checked with Sean and the female crashmates downstairs and they each gave me the thumbs up that Matt could spend the night. The last thing I wanted was someone calling the police if they saw a 6-foot 5-inch 280 pound white guy walking around in the middle of the night. Confident that everyone was comfortable with Matt spending the night, I called him and told him to book his flight for the next day.

He took the first flight out the next morning and I met him at JFK. We immediately went into Manhattan to run around Central Park and enjoy the day. When Matt was with me I actually liked New York. It felt like home. This was his first visit to New York City since getting settled in the crash pad so I was unsure of exactly where to put him. At first I told my crashmates he'd sleep on the sofa but by the end of the day I started worrying that Kader might make an unscheduled visit and get upset because there was a stranger in the house. I didn't want any trouble with Kader. I didn't like him and he didn't like me. Probably because I never kissed his ass like the other crashmates did. He also reminded me of the Taliban.

By the time we walked up the first set of stairs leading to the apartment I made the decision to let Matt sleep in the bunk bed with me. It would be horribly uncomfortable but I'd rather that than Kader finding him in his underwear on the sofa at 6 a.m. The less interaction I had with Kader the better. We walked into the apartment and it was dead quiet. Not a soul was home. That's hard to find when 16 people live under the same roof. I directed him upstairs and into my bedroom as quickly as possible. All my crashmates agreed to let him stay but I still felt the need to hide him. Have you ever tried hiding someone who has the nickname giraffe? It's nearly impossible.

"Schmoopie, hurry up and take your shower before anyone comes home."

He looked up from his overnight bag, "Why do I have to take a shower right away? I want to relax for a moment," he asked standing in the small bedroom. When he stood in the room it looked more like a walk-in closet than a bedroom.

Handing him a towel, "I don't want anyone to come home while you're showering and I need to take a shower, too. Can you please just take your shower now?"

"Can't they wait until I'm done?"

"No. Please just take your shower." He left the bedroom and closed the bathroom door with a huff. Would this be his last visit to the crash pad? If he continued with that attitude I guaranteed it. In all reality it was hard for him to understand, which I understood. A crash pad is a shared environment where strangers are forced to live together. He had no idea of what that was like. It's *The Real World* without cameras and a lot less fighting. The only fighting I ever witnessed was over dirty dishes and Obama being elected President. That was enough. If you are a thoughtful and caring crashmate you make every attempt to think about the other people sleeping around you. It was no secret that I hated being there; I hated it more than an empty bottle of lube before I was down for anal, but I still did my best to be polite. Was everyone like that in the apartment? No, they weren't. There was nothing worse than coming off a multi-day trip—wanting to wash away the airplane smell and jerk off for 10 minutes—and getting stuck behind a line of slow ass crashmates waiting for one of the two bathrooms to become available.

Matt finished his shower and I ushered him back into the bedroom. He hinted at having sex. I ignored him. Unfortunately, there would be no touchdowns in my end zone. Not with the chance of Mike coming home at any minute and sleeping above us. That bunk bed wouldn't shake uncontrollably for any other reason than us turning over. I grabbed my bathroom products and headed towards the bathroom when I heard someone downstairs in the livingroom. I walked over to the top of the stairs across from the bathroom, "Mike? Is that you?"

"Yeah. It's me."

I turned back to the bedroom and stuck my head in the door, "Schmoopie. Mike is downstairs."

73

"Ok. Is this news?" He put his shirt on, "You knew he was coming home, right?"

"Yes. I just wanted you to know.'

"I don't know why you're so worried about me staying here. Nothing bad is going to happen."

He was right. Worrying was oxygen for me and if I didn't do it I would most likely fall over and die. I agreed with him and headed back to the bathroom. I closed the bathroom door and turned the shower water on. All I needed was a few minutes alone under the running water to unwind and let the hustle of the day rinse away. The bathroom door was closed for around 30 seconds when I heard a large snap—like a tree trunk cracking—followed by a hefty thud. The thud of 280 pounds falling on the floor.

I didn't have time to shut the water off. I flung open the door and yelled, "What the fuck happened?" I came around the corner and stopped dead in my tracks.

The lower bunk was destroyed. Where my mattress and wood slats once sat perfectly attached to the bed frame was Matt, sprawled out on the mattress which was now on the floor. His face was hidden from view with his massive legs hanging over the only portion of bed frame that had not fallen over. My husband has massive legs but never did I think the girth of them could take down a bed. "Don't hurt yourself," I responded while standing over him not knowing what to do. Where did I start? Did I help him up? Did I clean up the debris? Did I start packing and looking for a new place to live? All of the above?

Stunned he slowly pulled himself off the mattress, "Jesus Christ. All I did was sit on the bed."

I just stood there staring at the devastation wondering how I was ever going to explain this to Kader. He'd most likely issue a fatwa on all overweight flight attendants. My life was officially over... there are a lot of fat flight attendants. My massive husband just ignited a war in Queens. Could I blame this on an earthquake? No. That was out of the question. There was no doubt that Matt's body slamming onto the ground registered on some seismic level but not enough to get me out of this wreck.

"What am I going to do?" I started to panic. "Oh my god! I am going to get kicked out."

Thoughts of having to drag my belongings through the snow and to the airport flooded my mind. "I should have flown home. Why did I let you talk me into staying here?" I began moving pieces of broken bed out of the way. The top portion of the bed remained intact but how long that would last was anyone's guess. All I needed was prison time for Mike falling to his death in the middle of the night. He'd most certainly be drunk at the time but I still didn't want that on my conscience. He was also younger and junior to me so the death of a fellow co-worker without the advancement in seniority was unnecessary.

"This is not my fault. I hope you're not blaming me for this." Matt grabbed the mattress and swung it around to place it against the wall. "This is a child's bunk bed anyway. Why does this guy have kid bunk beds for adults?"

"That's what I've been saying since I moved into this fucking place. This is why I can't sleep on the top bunk." Kids bunk beds for adults was absurd. Everyone knows there are bunk beds constructed of steel to hold an adult's weight.

During my banter with Matt, Mark snuck up the stairs unnoticed and positioned himself behind us with a glass of Malbec in his hand. "Damn. That must have been some rough sex."

Not even the best time to joke about something I would normally find amusing. "Mark. That's not even funny right now. Matt, seriously, I need you to fix this bed. I'm not joking."

"What? Joe, you are being ridiculous. I can't fix this bed." He picked up the longest piece of the bed frame, "Where do I put this?"

Sticking it up his ass was an option but I kept my mouth shut. Mark walked around the mattress along the wall, "Here," he opened the door inside our room that led outside to a portion of the rooftop, "just put it out here." He stood there sipping his wine and laughed out loud. "You fucked that bed up! Kader is gonna go nuts."

I grabbed a section of the frame that Hagrid from Hogwarts could have now used as a toothpick, "Fuck Kader. He should have beds that fit normal people and not toddlers." I threw the damaged slat onto the roof. *Thwack!*

The clean up from Matt's catastrophe went quickly with the three of us moving broken pieces of wood onto the roof. That night I stayed in one of the empty beds in the room across the hall while Matt slept on top of the mattress on the floor.

A few days later Kader showed up for his weekly inspection. I happened to be home which meant I had to man up and confess what happened. He would find out sooner or later so I just let it out, "I have to be honest with you Kader, my bottom bunk broke the other night when I went to bed."

Did I say be honest? I meant get out of this without a bomb detonating in the kitchen.

He stood at the sink checking the faucet, "What do you mean it broke?"

"I laid on it and it broke." I figured leaving Matt out of the scenario was for the best. He walked passed me and started up the stairs. I got off the sofa and followed. I felt like a teenager who was about to get the whooping of his life for horsing around while a friend spent the night. Kader stood in the door of the bedroom surveying the damaged bed. The jagged ends of the wood still fresh from when it snapped under the pressure of Matt's monster legs.

"How did it just break? Where's the rest of the bed?"

"It's on the roof." I was nervous, "I'll be honest with you, it broke because these beds are made for kids and not full grown adults."

He looked at me with so much hatred I'm surprised he didn't decapitate me on the spot. He stepped over a few pieces of scattered debris and opened the door to the roof, "How come nobody else has a problem but you? You couldn't sleep on the top bunk. You break the bottom bunk." He looked out at the wood strewn across the roof like a family of suicide bombers had blown themselves up after an afternoon picnic and shook his head in disgust. Slamming the door shut he said, "I will have to charge you for the bed."

Now I was ready to attack, "What? I'm sorry but I don't think it's my responsibility to pay for a bed that broke underneath me."

"You need to pay for the bed or you need to find a new place to live. I can't have my tenants breaking my property."

I was losing the fight. "Let me talk to my partner and see what we can do." I walked out of the room and into the one I had been sleeping in. "I will stay in this room until you replace the broken bed."

"I'm not replacing the bed. It still functions for the guy who sleeps above you." He didn't even know Mark's name. What a dick! "When I rent that other bed out you will have to find a new arrangement."

My goal was to get him out of my face, "Ok. I'll pay for the bed."

It worked. Kader walked down the stairs and out of the apartment; I was free for the time being. I never paid him for the bed. I figured if he was going to hate me I wanted it to be for a good reason. I avoided that dude at every turn. When he made one of his unscheduled visits I was either at work, out for a walk, or taking a shower. A few times I may have hid in the closet.

Weeks later I moved out of Kader's crash pad and into a two bedroom apartment in Kew Gardens. It was across the street from the airport shuttle stop and had only five crashmates. I loved it. There wasn't a single set of bunk beds in the entire apartment. Matt even spent many nights there without incident. All this luxury for only $25 more per month. It was crash pad heaven and I never had to rent from the Taliban again.

RESERVE (NOT FOR ME)

A raised hand from the back of the auditorium caught the attention of one of our flight attendant instructors, "What's your question, Sheila?"

"What's it like being on reserve? Can you give us some information on that?"

A question like that instantly pissed off the instructors. Our focus that afternoon was learning when and where to use the automatic external defibrillator (AED) on a child, not trying to understand the myths of reserve. Sheila's question quickly snapped the rest of us out of our emergency equipment trances.

"You will get an entire module on how reserve works before graduation," the instructor answered standing in front of the screen. Our class was notorious for asking the most off topic questions during lecture time. Often it was downright preposterous. If I was an instructor, I would have lost my cool a dozen times but these professionals kept their wits about them. I feared that at any moment they would snap and send us home wingless. I was hoping we'd get through graduation before that happened. She continued, "Can we please stay focused on how to properly use the AED on a child?

She was obviously crazy. AED? On a child? Who had time to learn about that? Understanding the big reserve picture was way more important than learning how to use the AED. Guess how many times I've had to turn on the AED and save a passenger's life while juggling beverages and salty nuts. None. Guess how many times I've had life altering shit happen to me while I was on reserve. So many I can't even count, but if you want a ballpark figure, I'd say somewhere between 100 and... one googolplex.

What was reserve? That was the $100,000 question buzzing around the auditorium the week before graduation. It was on my mind constantly. Not just mine—everyone's. How many hours were we required to work? How often would we be away from home? How much money should we expect to make? Was showering in the airport restroom a possibility? If you are wondering, the answers to those questions are: many, lots, nada, and you bet your fucking ass.

Our instructors kept their lips sealed tighter than The Go Go's. After Sheila's outburst during our emergency equipment module, if anyone even hinted at asking a reserve question our instructors announced a pop quiz. We were reprimanded like a lonely middle school student who may or may not have let their cock flop out of their shorts to get the attention of Coach Rodriguez in the 8th grade. Hypothetically, of course.

The day came for our reserve and scheduling module. It left us wondering what language they were speaking. An interpreter in the room might have helped because we had no fucking clue what they were talking about. Gisselle Grasa, an overweight lady from Crew Scheduling, stood up in front of everyone and rattled off so much information our pens couldn't write it down fast enough. "Let's talk about swapping your reserve days," she huffed and puffed walking back and forth in front of the entire auditorium. She resembled an over frosted cupcake, "because you can do that. Many other airlines don't allow you to swap your reserve days. We do." Señora Cupcake was proud of that. She pointed at the screen behind her which projected a grid filled with colors and numbers from the scheduling website, "If the reserve grid is in the red that means we are below minimums for the day."

Paul interrupted, "What are minimums?"

She frowned. We could all tell that being interrupted was not something she was fond of, "The number of reserves we have scheduled for the day," she went right back into her rehearsed speech, "and you can't swap out of that day. If the day is in the black you can't swap out of that day, either. You can, however, swap a black day to a red day but not a red day to a black day. Look for the color green. You can swap from a green day to a green day and a green day to a red or black day." She continued, "But never a red or black day to a green day." She finished with an enormous smile, "And that's how you swap your days on reserve. Any questions?"

Hands went up like a Nazi salute. Cupcake spent the next hour explaining the differences between red days, black days, and green days. I imagined she was talking about food coloring. My head hurt. I took four Advil and chased it down with a Bud Light when I got back to my hotel room.

It didn't take us long to understand everything we needed to know about reserve. It's easy: reserve sucks. Sucks more than a Mormon teenage bride on her wedding night. Masochists couldn't handle the pain that comes with being a flight attendant on reserve. I would rather be whipped with chains, fisted without Crisco, and left hanging upside down while someone pissed on me than spend a month on reserve. Actually, scratch that last part, that sounds kinda fun.

Reserve flight attendants act as the airline's safety net to cover for flight attendants who call in sick; that was what the airline told us in training. When we graduated and made it to our base city, we quickly realized the truth: we were airline bitches. Whores to be exact. Filthy whores pimped out by Crew Scheduling telling us where to go, what time to be there, what to wear, when to take a shit, and when we could leave the airport to go home.

On reserve you had to be ready to answer your telephone the moment it rang. No exceptions. There was no turning off the ringer and avoiding your calls like you do when your parents or in-laws call. Crew Scheduling was big brother, watching from a hidden camera, awaiting the most inopportune time to call. If we were shitting and missed the call we had a total of 15 minutes to call them back. If we miss that window the airline considered us AWOL. If that happened, we might as well keep running.

After training I received my first reserve schedule and cried like I had a hemorrhoid flare up. That was reserve for me, a hemorrhoid flare up that a Tuck's couldn't cure. I immediately began counting down the years until I was a line holder. I concentrated on nothing else. I fantasized about lines more than Whitney Houston. When my days off were over and it was time to head back to JFK for a block of reserve days, Matt literally had to throw me and my luggage out of the car on the departures level. He sped off and was lucky I couldn't run fast in my uniform. Before he dropped me off at the airport, I always suffered from excruciating abdominal pains and swore I had irritable bowel syndrome with the need to stay home.

"You don't have IBS. Go to work." Matt said annoyed.

"I do too have IBS. I'm literally about to shit myself right now. Why else I am in so much pain?"

"Because you're crazy?"

That argument ended quickly.

Everytime my block of reserve days were over and I was released from the painful grip of Crew Scheduling, I jumped on the first flight back home. When I left the crash pad my mind played tricks on me telling me I never had to return. My mind loves fucking with me. Going home made me so happy I worked myself into a frenzy whenever Matt picked me up from the airport.

"How was work?" he'd ask after I closed the car door.

"I'm never going back. I can't do this anymore."

As he pulled away from the arrivals curb he'd somberly say, "If you are that unhappy then quit," then he added, "but you need to have a job first."

"Why do you hate me?" I was convinced that he enjoyed my misery.

He'd look over and put his hand on my leg, "Joe, I don't hate you. I love you. But if you are unhappy you need to do something else. I hate to see you this upset because of your job."

There was no denying I was miserable. Reserve. Commuting to Queens. Being away from home. I was pathetic with my complaining. There were thousands standing in line wanting to become flight attendants, and here I was crying about every aspect of it. While I moaned like a little bitch, some of my flight attendant crashmates loved being on reserve. I did not understand them. I thought of them as sick and twisted fucks who tucked away a shitload of medications under their bunk bed. If this was true I never benefited from any of these meds. They either forgot to share them or I was working when they handed them out. Whatever the reason—they were a bunch of selfish bitches.

My prize was not a pot of gold at the end of a rainbow, but the thrilling moment when my seniority allowed me to say goodbye to life as a reserve airline bitch and become a line holding bitch—that was pure gold. There was a difference, an important one: the ability to know what flights I worked that month instead of blank days on a calendar. Where I would go on overnights and what time I started and finished each trip. Knowing what kind of clothes to pack instead of throwing my winter sweater in my luggage along with my white thong. Simple things that normal people take for granted when working a 9-5 job in the suburbs. And before you stop reading and ask for your money back—I do not own a white thong.

Being years away from the line holder prize was brutal for me. Not everyone felt that way. Evan bounced around cheerfully preaching. "We just have to do our time. Our day will come."

Really? That's what convicts say after they get 60 years behind bars for murdering a family at Disney. This actually was prison and Evan confirmed it to me while we watched the snow fall outside our prison pad. I figured the universe put me in this position as punishment for skipping so many days of Catholic Church when I was a preteen. Apparently, the universe did not take into consideration the ass whoopings my grandmother gave me when she found me loitering behind the church. Maybe I was waiting for Father Long to give me his Holy Sacrament. Did she ever take that into consideration? She didn't care.

I will go on record and state that I am shocked I was not terminated during my first six months as a flight attendant. Sick calls were my best friend and at my airline if you found yourself with six of them within a twelve month period, you were rewarded with a face-to-face meeting with your supervisor.

My supervisor, Myron Scarry, sat next to me shaking his head while tapping my name into his laptop. He reminded me of the fifth Golden Girl, Antigua, the one evicted for leaving her flat iron on and burning down Dorothy's bathroom. "Joseph. Joseph. Joseph," at least he knew my name, "what are we going to do with you?" I stared at him until he finished questioning me. I thought about crying but we were obviously both bottoms, so crying would get me nowhere.

Before I go any further, let me rewind back to the day prior and what ultimately led me to this meeting with Antigua... I mean Myron.

I was a bad reserve. Really, *really* bad. I am not exaggerating. I called in sick for everything. I didn't even have to address myself when I called Crew Scheduling; they had my telephone number programmed into the caller ID. I called in sick if I had a hangnail. Okay, that was an exaggeration, but in all honestly, I was quite the drama queen.

Crew Scheduling assigned me a two day trip with a layover in Charlotte. I had been to Charlotte a few times and the fear that this was Billy Graham country had subsided. During my first layover, I didn't want to let on that I was a homosexual so I used made-up sign language and kept my mouth shut. I didn't log onto any porn sites, which was the hardest part, and I said, "Thank you, Jesus," whenever I passed a Charlatan. Even if I found out their name was Bob or Loretta, I still looked up and prayed to the sky. While driving to the hotel we traveled along Billy Graham Parkway, which I was shocked to find out was an actual real highway. They have a fucking Billy Graham Parkway in Charlotte? I got off as quickly as possible. Thankfully, I had wet wipes in my tote bag. Get your minds outta the gutter, I am talking about getting off the highway. The wet naps were for the cream I squirted on my shirt from my airport doughnut.

This Charlotte trip had a late report time with only one quick flight from JFK. After waking up early, doing laundry, and picking up some nonsense items at the Queens Mall Target, Evan and I headed back to the crash pad so I could get ready to leave for the airport. One of the best things about being friends with Evan—and sharing a crash pad with him—was that he was the only person who had a car. When he went to Target, we all went to Target. It was the most exciting thing to do in Queens after running from muggers when leaving the J train. While we drove back to the pad I pulled up my schedule on my iPhone to see if my flight was on time. That was not out of the ordinary when flying out of JFK; flights are rarely on time. I punched in the information and was surprised to find out that my flight was canceled.

"What should I do?" I asked Evan while we drove down Queens Boulevard.

"Call Crew Scheduling to see what they are going to do with you."

"I hope they release me. I want to go home."

Evan continued driving, "Of course you do." He was over my complaining and bad attitude.

Calling Crew Scheduling was equal to me calling Irene when she was hitting the Budweiser cans too hard. The conversation never went well, there was always frustration—on my part—and I always hung up never wanting to call again.

After four rings a stern voice answered the phone, "Crew Scheduling. This is Devon."

Perky as a set of tits on ice I responded, "Hi, this is Joe Thomas, #01972.

"How can I help you?"

"My flight today is canceled. What do I do now?" This was my first cancellation. I had no understanding of how Crew Scheduling planned on abusing my testicles. I was hoping for a nice slow squeeze, or maybe a lick or two, not a steel-toed stomping.

"Please hold," and within a second, Celine Dion came on singing, *"...And that's the way it is."*

I should have taken that as a sign. One thing I knew about Crew Scheduling was they had no clue about what the fuck they were doing. Monkeys throwing paint at the wall could manage that department better than the twits answering the phones. I know that's harsh but it only took calling them once to come to that conclusion. These schedulers could have the flight attendant manual opened to the exact page and paragraph of the situation at hand and they would still—always and forever—place you on hold. I never understood that. It could be as simple as verifying a report time or as difficult as confirming a hotel change. Every question held the same importance which involved placing the caller on hold. What they were doing on hold was a mystery. Conversing with demons? Selling their soul to the devil? I would not be surprised.

A moment later Devon's husky voice came over my speaker, "Joe?"

"Yes, I'm here."

"The Charlotte's flight has been canceled." They loved stating the obvious, "You have been reassigned to do a Port-au-Prince turn this evening with a 2030 (8:30 p.m.) report time."

What did that mean? Thoughts raced through my head as the silence on the phone became awkward. A Port-au-Prince turn? What the hell was that about? I had an easy trip assigned to me with one leg to Charlotte and then one leg to the hotel and into bed.

"Is that a red-eye turn?"

"Yes. You will report off at o715 (7:15 a.m.) tomorrow morning."

"I've been up since eight o'clock this morning. I can't work all night."

His frustration was escaping through the phone, "You are good for two days, Joe, this is a legal trip. You have to work it."

"I-I can't work all night. I was assigned one leg to Charlotte tonight. That's what I am prepared to work." Evan looked over at me while we were stopped at a red light. I'd rather face Billy Graham's congregation than work a red-eye flight.

Devon took a deep sigh; instantly I knew my ass was in trouble. "You are on reserve. You can be reassigned to work anything we need you to work. Are you refusing the trip?" He asked point blank.

This was some serious shit. Refusals were bad. You were basically telling the airline, that took you over the other 10,000 applicants, that you were not working an assignment. I couldn't get a refusal, especially on reserve, but I was damn sure not working all fucking night. I was also wracking my brain with the question, where the hell was Port-au-Prince? Puerto Rico? Jamaica? Argentina? I didn't really care because my ass wouldn't be going there anytime soon.

"No." I had to think quick as Evan turned right onto Lefferts Avenue, "I'm fatigued."

"You can't be fatigued because you haven't worked yet."

Shit! Damn them and their specifics. "Then I'm sick."

"Alright. I will remove you sick. Please follow up with your supervisor before your next trip."

Evan parallel parked in front of our apartment, ."What happened?" Not letting me answer he continued, "Oh my god. You're crazy, girl. I can't believe you're not working the trip."

"I can't work all night." I was brave on the outside but shitting myself on the inside. I could not believe it either. What the fuck was I doing? Jeopardizing my job because I did not want to work a flight. I quickly thought about how other companies react to their employees not completing tasks assigned. Do people get fired from McDonald's if they refuse to salt the fries? Me thinks so.

"I will follow up with Myron this week," I opened the car door and squeezed myself out, "Looks like I am off tonight—let's go to the Kew Club for some drinks."

Never to turn down an opportunity to party, Evan was up for it, "Now you're talking. Let's put our shit away and get us some drinks." We both laughed walking up the stairs and he continued, "I need to flirt with boys."

When I woke up the next morning, with a headache and dry mouth, I was greeted with an assignment to work an Orlando turn and a voicemail message from Myron. He was requesting my presence in his office before I reported for my trip. Stress consumed me for the rest of the afternoon and no matter how I played out our conversation it ended with me being terminated. Fuck. Why didn't I just work the flight to Port-au-Prince? A Port-au-Prince flight from JFK couldn't be all that bad, could it? I packed my overnight bag, grabbed my flight attendant manual, and left the crash pad thinking I'd never return. That actually put a smile on my face. I hated that place. With no room to carry all my belongings, I told Evan to ship them to me or give them to a less fortunate reserve when someone moved in to replace me. I figured with how quickly Kader worked I would pass my replacement on the stairs leaving the building.

"Queen. You will be back," he tapped away at his laptop, "You are so ridiculous."

The Q10 bus pulled up to Terminal 4 and I was practically vomiting up my peanut butter sandwich in my mouth. It tasted much better going down. I popped an Altoid so TSA wouldn't think I was spreading chemical gas through the airport and started to the crew lounge. Our flight attendant crew lounge was secretly hidden from view. Probably a good thing. No need for passengers to hear the cries of terminated flight attendants throughout the terminal. It was located behind one of the gates and the only way to get through was to show our crew ID to the gate agent working that gate. It was like entering the Gryffindor common room, but instead of a fat lady singing, there was a fat gate agent yelling. Gate agents yell about everything. I don't know how they keep their jobs. Probably because if the airline fired gate agents for yelling, there would be no gate agents and passengers would run amok. When I stepped into the crew lounge there were a few lonely souls reclined in the overstuffed chairs watching television. It was quiet. I barely had a second to remove my tote bag from my shoulder and put it down when I heard Myron's voice echo through the lounge. "Joseph! Please join me for a moment."

Was big black brother watching? The answer was yes. He materialized out of the wall without warning to call me out in front of the flight attendants in the lounge. Maybe this was more like Hogwarts than I had first imagined. The few flights attendants planted in their chairs stretched their necks to see who Joseph was. That made me extremely uncomfortable. It also made me dislike Myron even more. I made a mental note to trip him if I ever saw him at a gay pride parade.

Walking into the office lined with cubicles was unsettling. I followed behind him like I did when I was young and ready to receive the belt from my father; head down and thinking of how I could get out of it. He sat down first and began tapping his stubby chocolate fingers at his laptop computer, "Joseph. Joseph. Joseph. What are we going to do with you?" He glanced up at me, "How are you feeling? Better, I hope."

He was playing mind games with me; I was sure of it. He knew I wasn't sick. Crew Scheduling records all telephone calls and if he was as thorough as he was playing himself out to be—he had memorized my conversation and was ready to recite it at any moment. I pulled up a chair and placed it to the side of his desk. I sat down, "I am fine. What do we need to talk about?"

"I'm looking over your sick calls and yesterday was your sixth one. Your sixth sick call. Did you know that?"

"Really?" I was playing dumb. New hire TSA employee dumb. Actually, any TSA employee dumb, "What does that mean?

"Well, Joseph, you are allowed five sick calls per year," he reached for a file folder and removed a tri-folded piece of paper handing it to me, "and this is your sixth. What that means is you're going on disciplinary action."

Disciplinary action? That sounded nothing like termination. Evan was right; I'd buy him a few beers at the Kew Club the next time I was at the crash pad. The hairs on my neck settled back down onto my skin and I felt this surge of excitement in my stomach. It could have been the need to take a shit, too. I am like a puppy when I get excited. I opened the tri-fold paper and glanced over it, "I get sick. I was a nurse for 15 years and I was sick a lot my first year."

He stared through me with his bulging eyes. It was awkward but I kept talking. Could he possibly have X-ray vision? Maybe his eyes bulged because he spent so many years willing clothes off skinny twink flight attendants. Either way, I was using my medical background to talk over him and hopefully confuse the shit out of him. "These things happen in this type of environment. Being around sick people or stuck in an airplane. It happens."

He exhaled, "That may be, Joseph, but you still have six sick calls and we have to document this. Have you thought about another job? Maybe this isn't the job for you."

I felt that surge again. This time I knew I had to shit. I had to wrap this conversation up before I was terminated for a gassing everyone in the supervisor's office. "This is the job for me. I'm sure of it." I wanted to ask him if being a supervisor was the job for him but I went a different route, "Are you saying I am not allowed to get sick?"

"You can get sick. If you are sick, you call in sick. I'm not telling you that you can't call in sick."

"But you told me I'd be in trouble."

"Yes. If you call in sick six times in a year."

"So I shouldn't call in sick?" I wanted him to tell me I wasn't allowed to call in sick. I don't know why I needed that information but it was the answer I was searching for.

"If you are sick, you call in. That is that."

"That makes no sense." I grabbed a pair of scissors from on his desk. What persuaded me to grab a blunt deadly object the moment my supervisor was placing me on disciplinary action, I couldn't begin to tell you, but I needed to have something to fiddle with and those scissors were in hands reach.

"I don't make the rules, I just enforce them." He grimaced, "You aren't gonna stab me with them there scissors are you, Joseph?" I smirked and then quickly put them back on his desk. Myron took them and placed them in a drawer furthest from me.

Without saying anything more about the scissors, he pulled out two pieces of paper stapled together from the file folder. He handed me the papers, "Please read this over and sign it on the bottom. Don't forget to date it. I will make you a copy."

The document was a list of things that I could not do while on disciplinary action. Violating any of the bullet points would result in the escalation of my disciplinary action. I took it from him and started to sweat.

My eyes quickly scanned over my six month action plan:

- Joseph cannot call in sick more than two more times
- Joseph cannot join any work related groups or committees

- Joseph cannot transfer to another department

My heart sank and I stopped at the third bullet point. I almost sharted in my polyblend uniform pants, "Will this prevent me from transferring to another base?"

"No. You can still transfer." He was excited to tell me that. Myron wanted nothing more than to transfer me as far away from him as possible. The feeling was mutual. Did we have a flight attendant base in Antarctica? I'd probably look good in a caribou hide.

I signed the form and placed it on his desk. He smiled. I didn't. I needed to get out of there as soon as possible. My report time was a few minutes away and I still had to unload this carry on that was about to bust out of my anal sphincter.

"Joseph, let me make you a copy."

"Just put it in my file," I stood up and moved the chair back to its original location, "I have to get ready for my report."

"Oh. I almost forgot to tell you," he stood to shake my hand, "Crew Scheduling called me to modify your pairing and you are now doing a later trip." While he looked down at his handwritten note I pulled out my cell phone to see that I had missed a call. Must have been while I was going through TSA. He continued with an evil grin, "Looks like you are going to Port-Au-Prince tonight."

Myron's hateful grin convinced me he experienced schadenfreude whenever the opportunity presented itself to make a flight attendant's life miserable; which I believed was every single fucking day of his life.

THE CRAZY BACARDI LADY

I was positioned in the middle of the airplane preparing to deliver the inflight safety demonstration when my eyes focused on the lady seated in 16B. I will call her Bonnie. How she slipped past me during boarding, I will never know.

Bonnie's hair was disheveled, her face smudged with dirt, and she was sporting an oversized brown winter jacket. A jacket three times too large. If it were January in New York City, it might not be bizarre, but this was August in Houston. It was blazingly hot. Standing outside for even five minutes was equivalent to being placed under a broiler. If she spent mere seconds outside in that jacket she would cook faster than a tilapia.

Her jacket was the first red flag. My instinct told me something was batty about Bonnie but I ignored my gut. In all honesty, I thought the angst in my belly was from the fried pickles I ate the night before. The checkered flag came down as I commenced the pre-flight safety demonstration. I pulled the life vest over my head and she mimicked my every movement from her aisle seat. I lost my focus on the cabin. It didn't stop with the life vest. Watching Bonnie was mesmerizing as she put an imaginary oxygen mask up to her lips and sucked the air through it. Did I look like that while I conducted the oxygen mask demo? Jesus Christ of Latter-day Saints, I hoped not. If I looked like that while sucking anything I would never put a dick in my mouth again.

We were on a smaller airplane with a 2x2 seat configuration. It's my favorite type of airplane because the lack of middle seat usually makes for content airline passengers. Sitting next to Bonnie in 16A was Cole; a tall, juicy, and an incredibly handsome Navy lieutenant. How did I know he was a lieutenant? Because, besides being an overly aggressive top who liked to make me oink like a piglet, lieutenant was his official position in the sexual fantasy I created while walking down the aisle towards row 16. He was most likely an ensign but if my sexually deviant mind promoted him, then so be it. Cole had a buzz cut, chiseled jaw, and was decked out in his military fatigues. He was the entire package. A package I was going to unwrap with my eyes as I made my way down the aisle. As I approached his row, my semi went completely flaccid as my eyes moved from Cole to Bonnie. Squashed against the airplane window, Cole looked terribly uncomfortable. It was my duty as an American citizen to move him to another seat— a more comfortable and spacious seat far from Bonnie. That proves I will do anything for my country, even in the great state of Texas, where my marriage was not legal at the time.

I stood at their row and looked at Cole. He was hotter than she must have been with that giant jacket wrapped around her. "Sir," I smiled and they both looked up at me, "please grab your things and come with me. I have a different seat for you."

He looked up at me and didn't move. I was worried. Did I stick my foot in my mouth? Was he with her? Was this his wife? Girlfriend? Mother? That was impossible. He still didn't move and my heart sank. For fuck's sake, was he Norman Bates?

"I'm fine." He finally spoke and gave me a slight grimace. At least he wasn't the victim of human trafficking. Obviously, he didn't want her feelings hurt. Hot and a gentlemen. My semi was back and hiding behind my demo bag. I refused to make him sit that close to Bonnie.

I repeated myself, "Please grab your things and come with me."

This time he listened. Faith in humanity and my loins was restored. Cole grabbed his bag from underneath the seat in front of him and with one long stretch climbed over Bonnie's legs. He managed not to touch an inch of her body. I was impressed. I was also impressed by his height as he hovered over me like a tall oak tree. I took a moment to take him in; he smelled like a Tom Ford fragrance. It was a fantastic smell. Cole had me so rock hard that a terrorist could have shot me point blank and the bullet would have simply ricochet off.

Cole followed me down the aisle to the exit row where I presented him with an entire row. Presenting him with my entire *hole* sounded better, but flight attendant uniforms are a bitch to pull down in a hurry. "Is this better?"

He grinned, "Thank you so much. I appreciate it."

I wanted to ask him how much he appreciated it but I had to get back to my jumpseat before we departed.

Watching Bonnie was like witnessing a train derailment. She was that intense. I fought the urge to gawk while strutting past her but it was impossible to turn away. She resembled a homeless person I once stumbled upon in Portland, Oregon who was confused and talking to the bridge she was sitting under. Bonnie wasn't far off from crazy Portland lady. She stared at Cole's empty window seat, having an intense conversation with herself. Listen, I have been known to chat myself up when I am alone but this was completely different. This was over the top extreme. She laughed, twitched, frowned, and then laughed again; all within the 30 seconds it took me to pass her while walking towards the back galley. I hadn't seen such emotional range since the cemetery scene in *Steel Magnolias*. I was ready to charge her imaginary friend a full fare for the flight.

After takeoff, and during our initial climb to cruising altitude, I envisioned Bonnie running to the back galley and wrestling passed me to open the airplane door. That, or standing in front of me, pulling down her stained panties, and pissing all over my new shiny black work shoes. I almost threw up in my mouth thinking about her stained panties. They probably smelled like fishy cat's breath. Talk about reasons to cancel beverage service for the remainder of the flight. Then, I thought, what could be worse than her cat breath? If she ran the opposite way to attack Cole for leaving her alone in row 16. There would have been no hope for me at that point. My only option being to stage dive over three rows and viciously attack her for even thinking about touching my imaginary lover.

Thankfully, none of that happened. I definitely suffer from an overactive imagination while seated on the jumpseat. After setting up my galley, I strolled up the aisle and started beverage service at row 13. Interacting with Bonnie was inevitable and I soon found myself handing her a napkin. She ignored me while watching an episode of *SpongeBob Squarepants* on her television. She wasn't just watching the episode—too normal for Bonnie—she was using her crusty dark stained fingers to outline the characters on the screen. Her concentration was unsettling. I imagined she looked that intense when she was coloring, working on a large puzzle, or cutting up the neighbor's cat. I considered fingering the screen was better than if she had a black sharpie in her hand. Wrestling a black sharpie out of her hand would have had me cursing myself for moving Cole to the exit row. Bonnie was stocky, strong, and I would need all the hot man power I could get prying that marker from her contaminated fingers.

I didn't know whether to take her drink order or throw spare change down on her tray table. I had put it off long enough. I had to talk to her, and to be honest, watching her with those fingers on the television screen made me mad. "May I get you something to drink?" I asked while waving the napkin at her. She snapped out of her psychotic trance and took the napkin. After a closer investigation of her fingers it was clear what she really needed was some kerosene and a match. It was time to set them fuckers ablaze.

She mumbled, "Coke." The way her request sputtered out, I thought for a moment that maybe she was deaf and not a raging alcoholic who smelled like yogurt left out in the sun. I quickly moved to the next row, took my drink orders, and started delivering the drinks. I am fast at beverage service. I don't fuck around. Some flight attendants take their sweet-ass time and practically crawl down the aisle serving drinks. Not me, I run over them bitches. I'm like Speedy Gonzales in the aisle, but instead of all the "¡Arriba! ¡Arriba! ¡Andale! ¡Andale! ¡Yii-hah!" bullshit I just yell, "Move bitches!"

When I reached Bonnie's row I placed the Coke on her tray table, careful not to make skin contact. I smiled and turned to the row across from her preparing to hand a cup of coffee to a male passenger. Out of the corner of my eye I saw her raise her hand attempting to grab my attention. Was she trying to touch me? I jerked so quick I almost spilled the hot coffee on 16C.

"One second, please." I placed the coffee on the gentleman's tray table, "Be careful, sir, it's hot." When I was done tending to him I turned back to Bonnie and cracked a phony smile, "Yes. What can I get you?" She pointed at her cup but didn't speak. Sadly for her, I don't understand real sign language, just the made up shit I use on layovers in Charlotte. I stared at her for a moment then asked, "Can I get you something else?"

She muttered something under her breath that I couldn't make out. I leaned in about a centimeter closer but stopped there. No way was I taking the chance of burning off my beard by getting my face near her skin. Standing at row one and yelling into the onboard bullhorn sounded perfect but that was not an option, "What was that? I couldn't hear you."

She finally blurted out, "Bacardi."

"Oh. You want a Bacardi?" I asked and she nodded. "That's gonna be $6.00. We only accept credit or debit cards."

Bonnie nodded and went back to coloring in the television screen with her imaginary finger sharpie. Before I went to the liquor cart, I stopped in the lavatory, turned the water temperature dial to scalding, and ran my hands under the water. Not wanting my screams to frighten passengers I bit down on a wad of airplane maxi pads while my epidermis turned bright red. It's just skin, right? It grows back. I'd much rather deal with third-degree burns than the hand-foot-and-mouth disease that Bonnie was trying to give me. When you interact with passengers like Bonnie, you make goddamn sure you burn your hands when you wash them. I don't care if the CDC recommends washing your hands for 20 seconds this was a 120-second project: 30 seconds to lather up and 90 seconds to kill any skin cells that tried jumping ship onto my life raft. Fuck universal precautions—these were Bonnie precautions—and I took them more seriously than a diabetic Dominican lady (they ask for 15 sugars per one cup of coffee) over the Caribbean Sea.

After I was sure my hands were clean, I returned to the scene and placed the Bacardi mini on her tray table with another cup of ice and a stir stick. I did not want to return. I had the credit card charging machine under my arm and immediately began ringing up the sale. She didn't move a muscle so I thought I'd remind her, "That'll be $6.00."

I hovered over the seat waiting for her to produce her credit card. With a quick movement, that made me jerk back again, she started rummaging around. She hastily opened and closed her overstuffed jacket and pulled the seatback pocket forward to look inside it. All these dramatics made me nervous. I try not glaring at a passenger when they dig for their credit card but it happens quite frequently and I honestly don't understand it. So I glare. Passengers know they will be charged for alcoholic purchases but the second you ask for payment, they act shocked and surprised. Do they act this way at the grocery store after their items are all rung up? I doubt it. I turned my head down the aisle to grab a glimpse at the top of Cole's head but I couldn't see him. He must have been sleeping against the window. I bet he was a cute sleeper. I'd never find out though because I was dealing with Bonnie, the crazy Bacardi lady. When I looked back down at her she was holding a plastic card between her fingers.

Staring at her government issued Texas state ID I thought about how to react—because let's face it—Bonnie was bonkers. My eyes scanned back and forth from the picture on the card to her disgusting fingers. I know I keep bringing them up- but they were atrocious. Each time I saw them I shuttered. Being finger banged by Edward Scissorhands for five minutes sounded more pleasant than shaking her hand for two seconds.

This brief moment with Bonnie brought me back to the time when I worked in the emergency department in the psychiatric triage unit. We saw every type of fucked up human being you could imagine. From the normal drunk person, who was brought in by the police, to the short young pregnant lady who went off her schizophrenia medication. She banged on the glass window in her cell until her hands bled. It was sad. This bitch had fallen off her rocker and there was no way to pick her back up.

She screamed at us every time we walked by, "This is Satan's baby. You'll all suffer at the hands of my child. He will be the next Hitler."

I just wanted this bitch to shut up so I could read my book and get through my shift without drama. After three hours in her small locked padded cell she convinced me she would stop acting like a deranged whacko, so I let her out to use the restroom. I didn't want to unlock the cell but the last thing I needed was some insane madwoman pissing on the floor, slipping on it, and aborting the next Hitler.

That doesn't sound so bad now that I think of it.

The moment I let her out of the cell she started running. I have no idea where she was going because we were in a locked unit. I tackled her hard but lost my grip and missed taking her down. We wrestled for a few seconds while yelling obscenities at each other. She called me a motherfucker and I called her a bitch, just your average Wednesday night in the psychiatric unit. When I finally wrapped my arms around her and pulled her to the ground she sunk her schizoid teeth into my arm.

It was that exact experience years ago that kept my sarcasm in check while dealing with Bonnie. In the psychiatric unit I was prepared for interactions with dangerous demented patients, but on the airplane, my patience for crazy went as far as someone angry that we were out of Sprite Zero. Not knowing how unstable Bonnie really was made me tiptoe around her row. One snide remark from me and she might have easily reached up, pulled me by my necktie, and bit off my nose. Or worse, stuck her thumb in my mouth. The Bacardi mini sat on her tray table and my instinct told me she had no plans on paying for the drink.

I smiled, "That is not a credit card, that's your ID." Her blank stare meant nothing to me at that point. Was she trying to destroy me with her mind? She had no idea she was already destroying me with her fingers. She placed the ID on the tray table and continued patting herself down. I thought about how many times she got away with stealing from 7-11 because the police refused to frisk her.

The farce went on long enough and I became annoyed, which was no good for either one of us. I decided that if Bonnie thought I was getting mouthy—and jammed her fingers down my throat—I would close my eyes and bite down really hard like I was grinding up a mouthful of almonds. I equated it to taking one for the team. If I could help another flight attendant, or the world, from ever having to look at those digits again I'd be doing the planet a huge favor. It would probably happen fast. I'd say something snarky, she'd jam—I'd bite—and then I'd wake up in the hospital attached to an IV antibiotic strong enough to kill the invasion of the Bonnie fingers that entered my body.

While she checked her jacket pockets for the fifth time I fought the urge to say, "Girl, the only thing you got in that jacket is dust mites and lost dreams." I kept my mouth shut. I guess I really didn't want to chew on her fingers. She continued fishing for her "lost" credit card and then abruptly looked up and said as clear as a Southern California day, "Sam has it."

Who in homosexual hell was Sam? Bonnie was tempting the evil demons right out of me, but I stayed calm. Deep breaths. Deep fucking breaths were my friend because I was mere seconds away from shoving my fist down her throat, "Who is Sam?"

"I'm traveling with him," she pointed to the front of the airplane, "he's up there in one of those seats." I honestly believed she expected me to walk up the aisle looking for Sam so she could drink the mini before I returned. Bitch, not on my watch. This was no fucking 7-11, this was my airplane.

"What seat is he in?"

"I don't know," she pointed again, "up there."

"Want to go find him?" My patience ran thinner than her hair. I had 49 other passengers to tend to and somehow this had become *The Bonnie Show*, a show that I did not sign up for. I was ready to cancel this shit faster than ABC cancelled *Pan Am*.

"No," she looked back at the television, "I don't know where he is."

Even though I was unhappy I smiled. Then with a swooping motion I grabbed the Bacardi mini off her tray table. This time it was her turn to jerk backwards from my cat like reflexes. I cheerfully responded, "Well, when you find Sam and get his credit card please ring your call bell. I'll gladly charge you for this drink." I placed the mini bottle in my front apron pocket and tried making eye contact. Her eyes never broke from the television. She seemed to play it off as if the entire conversation never occurred. I paused for an additional moment waiting for her to respond, but she never did. Once I realized she drifted back off to crazy land, I strutted away leaving her with her virgin Coke. There was never a Sam. There was never a credit card. And there was never a chance in hell Bonnie was getting a free drink.

THE UNDERCOVER DICK PILOT

Working with dicks can be dreadful. Well, unless you are a whore, then it's just a normal Tuesday. I've worked with dicks my entire life. Most likely—and I hate to admit it—I've probably been the dick a few times, too. Teachers deal with dick principals, nurses juggle dick doctors, and on most occasions flight attendants spend hours in a metal tube saving face with dick pilots. I spent 15 years working with difficult doctors and I'd much rather be locked in a medication room being injected with a Michael Jackson dose of Propofol than spend any significant amount of time on an airplane with a dick pilot.

Dick pilots come in all shapes, sizes, and colors. Some black, some short, a few Asian, but mostly white fat Republican fucks who have a God complex. There are two distinct types of dick pilots: mega dick pilots and undercover dick pilots. You can search the dictionary for these two definitions but you will be searching for a long time. Trust me. How do I know? Because I made these terms up after having the unfortunate experience of working with both kinds.

Let's tackle the ever demanding and miserable mega dick pilot first. I will be honest- you do not want to fuck with a mega dick pilot. Working with a mega dick pilot makes a diversion to San Antonio for seven hours seem fun and enjoyable. When I see them coming my first instinct is to run the other way. Mega dick pilots are usually under 5-feet 5-inches tall. There's always the off chance that a few of them will measure in at 5-feet 6-inches, but I doubt it. Something important to remember right off the bat is to never let these short fuckers fool you. These little guys are vicious. They have the ability to gnaw the skin off your kneecaps without having to bend over. They can lick your balls while doing double duty as a bedside table. I could name all the uses for these short fuckers but it might take up the entire story. If you haven't seen one of these petite guys yet don't beat yourself up. You probably walk with your head held high so it's easy to miss them as they shuffle by your feet like tiny elves. What these guys lack in height they make up tenfold in nasty attitude. That's why I call them mega dick pilots, not for their height, but for their ginormous attitudes. Attitudes so big they could be contestants on the *Biggest Loser*.

Why do these mega dick pilots think they know everything when their skulls are so much smaller than the average person's? Great question, right? The last time I came face-to-face with a mega dick pilot was in Raleigh, North Carolina. He didn't have to say a word; I could read his body language loud and clear as he walked down the jet bridge toward the airplane. At first I thought he was the first officer's luggage but then, once I made contact with his beady little eyes, I knew exactly what was up. Shorty Smurf had an appalling attitude, was a Federal Flight Deck

Officer (he carried a gun), and frowned like he was just stood up by a really tall prostitute. His sourpuss made me want to throw up my $10.00 airport sandwich. Shorty stepped onto the airplane with his chest protruding out as if he was riddled with osteoarthritis. The moment his size six shoe touched the airplane he started barking orders like Irene's chihuahua (you will learn more about her later), "We need to board 20 minutes early. I have a commute to catch and I need to get home." He adjusted his tiny belt and pants, "Also, give me a trash bag, a cup of ice with a Diet Coke, and I'd like a black coffee before we start boarding."

Correct me if I am wrong but I'm not aware that it is written in any flight attendant manual—or job description—that our duties included being the pilot's bitch. There are flight attendants that strive for this position, or any position a pilot can get them in, but not this flight attendant. Shorty was unaware of that so here we were, playing out these roles like a Broadway show, one that I'd have never auditioned for if I had read the script. I fantasized about dousing him with pepper spray and pushing him through the tiny crack between the airplane and the jet bridge.

"I don't have any brewed. We're about to board." I responded while pulling the trash bag out from the galley bin.

"Brew some." He lifted his suitcase and placed it into the flight deck behind the captain's chair, "Is that difficult?"

I couldn't concentrate on anything but watching him struggle with his luggage. How was he even able to lift his bag? It was gigantic compared to him. Where did this fucker commute from, Lilliput? I could only assume he wore the same clothes day after day and packed feathers in his luggage so he could easily lift the large bag without asking for assistance.

"No, sir. Black coffee coming right up." I hit the brew button on the coffee pot. I wanted to ask him if he wanted that served in a thimble but the idea of spending another night in Raleigh was out of the question.

Another thing about Shorty, he always had to have the last word. Yelling up from the flight deck he added, "If any of these asshole passengers give you a hard time let me know and I will take care of it."

Take care of it? That made me swallow my loud laugh and burp it right back up. I am perfectly capable of handling my own passenger confrontations. This mega dick pilot struggled reaching the overhead bin without stepping on a passenger seat. How would he help me? Kick them in the ankle, climb up their leg, and bitch slap them with his baby hand?

It's hard not cornering these types of pilots in the flight deck and reminding them, politely and professionally, of course, that anyone can do their job. They are pilots flying people around on vacation and to business meetings. They haven't saved the world. Call me when you find the cure for cancer.

With that said, not all pilots are dicks. I have had the pleasure of working with some of the kindest and most polite pilots at my airline. Pilots who treat their flight attendants like human beings, not just employees who they order around to get them cups of coffee and Diet Cokes with only one cube of ice in the cup. That's a true story. It didn't happen to me, but a fellow flight attendant confessed that a pilot asked her once for a cup with only one cube of ice. One cube of ice? Bitch, please. Get your fat ass up and get that shit yourself. That's totally the kind of shit a dick pilot does. If you ever encounter a dick pilot who's acting nice, it's probably because he just got divorced and his wife was awarded nothing.

I can always tell when I'm working with a nice pilot because they have excellent communications skills during the initial briefing. Let's face it, most pilots suck when it comes to communication which is probably the reason so many of their marriages end in divorce. That and the fact they don't know how to keep their zippers shut. I stand corrected, they know how to keep their zipper shut—they just don't want to. Flying with a pilot with great communication skills is like spotting a polar bear in a bank of snow; you know they're out there but they are so damn hard to find. The nice pilots, not the dick pilots, tend to go above and beyond to make their flight attendants feel special. Not just the flight attendants with the short skirts and big tits but even the male flight attendants, gay and straight.

Nice pilots take our bags down from the overhead bin. They help clean up the airplane between quick turns. They wait for us so we can all walk to the hotel van together. They offer to do a coffee run when we can't get off the airplane. Buying us a cup of coffee may be the nicest thing a pilot can do for their flight attendants. When this happens, I am so grateful that I have to fight off the urge to drop to my knees and offer up my blow job services. I feel that's the least I can do. It's my duty as the flight attendant to blow a pilot for a cup of coffee. Right? I've done it for far less so why not for a caffeine boost. As thrilling as that sounds, I don't believe the passengers in the front row want that type of show. Well, unless I am working a flight to San Francisco during gay pride. In that case, they'd give me a standing ovation after hot towel service. Nice pilots are exactly that: they are nice. They purchase donuts on a transcon flight, write in compliment letters to the airline on your behalf, and buy the crew brisket sandwiches from The Salt Lick in Austin, Texas.

A few years ago I had the pleasure of working with my friend Lyla. It was an easy trip with a long layover in Dallas, Texas. The pilots who flew us from Los Angeles to Dallas were continuing on to Orlando so we said our goodbyes as we walked off the airplane and found our way to the hotel van. We climbed into the hotel van and found ourselves greeted by two other airline pilots on their way to the hotel. One was older and one was hot. They noticed we were traveling without pilots and invited us out for drinks. We said 'yes' and immediately checked online to see if their airline was currently hiring flight attendants. They weren't.

After changing out of our uniforms into something more suitable for an afternoon of layover drinking, we all met downstairs in the hotel lobby and walked a few blocks to a local bar. The drinks were flying at us like dicks at a gay college frat party. My kind of party. Lyla with her long flowing brunette hair, white T-shirt, and large perky tits leaned over and whispered to me, "I think he wants to hook up with me."

"Which one?"

"The old one."

I had picked up on that too, especially when he tried showing her his collection of personal dick pictures on his iPhone. There was no way she was going to fuck him. That disappointed me. I was having so much fun and didn't want the free drinks to stop. For all the money he was spending on us, someone had to give it up. I thought about throwing myself into the equation but I was already too many glasses of wine in to stay awake for Captain Clyde— so oral was out of the question. So was anal. "Most likely," I said ordering another glass of Pinot Grigio, "just close your eyes and take one for the team."

"Joe! You are crazy," she said sipping on her third vodka and seltzer.

Lyla did not fuck him. I guess that was a smart decision. Even though she avoided all his advances he still got us wasted and paid the expensive tab. All that on a Wednesday night.

Situations with nice pilots, like the one I just shared, are rare. I shared that story so I don't come off as some pilotphobe flight attendant. I really don't hate pilots. In fact, I find most of them hot. I actually get along better with pilots than I do flight attendants. It's the dick pilots that I can't stand. Unfortunately, my interactions with these pilots tends to be over the top. I have dealt with an alarming number of dick pilots during my career as a flight attendant but none have left me wanting to commit murder like Jimbo Saks.

Captain Saks (Jimbo from this moment on) was the ultimate dick pilot. In fact, he was what I refer to as an undercover dick pilot. Mega dick pilots want you to know right off the bat that they are small, in charge, and don't like anyone taller than them, which comes out to roughly 92.8% of the population (or something like that). Heartbreaking, right? Almost makes me feel bad for those shrimps. Undercover dick pilots are the complete opposite. They play you like a banjo and pluck at your strings catching you off guard with their beautiful music. They are sneaky bastards with no soul. An undercover dick pilot hides his true feelings, judgements, and racist beliefs deep inside his Southern beer belly until the most opportunistic time. Their truth surfaces the moment you let down your guard and think they are cool. Suddenly, without warning and with the right amount of alcohol, they unleash the gates of hell on you proving that people living in the deep South should really be segregated from the rest of the United States.

I enjoy the flexibility of my job. Having the ability to bid for trips with layovers in different cities keeps me entertained. In one given month I can party with friends in Ft. Lauderdale, party with friends in Austin, and party with friends in Boston. As you can see, I like to party and I have many friends. On some trips it's a nonstop party from the moment we arrive at the hotel until bedtime. Some months our schedules are fabulous, and some months they are so terrible I contemplate tossing myself down a flight of stairs just to break a limb. It all depends. I enjoy trips with long layovers, in fun cities, and being assigned to work with flight attendants I get along with.

We might also find ourselves being awarded trips on certain airplanes we may—or may not—enjoy flying around the country on. The airline that I work for has four different airplane types. I usually don't care which airplane I work on because at the end of the day I am still doing the same shit; flying around at 37,000 feet, handing out sodas, and having my ass pinched by hot older men. That last part hasn't happened yet but I have high hopes it will. Honestly, I have no preference of which airplane I work, but if I had to choose I'd work the larger airplane. The main reason being the number of flights we have to work on the smaller airplane in a single day. On those airplanes we can work anywhere between two to four flights per day, and the airline expects us to be as happy and friendly on the fourth flight as we were on the first flight. Not going to happen. I don't care what anyone at the airline says, after working four flights in one day there's no flight attendant who will act chipper and friendly. That's an impossible assumption.

The Baby Jet, as most of us refer to it at my airline, has 100 seats and is the smallest airplane in our fleet. Because of the seat configuration the FAA (do I really have to explain who they are?) requires the airline to assign two flight attendants to work the airplane. When we're awarded trips on the Baby Jet we stay with the pilots for the entire length of the trip. That's completely different than our larger airplanes, where we stay with the same flight attendant crew for the entire trip but change out pilots like we change out liquor carts on a Las Vegas flight-each leg and often. Being awarded one of these trips can be fun if you are working with pleasant and friendly people. If you are stuck with asshole pilots, or a bitch flight attendant, then these trips can be soulsucking experiences that you wouldn't wish on a passenger traveling with four carry on bags.

When our monthly bid was published I was pleased to see a New Orleans layover on my schedule. The heat and humidity usually keeps me out of New Orleans during the summer but I hadn't visited The Big Easy in months. I decided to keep the trip. New Orleans layovers are fun and you'll know why if you've ever visited the city. Pairings at my airline range from one day to five day trips and this pairing was a quick two day trip with a 16 hour layover. We were scheduled to land at 11:30 p.m. and depart the following day at 5 p.m. This was just enough time to drink, eat, sleep, eat, shower, sleep, shave, get coffee, and head back to the airport. My kind of layover.

Most of the time I work with flight attendants I do not know. There are thousands of us so it's feasible most often I will work with someone I have never met before. That works out great as long as they do their jobs correctly. For this trip, the flight attendant Gods were watching over me. The initial person assigned to work with me dropped the trip which allowed my friend Abbie Seltzer to pick it up. The second she knew we were flying together she texted me threatening my life if I called in sick. I informed her I had no plans on dropping the New Orleans layover and I was thrilled she was on it. With her wind blown blond curls, tall stature, and dark rimmed glasses, Abbie was fantastic. Electric. She lite up the entire airplane cabin on a red-eye flight. Sure, she slammed the flight deck door louder than any other flight attendant I'd ever worked with, but if you could get past that—like I had—then working with her was a reward. I loved every minute of it.

The moment we reported in the crew lounge we started planning our evening.

"What do you want to do tonight? I was thinking about this jazz piano bar?" Abbie asked while repacking her tote bag with her flight attendant manual.

A jazz piano bar was not my scene but I went along with it, "Sure. Let's see what happens. Can we do shots there?"

She laughed. "Oh Joe. This is going to be so much fun."

This was not the first time I had worked with Abbie. A few months prior we had managed through a day from hell. A one day pairing that was originally scheduled to last only eight hours but ended up continuing on for 16 hours. By the time the airplane landed in Cleveland we were physically exhausted and beaten down by passengers. It was past midnight and although we were scheduled to report off several hours prior, we walked off the airplane laughing like we had just been paid to do nothing but drink wine and eat copious amounts of cheese. Two things I love to do more than anything else, I might add.

Our captain was shocked, "I can't believe it. I've never seen flight attendants so happy after a fucked up day like this."

"What are you gonna do? It is what it is." I responded. Abbie agreed and we continued laughing while walking through the airport.

Then the laughter stopped for a brief second. She added, "I missed the last fucking bus and now I have to sleep in the crew lounge." We paused for another second and then busted out laughing again. I can only imagine we were truly fatigued and didn't know what we were saying. Sleeping in the crew lounge was nothing to joke or laugh about. It didn't matter though because Abbie was the kind of person you wanted to work with on a shitty day. She spoiled you with her heart of gold and laugh so contagious you'd need a vaccine to prevent from catching the giggles when she erupted into laughter. If her career as a flight attendant fails to work out she can always aspire to be a divorce arbitrator, bringing her viral laugh to the most miserable divorces.

The day of our New Orleans trip we walked through the airport laughing, joking, and smiling at every individual we passed. If passengers waiting for their flights didn't know better, they'd think we were high on brownies sent from Amsterdam. That wasn't a far stretch for Miss Abbie Seltzer. I doubt she was actually high, but I have never met anyone so happy. I think that if we crashed into the sea and they found her strapped to the jumpseat she'd be grinning from ear to ear. When they found me they'd see a vodka mini stuffed in my mouth. After a quick stop for coffee we found our way to gate 15 and introduced ourselves to Jimbo and First Officer Kirby Kline.

Kirby was friendly, young, handsome, and easy to talk to. I informed Abbie that he'd hang out with us in New Orleans even if he didn't want to. It wasn't an option. Jimbo was a different story. He was talkative but left me with a bad feeling in the pit of my stomach, like I had just finished doing shots of habanero sauce in the desert; a feeling that a gallon of water couldn't cure. I immediately noticed his speech was slow and drawn out. More like an illiterate who failed the second grade twice or a guy who suffered a stroke and never fully recovered. I am no expert on genealogy, but I'd put my money on the fact that he was conceived by two first cousins fucking in the back of a beat up pickup truck. Like I said, I am no expert, but I do believe he was born in Kentucky, and don't quote me on this, but I do think inbreeding is that state's past time.

After we departed, and right before service started, I walked to the front of the airplane to talk it over with Abbie. Did she feel the same way about Jimbo? I had to find out. "I don't think I like this Jimbo character," I whispered to her while she set up her galley.

119

"I know. He seems weird." She responded pulling napkins and cups from the service bin.

I smiled. "I agree."

"But he already asked me what we were doing tonight so I invited him out," she replied taking a swig out of the clear plastic bottle she carried with her everywhere. The liquid inside was suspicious. It was some odd concoction that looked like day old urine. I doubt it was urine but the cloudy amber looking substance made me uncomfortable. I had no idea what was in that water bottle and I didn't care to ask.

"I can't believe you invited him out." I curled up my right lip leaning against the galley wall to block the nosy passengers in row from listening. They are always eavesdropping. "Why did you do that?"

She got flustered, "I don't know. I can tell him no if you want?"

And make me look like the asshole? I had to think about it for a moment. "No. He's probably not bad. I'm just being a bitch and my coffee hasn't kicked in." I only half believed that, "I just hope he looks better in normal clothes than that uniform. He's a fat mess."

She pulled her apron over her head,, "I'm sure he'll be fine. He doesn't seem *that* bad."

Our day consisted of three flights: Cleveland to Nashville, Nashville to Jacksonville, and then finally Jacksonville to New Orleans. We landed 30 minutes early which in the airline industry means free money.[1] Landing 30 minutes equates to having a drink in your hand that much sooner. It's really all I think about when I know fun will be awaiting

---

[1] We are paid for the original flight time. If we arrive early, we're still paid the full amount. That's right, bitches!

me once I get out of my uniform and change into something more relaxing. We said goodbye to the last passenger and then the four of us hightailed it out of the airport to the hotel van waiting for us.

The moment we stepped outside into the muggy Louisiana air, Jimbo stopped at the curb, dug deep into his pocket, and pulled out a pack of Marlboro reds. "Hey ya'll. I gotta have a smoke."

That motherfucker. The last thing he needed to do was smoke a cigarette, especially when his belly hadn't caught up to the rest of his body. I looked back and it was still rolling by baggage claim. He was that fat. I was sure that at some point in his life he got caught inside the revolving door at one of our layover hotels. Probably the reason we were kicked out of the Sheraton in downtown Philadelphia. I rolled my eyes as he stood to the side of the van and lit up his cigarette. If he had a heart attack at that exact moment I would tell the driver there was a $20 tip in it for him if he drove like Vin Diesel in *The Fast and the Furious*. Kirby, Abbie, and I placed our bags at the back door of the van for the driver and then the three of us climbed into the van waiting for Jimbo. He wasn't phased that we were waiting for him. I looked out the window while he puffed on his cigarette like a flapper from the 1920's. A fat flapper. That pissed me off.

I waited a few minutes, looked back and forth at Kirby and Abbie, and then my temper got the best of me, "Let's go! I need a drink," I made sure he heard me.

Dick pilots don't care about anyone but themselves. They especially don't care that the flight attendants patiently waiting in the van have spent their entire day serving hundreds of passengers sodas, cups of black coffee, and nuts in a pressurized tube. All we want is to leave the airport as quickly as possible; not wait for some obese pilot to finish his cigarette. An obese pilot who couldn't master the simple task of tucking his fucking shirt into his pants. It was at that moment I knew I would not be joining the Jimbo fan club. The three of us sat patiently in the van watching him hungrily puff on his cigarette until he finally threw the remains of the butt on the ground and squashed it with his heavy foot. Puffing the smoke into the air he shuffled his bags over to the young van driver—who had been waiting in the back of the van with the door open—and wobbled to the van door and boarded with the rest of us.

He climbed in (literally), plopped his ass down in a seat, and made no attempt at closing the door. He sat there catching his breath from walking five feet and climbing one step into the van. I was in the last row as far away as possible. I wanted to sit on the luggage in the back of the van but it wasn't an option. The sweat dripped off his brow like a draining faucet forcing him to push his glasses back onto the bridge of his nose every few seconds. It was sad. The driver walked around and slid the door with a force that made us all jump. When Jimbo jumped I thought the van shifted gears. He pulled a tissue from his pocket and wiped his forehead, "Sorry guys, but I smoke."

No shit. From his one cigarette the entire van smelled like the set of *Mad Men*.

With his messy hair, neck waddle, and beer belly, Jimbo was repulsive. I couldn't imagine any human being finding him attractive but the wedding ring on his finger begged to differ. Someone found him charming enough to marry and occasionally fuck because he boasted a few times about his kids. People like him reproducing proves there's no hope for humanity. The idea that some poor woman had to climb under him while he penetrated her had my stomach in knots and wishing I could reach the Pepto Bismol in my tote bag. I only hoped that she was usually on top, at least if not for comfort, for the sake of her poor squishy uterus.

While he continued to ramble on about who-knows-what the three of us kept our faces down and tapped away at our cell phones while passing the SuperDome. I secretly wished bad things on Abbie for inviting him out with us. Nothing too life threatening, just that her hair turn grayer or that the next time she had sex the guy had a micro penis. You know, shit that matters. My desire to push him out of the van increased every time he spoke. While he continued rambling, I wanted to stuff the pack of cigarettes in his front shirt pocket down his throat.

I texted Abbie: *"I can't believe you invited him to come with us."*

She looked back at me and frowned. Any lie she told him would have worked: we had headaches, we had horrible corns on the bottom of our feet, we had our periods and were bleeding out all over our jumpseats; anything was better than putting up with him for the night. I would have gone so far as to sacrifice any chances of witnessing Kirby naked with my own eyes. Anything.

The van pulled up to our hotel and we all filed out after Jimbo. He took forever to slide the door open with his ham hock arm. Kirby followed next, then Abbie, and I took up the rear. I grabbed my bags and started towards the hotel lobby to check in.

Jimbo pulled his bags to the side of the building and already had another cigarette hanging out of his mouth,, "Leave my key at the desk. I'm grabbing a quick smoke."

"Of course you are." I responded and pushed open the door and entered the hotel. Kirby and Abbie followed behind me.

The front desk clerk smiled, "Good Evening. Flight number?"

"456," I answered placing my hands on the counter.

She had three plastic key cards in one hand and a solo card in the other, "I have three rooms on the seventh floor and one on the ninth floor." We snatched the three keys on the seventh floor right out of her hand. Jimbo was still outside as we walked to the elevator. Kirby tried spotting him through the glass window, "Can you see him out there?" Abbie and I didn't say a word. We weren't looking, "I'll just text him and let him know the plans."

Did he really have to text him? I thought that was unnecessary. I had hoped the reason we couldn't see him standing outside was because he had already been mugged and left for dead.

Alright—just wounded. I'm not a monster.

Abbie asked, "What are the plans? What are we doing?"

I pushed for the elevator, "Let's meet down here in 15 minutes and then we'll decide."

"Sounds good," Kirby answered, "I need some food."

Abbie was giddy with excitement, "I am up for anything."

Was she up for a slap across the tits for inviting Jimbo? I wanted to ask her but I decided to leave that one in the back of my mind. My room was closest to the elevator and Kirby was right next door. I prayed for adjoining rooms—just in case—but as I walked in my room, instead of a friendly adjoining door, there was only a bare white wall. I parked my suitcase against the mirror and the moment my eyes made contact with the bed I had the desire to sleep. It happens often when I get to the hotel. I needed a recharge and because coffee wasn't an option, a shower would do. The shower would decide my fate of either waking up or just calling it a night. If that happened, I'd let Abbie know I was staying in for the night and if she found herself on the receiving end of a pilot bukkake, she could thank me in the morning. Well, thank me for Kirby. I'd expect her to throw up if Jimbo squirted his cigarette juice all over her.

The shower was a success and felt like a shot of B12. I changed into my favorite blue t-shirt, blue baseball hat, and khaki shorts. I snapped a selfie in the mirror, posted it on Facebook, and then let the door slam behind me as I walked towards the elevator.

The three of them each occupied one of the over-stuffed chairs in the hotel lobby and I was disappointed that Jimbo was still alive. Did I say alive? I meant not on his way to the emergency room for stitches. I forced a smile on my face and approached them. I didn't want to ruin Abbie's layover with my shitty attitude.

"Took you long enough. I thought you'd be down here first," Kirby jokingly said.

I smirked, "Needed to wash all the dirty airplane off me. Are we ready?" Without another word we stepped through the revolving hotel lobby door onto the uneven sidewalks of New Orleans.

All four of us had different ideas of how we wanted to spend our New Orleans layover. I shouldn't have been surprised. We walked one block from the hotel when Kirby spoke up, "I wanna grab some food and play pool."

Abbie joined in, "I hear there's a great live jazz bar in the French Quarter."

"I don't know if I wanna do that." I answered. She gave me a look but I gave it right back. I refused to back down especially when it was her fault that Jimbo was trailing behind us dragging his cellulitis legs. I added, "I just want some drinks and dance music."

"What you wanna do, man?" Kirby asked Jimbo who tracked behind us like an chain smoking elephant.

I was convinced the only thing Jimbo wanted to do was eat, smoke cigarettes, and annoy the fuck out of me. I came to that conclusion because he was still hanging with us and not in his room attaching his sleep apnea machine to his snout and going to sleep. Abbie continued clammering on about the live jazz band but I was distracted by the thought of running Jimbo over with massive farm equipment.

Jimbo put his cigarette out and caught up with us, we had to stop so he could catch up. I despised him. "There's a pool hall around the corner. The food is pretty good."

It was settled. As long as I had a gin and tonic in my hand in the next 10 minutes I didn't care. We entered the dark sports bar and it looked like they were about to close, and I don't mean for the night... forever. It reminded me of a bad vampire horror movie where the doors get locked and the hungry vampires feed on the drunk victims for the night. I would instinctively push Jimbo in front of us so the three of us had time to escape. I was pretty sure their entire coven could feast on him for a few days. I followed Kirby to the bar so we could order drinks. I'd be ready at the first sign of fangs. Kirby asked, "Do you have a food menu?"

"Sorry man. The kitchen closed fifteen minutes ago. Can I get you some drinks?"

Fuck. Now I would have to manage through Jimbo on an empty stomach.

"That sucks," Jimbo added with his cell phone in hand, "They have the best food here."

"Doesn't help us if the kitchen is closed." I spit out. It didn't phase him.

Jimbo asked Abbie to order him a drink and then he vanished outside for another cigarette. The time was well past 11 p.m. and after ordering our drinks Kirby moved the party over to one of the open pool tables draped by a wall of televisions.

"Who wants to play me?" Kirby asked grabbing a pool stick and sliding it up and down in the palm of his hand. I almost dropped my gin and tonic on the ground but composed myself so that I didn't make a scene. I was open for playing him until it was time to go back to the airport.

"I'll go first," Abbie giggled while taking a sip of her drink and placing it down on the round bar table. She laughed for no reason which made her more like a prepubescent teen than an older experienced woman. It was cute.

"Joe can play the winner." Kirby said as he entered the quarters into the slots on the table and released the balls. He moved to the end of the table and bent over while racking them up. I could hardly contain the drink in my glass from the excitement of him bent over. Thankfully, I don't spill alcohol unless it's going down my throat. I looked over at Abbie while we both took sips of our drinks and I mouthed, "Oh my god." We erupted into laughter and I was glad Kirby was intensely focused on making sure the balls were as straight as possible.

"Sounds good to me." I scooted myself up on one of the bar stools while he walked around the table and set up for his shot. His right bicep flexed as he moved his arm back and forth preparing to strike the cue ball with his long stick. Those balls placed perfectly together at the end of the pool table weren't the only ones looking for attention. The two in my shorts were about to burst and dribble down the side of my leg. When his long stick finally made contact with the cue ball and exploded into the awaiting balls at the end of the table, I shuddered. I sighed loudly. Abbie looked towards me and I grinned. From the way she glanced over I figured my pants weren't the only ones reacting to Kirby's fine ass. She probably needed a wet vac. And Kirby was right, he won before the game even started. She barely had a chance to play before he sunk the eight ball deep into the side pocket.

"You're up, Joe," He said pulling quarters out of his pocket and walking over to release the balls again. Jimbo had come back inside the bar from polluting the air outside. As he sat next to me at the bar table, I scooted over. In all fairness, he had just purchased a round of drinks so I was cutting him some slack even though my first instinct was to banish him to the other side of the bar. The side where I was certain the vampires would emerge from once they smelled his stench.

The four of us were double fisting and drinking like it was the end of the world. It might as well have been seeing the bar was officially closing in 20 minutes. We drank like we had just spent the last month on a deserted island. There wasn't a time that we didn't have two drinks at our disposal. One in our hand while the other one sat patiently awaiting our throats an arms length away. Kirby and I slapped pool balls around like professionals while Abbie talked to Jimbo about god-knows-what. I could have cared less. Maybe she was telling him that he was a fat fuck who should join Weight Watchers. I doubt it. She was too nice for that.

While we played pool, the Stanley Cup echoed from the televisions surrounding the bar. The Boston Bruins were hitting the ice against the Chicago Blackhawks and Kirby was fully invested in the game. He occasionally yelled at the television but for what team, I couldn't tell you. I really didn't care. I was fully invested in his arms and my gin and tonics. He beat me landing the eight ball into the side pocket again, all while barely paying attention.

I looked at Jimbo, "Are you gonna play?"

"Nah. Hey, let's go to Bourbon Street. I know this great piano bar we should check out."

We drank our drinks in quick gulps, ordered one more round for the road, and waved goodbye to the bartender. He was happy to see us go. Half a second after stepping outside, Jimbo lit up another cigarette. The way this dude smoked you'd think he carried a carton of Marlboro in his back pocket. My mind wandered to the image of him deeply inhaling the cigarette filter allowing the nicotine smoke to quickly surround his sizeable lungs while crushing his enlarged heart. It made me smile. On the other hand— my nicer hand—watching his attempts at keeping up with us in the muggy air made me almost pity him. Almost. If a stranger happened upon him they'd probably ask him why he'd been swimming with his clothes on. He was soaked from sweat and we hadn't walked a block. He struggled to walk down the sidewalk but held onto his cigarette like a fucking crutch. I even complained to Abbie about how loud he breathed. He sounded like a pack of wild boars running through the Everglades.

We turned onto the street that lead back to our hotel and Kirby paused for a moment, "Alright guys, I'm heading back to the hotel. Have a good night."

"What?" I stopped walking and stared at him, "You can't leave us." I sounded like a young child watching his dad go out for milk, destined to never return.

"Sorry, man. I've been awake since four this morning. I'm beat."

My puppy dog eyes did nothing for the straight first officer. He said his goodnights and disappeared down the street walking towards the hotel. My heart was broken for the night.

The humidity was disgusting. Every inch of me was screaming for ice water but there was none to be found. The only thing to refresh my thirst was the gin and tonic I held in my hand. To give my mouth a burst I'd occasionally suck on an ice cube before taking another sip of my drink. We followed Jimbo towards Canal Street and listened to his spiel about how we were about to experience the best piano bar in the world. Piano bars are not my thing. I find sitting in a piano bar surrounded by geriatric patrons to bring back memories of nursing school. A time I'd rather forget. Jimbo wasn't my thing either but here I was walking side by side with him and Abbie sipping my drink and agreeing with everything that came sputtering out of his mouth.

I had been daydreaming about Kirby as the three of us turned right onto Poydras Street. Now, I don't know if it was the humidity, alcohol, or nicotine overdose—or the fact that Kirby had abandoned us—but the moment we turned the corner Jimbo let his true self shine, "Obama is ruining this country. Destroying America. That's what he's doing."

It snapped me out of my Kirby fantasy and landed me smack dab in a nightmare on Poydras Street. How did we even get on the topic of Obama? I had no idea. While he continued his verbal assault on our 44th president, I racked my brain trying to remember how the conversation went from the piano bar to the president. How many drinks had I consumed? Was it enough to black out while walking down the street? Apparently it was. I looked over at Abbie while she worked on her best impression of acting like she gave a fuck what he had to say. I cleared my mind and started focusing on everything he was saying. Abbie walked between us as we made our way down the sidewalk. Jimbo finally let his guard down and I smiled knowing I had been right about him from the first moment I met his lard ass on the fucking jet bridge. We finally saw him for his true colors, I just didn't expect those colors to be such a nasty shade of bigot.

His anger went beyond the president, "What's this bullshit about gay pride month? Why do the gays get a month? The blacks get a month. The gays get a month. When is it straight guy month?"

Abbie turned to make eye contact with me and immediately saw the fury in my eyes. My blue eyes were red. My blood turned into the fuel that set off Delta rockets. I turned a shade of crimson that made a Red Delicious apple look pale. True, I couldn't actually see my face catching fire, but I could feel the heat rise from my pinky toe all the way to the tip of my bald head. I'm surprised my hat didn't combust.

I couldn't hold it in any longer and stopped walking, "Every month is straight guy month. Are you fucking kidding me?" I wiped the spit from my the side of my mouth. They both stopped two steps ahead of me. The entire world was outlined in red outrage. My brain was conjuring up words faster than my lips could get them out. I took a quick sip from my plastic cup and started walking again.

"Well you know what I mean, right?" Actually I didn't. "Everyone gets a month to parade around their flags, their pride, and all that shit. It's ridiculous."

I decided to keep my mouth shut. Any further interactions with Jimbo would land me in jail and terminated from my job. I focused on walking while counting my steps, coming up with a game plan on getting out of the situation. There was no way in hell I'd spend another moment with this douche bag. Like a bad date, I had to get out quick.

When I was single, and on a horrific date, I'd excuse myself to the restroom moments after arriving at the restaurant. It was there that I sneaked into the stall, called my friend Peggy, and whispered into my cell phone, "This guy is a troll. I can't be on this date. Call me in 30 minutes so I can get out of this."

"What do you want me to say?" She'd ask.

"Don't worry. I'll handle it. Just call me in thirty minutes."

"Why not five?"

"Cause I'm a hungry bitch and this restaurant is nice." *Click*.

Unfortunately, I was in New Orleans with no Peggy and no restroom. My first task was to find a restroom and use it as a distraction to end the night.

Abbie broke the silence lingering around like his stale smoker's breath, "Well, I think it's important that minorities have these types of events. They deserve it."

I interrupted, "I've gotta piss. Let's walk towards Harrah's to use the bathroom." There may be no Peggy to call but I had the next best thing.

We crossed to the other side of the street and continued heading towards the large purple disco shaped ball positioned on top of the casino. Normally, the dancing lights from the casino put me in a gaming mood but tonight I was nothing but a sour apple. My face frozen in what could possibly be a never ending scowl. The silence was welcoming for the few minutes it lasted. For a moment it seemed that Jimbo was done with debating, but who was I kidding.

He was only quiet long enough to collect the ignorant thoughts bouncing around in his Neanderthal brain, "What about me? I deserve it, too. You don't see me flaunting my lifestyle around, do you? It's not normal for that type of behavior."

I threw my drink on the ground. You know I'm angry when I waste even the smallest amount of liquor, "Are you kidding me with this? Are you FUCKING kidding me with this bullshit? You know I'm gay, right?"

"I know you're gay, but you are a cool gay guy. That's why I brought it up."

"You don't fucking know me," I stopped walking again, "You don't know if I'm cool or not."

Abbie's cat had ahold of her tongue like it was filled with fresh catnip. She stood between us with one arm on her hip and the other one holding her drink. She followed the conversation as it escalated while her head swayed back and forth like she was watching a live tennis match.

"Don't get offended, Joe." He pulled out another cigarette and struck the end of it with a match, "You're a cool guy. I didn't mean to upset you."

I couldn't conjure up any words. I was so mad my heart was vogueing inside my chest. My temples pulsated like subwoofers. I focused on walking fast and getting to Harrah's to duck inside the restroom. What was I going to do in there? I had no idea. Sneak out the back of the hotel? Hide in the restroom until he got tired and left? I hadn't thought that far ahead. I just knew that Harrah's was my escape from this backwoods pig.

My fight or flight response was working overtime. Technically, I was on a layover so I couldn't club my captain's head in with a baseball bat. Where would I find one? Probably from one of the homeless guys we passed on the street, but who in their right mind bashes in their captain's brains on a sidewalk in front of a casino in New Orleans? Can you imagine? I can see the headline, "Gay Flight Attendant Bashes Captain's Head In," on the front page of the *New Orleans Advocate*. Now that I think about it, the airline would most likely have handed me an award and presented me with my own month. A month I refused to share with any other minorities.

That wasn't how the night played out; I had to flee and go AWOL before fists started swinging. And when I talk about fists I mean mine attacking his chubby face. I wanted to punch him so hard that his double chin twerked. If that happened I would lose my job faster than Kirby ditched us at the sports bar. Don't get me wrong—I wanted to beat the shit out of him and leave him on the side of the road to be swept away with the rest of the trash, but spending the night in the slammer was not my idea of how I wanted to end my career. I always imagined my last official act as a flight attendant to be spilling hot coffee on some lady's tits who asked for an orange juice, seltzer, and coffee with cream and Splenda on a 35 minute flight.

When we finally arrived in front of Harrah's I continued up the steps leading to the casino and walked directly inside. I didn't look back to see if Abbie and Jimbo were behind me but I knew they were. When I stopped to hand my driver's license to the heavyset black girl at the door, I wanted to whisper to her that the fat dude behind me was a bigot and hated the month of February. I also wanted to warn her that he hated Martin Luther King, Jr., and decorated his bathroom with Confederate flag wallpaper. I kept my mouth shut. I guess there's a first time for everything.

The white devil followed me into the restroom and stood next to me at the stall. He instantly struck up conversation about the piano bar as if the last 30 minutes never happened. This was awkward for more reasons than just my dick being in my hand. All I wanted was a moment of peace from this troll. Would I ever get it? Not soon enough. I stared at the ceramic tiles while listening to Jay Z's song, *99 Problems* echoed from the speakers around the casino. I'm sure powering through 99 of Jay Z's problems was easier than the fucked up one I was dealing with.

While we both peed, I gave him the cold shoulder. What else was I supposed to do? Talk about paid time off at the airline? Winter was coming early in New Orleans, or at least at Harrah's, where I quickly washed my hands and rapidly shook them to dry. Waiting for Abbie to emerge from the restroom I tried to control my anger. It slightly subsided since we were on the street but I still wanted to destroy him. His arrogance was mind blowing and he proved that by assuming I would talk to him at the urinal.

Abbie walked out of the restroom and towards me, about to speak, but Jimbo changed her mind. She turned around facing the slot machines lined up like soldiers ready to take our money. I spun on my heels and moved towards the front entrance to evacuate the casino. The noise from the bells and whistles was annoying. It confirmed at least some people were having fun in New Orleans. Stepping out of the hotel I held the door for a few patrons which allowed Abbie and Jimbo to walk outside. If only I could have slammed the door in his face. Who am I kidding? What would that prove? That I was a just another crazy gay guy who fell part while debating with a prejudiced right wing Republican. He never admitted to being a Republican but that was a no-brainer.

With my buzz officially wearing off I could finally think clearly. It was time to be intelligent and level headed. I didn't know if it was due to my racing heart beat, the evacuation of my bladder, or the sweat from the humidity but as the three of us walked towards the steps leading to the sidewalk I realized how crazy this entire night had become. It needed to end. Kirby would never believe it when Jimbo took the time, behind the secrecy of the flight deck door, to recall word for word what went down on the urine soaked streets of New Orleans. It was clear that nobody should have an all-out war after ingesting four gin & tonics in the course of 45 minutes. Especially someone like me with someone like him.

We reached the steps and filed down one right after another. While pulling out another cigarette he surprise us both by continuing the conversation where we left off before entering the casino, "Jesus Christ says in the Bible that homosexuality is a sin. Same-sex marriage is wrong."

Abbie spoke up when she reached the sidewalk, "There's nothing wrong with two loving people getting married."

"Of course there's something wrong with it," he took a long drag from the cigarette crushed between his sausage fingers, "it's not a lifestyle the church agrees with."

Did I say I was thinking clearly and needed to be intelligent? That idea flowed with the murky street water right into the gutter. "I can't believe how fucking stupid you sound. Listen to yourself, standing there smoking and preaching, I'm not even a fucking Christian." I was on a fantastic roll, "You and your crazy beliefs don't matter. You know what does matter? That you've ruined my fucking layover. That's what matters." If he reported me for insubordination I would have accepted that termination letter proudly and with my head held high. If he had the right to express his feelings and hate towards minorities than I sure as fuck had the same right to call him out on his preconceptions of homosexuality.

"I'm just—"

"You're just what?" I had no plans on letting him finish his sentence, "Fuck it. I'm done with this evening." I was too irate with Jimbo and the red hue of the world was back in focus, "I'm going back to the hotel. I've wasted enough time talking to you."

"What do you mean? I was thinking we could go back inside and gamble?"

I stared at him and looked over at Abbie. She showed no emotion and looked exhausted and weathered from our nonstop bickery. Was this dude high on crack? Did someone slip this fucker a roofie? Was it Kirby? And if so was the roofie really meant for me? I had no idea. When Jimbo dropped that bomb I wanted to run for cover. "No. I'm not coming in to gamble. I'm fucking tired. I'm going back to the hotel," I turned to Abbie, "Are you coming with me?"

"Yes." There was no hesitation. She was already facing the way back to the hotel.

"Man, Joe, I wished you weren't mad. I was hoping to still have some fun."

We both ignored him while passing the garden beds and palm trees outside the casino. Abbie placed her arm inside mine and held me tight as we took a quick left and followed the length of the building until it was time to turn right onto Convention Center Boulevard. Our hotel was along this road and we briskly walked hoping to put some distance between us and Jimbo. I was shaking with anger and couldn't help but yell and scream about Jimbo the entire way back to the hotel. Abbie pet my arm and laid her head on my shoulder to calm my nerves. It worked.

The next morning my neck was still bright red from my blood pressure explosion the night before. After my shower, I went downstairs to get a cup of coffee and reflect on my behavior and how I reacted to his ignorance. I strive to be a decent person. A person who takes pride in myself and stays above stupidity. Jimbo broke me down like nuns do to Catholic elementary students. Raw emotions flooded over me like water breaching a levee during Hurricane Katrina. I may not be perfect but I am no fucking Jimbo. I've always considered myself to be a lucky gay man who has not had the misfortune of interacting with ignorant people when it comes to homosexuality and equality. In high school, yes, but not as an adult. I guess my luck finally ran out. This wouldn't be the week to gamble in Las Vegas.

I found myself a quiet chair in the corner of the hotel lobby and camped there enjoying my morning coffee. I heard the elevator ding announcing a new arrival but I was too preoccupied with my cell phone to look up. My instinct got the best of me and when I looked up Jimbo was making his way over. I kept perfectly still but that trick only works on a Tyrannosaurus Rex. I was not ready for this, nor did I want to rehash anything from the night before, but Jimbo had other plans.

"Morning, Joe, " he said in a soft voice as he approached me and stood to my right. I didn't look up from my cell phone. "I'm really sorry about last night. I guess it's not smart for me to talk about religion when I'm drinking."

"You know," still not looking up from my phone, "It's probably not a good idea for you to talk about politics, religion, or minorities when you are drinking."

"I know man. I apologize. Are we cool?"

Placing my cell phone on my lap I finally broke down and looked up at him. He looked like he spent the rest of the evening being dragged behind a wild horse along Canal Street. Good. I hope it fucking hurt. "Well we have to work one leg together tonight so I guess we're cool."

To clarify: we were not cool. We were never cool. My distaste for this man was unmeasurable. As the words, "I guess we are cool," came out of my mouth I knew I had instantly betrayed myself for even talking to him. The need to maintain my professionalism on the airplane and on a layover kept me grounded. I had to fight the urge to throw my coffee in his face but that would be so unfair to my cup of coffee. He thanked me, reached into his pocket for a cigarette, and walked out of the hotel.

Later that evening, we arrived at the airport to find out our flight was slightly delayed. The idea of having to spend one more second with Jimbo worsened my already pissy mood.

The four of us meandered towards the food court inside the airport. I wasn't hungry, neither was Kirby or Abbie, but you guessed it, Jimbo needed to gorge himself on Popeye's Chicken before our flight. If he had a heart attack in the flight deck, I was counting on Kirby to land us safely. We can't bring the AED into the flight deck and I wasn't strong enough to pull Jimbo out of his seat and into the galley to perform CPR. We followed him to the restaurant and the four of us found a wobbly table and took a seat. Our conversation was uninteresting while Jimbo stood in the endless line ordering his three piece chicken basket with two biscuits and an extra jumbo sweet tea. I am pretty sure he had a few add ons to that order.

Watching him devour that meal made me want to help the starving children throughout the world. His groceries alone could no doubt feed the entire population of Rwanda for a three day weekend. We sat in silence while he sucked the last remaining bits of chicken off the bones. His slurping, moans, and loud grunting almost made my coffee come up. He sounded like he was performing cunnilingus while drowning. Once he was satisfied that an ant couldn't feed off the chicken carcasses, he drank the remainder of his sweet tea and stood up. Without a thought he grabbed the handle of his suitcase and exclaimed, "I'm getting another cigarette before the plane lands," and walked off.

The three of us looked down at the orange tray filled with chicken bones and crumbs left behind for the Popeye's employees to clean up. I shook my head in disgust. His curtain call undercover dick pilot move stunned all three of us. Should we have really been surprised? No, but that's not to say we weren't taken aback by his disregard for the airport employees. Being the professional flight attendant that I am, and because I was embarrassed by my coworker, I grabbed the tray and disposed the chicken remains in the trash can. We grabbed our luggage and walked side by side through the terminal towards security. Kirby had been quiet about his feelings towards Jimbo. We had no idea what his impression of Jimbo was but if he had the brains to go along with the brawn it probably wasn't much different than ours. Something everyone should know about pilots is their strong bond. They are known for sticking together no matter what the circumstances. You practically have to torture them and threaten to remove a fingernail just to get them to rat each other out. It's fucking annoying. They are nothing like flight attendants. We'd throw our best friend under the bus to move up one spot in seniority.

While standing in the TSA line waiting for our luggage to go through the conveyor belt Kirby finally spoke out, "I can't believe what a dick that dude is. He left that mess behind for us to clean. What a fucking slob."

I HATE COMMUTING

Commuting can suck a dick for Jesus Christ. I could have easily gone the Mohammad route but I'm no fucking idiot. Christian radicals have nothing on Islamic radicals. What's the worst a Christian radical will do? Refuse my request for a marriage license? I rest my case.

Commuting to work is dreadful. Dreadful! If you consider spending 20 minutes parked on the highway during rush hour as a painful commute, you are sadly mistaken. I am not going to say that it's not abysmal, believe me—I've done it, but there's something to be said for having the ability to get behind the wheel of your car, drive at your own pace, and arrive at your destination with only a few feet between you and the start of your work day. The freedom to get behind the wheel of your car ultimately controlling the outcome of your commute is powerful.

Everyone has commuting hardships they must endure. Some people walk in the snow. Some ride a bike. Some take the bus or train. Some, like me and many other airline employees, board an airplane and fly thousands of miles before we even start our fucking day. That's what I am talking about here: crew commuting and how much I fucking loathe it.

I probably hate commuting as much as I hated being on reserve. It's hard to tell. I will say that I hate them equally; like cilantro and passengers who have chihuahuas as service pets. If being on reserve sucks out your soul, commuting then takes it and rips it to shreds. They work in tandem making your life a living hell. Reminds me of my first ex-boyfriend and his ornery mother. She's dead now.

In the event a flight attendant ever tells you that commuting is easy, you should be wary of this person. Stay as far away from them as humanly possible because this person has no soul. Did you hear me? NO SOUL! Seriously. Run to the basement of the nearest Catholic Church, drag Father Pedophile off an innocent four year old boy—the boy will thank you, Father Pedophile will not—and beg him for a few crucifixes and some holy water. Don't forget the holy water! You should carry that small bottle of holy water in your pocket and be prepared to splash the evil right out that flight attendant like my grandmother did to the Jehovah's Witness who knocked at her door. Anyone who thinks commuting is easy should have their asshole bleached with undiluted Clorox. Trust me, it won't hurt them. They have no soul so they obviously won't feel bleach turning their insides out. These flight attendants are soulless demons straight from hell and will do everything in their power to suck out your soul to replace theirs. I've actually worked with a few of these bitches before and it's not a pretty sight. Luckily, as told by many pastors and preachers, I am gay and don't have a soul. Even if I did, no demon soulless flight attendant would try and steal a gay man's soul. Are you kidding me? That's like trying to pry the Miss Gay America crown away from a drag queen. You better bring lots of backup glitter to blind them in that cat fight. In their defense—not the drag queens but the soulless flight attendants—I doubt they were always soulless. Early on in their careers I bet they had enormous souls. Souls large enough to be stored in an aircraft hangar. Ron Jeremy sized souls. That's the kind of soul you want. The kind that you can fling over your shoulder and smirk at the captain as you exit the airplane. But shit changes after spending decades serving airline passengers. Those perky souls tend to vanish and fade away right along with taut skin, likeable attitudes, and tits.

I never thought I'd commute again after transferring out of JFK. Never! It wasn't a passing thought. It was never entertained or discussed. It didn't exist in my realm of possibilities. Why would I commute again when the airport was a 15 minute drive from my house? Ten minutes with no traffic. Even as a joke, if anyone had hinted hypothetically about me commuting again—say from San Francisco to Cleveland—I would have pinched their nipples to the point of reconstructive surgery.

It happened though. It sure did. I became a West Coast commuter. Came out of left field like catching a nasty case of gonorrhea while partying in Las Vegas over Labor Day Weekend. But instead of screaming for hours over that painful pissing glass sensation, you spend the same amount of time fighting off the urge to scream in the airplane lavatory on your flight to work. If only there was an antibiotic strong enough to cure the transcontinental commute like there is to cure the occasional weekend case of the clap. Maybe one day.

Long story short, we moved to California. And I transferred to Cleveland. The major adjustment to commuting was the amount of free time I lost. And sitting on an airplane for what seemed like endless hours while not being paid. That was the hardest pill to swallow and the one aspect of cross country commuting that I detested. When your job includes flying hour after hour, day after day, your top priority should be reducing the amount of time you spend on airplane not getting paid. Unless you are going on vacation to Puerto Vallarta or Cabo—then it's doable. I did the math flying over Iowa one afternoon and calculated the amount of cash I was losing sitting on an airplane commuting.

$$\$37.00 \times 6 \text{ hours} = \$222.00$$

That was a one way flight. Multiply that times two for the round trip; three for the amount of times I commuted in a month; and 12 for the number of months in the year.

$$\$222.00 \times 2 = \$444.00 \times 3 = \$1332.00 \times 12 = \$15,984$$

That's how I computed my time commuting, as money lost. After my first month living this commute, I battled with Matt over the topic while we sat on our new sofa. The new sofa that we bought at some downtown hippy store. My love for the sofa lasted until I returned home from my first miserable commute. There was no love in my heart, only frustration. I may have mistook Matt's attitude but he projected to have no empathy for my struggle, "What's the problem? You sit on an airplane and go to work. Big deal."

I fought the urge to punch him in the throat, "It's called wasting my fucking time. I work on the airplane so when I'm on the fucker and not getting paid I don't like it."

145

"I just don't understand. All you have to do is sit there and read a book. It sounds easy."

I reeled in my emotions. Being arrested for assault after only living in California for one month didn't seem like the responsible way to introduce myself into the community. He was lucky our conversation didn't include us standing in the kitchen while I sliced an apple, "Ok. Think about it like this for a moment, alright? What if you went to work six hours early and sat in the lobby. You just sat there. You weren't getting paid. You were just sitting there. Then you go up to your desk and you work for eight or nine hours. Okay. Easy, right?" I took a sip of water and continued, "Then you go back down to the lobby and sit for another six hours. And then you go home." He looked at me intently the entire time. I could see the gears working in his brain, there was practically smoke escaping his ears, "How would that make you feel?"

He shook his head, "I see your point."

By the second month commuting cross country I blamed him. The entire situation was his fault. Why wouldn't it be his fault? He brought us out here to California resulting in my work life becoming an utter living hell. It was worse than hell, it was like being gay and living next door to the Westboro Baptist Church. On average most of my commutes were uneventful. I don't want to confuse anyone with that statement. Even though they were uneventful they were still terrible. A broken record of sorts: arrive at the airport, take my seat, fly to Cleveland. Then repeat. I'd work the trips assigned to me and then commute back home. It was the normal commutes that left me in a state of amnesia for when commutes went from good to bad within seconds. And that's how it happened, like a F4 tornado sweeping through the airport and whisking me off to die. There were countless unpleasant experiences commuting from San Francisco to Cleveland. Each time Matt picked me up from the airport, I'd spend fifty percent of the ride complaining about the commute and the other fifty percent gushing over how happy I was to be home. It really was reserve life all over again. As horrible as the most mundane commutes went, nothing prepared me for the onslaught of bad misfortune awaiting me on my commute home after working a red-eye flight from Las Vegas to Cleveland.

We all have moments that define us or change our way of thinking. This was that moment in regards to commuting. It was actually less of a moment and more of a breaking point. Moments pass, this experience stayed with me like genital fucking herpes.

The story goes a little something like this…

7:10 a.m. — My Las Vegas flight lands in Cleveland 20 minutes early. I'm excited because the flight home to San Francisco is at 7:45 a.m. I feared I'd miss the flight so this early arrival has me grinning like the Chesire Cat. The captain calls the back galley to inform me we will have a short taxi to the gate and I should make my commute flight. Excellent!

7:22 a.m. — We are still on this motherfucking goddamn airplane. Deep breathing and trying to stay calm while I rock back and forth in my back galley jumpseat like I'm autistic. Missing this flight is not an option. I will need to resort to plan B and I don't have a plan B. Such a novice. Did I just start commuting? I am an embarrassment to every pilot and flight attendant who commutes. The Captain comes over the PA again and informs the entire airplane there's a traffic jam at the gate we are awaiting. A fucking traffic jam at 7:22 in the morning? This is Cleveland Hopkins International Airport not LAX. What the gay fuck? I am sweating through my uniform.

7:25 a.m. — Pull up to the gate. Finally. It takes forever for these assholes to grab their luggage and make their way off the airplane. I am pacing in the back galley and look manic. My first instinct is to pick up the interphone and start screaming at the passengers like the Gunnery Sergeant from *Full Metal Jacket*. Panic has kidnapped me. The captain calls the back galley a second time letting me know the San Francisco flight hasn't started boarding. I'm relieved… for the moment.

7:37 a.m. — Off the airplane. It's been 27 minutes since we landed and I need to focus on the task at hand. I run to the gate a disheveled mess. If I had hair it would look like I just got fucked in the back galley between handing out Diet Cokes and informing passengers to fasten their seat belts. The gate agent frowns telling me the flight is delayed. I ask if standby seats have been assigned and she says no. Then I ask if any window seats are available and she snickers, "This bad boy only has middle seats available." I fake a smile and walk away hiding against the wall between the machine that sells iPads and a family of four praying the airplane doesn't crash. First off, who the fuck buys an iPad in the airport? Has anyone in the history of flying ever passed through security and said, "Holy shit, I forgot my iPad. What am I gonna do? Oh look, there's a pop up kiosk over there selling them for $500." Nobody with a functioning left brain. I debate whether to ask the zealots to include me in their superstitious prayers but change my mind and simply stare a hole through the gate agents head waiting for her to call my name.

8:05 a.m. — I'm still against the wall between the iPads and Christians. I fight the urge to lean over and whisper to the two brats that there is no God. How do I know there's no God? It's simple. If there were a God we wouldn't be standing here like suckers waiting for the airplane to depart. That's how I know! Anyway, I am beyond tired and it doesn't help that my right ankle is swollen and throbbing. I didn't injure the ankle this morning running to the gate, although I did sprint faster than a elementary school kid running from a priest. It was injured last week while on a leisurely jog in the park. Getting old is worse than your cell phone battery dying while jerking off and chatting on Grindr at the layover hotel. Scratch that - midjerking disruptions are catafuckingclysmic. My ankle is wrapped with an ace wrap and has been on all night. It could be cutting off circulation to my foot. Can that make you go insane? I'm starting to think that's a possibility. Why am I worried about all this nonsense? The most important question is when will this fucking airplane depart?

8:15 a.m. — The gate agent announces, "Ladies and gentleman, I have some good news and some bad news." Stabbing that bitch in her neck would be great news but her announcement makes me perk up and pay attention. I am no longer standing where I was 10 minutes ago. After the Christians pulled out their Bible and started reading verses from Deuteronomy, I hightailed it over to stand next to the shoeshine guy. The gate agent adds, "The bad news is that this airplane will not be taking you to San Francisco. The good news is the airplane taking you to San Francisco has just landed at another gate." Victory! She directs all the passengers to gate A3 and I follow the mad dash to the new gate.

8:35 a.m. — The same gate agent magically appears at gate A3. I approach the counter and she gives me my seat assignment. It's 15A—a window seat. My pain and suffering has been rewarded with a great seat. This has nothing to do with God and all to do with my good luck. I bet the Christians are in row 30. This morning may be turning around. I feel it in my ankle. I smile and stop myself from questioning the gate agent about her false information on only middle seats being available. The idea of her snatching the boarding pass out of my hand and taking it away from me is too much to handle. I'm not saying she would take my seat away but from across the counter she looks hangry. I hobble to the restroom to change out of my uniform. It's been on since last night and I feel gross. Fatigue must be setting in because I left my crew ID hanging in the restroom stall and had to run back in to get it. Glad nobody was taking a shit because that's always an awkward conversation.

9:05 a.m. — We are finally allowed to board the fucking airplane. I introduce myself to the flight attendant and start down the aisle. There's a mother, father, and toddler in my row and I am thankful it's not the Bible thumping fucks from the other gate. The mother and toddler are in the window seat. I get to row 15 and stare at them like they just stole the only thing that will make me happy in life, the ability to put my head against the window and sleep. The mother asks me to sit in the aisle because she believes children shouldn't sit in the middle seat. I correct her—because I am a bitch—and tell her that children can most certainly sit in the middle seat. But I am not in the mood to interact with them so I take the aisle seat. It's for the best because I really don't want to be prisoner to these three while sitting at the window.

9:19 a.m. — I grab my earbuds from my tote bag and start settling in for the long flight. The first officer's voice startles me over the PA, "Looks like we're all having a bad day today. This airplane has a mechanical and we are looking at a four hour delay. Please grab your belongings and deplane." I stare blankly up the aisle at the pilot and refuse to hear what he is saying. I know it's true because I just heard him say it but I don't want to believe it. NO! NO! NO! Motherfuckingcocksuckingbabyrapingasshole! They need a third plane? What kind of Howdy Doody bullshit is this? Do I work for an airline or the Republican Party?

9:22 a.m. — I wish I could reach around and kick myself in the ass for not having a plan B. Who doesn't have a plan B when they commute? I need a plan B like a whore needs a Plan B One -Step after a gang bang. I probably need it more because what I'm dealing with here is much worse than an early morning toilet abortion. If this flight cancels I will be stuck here for the the entire afternoon. Probably the rest of the night. I want to scream 'Goddamn it!' but there's a toddler sitting in the row. Even I'm not that crass. I grab my shit and stand up to deplane. The father asks, "Will this really take four hours?" I just shrug my shoulders and walk away. Don't fucking talk to me.

Dick! Getting off this broken down excuse for an airplane I run, with my throbbing ankle, to an empty gate and log into the computer. I pull up a list of other airline flights to San Francisco and list myself on the first one I find. The next flight departs in 55 minutes so I shuffle faster than a fat kid chasing an ice cream truck for the other airline counter.

9:35 a.m. — Arrive at the new gate and the agent checks me in but sadly informs me that the flight is full. I am number ten on the standby list and there's a weight restriction on the flight. Unless I weigh less than a newborn and can sit on some hot daddy's lap, I am not getting on this flight. She's not even friendly about it which makes me hate her. Grab a seat across from the gate and realize this shit ain't-a-working. Looks like I need a plan C. How many letters are in the alphabet? I'm on a time crunch because each moment I'm wasting in Cleveland makes it more difficult to get back to California.

9:39 a.m. — I text Matt, *"I'm gonna have a nervous fucking breakdown. I can't do this commute."*

9:40 a.m. — Matt attempts to call me but I miss his first call because I am too busy looking up additional flights home. Call him back and can barely speak. I lash out at him, "Hi. Can't talk. Life is fucked. I hate this. I will call you later. Have a nice day." *Click!*

9:45 a.m. — I find another flight to San Francisco via Los Angeles. Run into the nearest restroom to put my uniform back on since I have to exit out of the A gates and make my way through security to the C gates. In a frenzy I pull my ID over my head and it snaps off the lanyard. In all honestly, it's not that big of a deal but I am irrational at this point. I hold it in my hand and fight the urge to drop to the floor of the stall and cry but the lake of manpiss around the toilet stops me in my tracks. I should cry. I want to cry. Fuck it! I will cry… but not right now.

9:55 a.m. — I run from the A gates to the C gates to catch the flight. Is this plan C or D? I've lost fucking count. My suitcase handle comes off in my hand while I am bolting around old people meandering through the main terminal waiting for the shuttle to heaven. I stop for a second to search for the screw that came off my luggage but I can't find it. I have no time to waste. The screw is gone like my sanity. I grab the bag by its side handle and spot an airline employee walking towards me. I stop her asking if I am going the correct way to the C gates but her facial expression catches me off guard. She must have been on her lunch break because she looks ticked off I interrupted her. She says, "No. You need to walk straight to the C gates. It's that way." What am I thinking? When did I forget how to navigate through the airport I'm based in? It must have been the same time I forgot how to read signs. I continue to the C gates, get through security, and come face to face with gate agent Angel at the counter.

10:05 a.m. — At this point in the game I am a fucking mess. An Eastern European passenger train derailment doesn't look this bad. My crew ID is hanging out of my mouth while sweat cascades down my bald head like a Yosemite waterfall. I can barely speak. Angel, the gate agent, should have big fluffy white wings attached to her back because her name says it all, she's an angel. My angel. I wipe off the saliva from my ID and hand it over the counter to her. There's no doubt she wants to vomit but she never digresses from her focus. Angel puts me at ease while tapping my employment information into her computer. We engage in small talk while she completes my transaction. I explain why I moved to San Francisco and spend most of the conversation blaming my husband for putting me through this nightmare. She laughs. I don't. I unload on her like she's my therapist and she takes it with a smile. A professional. Assuring me that my day will get better she lists me on the Los Angeles flight and then the connecting flight to San Francisco. "The flights are wide open all the way through," she advises. I'm feeling better.

10:20 a.m. — Standing at the gate awaiting my name to be called and for my seat assignment. Rocking back and forth in place from all the stress. It's a nervous habit I've had since I was in the third grade. I usually try reeling it back a little when I'm rocking in public but today I don't give a fuck. Let people watch the crazy guy rocking back and forth. Maybe if I rock fast enough people will keep their children away from me. I will remember that. My cell phone battery needs juice so I find an empty plug a few feet away and charge it. Starting to feel like everything will work out. If I think about it, nothing bad has happened yet. All this sweating and overreacting is unnecessary. I fantasize about taking a nap on the airplane and the two hour shower awaiting me at home. Make that three hour. My uniform is still on because I can't go through another costume change again. I'm not a Madonna backup dancer for Chrissakes! I text Matt updating him and reassuring him that everything will be fine. Let's cut the bullshit, I'm really just reassuring myself.

10:37 a.m. — The gate agent calls my name for my seat assignment and it is in the exit row. Jackpot! Extra leg room and it's a window seat. Nap time here I come. I make my way down the aisle behind a slow family. The blond muscular guy turns around and it's an actor from the television show Dawson's Creek. You know the one. He's traveling with his wife, nanny, and two kids. I am too exhausted to care and I don't think about snapping a picture. That's just rude.

10:42 a.m. — I am on the airplane in seat 9F. My seat doesn't recline but I will make due. The older man next to me comments that I am in my uniform and asks me if I will get in trouble for flying on another airline. I'd normally think that's cute but not today. Leave me alone and don't talk to me. I hate you right now because you are in my row and I can't lay down so just shut up and read your book.

10:49 a.m. — The guy behind my seat pushes his touch screen too hard and every few seconds my seat leaps forward. I hope this doesn't happen the entire flight. I would hate to have to divert to Omaha because his face was embedded into the screen.

11:00 a.m. — Take off. LAX here we come. I enjoyed free food, watched *This Means War*, and I may have napped. Maybe I slept more than I realize because I can't remember anything else happening on the flight.

1:49 p.m. — We land in LAX and I am happy to be in California but sad that I still have another flight home. When will this end? I have been awake for 29 1/2 hours and that is just insane, I can barely stay awake for 10 hours before requiring a lengthy nap.

2:24 p.m. — I decide to get something to eat. The only restaurant open happens to be Burger King so I stand in line, order a greasy Junior Whopper, and sit down in the corner of the restaurant for a quick lunch. I have to be back at the gate at 3:35 p.m. so I take my time with lunch. This never happens.

3:00 p.m. — After finishing my lunch I head over to the gate area and find myself sitting among hipster LA douchebags. Disgusting. My lunch wants to come up but I force it back down. Instead of looking at my surroundings I pull up the Facebook app on my phone and stare at that. Anything's better than having to witness one more Ed Hardy t-shirt on some twenty-something asshole. Not much time passes before I act on an impulse that nobody should act on when they are tired or angry, I blow up Facebook with emotional and negative comments about my day. What the fuck was I thinking? This is worse than drunk texting. At least with drunk texting only the individual on the other end of the phone gets the emotionally awkward tasteless drunk text. When you erupt all your emotions on Facebook everyone experiences the madness. What started out as an innocent bitchfest (is there such a thing?) complaining about my commute turned into a verbal assault against Joe. I start receiving unpleasant comments and my first reaction is to blast these fuckers right off my Facebook page. A few "friends" tell me to "chill out," and "stop bitching." I restrain myself from commenting. The ego stroke I was searching for turns into a bitch slapping event. I hate my life. I hate my job. I hate LA. I hate everyone. I just want to be home. At least I am sober and still have a shred of dignity not to respond.

3:33 p.m. — I walk up to the gate and the gate agent barks at me to come back at 3:35 p.m.. Is this bitch serious?

3:35 p.m. — Two minutes later, I return back at the gate. Two fucking minutes! Why are so many gate agents nasty to me? Like seriously, why? I smile. I say thank you. I usually bring treats. Are they forced to take How to Be Cunty 101 in gate agent school? This makes me miss Angel. My seat assignment is the same as my last flight. I proceed to the gate and stand in line watching the gate agent checking to be sure each and every passenger places their carry on bag into the sizer next to the podium. Love the efficiency but I don't have time for this diligence. It's a time waste. At least five bags get pulled to be checked while I am standing there waiting in line. These passengers are furious. A few of them recite, "It fit the last time," but the gate agent could care less. My boarding pass is scanned and my bags are overlooked. Thankfuckinggod! I knew it was a smart idea to keep my uniform on. I board a smaller airplane so even though my seat assignment is the same, it is sadly not an exit row. I take the window seat and my legs are crushed against the tray table. Fun. I happily sigh for a moment thinking boarding has concluded but then some last minute passenger runs onto the airplane and takes the aisle seat in my row. I hate Tuesdays.

5:30 p.m. — Land in SFO and I literally throw myself off the plane. I am happy to be home but my face resembles someone who has won the lottery but their toddler ate the winning ticket. That kind of miserable. My uniform smells. I stink so bad the lady in front of me looks back with a raised lip as if I am trying to smuggle skunks into California. I run into the restroom and change into shorts, a polo shirt, and my sneakers. I smear some deodorant under my pits leaving the restroom like a new man. I need to find the Airtran so I stop and ask an airport employee for directions, again. I've reached the point of requiring constant supervision at the airport. Why do I fall apart and act like I have never been inside an airport before? Something to talk to my therapist about. Hopefully, she'll take my calls after my Facebook rants. If not, there's always Angel. The airport employee is helpful but he takes 20 minutes to explain. English is not his first language. It's not his second, either. All I need is a pointed finger and a smile, not a dissertation in a foreign language.

5:45 p.m. — Through his broken English I find the train station and take the Airtrain to the BART and finally make it to the CalTrain. It's prime traffic time in the Bay Area so I didn't even bother asking Matt to pick me up from the airport. I swipe my Clipper card at the CalTrain station and it deducts $10.50 for a $5.00 train ride. I lose it.

6:02 p.m. — I texted Matt: *"I'm having the worst fucking day ever."*

6:05 p.m. — He calls me while I'm waiting at the track for the train to arrive. My speech is incoherent when I answer the telephone. A stranger looks over at me probably questioning if English is my first language. I deserve that. Attempt to break down my entire day to Matt in 11 minutes before the train arrives. Tell him I am ready to throw myself on the train track. He calmly tells me to take a deep breath and then reassures me that I really won't throw myself on the track. True. I'm a drama queen and right now I am going for best lead actor in a drama. Totally Meryl Streeping the fuck out of this experience.

6:16 p.m. — I push my way onto the train and drag my bags with me. I can barely get on the train before the door closes. Nobody will move out of my way so I am forced to yell, "Move out of my fucking way. I've got a suitcase here." They all look at me like I am on drugs and go back to reading their books and texting their friends. Most are Asian so they don't even understand me. Nothing worse than being on a tirade and nobody even understanding how pissed off you are. Assholes.

6:20 p.m. — There are no seats on the train; it's standing room only when I board. It's crowded to the point that your breathing may annoy the person standing next to you. My suitcase goes between my legs and I hold position in the middle of the train. Fuck it. If a passenger wants to get off at the next stop they will have to fling themselves over me because I am not moving. It's that jam-packed. There's nowhere to go unless I crawl up inside someone's asshole. That doesn't sound too bad as long as there's extra leg room. I'm officially fried. Not fried like chicken because that sounds great—fried like a sunburn on your first day of vacation. My cell phone is dead so I have no communication with the outside world. If Matt's texting me with no response he might be watching the local news to see if I went through with my train track threat.

6:28 p.m. — At our third stop a shitload of passengers disembark. I scan the train car and see a single seat available. Place my suitcase onto the luggage rack and race to snag the seat. I won't deny that an old lady might have been pushed out of the way or not. Let's just say I didn't and that I haven't lost all my self-respect. I take the seat next to some Chinese lady playing sudoku who covers her nose when I sit down next to her. I think it's illegal to treat white people this way; I will check that out online when I get home.

6:48 p.m. — I get off the train a few blocks from my apartment and walk the short distance to my building. I am spent. As much as I love a healthy confrontation, I don't have the energy to push a toddler off their tricycle. If a Scientologist approached me I'd give them all my money even though I'm not awaiting Xenu's arrival. I'd even hand over my luggage so I wouldn't have to pull it anymore.

7:05 p.m. — I walk into the apartment, look at my watch, and realize it has been over 14 hours and 45 minutes since I made my first attempt to get on a flight home. I could have flown to fucking London and back. I've also been awake since 8 a.m. yesterday which is over 36 hours ago. Giraffes running from lions on the African savanna get more sleep than me. I say outloud to Matt that I can never do this again. I quit. I quit. I QUIT!

7:20 p.m. — I don't even bother unpacking, I will do it in the morning. Plug my cell phone into the charger, peel off my uniform, and start running the shower water. The decision has been made. I need to transfer to a West Coast base as soon as humanly possible. Fuck. This. Commute!

THE F-BOMB

The rain pelting against my hotel window woke me up before my 5:30 a.m. alarm. That's painful. Extremely painful. Nobody should be required to wake up at that blasphemous hour. Waking up even 30 seconds before the alarm buzzes sets me down the path for a cantankerous morning. It's like an explosion to my mood. Wake up calls from the hotel staff have the same type of effect. This morning it wasn't a mere 30 seconds of crucial sleep deprived from me but a solid eight minutes. Do you know how important eight minutes of sleep means to someone when they have to wake up at 5:30 in the morning.? It changes your entire day. I should have taken this as an omen, picked up my cell phone, and called in sick to Crew Scheduling. Why don't I follow my gut? I really should. It's big enough to lead a gay pride parade.

While the wind howled outside my window, I recoiled under the sheets of my king-size bed. I felt safe wrapped in its fluffy arms sheltering me from what sounded like armageddon only five feet from where I lay. The bed and only a few inches of glass protected me from being swept out 20 stories above San Francisco. I didn't have to get up from the safety of the bed to know it was a harsh environment outside. The gusts echoed through the glass and surrounded my entire room sounding like two Tyrannosaurus Rex fighting over who was going to get to devour me first. While concentrating on the wind I was startled when my alarm finally went off. That was a quick eight minutes. My cell phone chimed, jingled, and jangled forcing me to throw my soft down comforter to the other side of the bed. I heaved the blanket over in one motion to not feel it's comfort any longer. If I don't immediately pull myself out from under the blanket I'll be forced to let the sandman drag me back down into a blissful slumber.

I am so easily persuaded to sleep that while writing this I am fighting off the urge to lay down and take a quick catnap. As much as my heart, mind, and body tell me to, I can't because—goddamn it—I have to finish this book.

Grabbing my cell phone and shutting off the alarm, I slide my legs over the side of the bed. While sitting there with my feet firmly on the carpet I wondered how my day was going to play out. I often do this on work trips. I run through the entire day; from catching the hotel shuttle van to the airport to eventually driving home in my car. My day never turns out how I anticipate it will. Stopping this practice all together might be helpful, but now it borders on an obsession.

I stood up tall, stretched my fingers to the sky, and proceeded to the floor-to-ceiling red curtains that hung in front of the vertical window. With a swift tug I pulled them open to reveal absolutely nothing. I knew the sun had started to rise but the entire San Francisco skyline was cloaked in a white fog. If my room had been equipped with a deck I could have stood outside allowing the marshmallow clouds to prevent me from seeing my hand three inches from my face. Placing my hands on my hips and staring out into the void for a few moments I tried making out any sign of life. A building? A bridge? Nada. The view was void as if a large eraser swept away the city.

I took my shower as quickly as possible. From the second I shut off the water I noticed the wind had stopped howling aggressively outside. That was reassuring. There was no way to tell if it was raining so I figured I'd find out when I stepped outside. The van to the airport was scheduled at 6:15 a.m. so I needed to move fast. When I wake up that early I never give myself much wiggle room. Everything happens fast: shower, shave, teeth brushed, luggage packed (which I always do the night before), and then down to the hotel lobby. In that precise order. I don't falter from my routine. I also never factor in a morning shit, which if that situation unfolds, all hell breaks loose.

With my luggage dragging behind me I exited my hotel room and proceeded to the bank of elevators to take me down to the lobby. I rode the elevator alone wishing I could go back to sleep, even if I had to defend myself from the dinosaurs should they return. The elevator stopped on the lobby floor and I shuffled out of it with sleep still encrusted in my eyes. This exhaustion would last until I was well on my way home. That was a guarantee. We were finishing up a four day pairing with only one flight left back to Cleveland. One-leg days at the end of a pairing are equivalent to laying by the pool after a rigorous workout. It's a reward. Flight attendants can handle anything the universe throws at them for one leg. When so many pairings have two, three, and four legs in a day, one leg on your last day is the buttercream frosting on a three-tier cake. I shouldn't have said that because now I am craving cake.

I made my way around the elevators and briskly walked to the oversized water fountain in the center of the lobby. That was the designated location where all crews met to wait for the hotel van. I didn't see any flight attendants waiting so I figured I was the first one downstairs. After arriving at the fountain, I noticed my entire crew, pilots included, seated at the restaurant to the right of the fountain. It was an open seating area inside the hotel lobby with a buffet style continental breakfast spread. Did I miss the invitation for an early morning breakfast rendezvous? Could it be possible that I wasn't invited? I shook the thought out of my head. Impossible. I simply missed the memo. They probably forgot to slide it under my door last night. Why was I even entertaining the idea? I would have never made it downstairs for breakfast.

The two flight attendants working this pairing with me were Misty Grant and Ursula Lie. Working with Misty was delightful. I relished just being in her presence. She had a warm and compassionate vibe that drew you towards her. It was a mom vibe. A hot cougar mom vibe. Let's just say she was hot enough for me to question my decades long vagina free diet. Ursula, on the other hand, was a back stabbing whore who deserved a swift kick in her lady parts.

I should stop there. I'm getting ahead of myself. There will be plenty of Ursula-bashing to come later. Trust me on that; I hated that bitch. But just for the record, and before you protest in support of my castration, I never kicked Ursula in her lady parts. Even though I fantasized about someone doing it while I watched from the sidelines drinking a glass of Pinot noir. Pinot noir? What am I thinking? If kicking Ursula in her lady parts was on the menu I'd need something bold and strong—like a bottle of Merlot.

Misty, Ursula, and the two pilots were paying their checks when I made eye contact with Misty and she happily waved at me. I smiled and faintly waved back but decided not to walk over. It was too early for me to be that nice, so I just stood by the water fountain playing on my cell phone.

Within seconds they swarmed around me with excitement in their eyes and drama on their lips, "Our airplane never landed in SFO last night. It diverted to San Jose because of weather." Ursula blurted out placing her luggage next to mine. I stared at her while she chattered on, "We have to take a van to San Jose. This is so ridiculous."

Her makeup was ridiculous but I kept that thought to myself, "What about the passengers?"

Captain Emerson spoke up, "They're all being bussed."

It was too early in the fucking morning to be this unhappy.

The five of us boarded a large black Escalade bound for San Jose International Airport with another crew of five. Six flight attendants and four pilots packed into what would normally be a comfortable ride for seven people. Eight, if two were bulimic. If only one of us idolized Karen Carpenter enough so I might have avoided traveling with my knees on my chin—like a set of hairy balls—my mood might have been a little less bitchy. There were ten of us packed into the Escalade and if I was Jewish I'd have sworn we were on our way to Auschwitz.

I tried timing my climb into the SUV to sit by Misty but I ended up crushed between the window and a flight attendant I had never met. She smelt like cigarettes and cheap perfume. A floral headache-inducing fragrance created by some slutty pop star and sold at Walmart. I wanted to eject her from the van as we drove down the highway. She was lucky we were seated far from the door. When the van door slid shut I fished out the earbuds and started listening to Madonna. It was too early in the morning to even entertain the thought of listening to the four pilots complain about whatever it was they were complaining about. To be honest, I couldn't even tell you if they were complaining. They might have been silent. I don't even remember but from my experience, pilots are always moaning and groaning. If they get the chance, they will bellyache about something and trust me—many of them have big bellies. Virtually every single pilot I have worked with will cry and grumble on more than a gay 17 year old taking it up the ass for the first time. That's exactly what pilots do in van rides to the airport—not take it up the ass (although I wouldn't be surprised)—but complain. They complain about the airline. They complain about politics, religion, and anything else that will get a conversation in motion. It doesn't even matter if the occupants in the van are paying attention. If the flight attendants don't add fuel to their fire they will strike up conversation with the van driver and bitch to them. I had no time for that bullshit. There were bigger fish to fry, like fighting off the cancer stench coming from the flight attendant seated next to me. And the fact that my day was already starting off badly. This couldn't be good. I sat with my head against the glass, closed my eyes, and silently lip-synced the entire way to the airport.

When we arrived at the airport the van door slid open and we all fell out like circus clowns. It must have been quite a sight for anyone standing curbside to witness this madness. Without worrying about anyone else I quickly grabbed my bags from the driver, gave him a dollar tip, and dodged the raindrops briskly walking towards the terminal. Once inside and out of the rain, I made a beeline for the employee TSA line. The security checkpoint was buzzing with passengers trying to recover from their previously canceled flights. It was pandemonium. All of our passengers shuttled over on buses were most likely in one of these chaotic security lines. I figured I lost Misty, Ursula, and our pilots as I rushed to the TSA agent to show my crew ID but when I turned around they miraculously found their spots behind me.

"Don't worry," Ursula said, "We're right here."

My attempt at smirking wasn't convincing, "Oh good. I wasn't trying to lose you guys, just get ahead of everyone else." She knew I was lying but I didn't give a fuck. Nothing could put me in a pleasant mood, especially after that hideous van ride. The entire right side of my uniform smelled like a pack of Newport Menthols.

I flung my suitcase onto the conveyor belt and flashed my ID to another TSA agent while he yelled out commands to passengers like a drill sergeant; a drill sergeant who only two weeks prior worked as a roast beef slicer at Arby's. The five of us zipped through security theatre and then walked over to the departures board to find our departure gate was 20. It was at that moment I realized I had not eaten breakfast. What the hell was I thinking? Never mind about breakfast, I hadn't had any coffee. If you've met me then you know that's dangerous. Not a sip of caffeine had touched my lips since waking up and I was already ankle deep in a shitty assmunching day. Unfortunately, there wasn't enough time for me to get breakfast or even a tiny cup of coffee. While my coworkers walked ahead of me through the terminal with their heads held high and bellies full, I fought the urge to sift through trash cans searching for half-eaten glazed donuts and coffee grounds. I don't know how likely this is but if you happen to stumble upon me eating garbage out of an airport trash can and it's not the apocalypse—please be kind and report me to airport security so I can receive the mental health care I need.

When we arrived at the gate there was no airplane. Shocked? Not really. We weren't alarmed, rarely do things work out as you'd expect them to in the airline industry. A genuine smile crept across my face after realizing I might have time to squeeze in a cup of coffee, and an even bigger grin when I realized I might even get a scone. A scone and a coffee before departure may be more rewarding than masturbating at the hotel after a long day on the airplane.

When the gate agent spotted us lining up our luggage against the wall she threw her hands up in the air and announced, "Oh, thank God you guys are here. We didn't know where the crew was?"

I looked over at Misty, "I'm gonna get some coffee. Can you watch my bags?"

"Of course," she answered, "take your time."

I turned to walk away and overheard the gate agent inform Captain Emerson, "The airplane is at a hard stand and we are already running late. We need to get you guys out there and start boarding as soon as possible."

I spun back around crushed. It was the equivalent of having my pants down around my ankles, a hotel towel within reach, good porn on the laptop, and hearing a weak tap on the door with a faint accented, "Housekeeping."

We grabbed our bags and followed behind the gate agent like little ducklings as she led us down the jet bridge. Once we were all piled up at the end she pushed in the secret code and opened the door leading down to the tarmac. The five of us lifted up our bags and slowly descended down the unstable and slippery metal stairs. So fucking dangerous. Was the airline looking to fill out five on-the-job injury claims? It seemed that way. Even though I wasn't in the mood to deal with any injuries, I secretly wished Ursula slipped and fell to the tarmac. I didn't want her to die or anything dramatic like that. Maybe just a little whiplash to knock the slut out of her.

The airport shuttle was waiting and immediately whisked us off to the airplane. It was still overcast as we left the terminal for an unknown location somewhere on the tarmac. Although pleased there were no passengers on the shuttle, the dense fog and drizzle hanging over the airport made me question whether we'd depart safely.

"It's so depressing here today." Misty said while riding towards our airplane. I nodded my head in agreement. We had no knowledge of the number of airplanes that diverted to the airport or how many were lined up along the runway awaiting their crews. We couldn't see anything out the window but I knew the airplanes were out there. It was as if the blanket of fog that greeted me earlier in the morning followed us to the airport. A few minutes went by before a break in the fog revealed the outline of an airplane and then a hint of color before it came into view. Our airplane was parked alongside two other airplanes with the airstairs truck parked a few feet away. For safety measures the airstairs are moved away from the airplane when it's out on a hard stand overnight. The shuttle pulled up to the side of the airplane and we filed out, grabbed our luggage, and waited for the gate agent to pull the stairs closer to the airplane. She walked up the stairs first, opening the airplane door, and then we all climbed up in a single file behind Captain Emerson. I immediately felt like a movie star walking up the shaky stairs. Even though we had a rocky start to the morning, strutting up those stairs and onto the airplane put me in a better mood. I'm not saying that I was completely cured of being a curmudgeon old bitch, but I was on my way. One more flight. One more flight. One more *fucking* flight. If I kept telling myself that for the next five hours I was sure I'd make it through the rest of the day. I stopped in the middle of the airplane, hoisted up my suitcase into the overhead bin, clicked my black size 11 Dockers from JCPenney together three times, and whispered to myself, "One more flight."

"One long leg and we will be done, Joe." Misty stated as I caught up to her in back of the airplane. Was she psychic? Could she read my mind? I hope not or she probably already knew I had undressed her with my eyes. I may be gay but I am not stupid.

"Yes. I need this trip to be over. I'm tired. I didn't sleep well last night." I blamed my mood on sleep but in reality it was Ursula that I was tired of. I kept that information to myself. Misty and Ursula were friends and I've learned that when working with flight attendants who happen to be friends you don't offer your opinion if it's a negative one. You keep your mouth shut. Too bad Ursula didn't live by that rule. I opened and closed overhead bins verifying the emergency equipment was present and secured when I heard the PA come alive throughout the cabin.

Ursula's voice boomed from my right eardrum to my left, "Do you guys want to come up here and brief? They want to start boarding right away."

"Of course they do," I mumbled while smiling at Misty. She followed me up the aisle to the front of the airplane where Captain Emerson, Ursula, and the gate agent patiently waited.

The second Captain Emerson finished briefing us on our flight time and weather to Cleveland the gate agent rudely interrupted, "Are you guys ready to board?" She stood on the top of the airstairs looking into the airplane with her walkie talkie in hand anxious to push the talk button.

"Are you guys ready in the back?" Ursula asked pushing her mismanaged hair out of her face.

Starting towards the back of the airplane I answered without turning to face her, "Yes. Send them up. I need to get out of here." I continued to the middle of the airplane and took my position in the exit row. Misty raced to the back galley to finish her security checks and Ursula stood up front with her half crooked smile and smeared on lipstick.

The buses carrying all our passengers arrived quickly and it took only a few minutes before they were awkwardly climbing the airstairs and walking onto the airplane. The drizzle had turned to full blown rain by this point and I assumed these passengers were miserable. I couldn't blame them. I later found out that the airline never contacted any of them to advise on the status of the airplane and that it never landed in San Francisco. These passengers woke up at the asscrack of dawn and drove all the way to the airport to find out that they were being bused an hour away to another airport. By the time the first passenger approached me in the exit row I had my game face on. Which at this point was faker than Ursula's eyelashes. My cheeks were ready to crack from the Joker smile I painted on. And just to confirm, Heath Ledger's Joker—not Jack Nicholson's.

"Good morning." Smile. "Welcome." Nod. I alternated greetings and gestures to each passenger stumbling passed me down the aisle. I don't want to brag but I am a certified bullshit artist when it comes to greeting people on the airplane. My greetings are perfected to the point where no passenger could ever guess I hated them all. Without thinking, and probably because I was caffeine deprived, I added, "How are you?" to one guy who looked like the only thing he wanted to do was punch the grin right off my face. What was I thinking asking one of these passengers an open ended question?

Right on cue he spit out, "I love being delayed." He paused for a moment when I didn't instantly respond. Then he added, "Just glad to finally be on the airplane and out of the rain."

My smile grew bigger. "Yes, sir. This weather is terrible today. We were bused over from San Francisco, too." I can't begin to wonder why I added that to the conversation. It brought nothing but an avenue for him to continue talking with me. He didn't give a damn if I walked the entire way in my bare feet over broken glass. Luckily for me, the line began flowing so he continued past me while I smiled the entire time. It's all so exhausting.

Keeping on my toes and not letting these passengers know I was just as disappointed as they were about our morning was front and center in my mind. Besides the one guy who stopped to talk to me, most of the passengers— even with the hassle of a bus ride from San Francisco—had a positive attitude.

Travel delays suck. I understand. Honestly, I am not innocent of having my share of meltdowns due to an extended airport delay. I've been known to get crazy with the best of them (did you read the last chapter), but I'd rather get to my final destination late than have the airline cancel the flight. Do you agree? I assume most people agree. There are probably a select few who'd rather have the flight cancelled to start fresh the next morning but fuck that.

Whenever I have waited at the airport because of a rolling delay, all I focused on was getting home. Spending another night away from home was never an option. I'd find a nice quiet carpeted corner of the airport, get on my knees, and pray to God that the flight wouldn't get cancelled. It never got cancelled. Why? Because God always answers the prayers of a gay guy on his knees. Don't believe me? Do you think it's a coincidence that porn is available online for free? What about our friend Barack Obama. How do you think he became president? The gays. There were more cocksuckers on their knees praying during those two Presidential campaigns then all the gay pride parades combined.

As more passengers boarded I was displaced and forced to move from the exit row towards the rear of the airplane. I made it to row 19 when an older female passenger asked me to lift her bag up into the overhead bin. Normally, we are not required to lift a passenger bag without their assistance, but this decrepit lady was tiny and I was being nice. She looked like an older Jessica Tandy. Why was she traveling alone? I had no idea but my generous attention and kindness towards her proved that I can still be nice even when I haven't had my morning coffee.

Stepping halfway into the row to place her bag in the overhead bin I heard a faint voice in my left ear. Was someone talking to me? It was a female voice, that I could tell, but whoever was delivering the message couldn't possibly be talking to me. They must have been talking to someone else because I had a large piece of luggage hanging over me and Jessica Tandy's head. The option of lending a hand to another passenger at that moment was out of the question. Dropping the bag on my head, or even worse, on Jessica Tandy's doppelganger was not part of my morning plan. I had enough paperwork to complete due to our airplane diverting the night before. Filling out any further incident reports would have to wait for the next time I worked. The female voice swam inside my head for a fleeting moment and then it was gone. My focus was on placing the bag into the overhead bin and stepping out of the way. I turned the bag around so the wheels were facing out and looked down at Jessica's warm face. "There you go."

Without thinking I stepped back into row 19 and began greeting passengers. Then it happened.

The same female voice blasted, "GET THE FUCK OUT OF MY WAY!"

Allow me to paint a clearer picture with brighter colors so you fully understand the situation. The area of the airplane we were standing in was a total cluster fuck with passengers getting themselves settled. Luggage was being tossed into any open space available in the overhead bins while children screamed from their car seats after being strapped in by their parents. Controlled anarchy should always be expected on an airplane. It was hard focusing on any one person while everyone in the surrounding area thought they were more important than the person standing next to them. As turbulent as it was, I never expected an explosion of that magnitude to go off right next to me. That bitch might as well have been a suicide bomber because the moment her sentence detonated out of her mouth—row 19 became ground fucking zero.

My neck swung around so fast it still hurts. I became possessed with Willow Smith. If I had hair I'd have whipped it back and forth and knocked her fucking lights out. I turned to face this unknown villainous creature (not knowing what I'd find) and immediately stopped after coming face-to-face with a petite-sized woman. The power projecting from her deep voice had me expecting to throw down with Xena. Or a woman who doesn't fuck around, like Hillary Clinton. Someone who starts a fight and can finish it. This bitch couldn't finish a cup of coffee without assistance. She sported short brown hair, black framed glasses, and if I passed her on the street I'd assume she was on her way to volunteer at a soup kitchen. She looked innocent until we made eye contact. Then she scowled so angrily I instantly wished her mother had aborted her.

The kicker was she had a baby in her arms. She actually produced an offspring? Are you kidding me? Can you imagine the level of demonic forces flowing through those little veins? I've probably been two feet from the Antichrist and I was too shocked to snap a picture. I was dumbfounded that she spoke to me in that tone. I'm the flight attendant. The male flight attendant. The male flight attendant with a beard, bald head, and thick neck. Was nobody afraid of me? If I sported a few tattoos on my arms I might look like I had recently been released from prison, not asking you if you'd like cream and sugar in your coffee. My neck immediately turned red which is something that happens when I'm ready to attack. This lady was a fluffy white poodle who ventured too close to the water's edge and I was the hungry alligator who was moments away from devouring her. My adrenaline kicked into high gear. Think of it as that moment you are walking along a desert trail and hear the warning sound from a rattlesnake a few feet away. Has that happened to you? Me neither. But if it did I'd expect my heart to gallop just as fast as it was while standing at row 19 facing off with this demon.

It may seem from my yammering on that minutes—or even hours—passed while we stood there staring at each other. That was not the case. Once I heard the word *'fuck'* broadcasted louder than a touchdown during Monday night football, I yanked my glasses off my face and leaned in closer, "What did you just say to me?"

She ignored me which infuriated me. Completely forgetting I was a working professional, on an airplane, unable to get crazy, I leaned in again and stopped a mere five inches from her face, "You don't need to talk to me like that. Do you hear me?"

Her eyes flickered with an evil I hadn't seen since the nuns at Our Lady of Sorrows. I backed away for a moment but didn't break my eye contact with her. I usually refrain from talking to passengers like that, but what can I say, I am only human. She, on the other hand, was a horrid succubus who sucked the life out of anyone who spent more than five seconds with her. I concluded that she had come from the netherworld to steal my happiness and fuck up my morning more than the weather had already done.

I stepped out into the aisle but didn't move past row 20. I hovered there waiting for her to respond but she gave me nothing. Nothing. She slide into row 19 and took her aisle seat as if I had vanished into the overhead bin. A second later the man behind her, a gray hair gentleman, walked up with multiple bags in his hands and said, "Don't get into it with her. It isn't worth it."

Was this her therapist? Maybe it was her priest, although I doubted that. No God-fearing man could withstand such close proximity with that level of evil without combusting. It had to be her father and if he was telling me to let the incident go, I should have taken that as a warning to stop poking my stick at this hornet's nest. Coming down the aisle behind him was a well dressed older lady who I assumed gave birth to this serpent from the abyss. I'd hate to see the inside of her vagina; it's probably got more claw marks than a cat's scratching post. I defended my spot at row 20 while watching the entire family crowd around and take their seats at row 19. The mother and father sat across from my nemesis in seats 19 B and C. I kept my eye on the three of them, four if you included the Antichrist sitting on his mother's lap, and then casually looked up to see her battered husband making his way towards me with the child's car seat. If body language was processed through our ears I'd have needed ear plugs watching this guy warily stroll up the aisle. His darkened eyes, low hanging head, and somber expression gave the impression of someone who'd rather be put out of their misery than spend one more millisecond married to this lady. First impressions are powerful and it was clear that this guy didn't get much sleep. How could he? He was sleeping with the enemy. I imagined most nights he laid awake with one eye opened resulting in his physically exhausted looking state. He made it to row 19 and glared at me with this gloom that mimicked how a human trafficking victim might make eye contact with you while they internally scream for help. He awkwardly secured the car seat against the window. His evil wife didn't offer to help him; I wasn't surprised. After he attached the seat belt through the car seat, she handed the baby over never once acknowledging him. She didn't say one word. He was treated like the hired help. If I had a few matches, some gasoline, and a DVD copy of the *The Burning Bed,* I'd have slipped it to him whenever he got up to use the lavatory and wished him luck when he got to the hotel. He most likely had a copy in his checked bag.

I was torn on how to handle the situation. I love saying fuck. I say it all the time. It's my second favorite word after bukkake. Honestly, there's really no better word than bukkake. Just saying bukkake makes me smile. If you don't believe me just know I am smiling at this exact moment. But I am talking about the word fuck. Repeat it with me, "Fuck. Fuckity, fuck fuck!" Almost heals all your aches and pains just saying it outloud. Like the weight of the world has been lifted off your shoulders.

> I say it when I am happy.
> I say it when I am sad.
> I say it when I am frustrated.
> I even say it when I am mad.
> I say fuck - Joe I am.

I figured resolving this conflict with 19D involved removing her from the flight. No question. She was a migraine with no Excedrin. I couldn't possibly manage through the flight looking at her face each time I walked by. What if she stabbed me while I zipped by with a cup of hot coffee? I couldn't let that happen. Clearing my head and releasing my anger was my top priority. I turned around, took a deep cleansing breath, maneuvered myself through the few passengers standing behind me in the aisle, and marched to the back of the airplane. While approaching the back galley Misty instantly picked up on my temperament. "I'm so angry," I put my hands on my hips while standing between the two lavatories, "The lady in 19D just told me to get the fuck out of her way."

"What? Why did she say that?" Misty asked stepping back to allow me space to walk into the galley.

"I don't know." The volume of my voice never lowered, "I was helping some old lady with her bag and I guess I didn't move fast enough."

She shook her head, "I swear. These people are ridiculous. Call Ursula and tell her. Nobody should talk to us like that."

Moving over to the jumpseat across from Misty I threw my hands up like a drama queen, "Who the hell does this bitch think she is?" I didn't give Misty time to answer. Without warning I violently started punching the headrest of the jumpseat. Left. Right. Left. Right. All while passengers were still boarding the airplane. I imagined her bloody lips and swollen eyes each time I struck the jumpseat violently. The harder I punched the better I felt. Misty laughed uncomfortably while wondering what the hell I was doing.

After what seemed to be a few minutes I stopped striking the jumpseat and looked over at Misty, "I bet if I punched her in the throat she'd never think of dropping the f-bomb on another flight attendant again. What do you think?"

"I think you need to have some water and chill out." She started walking away, "Cool down and call Ursula. I'm gonna check out the cabin. I'll be right back."

She left the galley and made her way up the aisle closing full overhead bins. I contemplated walking up to row 19, grabbing the bitch by her neck, and throwing her out of the airplane directly onto the tarmac. I let that thought pass through my mind and smiled for a brief moment. After I downed two large bottles of water I picked up the interphone and called Ursula to brief her on the situation. She didn't say much and listened to me rant. We hung up and a few minutes later Captain Emerson called me in the back, "Hey Joe, do you want this passenger removed from the flight?"

What an idiotic question. There was no questioning she was gone off the flight. I'd smile and wave at her as we took off wishing the Antichrist vomited on her neck. "Yes. She told me to get the fuck out of her way. I'm not dealing with that type of behavior from a passenger."

"Is she traveling alone?

"No. She has her family with her. She's in 19D."

"Ok. Just keep Ursula informed on what's going on and if we need to get security."

"I will. The gate agent will need to come down once the aisle is clear to talk to her."

He responded, "Copy that." and I hung up the interphone. I punched the jumpseat a few more times, for good luck, and waited for Misty to make her way back from the aisle so I could continue helping passengers with their bags. While standing there watching Misty, and all the commotion from boarding started to die down, I questioned why this dreadful woman lashed out at me. Was she just frustrated like the rest of us? What happened to her before she boarded the flight? Did I really want to kick a passenger off the flight who had her child with her? Even if that child was to grow up to feast on the flesh of Christians? Was I having a change of heart with this lady?

I tried remembering if there was ever a time I said fuck inappropriately. I didn't have to think about it for long. I use the word so often that I'm convinced it accidently, at one time or another, slipped out when something else should have been said. But I have never directed it at an employee or a complete stranger for no reason. There's a time and a place to say fuck and it's not on an airplane directed at your flight attendant.

While I stared out among the passengers, Misty made it back to the galley, "We are almost done boarding," she said folding her arms leaning against the galley counter.

"Good. Thanks for helping me out and giving me a moment to calm down. I needed it. I called Ursula and briefed her on what happened," I paused for a moment, "I think I'm gonna try and talk to this lady so we don't have to kick her off the flight." Misty gazed at me processing my words. A look of concern furrowed her brows and I nodded in agreement without saying another word. I was just as confused as Misty at how quickly my attitude changed. Maybe it was that last jumpseat punch, but letting out some of that anger and frustration soothed my mood. I wanted to resolve this problem. Honestly, I can't put my finger on how this conclusion came to be—it just did. Perhaps taking a bus from one airport to another was too much to handle and she snapped. We've all had delusional moments; just look at the flight attendant who decided to end his career by going out the wrong airplane door with a couple of beers. Giving 19D the benefit of the doubt made me the better person and I wanted at all costs to save her from deplaning and leaving her family behind as they jetted off to Ohio. I stepped into the aisle and walked up to row 19.

My first challenge was to stop referring to her as a demonic creature even though she was. Turning to face the back of the airplane, I knelt down on my right knee and took a deep breath, "Ma'am, I am a nice person—."

Looking straight at me she screamed, "Stop harassing me. Leave me alone! I wasn't talking to you, I was talking to my father." With a snap of her neck she went back to staring straight ahead towards the seat in front of her.

Talking to her father? During our brief interaction in the aisle her father was walking behind her so I was pretty fucking sure she wasn't talking to him, especially when she was looking straight through me with her fiendish eyes. "You can't talk to a flight attendant like that," I blurted out, "I can have you taken off this airplane for speaking to me like that." She continued to look ahead. I looked over at her husband, who barely made eye contact with me, and then kind of forgot where I was, "You are lucky to be here, do you hear me? She definitely heard me. It seemed everyone from row 15 heard me as they simultaneously turned to see what the excitement was behind them. Misty heard me. I wouldn't be surprised if the ground operations guy heard me from inside the cargo hold. Who needs a megaphone when Joe is your flight attendant?

At this point the airplane was fully boarded and the gate agent was waiting to close the airplane door. Misty picked up quickly that things were not working out and started walking back up to row 19. I stood up to intimidate this lady but she was harder than masonry nails. Her husband stared at me, trying to calm down his screaming baby, with an I'm-so-sorry look. I wanted to ask him if she forgot to take her lithium.

She broke her position, looked over my shoulder as Misty approached, and announced loudly, "I refuse to talk to him anymore! I will only talk to you." If her goal was to aggravate me she had successfully just crossed the finish line.

I was over this fucking lunatic. Done. The fiery tension coming off my head, neck, and chest could have melted the entire Ice Hotel. If I bursted into flames at that exact moment, my only wish would have been to take her down with me. Not the husband and Antichrist though, they'd need a fresh start. On second thought—scratch that plan— no love lost if the Antichrist went up in flames with us. Let's face it: in 20 years he'd be exacting revenge on every flight attendant he could get his claws on. I'd be doing the airline industry a favor if a flicker of my embers found their way onto his diaper.

Misty approached me concerned but I was blind with fury. I couldn't speak. There was no doubt in my mind that the creature was about to be escorted off the airplane by security and await the next flight. Sitting at the gate area for an extended amount of time would be the perfect opportunity to evaluate her treatment of human beings, even if she wasn't one. When you live among humans you better know how to fucking treat us. Her hatred for me would last an eternity and I relished in that idea. I'd sleep with one eye open for the rest of my life but it was worth it. Furthermore, if her family wanted to stay behind and stand by her side, so be it. I turned away from the situation and proceeded to the front of the airplane.

"Are we ready to close the door?" The pushy gate agent asked while standing outside on the jet stairs.

"Nope!" I addressed this directly at Ursula, "The lady in 19D is coming off the airplane. I will not fly with her." I theatrically stated for the entire first three rows to hear. My delivery was so climactic if I curtsied after my lines I'd have received a standing ovation. A reaction ultimately pissing me off because the seat belt sign was illuminated. You know when my anger overpowers my desire for attention and praise I'm fucking outraged.

Ursula moved from the space between the galley and the flight deck, "What's going on?"

I planted my feet in the aisle at row one, "The lady in 19D is what's going on. I want her taken off the flight. She's being disrespectful and dropped the F-bomb."

"She's traveling with her family, right?"

"Yes. Her mother, father, husband, and baby. That doesn't matter." I was confused as to the point of her question.

"It actually does," Ursula answered while leaning towards the flight deck, "Captain, can you come out here?"

What the fuck was happening? And why was Ursula looking at me like Lord Voldemort after he summoned his Death Eaters? I had previously spoken to Captain Emerson and I was under the impression we were in agreement with reference to this passenger getting the boot. My eyes panned back and forth from Ursula to the gate agent, and then Captain Emerson climbed out of his seat, stepped out of the flight deck, and squeezed past Ursula.

"Come over here so we can talk." He walked through the galley and waved me to follow him onto the wet platform. While standing between him and the gate agent he continued softly, "I spoke with Ursula. We've decided not to remove that lady. She's traveling with her entire family and I'm not kicking off some lady with a baby. I don't care how much of an asshole she's being."

I peered at him while the drizzle danced off my bald head. He's lucky laser beams weren't attached to my fucking eyeballs or he'd be incinerated. I looked over at Ursula standing in the galley while innocently looking down at the manifest. She was obviously listening to our entire conversation but trying to look preoccupied. I fought the instinct to haphazardly shriek,"Hey Ursula. You're a big fat fucking cunt!" I swallowed it down like it was a balloon full of coke and I was crossing from San Diego to TiDiegoa. I figure that's difficult, right?

"Who decided?" I conjured up a perplexed facial expression, "You and Ursula? I thought I had a say in this too."

His forehead crinkled, "I decided!" It was easy to see how offended he became after I added Ursula to the equation, "Let's not forget I'm the captain. If you have a problem with that we can remove you from the flight and get another flight attendant."

I was flabbergasted and had no words to express myself. That's a fucking lie; I had the exact words to express myself but swallowed them down again. This time it being slightly more strenuous than just a balloon of coke—this time like a brick. Instead of reciting all those lovely adult themed slang words I shook my head in disbelief. Disbelief that this passenger was getting away with talking to me the way she did and that Ursula had just slipped it to me with no lube.

Captain Emerson watched me and reiterated, "Are we going to be alright on this flight today? I'd like to go home."

"I guess." I stomped back onto the airplane making brief eye contact with Ursula. Not too long, just enough to let her know my blood was bubbling up like hot magma. She also needed to know that she was the enemy now. Fuck 19D—I had bigger cunts to fry.

Unity as a crew on the airplane is vital for a successful flight. Even if at that exact moment you don't 100% agree with the person you are working with, having their back when surrounded by passengers is beneficial. Standing strong as a crew sends a powerful message to the passengers on the airplane. It sets the tone that flight attendants are not parents and passengers can't play us. You will get the same response from me that you will get from Misty, and so on. You notice I didn't say Ursula, right? It was hard to include Ursula while I maneuvered through the airplane trying to pull her jagged knife out of my back.

My policy for handling altercations with coworkers is simple. Support each other in front of passengers and when you're finally alone behind closed doors—beat the shit out of them. Clean and simple. That's a joke. Calm down. I am not encouraging work related violence. Just handle those critical conversations behind closed doors or in the back galley. It really depends on how long you can hold your tongue. Bottom line is that flight attendants should look out for each others at all times. It's basically sink or swim.

News flash to the reader and anyone who might actually ever work with me: I do not like sinking. Second news flash: if every flight attendant working with me from this point moving forward can have my back when dealing with asshole passengers, I'd forever be grateful. While I'm thinking about it, I should also add it's influential when the captain has your back too. It makes working in a tube at 37,000 feet easier if the entire working crew agrees on how to handle different passenger concerns and issues. I am not saying all flight attendants and pilots get along. Trust me, they don't, but when it comes to dealing with passenger issues it's important to stick together. I walked through the airplane towards the exit row to give my standard briefing. It was hard to concentrate. My plastic smile flashing from passenger to passenger and row to row all while struggling to erase the smug look on Ursula's face from my mind. It might have been easier to grab Ursula's wavy long hair—which was out of uniform compliance, I might add—and beat her to a pulp with an oxygen bottle. It was official: Ursula was a bigger bitch than the lady who told me to get the fuck out of her way. At least she was upfront and direct with me. Ursula slithered behind my back like a poisonous serpent.

After conducting the exit row briefing I went right back up to the front galley. By the time I reached the galley the main airplane door was closed. I positioned myself waiting for Ursula's cue to arm the doors.

Without looking at me she picked up the interphone, "Flight attendants prepare for departure."

I whispered to myself, "Eat a dick, Ursula. Eat a big fat hairy dick!" She didn't hear me, which was good. I moved away from my armed door and before she asked I answered, "My door is armed and cross checked."

I stepped out of the galley and opened the first overhead bin to grab my safety demonstration kit. I tossed the kit through the air and it landed on the galley counter with a thud. Fuck it. I didn't care. Let her say something. Please. I was waiting. It's that instant when you regret not verbally attacking someone who has wronged you. My pride was hurt. My ego fucking destroyed. I didn't even feel like a man. My dick and balls packed up and went searching for an eager pre-op transitioning male who'd actually use them. Like Chaz Bono. Chaz Bono would use the fuck out of my dick. Sadly, I just carried my dick and balls around like luggage. Ursula sat in her jumpseat preparing to read the safety demonstration. I stood in position at row one and plastered on my fake smile. I should have won a Tony Award for this shit.

Her voice drove me to the brink of insanity. I knew discussing my feelings with her was my only option. Simply looking at her made me want to wrap the oxygen tubing around her neck. After the safety demonstration was complete, I arranged the equipment back into the black leather bag and placed it securely into the overhead bin. No words were exchanged. She stood up putting her stuff away but I ignored her. I'd need a minute to construct my thoughts and words before confronting her. I had to brace myself. With how upset I was, if I started talking without a formulated plan, security might have been needed out on the tarmac.

Matt says that when I am mad I have the tendency to go from zero to 10 within seconds. Probably more like zero to 1,000. I have no filter. He also says I have no control over how angry I get. My anger knows no limits. It's all true. But at work it's different. There's a switch somewhere in my brain that deciphers when it's alright to go batshit crazy on someone and when it's not. I am no doctor but if you cracked my skull open, peered deep inside my brain, you'd most likely see synapses firing all out of sync. I have no fucking clue. Knowing all that about my anger I had to carefully think about how to approach her. Ignoring her sounded perfect, but that was unprofessional. She may not be professional but I am. And if I gave her the cold shoulder I'd miss out on letting her know how disgusted I was with her behavior and her short skirt. Being honest and letting her know how I felt was way more professional than just ignoring her for five hours. It was settled. I had to confront her; I couldn't live without my dick and balls. Even if they had already moved on to Chaz.

I started to the back of the airplane to talk things out with Misty. We just pulled away from the gate so I figured I had plenty of time to give her the rundown on Ursula's behavior and get some feedback. Worry about their friendship had vanished. Even if Ursula had been the maid of honor at her wedding—I had no idea if that's true or not—I was ready to unleash my opinion. I never got the chance. As I approached the fifth row Captain Emerson's voice came over the PA, "Flight attendants, please take your seats for departure."

I spun around and marched back up the few rows to the front galley. Without us making eye contact, I lowered my jumpseat and sat down. She was seated next to me. Five inches away. I tried not touching her crusty skin while fastening my seatbelt and pulling the harness over my shoulders to lock into place. My plan on coming up with a plan to approach her was unsuccessful. Who fails at the pre-plan stage? Me. That's who! I sat there staring ahead hoping to remain silent until I was in the back galley reactivating my plan. My wish was not granted.

"I'm sorry, Joe. I just didn't want to leave that mother behind with her baby."

"Listen," I used muscles I never knew I had keeping my voice down. It was painful. The six passengers in the front row watched us like we were being broadcast live on Bravo. "you could've talked to me about it. Going behind my back like that, I can't believe you did that. You pulled the rug out from under me. I wouldn't have done that to you."

She pushed her hair out of her eyes, "I spoke with the captain and we decided that it was best if you just keep your distance from that lady. She's not in your section anyway, right?"

"Ursula," my voice raised and I quickly brought it back down and started smiling again, "that's not the point. You know what?" I recollected my thoughts, "Never mind. How would you feel if that lady treated you like that?"

She fidgeted with her watch for a few seconds, "It doesn't matter. The decision was made."

"Yeah, I was there. I know." I broke eye contact with her and looked at the passenger in 1C and whispered, "It's probably best if we only talk if it's work related."

"I'm sorry."

An electric pulse shot through me, "No you're not!" My voice escalated leaving no doubt passengers heard me,

"Or you wouldn't have done it in the first place." The engines roared and we started down the runway. I turned my head as we took off and didn't speak to her again for the rest of the flight.

When the airplane reached 10,000 feet and I heard the double chime alerting us it was safe to get up from our jump seats; I unbuckled my harness quickly and proceeded down the aisle to the back galley. Misty was informed of the entire situation while she set up the galley for our beverage service. All she did was apologize while I insisted it wasn't her fault.

"I don't plan on going anywhere near the front of the airplane. So if the pilots need to come out can you go up front?"

"Of course." She slid her glasses to the top her head to hold back her bangs, "I'm surprised that Ursula didn't support you. I'm a little disappointed in her."

I pulled my apron over my head and wrapped the strings around my waist, "I'm disappointed in her and the Captain. What a fucking asshole." My bad attitude stayed with me like a pulled muscle. An entire tube of Bengay couldn't cure my pain.

Misty tried her best to make me happy, "I cleaned out the coffee pot really good so you can have a cup of coffee."

I curled my lip, "Coffee from the airplane? Gross. I think warm piss tastes better."

Our laughter erupted in the galley. It felt much better than anger.

Throughout the five hour flight, whenever I tiptoed by 19D or thought of Ursula, I felt defeated. Nauseated. Antichrist's mother curled up in the fetal position, laid her head on her husband's shoulder and slept the entire flight. She never asked for anything to eat or drink. And if my memory serves me correctly, she never got up to use the lavatory. Evil must only piss once a month. After passing by their row a few times, her husband eventually stopped making eye contact with me. That was fine. The only person who smiled at me from row 19 was her father. Was he flirting with me? I hope not. Although a little old man flirting would have distracted me from this terrible day. Misty calmed me down for most of the flight but nothing prevented me from dwelling on the repugnant way Ursula handled the outcome of this situation.

When we landed in Cleveland, I anxiously awaited 19D to make her way to the front of the airplane. I stood behind the bulkhead fake smiling at the passengers walking off the airplane. Would she apologize? Would she step out onto the jet bridge and start yelling at me? Would I just fucking lose it and punch her in the throat?

None of the above. She strutted up the aisle with her sunglasses covering her subhuman eyes, ignoring my existence. I was hopeful she'd apologize for treating me with such disrespect. But no such luck. That was asking too much. Instead she disregarded me like I was transparent. Obviously, it wasn't worth her time to offer up an apology for ridiculing me in front of Misty and anyone else who wasn't hearing impaired.

Standing there watching her step off the airplane, I focused all my energy on willing her to trip and chip a tooth. It failed. What can I say? My telekinetic abilities need some work. One after another her family filed out of the airplane behind her. The husband refused to make final eye contact with me which confirmed he was a piece of shit just like his wife. Her father, last off the airplane, looked at me and gave a mumbled, "Thank you," under his breath. He said it flimsy so I don't believe he meant it. Either that or he was simply too afraid that a member of his entourage overheard his kind gesture.

After the last passenger walked off the airplane I sprinted down the aisle to grab my luggage out of the overhead bin. Captain Emerson picked up the interphone one final time, "Hey guys. We're outta here. Sorry today was such a rough day, Joe. Time to just let it go."

Refusing to look towards the front of the airplane I ignored his well wishes. You can call me a bitch if it makes you feel better. You can call me a megasuperduper-cuntybitch if you want; I really don't care. The second the last passenger deplaned my only goal was to get as far away from Ursula and Captain Emerson as possible. Anything they said at that point fell on deaf ears. My job as the friendly smile-at-all-costs-no-matter-what flight attendant day was over. My priority was feeling better about myself because carrying around work related anger for the rest of the day was not an option. Did I say a day? Silly me. I didn't carry this anger around for one day. I carried it around for months. Years. Why else do you think I am taking the time to tell this story in such detail?

It took weeks of soul searching and self analyzing to realize my rage was not towards 19D or Ursula. Don't get me wrong, I'd instantly run them both over while they jaywalked in front of me. No, I was angry with myself. Disappointed that I allowed a passenger to speak to me with such contempt. As if I was nothing more than one of the seats on the airplane. Appalled that I didn't stand up for myself against Captain Emerson and Ursula's backstabbing decision. A decision I should have been invited to take part in. Saddened that I continued playing the victim days after everyone else went on with their lives. Because I am sure that's what happened. I bumped into Ursula a few weeks later in the crew lounge and she acted like nothing happened. Did she fall and strike her head? Was it amnesia? Nope. It was her moving on with her life and being a bitch about it while I dug a hole deeper with regrets.

I expected a complaint letter from a member of the Antichrist's family. I anxiously waited to be called into the supervisor's office to recount this miserable flight. As days turned into months and then years, a complaint letter never came. Hopefully, when they checked into their hotel, she took a nice hot bath, a long nap, spent a few days thinking about what occurred on that rainy day in San Jose, and finally realized her wrongdoing. I have to believe that's why I never received a complaint letter. 19D finally came to her senses about her disgusting behavior.

I still believe that to this day. If I didn't, I'd never have found closure regarding this onboard altercation.

DIVERT TO HARRISBURG

When it comes to working flights to Orlando, I usually want to hide in the lavatory ignoring every Disney princess that makes her way onto the airplane. If you've seen one seven year old Elsa, you've seen them all, right? I know I have. My attitude might do a complete 180 if, say, a 24 year-old muscular blond Kristoff strut onto the airplane. Now that's my kind of distraction. Talk about standing fully erect during boarding.

How can I describe an Orlando flight to someone who has never experienced one as a passenger? Loud, chaotic, disorderly, excessive amounts of carry on bags, children, Disney merchandise... Did I mention children? They practically outnumber the adults. Never will I understand how a family of six travels to Orlando spending a week bleeding out money on airfare, hotels, theme parks, souvenirs, and food. I can barely afford a cup of coffee at the Las Vegas airport.

Lucky for me, on this day I wasn't working the flight from Orlando to New York City, I was traveling there for a flight attendant meeting. Before I go any further, let me explain about these meetings so that it makes sense why I was traveling to JFK as a passenger.

Everyone desires to be heard and have a voice at the table. There might be a select few who disagree with me and if so, that's their right. If communicating and getting your point across doesn't satisfy you in the way it does me then we can agree to disagree and move on with our lives. Agreed? However, if you do disagree—I don't fucking get it. It makes no sense to me. As human beings we have been striving to be heard since we crawled out of our cave uttering nonsense to our cavemen neighbors. I'd rather be loud and proud letting it all out than sulk in the corner disappearing into the wallpaper never to be heard. Having the opportunity to express ourselves stretches back to our early childhood. At least for me it does. I faintly remember being a young teen sitting at the dining room table eating dinner with my entire family, vying for the exact moment the spotlight shined on me so I could interrupt whoever was speaking and have my say. I wanted to tell my story and share my experience, but mostly share my opinion. Maybe talk about how Jason Billings aggressively tried making me eat his snot in the back of the school bus on the way home. Confess I finally had a girlfriend but leave out the part about how she ignored me in school and only called late at night after her parents went to bed. Shit like that. Even if I couldn't make the topic about me, I fought for the opportunity to hand out my personal opinions on everything from naming the family cat to vacationing in Canada.

With my ambition to express my every idea and thought since childhood, it should come as no surprise that when I became aware that there was a way to communicate and interact with the management team at my airline, I leapt at the chance to get involved. I jumped on it quicker than a wide-open standby flight to Paris.

I bet you thought I was gonna say big fat dick, but I didn't.

The Standards Advisory Team-SAT for short-was conceived a few years after the airline's inaugural flight. A creative and brilliant way to allow flight attendants, pilots, ground operations, and airport employees a safe and effective outlet to speak their mind and have a say in their daily work rules without losing their jobs. Each department's SAT had a different goal. My knowledge for the other departments was minimal, but the flight attendant's SAT was broken into five different subteams: Airplane Products, Hotel/Van Accommodations, Uniforms, Security & Safety, and finally, the one that made me stiff in my uniform pants, Scheduling.

I honestly don't know why I had a boner for the scheduling aspect of my job but I did. The entire process was a mystery to me from the moment I started my airline career. How were pairings created? Why were there layovers in one city in lieu of another? Why did we always stay with the same flight attendants but never the same pilots? So many questions that never got answered. It drove me fucking crazy. I became eligible to apply after being liberated from my six month disciplinary action sentence. I filled out the online survey, interviewed with management, and was officially elected by my peers to represent them as their voice for the scheduling group. I was ecstatic and took my role as seriously as Catholics take fasting during Lent. Scratch that last part, I took it way more seriously.

Our SAT meetings were scheduled on a quarterly basis and often held in a conference room on the fifth floor of our headquarters building. It was an event. A special occasion that gave everyone involved the opportunity to speak—not only for ourselves—but on behalf of thousands of other flight attendants. I can't deny, I was cocky as fuck about it. Whenever I attended one of these meetings I always flew up from Orlando the day before. When the airline pays for you to be in Manhattan for a work meeting your goal should be getting there as soon as possible. That way you get the most bang for your buck. Because I fly for free, my buck was zero; the more bang I got, the better.

On this specific occasion, while I packed for my trip, Matt sat on the sofa stewing like a pot of bolognese. He loathed the fact that within a mere four hours I would be checking into a boutique hotel and spending the evening frolicking around Manhattan. Did I say frolicking? That's definitely the wrong word. If history repeated itself, as it often did when I was in Manhattan for work meetings, I'd finish the night stumbling through the streets inebriated. I don't want to give the wrong impression of my behavior when I visited Manhattan, but I usually got mortifyingly wasted. There's nothing frolicky about narrowly avoiding being squashed by speeding taxi cabs trying to cross 8th Avenue in Chelsea.

"Why do you always go up the day before?" He asked from the sofa while I ran around packing my suitcase. I couldn't tell if he was joking or being serious. If I know him, and I do, probably an equal share of both.

"Because I enjoy the city and have dinner plans with friends." I answered while kissing him goodbye. Nothing more. Nothing less.

My flight was showing an on time departure, so I raced to the airport to have the gate agent assign me a better one. The travel department was notorious for booking us in middle seats all the way in the back of the airplane. Never in economy plus or first class. That annoyed the fuck out of me. Seriously, it never failed. Even if every upgraded seat was unoccupied I found myself sitting between two overweight passengers in row 28. The trick was getting to the airport before the flight started boarding and simply asking the gate agent for another seat. It worked every time. I know what you are thinking and you are correct: I am a spoiled brat and like Rosa Parks, the thought of sitting in the back of the bus angers me. But before you send me off to the pyre to do my best Joan of Arc impression, I am not saying that Rosa Parks was a spoiled brat. She was a brave women who fought for her freedoms and the right to sit wherever the hell she wanted—I on the other hand—just wanted a better seat.

Boarding was underway as I approached the gate. I slapped on a smile and approached the gate agent while he madly tapped at the keyboard, "Hey Rusty, have you assigned seats already?"

"No!" Refusing to look up he continued, "We will call you up when we do."

"Is the flight full?" I politely asked. It was an important question when calculating my chances of an upgraded seat.

Silence. I took that as a yes and stepped out of the way banishing myself to a row of empty seats against the wall. As a standby traveler you learn pretty damn quick not to piss off the gate agent. I hate to admit it but they hold all the power and they know it. If you annoy them too much you'll find yourself crushed in the last row among passengers who travel with garbage bags as luggage. You do not want that happening to you. Trust me. I've learned from personal experience that if you stalk, harass, or raise your voice to the gate agent while flying standby you'll most likely find yourself with a dreadful seat, no seat, or even worse—having your free flying privileges suspended by management. And let's face it, the only reason I sling cans of Sprite and pretzels around is for free airfare.

From my interaction with Rusty, I figured an upgraded seat was not in the cards for me that morning, and because I ran to the gate and ignored my stomach screaming at me for breakfast, I lost any chance of eating for the next few hours. A double whammy. When I arrived in Manhattan, the first thing I'd do was check into my fabulous boutique hotel; second was get something to eat.

"Joe Thomas?" He called over the loudspeaker. I walked up to the counter to collect my ticket avoiding eye contact with his distressing gap-toothed smile. An arduous task but one I prepared myself for. The blank slot wasn't only a mere space separating his two front teeth, I could handle that, but an entire tooth missing in action. Gone. It went out for a gallon of milk and never came home.

I stared down at the piece of white paper in my hand, "22A? That's all you've got?"

"Yup. That's all we got. Be glad it's a window." He smiled immensely making me flinch. Did he smile to make me uncomfortable? It worked. If I was missing a central incisor the last thing I would do was walk around grinning like I had won the Powerball. He continued, "Maybe if you bring that hot husband around next time you'll get a better seat."

The idea that Rusty lusted after my husband made me want to heave up my gallbladder. I don't mind men craving the pleasures of my husband but not if they can slide an entire chicken tender down their throat without unlocking their jaw. I grabbed the handle of my luggage and responded in an abusive tone, "Watch it, Rusty, or you'll be missing more than just one tooth." I flashed one final farewell smile as I walked passed him rubbing it in that I had the two things he didn't: a hot husband and a mouth full of teeth.

After introducing myself to the flight attendant, I dragged my bags down the aisle to row 22 to take my seat and patiently await my lucky seat companion. There had been a few hotties standing around the gate area, so I daydreamed about one of them sitting beside me so that our hairy arms could sword fight for the duration of the flight. Sitting far enough back I was able to watch all the passengers walk down the aisle, take their seats, fight over a pocket of space for their carry-ons, and stand in the middle of the aisle blocking other passengers while trying to find a spot to place their jackets. Boarding an airplane should be easy: walk on, place your bag in the overhead bin, and sit down. There's nothing else to it.

My eyes fixated on this tall, attractive, Italian guy making his way towards my row. He sported a black baseball cap—placed backwards for extra hotness—tight white plain t-shirt, black Adidas gym shorts, and good-looking five o'clock shadow. It may have been hours away but it was five o'clock somewhere and that somewhere was right in front of me. This guy projected manliness. It oozed out of his body from every visible pore. If he was smart he'd bottle his essence, sell it at every gay pride parade in America, and make millions. He was that gorgeous. Goddamn he was hot. My mouth watered just looking at him fully dressed; I'd probably bust a water main if I saw him full monty. He was a mature sexy man and if things went well he'd take the seat next to me for the next few hours. This Italian stallion was a beautiful stranger and I fantasized about us holding hands, tongue wrestling, him feeding me peanuts, and us sharing my ginger ale during the flight. What? I may be married but my ashes aren't blowing in the wind. When a fine ass hunk of Italian sausage walks your way, you better get your buns ready just in case. My fantasy was at full throttle until he stopped at my row and stepped out of the way. A repulsive sound rang through the entire airplane and broke my focus on his handsomely structured face. I jerked my head away and quickly looked out the window.

What snapped me out of my mid-morning wet dream was the high-pitched New York accent projecting from behind him, "Where we sittin'? I ain't sittin' all da way back hea!"

I looked back at them to watch the disaster unfold, "Shut up, aight," he barked while taking her bag, "Give me ya bag and sit down."

"We gotta sit back hea? Oh my fuckin gawd, this is horrible." She eyeballed my row with a look on her face as if she just shit her pants. Then she looked at me for a brief second to acknowledge that someone was actually sitting in the window and went right back to her man, "I ain't sittin in no middle seat, babe."

"Yes, you are."

The hairs on the back of my neck stood on end while they argued back and forth about who was going to sit in the middle seat.

"No. I ain't. You ain't making me."

He flung her bag into the overhead bin, "Reeta, sit da hell down. Why you gotta make everything so damn difficult, eh?"

"Babe, Don't tawk like dat." She screeched, "I need to be on the end so I can get up to pee." Her chipped painted fingernails flew around in his face in what seemed to be her way of getting her point across.

He mumbled under his breath, "Sit da fuck down and shut up. I ain't sittin in no middle."

I quietly wished that he had won the middle seat because sitting beside me was probably the best thing that would happen to him for the rest of his life. Or at least this flight. He won. I lost. She sat down in the aisle seat and scooted herself over into the middle pouting the entire time. We both pouted but for different reasons; my reason being I was left sitting next to a loud mouth. And that's saying something coming from me.

Reeta was an aged cut-out character from the since cancelled MTV television show *Jersey Shore*. Actually, she was more like a dilapidated cut out who had been bent in half, kicked a few times, and left in the attic for years only to be brought out again and placed next to me on this flight. I know, I am a lucky guy. Even after sitting down she continued talking—if that's what you called it—but her words sounded like Charlie Brown's teacher. Not because she mumbled but because my mind was fixated on her husband's muscular arms. Her voice became background noise while my mind focused on nothing else but swinging on his arms as if they were thick oak branches. I haven't climbed a tree in over 25 years but I was willing to give it my best try. His limbs were powerful. I am not exaggerating either, these were no ordinary, run-of-the-mill kinda arms. Oh no. These were beefy tattooed arms that belonged in a museum, or around my neck, preferably the latter. Instead, his left arm was wrapped around Reeta's shoulder while the right dangled playfully between his legs. I damned him for sitting in the aisle so far from me.

Her shrill voice sounded like Chandler Bing's girlfriend, Janice, from *Friends*, "Do you tink da girls are aight?" She didn't let him answer, "Bobby, the weatha is so bad at home. I hope our babies are ok. If my babies aren't okay I swea I'm gonna fuckin lose it."

Whatever she was going to lose I hoped it was lost before we took off so we could return to the gate and drop her off. Bobby could stay. Bobby could always stay.

"Don't worry, babe, da girls are cool. Just fuckin relax."

I silently agreed with Bobby and thought to myself, "Yes, please, just fucking relax. And shut up." They noisily unwrapped McDonald's breakfast sandwiches from a bag and the smell made my stomach bitch slap my esophagus for being late and not eating breakfast. The thought of pretzels and nuts for breakfast was unpleasing but a true reality. I pretended to watch television but kept glimpsing over at the two of them with envy. Reeta had the two things that I wanted more than anything at that exact moment: McDonald's and the handsome stallion Bobby. The universe was paying me back for being such a cunty bitch to Rusty. I deserved this treatment but I didn't have to like it.

My earbuds were tightly in place but nothing blocked her annoying voice only a foot from my right ear. She was a human megaphone getting louder and louder with each word she uttered from her cracked lips. She attacked her Egg McMuffin sandwich, with bits and pieces spraying all over her tray table and shirt, and I thought for a moment that if she started choking on the rubbery English muffin, I'd lay my head against the window and watch the drama unfold.

The airplane pulled away from the gate and during the flight attendant safety demonstration, Bobby texted someone which made her howl. "You gonna crash the fuckin plane. I'm tellin on you, babe." She reminded me of a monkey who was trained to speak. I wanted to give her a banana and see if she could peel it. They were full grown adults but their thick child-like accents reminded me of two toddlers who had escaped their playpen.

"Calm down. My phone is off. Go to sleep, will ya," He ordered her and I fell in love with him a little more each time he verbally abused her. I am not proud of that admission but his aggressive behavior fit in perfectly for the role he'd played in my sexual fantasy. For one thing, Bobby wasn't blind to her ignorance. She was a big set of tits carrying around the brain of a turkey. Great to have around for Thanksgiving, but terrible to sit next to on a 2 1/2 hour flight. Clearly, he let the power of her tits and vagina guide him into this relationship. There was no other explanation. Nobody from the planet Earth would look at Reeta's face and confess their love. Impossible. Her adult acne would put ProActive out of business.

The flight to JFK was uneventful and they slept. She curled up in his armpit and I was relieved that she was hiding her face... and not talking. He held his head down and his eyes were closed with his big masculine left hand placed carefully on her leg proclaiming his property. A piece of property that lost value every second of the day.

As we got closer to JFK the air became more turbulent. The Captain came alive on the PA, "Ladies and Gentlemen, due to the weather over JFK we've been put into a holding pattern while we wait for the weather to do it's part so we can land safely. It will get a little bumpy so please remain seated while the seatbelt sign is on." The seat belt instantly lit up as the airplane vibrated and bounced through the clouds.

This was common and nothing to fear. Holding patterns are a part of life when you fly in and out of JFK. When the weather cockblocks airplanes from landing safely, Air Traffic Control contacts the pilots and arranges them in a holding pattern. I'm baffled by how airplanes can fly around in circles and not crash into each other. I can barely merge into the next lane without running someone off the road and here you have multiple 16 ton airplanes traveling at ridiculous speeds, dancing around the clouds waiting to land once the weather clears. Fuck that! It's choreography that boggles my mind. Honestly, there's really never a good time to land in JFK. The weather above New York City will make the most seasoned traveler weak in their bowels. I haven't even taken into account that there are three major airports within 25 miles catering to the friendly and loving citizens of New York City. That's a lot of mayhem flying above your head during a thunderstorm.

It didn't take long for the turbulence to wake Reeta and my Prince Charming from their naps. She became unhinged and spilled her hysteria all over our row, "We are gonna crash. I knew we shoulda like drove back from Orlando. Why do I fuckin' listen to you?" She snapped her head from looking out the window back to Bobby, "You are so fuckin stoopid," She tugged desperately on his arm while he stared blankly at the television screen.

At that moment, and I am not exaggerating—at that EXACT moment, the airplane hit a pocket of air and we plummeted hundreds of feet. It caught me off guard to the point of clutching my pearls and gasping like I was watching an episode of *How to Get Away with Murder*. And I work on the airplane.

Before I go any further, let me break down turbulence in my own words. This will be a quick explanation so pay close attention. Ready? When it comes to air travel there are three levels of turbulence: light, moderate, and severe.

Or as I like to call them: damn, oh shit, and FUUUUUCK! You may be lucky and go your entire life without experiencing turbulence. Every one of your flights reminds you of peacefully floating in a canoe on a lake during summer visits to Vermont. If that's you, I don't want to hear about it. My flights are prone to experience some level of turbulence. In my history, I have had hundreds of damns, a few serious oh shits, and two uncomfortable FUUUUUK!s.

My first FUUUUUCK! was on a flight from JFK to Jacksonville. Surprisingly, it came out of nowhere and was over quicker than I had expected, just like the fuck that took my virginity. We were flying at 38,000 feet, somewhere over North Carolina, when out of nowhere we flew straight into a pocket of air that sent the airplane rolling to the right. Let me say that this was no slight roll. This roll was dramatic enough to win an Oscar. For a brief second we were flying sideways. Nobody on the airplane was prepared, pilots included. When we flew through the turbulent air, I had been standing in front of my jump seat chitchatting with a coworker from our human resources department who I had known from my time on the Standards Advisory Team. She leaned against the back galley counter looking down the aisle towards the front of the airplane while I stood slightly to her left and another flight attendant was flanked to her right next to the coffee maker. All three lavatories were full with passengers and a few were lined up waiting their turn. The flight was uneventful from our departure out of JFK. This was our canoe and the smooth air was our Lake Champlain. Then the wave came and it was pandemonium. The human resource employee and the other flight attendant dropped to the floor. I say dropped because that's exactly what it was—one minute they were standing and the next they were sitting with their legs crossed. I grabbed the oh shit bar on the galley counter—in this case the FUUUUCK! bar—and immediately sat down in my jump seat and secured my harness. The passengers in the lavatories were tossed around like dice during a game of Trouble. Screams and howls came from every seat on the airplane. After we leveled off one lady refused to come out of the lavatory and sat in there squealing like a stuck pig. Like I said, Oscar worthy drama. After all was said and done nobody moved from their seats for the rest of the flight. I loved that part.

Back to row 22. The turbulence I had just shared with Princess Fiona was of the FUUUUK! caliber. This was my second FUUUUCK! and honestly, after that last one, I'm all FUUUUCK!-ed out.

Reeta started crying and buried her face deep into Bobby's arm. I was scared too but was I thrusting myself into his sweaty greasemonkey pits? No. Did I want to? Yes! Sure, I would have walked off the airplane with his fist imprinted on the side of my skull, but that's not the point. The point was he was gorgeous and probably worked on cars somewhere in Brooklyn.

The working on cars is a total fabrication on my part. It was obvious Bobby was on welfare.

It was time to take control of row 22. I pulled out my airline ID from inside the seatback pocket and tapped Reeta on the arm, they both looked up at me—he was so fucking sexy. "Hi, I'm Joe. I'm a flight attendant at this airline. This is just from all the bad weather. Everything will be ok."

She looked at me and for a moment I felt bad for her. She gave me a half smile, "Thank you. I'm like so fuckin' scared. These pilots better know what they are doin. I have babies at home."

I reassured her, "The pilots are trained for this type of weather. We'll be fine." Then I added that she would soon be safely on the ground and home with her babies. I wondered what her babies might look like and it gave me a sharp chill. All I will say is I hope their daddies genes were stronger than their mothers. I imagined them to be little hairy Neanderthals running around their backyard half-naked, eating out of the trash can, and yowling, "Where foooooooood?" Reeta was that unattractive. She wiped her mascara-stained cheeks with the back of her hand and shoved her head back into his arm like an ostrich. He shrugged his shoulders, smiled, and winked at me.

That wink sent my balls into overdrive. My swimmers paddled around thinking it was the Summer Olympics as they prepared to shoot out of my canon at top speed. I was three strokes away from winning the gold. Even though he went back to watching the television I stared at the side of his face and thought, "Can I hold your hand please? I'm just as frightened as her." I actually heard the words aloud in my delusional mind. He never turned to look at me so I am pretty sure my inner monologue didn't fail me. Maybe it did. Maybe he actually did hear me but decided to simply ignore the crazy gay guy seated next to them. I will never know.

That was the melodrama happening inside the airplane. Outside, the scene was just as grim. The white and gray fluffy clouds surrounding the airplane obscured any view of land or sea below and the vibrating airplane became unsettling, even for me. The turbulence level switched from oh shit to FUUUUCK! and then back to oh shit all within 60 seconds. And then repeated the same pattern numerous times reminding me of a bipolar patient off their medication. Although I have persevered through my fear of flying, there are still rare occasions when I get nervous barreling through the sky in a tube; this was definitely one of those times.

I turned the television channel to the live map to monitor our progress. I expected the airplane to break through the clouds soon to attempt a landing. The cloud coverage did nothing to ease my anxiety and I was not the only passenger who felt that way. The murmurs increased over the safety of the flight. The extreme tension outside the airplane had found its way inside the fuselage and whispered into our ears, "Something is wrong. Prepare for it."

Every few seconds I turned from the map channel to the window and then back to the map channel for perspective on our location but my attempts were unsuccessful. The cloud coverage was too blinding. The map clearly showed us at an elevation of 2,000 ft and heading towards northern New Jersey. Were we going to attempt a landing in Newark? I never got an answer.

A few moments later the airplane burst through the clouds giving me a crystal clear view of the Statue of Liberty. There she was, waving her green torch like she was trying to grab my attention. She didn't need to wave too hard, I was quite aware she was right outside my window. I had never seen her from an airplane window. On second thought, I had no idea airplanes were even allowed to fly this close to her. I internally freaked out when I realized we were flying towards downtown Manhattan at a very low altitude.

We reached 1,800 ft and turned right allowing lower Manhattan to come into view. I couldn't believe how low and close we were to Manhattan. The airplane kept descending and it seemed to me that we were too far from JFK to attempt a landing. I am no pilot but when it seems like you can step out onto the wing and do a somersault into the water, you are flying too low.

Then it hit me upside the head like a bag of minis: we were ditching in the Hudson River.

The word ditching hurts my ears. It really does. When I hear it the hairs on the back of my neck stand up. When I say it, those same hairs whisper into my ear to shut the fuck up. Ditching is just a nicer way to say death. It's that simple. There's nothing cute about it. Most likely, the National Transportation Safety Board (NTSB) came up with this term because, let's face it, to the normal ear it does sound less painful than the word crashing. But it's the same fucking thing. Actually, it's much worse than crashing. Have you ever dove off a diving board into a pool and accidently experienced a belly-flop? Screams of pain and torture flood my brain remembering my horrific belly-flops as a child. It's excruciating. Now take one of those experiences, but this time add about 500 miles per hour to it. That's ditching. They should really change the name from ditching to crashing violently into a body of water and dying. *That* seems more on point. When I was in flight attendant training one of my instructors stood up and said, "Well, if you ditch you probably won't make it anyway." She's no longer an instructor and for good reason. It took all our energy to stay seated and not run for our lives.

Crazy thoughts scrambled around inside my head as we continued to descend, "They won't make it to the airport. The winds are too strong. I am going to miss Matt and the cats. We are in trouble."

Our pilots hadn't given us a report in approximately 20 minutes and I figured they were in the flight deck trying to save the airplane and all 155 people on board. As scared as all this was, I knew I had to stay calm because I had the Mad Hatter sitting next to me and if I showed any signs of fear or uncertainty, she might freak out.

I imagined her yelling, "You told me everything was going to be ok!" as she shook me and splattered mascara all over my face.

My focus was on surviving and getting out of that airplane. Nothing else mattered. I quietly planned what to do once we splashed down into the water, if we weren't in a few dozen pieces. Flight attendants are trained for this type of emergency, but not from seat 22A. My quick actions meant everything. I figured the tail of the airplane, and the two back doors, would be submerged under water so going out the back was not an option. The only way to save my own ass was to climb over twelve rows of seats to get to the overwing exit windows. I made the decision to climb over children, women, and men to get to the exit. I'd use Reeta's body as a weapon if I had to.

I was not going to die.

All my focus was on my escape plan. And it was a good one. If executed quickly and correctly, I'd be out of the airplane, on the wing, and assisting other passengers to safety. With my legs I pushed my tote bag as far under the seat in front of me and tightened my seat belt just short of cutting off circulation. I slid my cell phone deep inside my front pocket figuring that it might come in handy if I didn't get wet. I knew that was a long shot; I would be in the freezing Hudson River in only a few moments just like the passengers and crew on US Airways Flight #1549.

Do I need to explain what happened to Flight #1549? If you haven't been living under a rock, and watch the news, you are well aware of this heroic flight. But for the minuscule few who have no idea what I am talking about, here's a brief explanation: In 2009, Flight #1549 departed LaGuardia Airport for a nonstop flight to Charlotte Douglas International Airport. After being airborne for only three minutes the airplane struck a gaggle of geese which ultimately took out both engines. Captain Sullenberger and First Officer Skiles, realizing they wouldn't make it to the closest airport, ditched the airplane in the Hudson River. There were no casualties. It was so fucking impressive that Kitty Higgins from the NTSB stated it was, "the most successful ditching in aviation history."

I know what you are thinking and I am right there with you, the amount of pussy thrown at these two pilots after this successful ditching must have been staggering. Just imagine all the mothers, daughters, grandmothers—that transgender aunt you only talk to on Facebook—being so enamored with these two that they just laid out their pussies like an endless shrimp buffet at Red Lobster. Trust me, that's a lot of pussy, even for two pilots.

I looked out the window at the water below and thought to myself, "I am not going to die. I am not going to die. I AM NOT GOING TO DIE!" as we continued to descend with JFK nowhere in sight.

Matt crossed my mind while my head swept from the television, to the window and ahead to see how tall the people were in front of me. Making my way up to the over wing exit looked remarkably challenging but none of that mattered if the airplane broke apart once we hit the water. The rain was coming down violently, something that was not a factor when Flight #1549 ditched safely in the Hudson River, and the wind was howling mad all around us.

The Captain came back over the PA, "Ladies and gentlemen we will be landing in JFK shortly, flight attendants please be seated for landing."

My head swung back to peer out the window, we were somewhere over Brooklyn. Land. That was reassuring, I guess. Were our chances better ditching in the water or crashing into row houses somewhere in Queens? I had no idea. The negativity and ideas of certain death were warping my reality. Why do I let these dubious assumptions take control of me? The captain had specifically stated that we were landing at JFK so why did I still have doubt? I shook my head hoping those negative thoughts escaped my mind as quickly as they appeared. I forced myself to think about being safely on the ground, at the gate, and on my way to my fabulous hotel in Manhattan. It worked for a moment.

The landing gear came down and the rotating sound of the wheels hitting the air was soothing as we continued our descent towards the airport. I stayed quiet while my insides screamed, "land this fucking airplane." I leaned my head back against the seat and took deep breaths counting the minutes until we touched down at JFK.

Without warning, the engines roared loudly and everyone looked up from their televisions as the airplane started ascending back into the sky. I heard the wheels retracting back inside the belly of the airplane. I looked out the window to see the ground quickly disappear again due to the white clouds. 2,000ft. 3,000ft. 4,000ft. 8,000ft, 10,000ft—What the hell was going on? On the live map, it seemed we were heading northwest. The airplane breached the 10,000ft mark as we made our way out of New York City and towards New Jersey. Still with no word from our pilots, three things quickly became clear: we were not landing at JFK, we were diverting, and we were running out of fuel.

Where were we going? Newark was south of us, but we continued on a northwestern route. It was clear that Newark was not our destination. Pittsburgh? That made sense. It was the next city we flew to in our flight path but Pittsburgh was approximately 400 miles away. Did we have enough fuel for that distance? So many questions and no fucking answers. I understood the pilots were busy but a little message would have put everyone at ease. My mind raced right back to the fuel. We had been circling in a holding pattern for over an hour and our fuel reserves were most likely depleted. I honestly didn't know if that was true or not but at some point the airplane runs out of fuel. We hadn't boarded an electric-powered airplane.

To be honest, I am ignorant to the ins and outs of fuel on the airplane. I am serious. There are two things I know for sure: fuel is stored in the wings and that it's crucial so the airplane doesn't fall out of the sky. After that I hit my fuel wall. I suppose that's really all the flight attendant needs to know, right? Who has time to worry about airplane fuel while dealing with real issues on the airplane, like managing passengers' emotions after running out of Dr Pepper on a flight to Texas. If you want to enrage a Texan, tell them you are all out of Dr. Pepper. And that there's a black president. And that same-sex marriage is legal throughout the United States. And that an abortion should be the decision of the woman involved and not the government. You get my point, it's not pretty.

When I sat down to write this chapter I contacted my pilot friend, Trick Daddy, asking for a quick tutorial on airplane fuel. How much fuel does each flight need? Who is tasked with this important responsibility? Is there a mathematical equation deciding how much goes onto the airplane or do they just pull up to the gate, open the flight deck window, and yell out, "Fill 'er up," like at a gas station in New Jersey? It was imperative that I find out these specifics. We spent over an hour talking about airplane fuel. While he lectured on, I feverishly filled my steno pad with important notes. Trick Daddy was so on point with his feedback I should have been able to hang up and immediately go to work for an airline as a fueler. But that wasn't the case. When we finally hung up the phone, I sat blankly staring at a bunch of words that still made no sense to me. I am a terrible note taker. A few weeks later I called him back and asked for an even shorter explanation. He was up for it and just as enthusiastic as the first time. His reaction was not a surprise, pilots love to explain their jobs to any layperson who will listen. They also love to lay any person who will let them—but that's a conversation for later.

After his second attempt at drilling the information into my head, I came out with a little more understanding than the first time. It's actually quite simple. For each flight, dispatch works with the pilots and fuelers to guarantee there's more than enough fuel on the airplane at any given time. This includes: taxiing fuel, fuel for the scheduled destination, extra holding fuel for bad weather, alternate airport fuel in case of a diversion, and finally an additional 45 minutes of fuel required by law. That additional 45 minutes of fuel should never be used except in a dire emergency. The airplane should take off and land with that 45 minutes of fuel. That last sentence must be a crucial point because it was written down in my notes three times and underlined with a black sharpie.

As we flew to our unknown destination I'd bet all Reeta's tears that we were in a dire emergency and had already burned through 35 minutes of our 45 minute reserve. The reserve that you are never supposed to tap into. I wondered who else had fuel on the brain but there was no further chatting or murmuring going on around me. Everyone was silent and waiting for whatever was going to happen to happen. Survivors of airplane disasters have gone on record stating that before the airplane crashes everyone onboard becomes eerily quiet and preparing for the worst. I just wanted to scream.

"Ladies and gentlemen," our captain announced, "seems like mother nature is giving us a difficult time today. We had a short window of opportunity to land at JFK and due to the winds we missed it. We are running low on fuel and will be diverting to Harrisburg to refuel and wait for a new window to take off and land safely in JFK. Just so you know, our airline doesn't typically fly into Harrisburg so there are no airport employees here to let passengers off the airplane."

You could almost feel the passenger's level of anxiety lower inside the airplane. My first thought was, "no shit we are running low on fuel," but I smiled knowing that my panic was warranted. Once the other passengers realized we weren't going to die-even though diverting to Harrisburg is almost equal to death-the chatter began and most passengers understood that safety was the most important thing. Diverting is much better than landing in bad weather and have my body ripped to shreds while the airplane cartwheels down the runway in a ball of fire and debris.

Of course, to no surprise, Reeta did not feel the same way.

When the airplane finally landed safely at Harrisburg International Airport and rolled to a stop away from the runway, Reeta became a different person. That's not a good thing. She wiped away her alligator tears smearing her mascara and immediately began bitching about what had happened. "We just almost fuckin' died. This airline is ridiculous." She looked over towards me but I continued looking out the window. I knew she was gawking at me because I could feel the heat from her breath on the side of my neck. Definitely a reason to pull out the air sickness bag and fill it up. My empathy for her vanished; I wanted to punch her in the face. That was a sure way to keep her husband from becoming my Facebook friend so instead I turned on my cell phone to send off some text messages. A few coworkers were waiting for me at JFK so we could all commute into Manhattan together on the train. My entire day was being swallowed up by this diversion.

When Reeta got zero response from me she went back to Bobby, "This is fucking bullshit. Right? I'm not flyin' to New York babe. Rent a car. I want off this fuckin plane."

He ignored her.

"I thought we was, like, gonna die. Babe? Babe, listen to me." She snarled when he started punching numbers into his cell phone, "Who you callin?" Bobby continued on his cell phone like she wasn't there. I wondered if he secretly wished we ditched in the river so he could have sat on her head until the bubbles stopped.

Most of the passengers remained calm and kept their spirits up. Our captain updated us with good news and bad news. The good news was refueling was completed and we'd take off for JFK as soon as ATC allowed us. The bad news was that it could take up to four hours before we were granted permission to leave. It was a grim thought being stuck on board the airplane next to Reeta for an additional four hours.

"I'm hungry. I haven't eaten all day," she howled at Bobby. She reminded me of a pull string doll that said everything you didn't want to hear. I was irritated with her bitching about food because I was the one who hadn't eaten all day. It took all my strength not to remind her of the Egg McMuffin she abused only three hours prior.

"Bobby. Bobby?" She shook his arm, "Get me a snack. Fuck, you'd think they'd bring some water or something." She ranted with no response from Bobby while he continued whispering into his cell phone.

She continued pulling her own string and verbalizing every passing thought, "I want off this fuckin' plane. We can drive. They can't hold us hostage."

He finished his phone conversation and finally responded, "We aren't driving. I told you to chill out." Then as if he was sharing the weather he said, "The girls stayed home from school today. They are sick."

Reeta's response led you to believe the airplane landed on their house.

She screamed, "What? What's wron with my babies. I don't like this, Bobby. We have to get out of here. I want to drive back to New Yawk."

"Everything is aight. My motha said they were runnin' fevers dis mornin' but they are fine now." He tried to reassure her, "and we are not rentin' a car and driving to New Yawk."

After watching the rain come down for an hour my ears were bleeding from Reeta's venting. They weren't really bleeding but they should have been. She wouldn't shut up. Did she talk this much when a dick was in her mouth? I was jealous just thinking about Bobby's dick in her mouth. I thought about how much I truly hated the dentist but drilling, pulling teeth, and enduring a root canal was less painful than being stuck on a runway, in the middle of Pennsylvania, sitting next to Teresa from *The Real Housewives of New Jersey.*

Many passengers were standing in the aisle waiting for the lavatories and at this point in the game I was hungrier than a Guantanamo Bay hostage. My hunger took a turn for the worse when I realized I was secretly searching the carpet for crumbs from Reeta's Egg McMuffin. I was so desperate I fantasized about snacking on anything, especially the deliciousness of an English muffin's nooks and crannies. It was for the best she destroyed every morsel of that sandwich. Explaining my actions while she looked down at me rummaging through her McDonald's bag might have been tricky.

My left knee became stiff so I decided that it was a good time to get up, stretch, use the lavatory, and purchase an airline meal. I smiled and looked over at Reeta, "Excuse me," I unfastened my seatbelt, "I have to use the bathroom."

"Babe, he's gotta get up," she pushed at his arm, "Get up. Move!"

I wanted to stuff my sock in Reeta's mouth to shut her up. My only reward for enduring this entire day was the chance to glide across Bobby's lap while getting out of the row and she managed to fuck that up.

Inside the lavatory I was reminded of how human beings react in a crisis. It was appalling. Practically nothing was left. A few more diversions like this and the airline might go bankrupt. These passengers had resorted to looting the airplane lavatory during one diverted flight. I was surprised the lavatory mirror had not been dismantled and carried off to the overhead bins. They confiscated the toilet paper rolls, the paper napkins, and tissues; anything that could be used to wipe someone's ass. They even took the tampons. Gone. I could understand the need to hoard tissue and napkins, but tampons? Were all the female passengers on the same cycle? I hoped not. People are capable of the most random crazy behavior when faced with disaster, albeit this was far from a disaster. But what do I know, I've never had to worry about Aunt Flo and Cousin Red knocking at my back door during an unscheduled diversion. What I did know was that the Grinch was on board the airplane and decided to give up on trying to ruin the Whos' Christmas and instead just piss off any Who on their period.

I washed my hands, dried them on the front of my pants, and abandoned the lavatory to spend a few minutes in the back galley with the flight attendants. These flight attendants had been through the mill. A short day trip to JFK and back turned into a long day nightmare. One of the flight attendants working in the back had tears in her eyes. "What's wrong?" I asked making eye contact with her and moving out of the next lavatory occupant's way.

She didn't say a word. She flashed a crooked smile and pointed to the floor beneath her and I saw the mess. She was standing on an airline blanket that was draped over what looked like a pool of vomit, make that a lake. I understood why she was at the brink of tears.

"That's disgusting. What happened?" I questioned leaning against the jumpseat and staying out of the way.

She recited the tale in a deadpan tone, "A passenger pushed his way through the aisle and instead of making it to the lavatory he projectile vomited all over the galley, carts, and floor. And me." She pointed to her shoes. It looked like a crime scene but I kept that to myself. Whoever made this mess decided to give back all the red wine they ingested during the flight. Another flight attendant was passing his cell phone from passenger to passenger so they could make phone calls to their family.

Witnessing all the chaos inside the airplane from the terminal might have led people to believe the airplane actually crashed. I was in the middle of a war zone in Harrisburg, Pennsylvania and all I wanted to do was get to Manhattan so I could go get dinner in Chelsea like every other gay guy in New York City. Was that so fucking hard? After a few minutes the flight attendants ushered me back to my seat for some extra elbow room. There wasn't enough room for me, them, the never ending line of needy passengers, and puke soaked blankets in the back galley. I understood but I hated leaving, standing in the middle of Lake Vomit was better than sitting next to Reeta.

After climbing over Bobby's thick muscular hairless legs—he didn't get up this time—I leaped over Reeta—she had fallen asleep again—and I plopped back into my seat. I fastened my seatbelt and then realized I forgot to purchase an airline meal while I was in the back galley. It was probably for the best because after witnessing the galley disaster my hunger subsided. I tried focusing on anything other than my situation and the fun night in Manhattan stolen from me. My attention drifted to the little frail black lady seated directly behind me making phone calls. She was calling friends to update them on our current situation. At first, I thought she was calling the person picking her up at JFK, but I was wrong.

"Mildred? Yes, it's me honey. We landed somewhere in Pennsylvania. What? Girl, I don't know. Yes. Something about weather. How's the weather in Oakland? It's raining like cats and dogs here. I know. Can you imagine? Ok I gotta run. I will talk to you later."

There was a brief moment of silence before the next caller picked up, " Hi Marisa? Can you hear me? I'm in Pennsylvania. Did I say New York? No. I said Pennsylvania. Turn up that hearing aid, you know you can't hear nothing when you don't turn that thing up," she coughed into the phone, "Yes. PENNSYLVANIA. Well I know safety's important but I think my blood sugar is getting low. What was that? I know you're right, I wish I had my Bible too."

It didn't end there. She continued hitting buttons and speaking to whoever answered. By the fifth call I questioned why anyone in Tulsa cared about our diversion. I was traveling with the residents from the island of misfit toys. How did they escape and end up on my flight?

After spending only an hour on the runway in Harrisburg—it felt more like a week—the captain came over the PA and updated us on our new take off time. He added that everyone needed to be in their seats within five minutes—with their seat belts fastened—and that if the airplane had not departed by that time, our next opportunity to leave would be in three hours. I've never seen adults move so fast in my life.

The airplane shot into the sky like the space shuttle. As our airplane lifted off from the tarmac we got a clear view of three other airplanes from my airline that had diverted to Harrisburg. When Reeta saw the matching tail fins outside my window she started screaming,"They're lyin' to us. There are otha planes here just like this one. We could have gotten off the plane."

My patience had worn thin with this women. I turned to her, "They diverted like we did. That is why they are here. They couldn't land safely either."

She stayed quiet for the short flight back to New York City. As we made a turbulent, but safe, landing at JFK she cried the entire time threatening to never fly again.

That was a threat that I hope turned into a promise.

WHEN FLIGHT ATTENDANTS ATTACK!

"Ladies and Gentlemen, welcome on board flight 666 with service to LaGuardia. My name is Joe and it's my displeasure to be working with Carol. She's the nasty looking she-devil standing in the middle of the cabin. She's also a total bitch so feel free to throw your empty cups of ice, dirty diapers, and any other trash at her whenever she walks up and down the aisle. In addition, there's a free drink in it for you if she cries. Thank you. Please sit back, relax, and enjoy your flight."

That was the safety demonstration running through my head while standing at the front of the airplane preparing to work a flight from Tampa to LaGuardia. Working a flight to LaGuardia is difficult enough, just ask any flight attendant, but adding Carol to the mix made it unbearable. Flights to LaGuardia-or LaGarbage (which is how I will refer to it from now on)—are not my favorite. Every flight I've ever worked in and out of LaGarbage the passengers were demanding, rude, and took enough beverages off the airplane to last them through another Hurricane Sandy. What made the entire flight worse, if that was possible, was knowing I'd be stuck in a metal tube with the evil Carol. Carol can only be described as vile, disgusting, and so unfriendly I can't fathom how she's continued her employment as a flight attendant.

I don't know many of the people based in Cleveland and I am perfectly okay with that. Some of my coworkers treat this job as a high school repeat. Fuck that! I struggled enough as an outcast throughout my four years in high school, who the hell wants to relive that nightmare? The popular flight attendants make it a point to know every pilot and every flight attendant in the base. They've worked with most of them, slept with a few of them, know all their personal business, and share it on the airplane as galley gossip. It's like third period study hall but with a lot less pounding of erasers and a lot more pounding of sphincters.

Now that I think about it, there could be some benefit to knowing more people at work. If I knew I didn't like someone, it would help me decide whether I wanted to work the assigned trip or trade it for another one. At my airline, flight attendants and pilots receive their monthly schedule weeks before the new month starts. Even though I have the names of all the flight attendants assigned to my trips, I usually have no clue who they are.

I often find myself sitting on Evan's sofa calling out names like a game show announcer, "Who's Beau Dawkins? How's he to work with?"

He'll look up from his laptop with a chuckle, "Ewww. Beau Dawkins? You won't like him."

He's always right.

Airline crew lounges have a multitude of flight attendants and pilots filing in and out at all hours of the day. With crew briefings being conducted, lunches being devoured, and gossip broadcasted from one ear to the next, it's a challenge tracking down the people you are working with. It's not until I've printed out the flight details, stood in the middle of the crew lounge, and yelled out to anyone who happens to be listening do I finally meet the flight attendants I'll be spending countless of hours with for the duration of the trip.

That was how it happened a few years ago when I was assigned a three day trip with layovers in Tampa and LaGarbage. Two cities that I don't like flying into, but I'm not senior enough to put on my avoid list.

Standing in the Cleveland crew lounge I yelled, "Who's going to Tampa?" awaiting a response from the dozen or so people fluttering around the expansive room. I quickly saw two hands raise at the back of the room. With my big smile, I collected my required items from the table and walked over to the computer station where these two ladies were seated. Our required items must be with us at all times during each flight. These include such things as: our flight attendant manual, a flashlight, a working watch with a second hand, and our employee ID. To name a few. There are also a few off-the-record required items you should bring with you as a flight attendant, and those are: a friendly smile, patience, a can of mace, dollars to tip the van driver, and a desire to drink. The mace is for walking to your car late at night in the employee parking lot or to blind horny pilots who get too touchy in the hotel elevator. When our trip starts, we must prove to each other that we've brought our items before we step onto the airplane. It's adults babysitting adults. Imagine working in an office building and stopping each person that enters your cubicle area checking to be sure they brought their laptop, stapler, and that they are dressed appropriately and not like homeless gutter trash. It's annoying. It's childish. It makes me feel like the hall monitor ready to report anyone who steps out of line. Sure, some flight attendants need supervision (okay most flight attendants) but my stance is this, if the FAA walks onto the airplane demanding to see a flight attendant's manual and they don't have it, then they should be held accountable. Agree?

But let's get back to the story. I made my way across the room and walked up to the two flight attendants, "Hi. I'm Joe. How you guys doing tonight?" There were three desktop computers sitting on top of a chipped gray formica counter that was attached to the wall. I placing my oversized flight attendant manual on the counter next to a computer that nobody was using.

"Doing great, Joe." One of them answered. She had a beautiful smile and warm greeting. "I'm Amber. Are you new to the base?" I liked her right away.

"No. I've been here awhile. I guess we just haven't worked together."

That was as far as I'd get to liking anyone on this trip. Sitting to Amber's right was a frizzy blond-haired flight attendant who had yet to look up from the computer screen. She pounded furiously at the keyboard and I wondered what the keyboard had done to put her in such a grumpy mood. It wouldn't take me long to learn that the keyboard was just an innocent bystander like the rest of us. Plain and simple, Carol was a vicious cunt.

She still refused to introduce herself. After a second or two of silence I continued the conversation, "Are you guys ready to brief?" I lifted my manual off the counter, "Do you have your manuals?" I asked ignoring the steamy attitude protruding from Carol.

She came to life, "Really? You wanna see my manual?" Her sarcasm leaped out and scratched the surface of my skin without us touching. Amber simply reached into her bag and removed her manual.

I told you I liked Amber.

"Yes," the aggravation in my tone harder to hide, "I would love to see your manual."

Carol rolled her eyes as if I was her father telling her she had to finish her homework, clean her room, and pray to Jesus for a better attitude before she would be allowed to go out on her date. Sadly, not even the little baby Jesus could help this girl out.

She was pissed, and I will be honest, I loved every fucking minute of it. Without her speaking one syllable she pulled out her flight attendant manual and the three of us completed our crew briefing. The instant we finished she began banging at the computer keyboard and added, "I still have work to do on the computer, Amber. I'll meet you at the gate."

I smiled while packing my manual into my tote bag. Did this little kinky haired bitch think she was upsetting me? She had better think again. Her disdain gave me the power and ammunition I needed to verbally attack her later on the flight. I grabbed my bags and started walking away, "I'll meet you guys at the gate. It's B9."

Amber stood up, grabbing her bag, "I'm coming with you. I need to get some coffee."

We were scheduled to fly from Cleveland to Tampa and then up to LaGarbage for the night. Sadly, I was ready for the trip to be over before it even started. Carol arrived to the gate at the last possible moment (not a surprise) and the three of us boarded the airplane and conducted our security checks. As I was placing my cell phone in my tote bag I remember that I had forgotten to brief them on electronic devices. Each airline has specific rules regarding flight attendants and pilots using electronic devices while they are working on the airplane with passengers. The rules are simple—we are not allowed. Electronic devices included are: laptops, iPhones, iPads, cell phones of any type, tablets, e-readers, and anything else with an on and off switch. Surprisingly, not vibrators. That's important to know when working a red-eye flight. Cell phone—NO! Vibrator—YES! Some airlines are more lenient than others, but the airline I work for forbids it. There are no chances. If you make a mistake and get reported by a passenger, caught by management, or tattled on by a ruthless flight attendant for having any electronic device on while passengers are present then it's *adios amigo*. I have known a few amazing and talented flight attendants fired for simply forgetting to turn their cell phone off and putting it away in their tote bag. The repercussions for using electronics during the flight are equivalent to a positive drug test, which is something I have questioned since my first day on the job. In my opinion, an electronic device in the on position during a flight can't compare to a flight attendant doing a line of cocaine off a Cuban dancer's ass on a nine hour Miami layover. But what do I know?

Carol and Amber were standing in the back of the airplane by the last row as I sauntered down the aisle to remind them about the electronic device policy. Whatever conversation they were having came to a quick halt the moment I passed row 22. This happened for the remainder of the trip every time I stepped within earshot of their conversation.

"Hey guys, I just wanna remind you to be careful with your electronic devices during the flight. Be smart if you take them out. I don't want anyone to get in trouble."

Amber nodded in agreement. Carol's head spun around like it wasn't attached to her spine, "I've signed a union card so don't worry about me!" She turned and walked to the back galley.

What was up with this asshole? Why was she so hostile towards me? Did I remind her of an ex-boyfriend who broke her heart by fucking her high school best friend? A pregnancy test that came back positive? An abortion that didn't keep? Maybe she had a bald uncle who slipped into her childhood bedroom one night and tried playing hide Uncle Bob's salami. I had no clue but I was starting to question if I actually did work with Carol at one point and that we left the airplane as mortal enemies instead of best friends. I racked my brain for a split second. Nope, I did not know this fucker. One doesn't forget meeting Satan's illegitimate offspring. And I say illegitimate because even Satan wouldn't claim Carol as his own. I forcefully gripped the top of an airplane seat and blasted out, "I didn't mention anything about the union but you go ahead and do whatever you want."

I released the seat cushion, leaving an indentation, and stormed up the aisle like someone just asked for a cup of coffee on a 30 minute flight. All I wanted to do was tear that untamed fucking mop out of her head one strand at a time. I'd even take a delay to make sure I got every last lock.

A union card? Who even brought up anything about the union? If throwing that up in my face was her war tactic, this would be a slam dunk battle.

My airline is one of the last few airlines that do not have union representation for flight attendants. Some days I like this; some days I don't. But officially, I am not on board with welcoming a third party union into my workplace. That's my own belief. I refuse to push my anti-union beliefs on my fellow flight attendants and I appreciate it when they do the same by not shoving their union beliefs down my throat like an unwanted dick. What am I saying? Have I lost my mind? Is there really such a thing as an unwanted dick?

The answer is no. There is no such thing as an un-wanted dick. Just in case you were wondering.

Union talk is very dangerous territory at my airline. There are union pins, union bag tags, and a union website for union representation that doesn't even exist at the airline. Conversations regarding unions should be left on the jet bridge along with other topics like: religion, politics, and if you blew the first officer on a layover in Salt Lake City.

When I approached the front of the airplane I fought the urge to smack my head against the overhead bin for not delivering a juicier quick-witted response. Anyway, I had no time to dwell. Within seconds passengers started filing in one right after another. As I smiled and welcomed them onto the airplane I couldn't help but see the words flash across my brain like a billboard, "You dirty whore, nobody cares if you signed a union card. You should be signing a letter of resignation."

By the time the last passenger stepped onto the airplane I was beside myself. Carol's voice over the PA was like fingernails across a blackboard. How was I going to manage through a three day trip with this monster? I ignored the urge to hammer a stake through her heart. Although nothing would have made me happier than to impale her with a blunt instrument, I decided against it. The last thing I needed was to go back on disciplinary action. The best way to forge ahead was to stay in the front of the airplane for the entire trip. I'd refrain from passing row 12 unless someone was dying. And hopefully that someone was named Carol.

My plan didn't last long and I quickly found myself in the back galley talking with Amber whenever I passed through the cabin doing a security check. At least Amber treated me like a human being and not part of the fuselage. When I stepped into the back galley, Amber attempted to strike up conversation with me. Carol, on the other hand, had her nose so deep into the crevice of her book I wanted to ask her about the fragrance of the pages. Once we landed in Tampa, reboarded, and started preparing to take off for LaGarbage, I had had enough.

After my front airplane door was closed and all the evacuation slides were armed, Amber and I began conducting our cross check. During this brief moment,

Carol attempted to call me on the interphone. Her calling to the front of the airplane was not an uncommon practice, that's how we are trained to do a verbal compliance check. I never hesitate picking up the interphone when the signal dings but I was actively speaking to Amber and it took me approximately three rings before I picked up.

She didn't allow me to speak. "I'm armed and cross-checked. Does it always take you that long to answer the phone?" she questioned acerbically.

Without skipping a beat I responded, "I will pick up the phone when I'm ready. Armed and cross-checked." I hung up. *Click!* Actually, it was more like a SLAM!

My blood pressure was palpable. It became clear that a Carol vs. Joe confrontation was inevitable. My neck was red, my ears were burning, and if I didn't stand my ground and put this bitch in her place I'd wind up killing her and that's really no way to end your career as a flight attendant. I held my tongue until service was completed. Before I made my move I called the flight deck to ask the pilots if they needed a lavatory break. They declined. I swiftly cleaned up the galley, did one quick trash pick up in my section, and headed to the back galley to talk to Carol. I rehearsed exactly what I would say once we were face to face. I wouldn't let her get away with disrespecting me. No fucking way. After Amber finished helping a female passenger in the aisle, and she was positioned in the back galley on her jumpseat, I headed down the aisle towards them. Confronting Carol without a witness would be a foolish action. And I'm no fool.

Flight attendants and pilots are encouraged to confront each other when it comes to work related conflicts.

Do they actually use the term *confront*? I don't recall. Probably not. Most likely they use a fluffier more politically correct term. Words like: approach, discuss, and hug it out, come to mind. Unfortunately, that shit was not going to work on our way to LaGarbage. I needed a knock-down, drag-out confrontation with Carol and I was ready to deliver the first punch.

When I stepped into the back galley she was in her jumpseat, feet up on the trash bins, and reading her book. Her worn down black flats were falling apart like she either ran the Cleveland Marathon or picked them up at Goodwill. Amber sat in her jumpseat fishing through her lunch bag, preparing something to eat. I stopped once I reached the galley counter and stood between the two of them. I folded my arms as gay as possible, spun around to face the aisle, and just let it out, "Do you have a problem with me?"

Amber instantly looked up; Carol refused to peel her eyes away from the paperback book she held in both hands. I glanced over at Amber, made eye contact with her, and then shifted my gaze back to the top of Carol's dirty blond thinning hair. Did she realize her hair was thinning? If not she was in for a rude awakening. From this angle she reminded me of Larry David. The idea of her turning into a female version of Larry David made me smile. Her sadistic voice snapped me out of it, "Are you talking to me?" she asked closing her book and placing her feet firmly on the uneven plastic floor covering. She also turned her book over so the cover was hidden. My guess she was reading *The Satanic Verses* by Salman Rushdie. Anything to try and get on her biological father's good side.

"Yes I am," I answered leaning against the back counter, "Listen, I don't know you. I've never even met you before. This might be the way you act with everyone you work with but it's like you've got a problem with me." She peered at me without fluttering her eyes. I continued without relaxing my stance, "From the moment we've met you've been very nasty. Do we have a problem?"

Staring me down like a cat she answered, "Nope. I don't have a problem with you."

She threw me off guard. What the fuck? Was that it? How disappointing. Here I was preparing for World War III3 and she barely shot a bullet at me. I wanted her to argue or at least confirm her feelings towards me. But I got nothing. We glared at each other for a few more seconds and all I was able to muster up was a weak, "Good."

Without saying another word she opened her book and went back to reading. My first instinct was to stab her in the eye with my pen but I took the high road and simply walked away. As much as I wanted to shake her like a baby who refused to stop crying, I had to control my temper. She was a challenge that I had to overcome and I'd have to dig mighty deep for the strength not to end up in jail for punching her in the face. I spent time in the front galley creating stories for why she was such a bitch. Maybe she spent her days off rescuing kittens from burning buildings which left her tired and cranky. That would make her a hero in my eyes and give her a pass for being so mean. Perhaps she did know her hair was thinning and decided to punish all bald men. That made perfect sense. I sat down in my jumpseat to eat my dinner but my mind continued to wander about Carol. What was her fucking problem with me? Could her bitchiness be coming from an accidental over crimping situation earlier that day? Jackpot. That was most likely the issue. No white girl's hair is that frizzy on purpose.

Amber pulled me back into reality when she walked up to the front galley to do a trash pick up. She reached into the front bin and grabbed a garbage bag, "She just doesn't like you," she clarified as she opened the garbage bag and sat next to me on the jumpseat, "so stop trying."

"But why? I don't get it."

"I don't know, Joe. I like you; she doesn't." She stood up and started down the aisle collecting trash ending the conversation. I sat there staring at my cup of yogurt realizing I forgot to grab a spoon. Most likely Carol stole it. I'd blame her for everything. My missing spoon. The inconsistent temperature in the airplane. A disastrous mid-air collision. Everything.

Carol and I didn't interact for the rest of the trip. I guess that was a good thing. Her body language screamed that she loathed me. Too bad it wasn't screaming from being thrown into a rotating Pratt & Whitney engine. Too harsh? Not really. I'll go out on a limb and say we've all worked with a Carol at some point. We've all dealt with a miserable coworker. And we deal with our Carols in our own special way, mine being to witness her experience a quick death at the hands of an airplane engine. I see nothing wrong with that.

During the rest of the trip, to make myself feel better, I speculated Carol was a lesbian. A full-blown carpet muncher with an appetite for Birkenstocks and strap ons. How's that for stereotypes? To be honest, I had no proof of her being a lesbian. It's not like I witnessed her do a face dive in Amber's crotch in the hotel lobby. Although, if I had, I'd guess she was just curious about her brand of panties and nothing more. Seriously, my poor gaydar knows no boundaries. I figured Carol to be lesbionic because she constantly ignored me but chatted with Amber every chance available. I know for a fact-or maybe I read it on a Ted Cruz website-that all lesbians hate talking to men. And sucking dick. They hate that even more. Carol and Amber's laughter and giggling echoed all the way up to row 20. It drove me insane. I felt like the little kid invited to a birthday party but shunned to the corner because the gift I brought was a regift. At least if there was cake on the airplane I could have drowned myself in cake frosting. Who cares about two chicks gossiping when you are knee deep in buttercream frosting? I'd step into the back galley and they'd both go silent. I know how it sounds, but this wasn't my imagination. I even snuck up on them a few times but the moment my right foot hit the galley floor—they went dark. Noses in their books and purses. What made me feel even worse was that Amber would openly converse with me on the jumpseat during departures and arrivals but she shut down around Carol. Now, I know it's terrible to go directly to the, "she must be a lesbian because she doesn't talk to me," conclusion—but I did. Guilty.

I am no lesbian hater so please delete all those angry emails you are preparing to send off to Rosie and Ellen. Stop it right there. I am gay. How could I possibly hate lesbians? That's like being a cop and hating donuts. It's not conceivable. The last thing I hate are lesbians. I love them. I just don't understand why they hate dick, but I love them.

My first conversation with a lesbian was when I was 16 years old and worked at McDonald's.

It went something like this:

Me:"How do you have sex without a dick?"

Big Butch Lesbian: "It's easy. Use your imagination."

Me: "Is it like eating sushi?"

BBL: "We have ten perfectly good fingers and a strong tongue."

Me: "Oh. Ok. Excuse me while I go throw up my Big Mac and cry myself to sleep."

But there's a twist in this story. Not the story about the lesbian giving a young 16 year old Joe life lessons on lesbian sex. The only twist happening there was from my stomach in the nasty bathroom of a dirty McDonald's. I am referring to the story about Carol and Amber. Carol was no lesbian (Carol, if you are reading this right now please go ahead and cancel the lawsuit. I've delesbianized you). She was just a bitch who despised the fact that I was alive and taking up valuable air. She also dated a pilot at my airline. That surprised me. Well, not really. I presumed he was an undercover dick pilot and then it all made sense.

Drumroll… the lesbian was Amber. Did you get that? She was a lipstick lesbian who'd trade in a pair of Birkenstocks for a pair of Manolo Blahniks anyday. I told you my gaydar was useless. Here I created an entire story in my head about Carol being some man-hating lesbian and she was the straightest person on the flight. She was still a bitch though. Let's not forget that.

See what happens when you allow your emotions to control your thoughts? Your brain makes you out to be a bigger asshole than the asshole making your life miserable.

All this negativity towards Carol made me question myself and how I interact with others. Even though she was a super bitch towards me, I should have handled myself better.

I will confess something to you at this very moment. Are you ready? If you didn't pick up on this, I am not perfect. I can be an asshole just like Carol. Take it all in and just accept it. I had to. I have been told multiple times by close friends that I have a difficult time getting along with strangers and that I find fault in almost every new person who crosses my path. How dare someone say that? It's slightly true, but how dare they? Sometimes it's just best to keep shit like that to yourself.

Once a good friend and I were at the bar and he confessed, "I get nervous introducing you to new people. You just don't like anyone."

"Is that true?" I turned my head, "That's not true."

"Yes it is." At that exact second he looked over to the other side of the bar, "Oh look. I met that guy last week. You wanna meet him?"

"Ugh. No thanks. I'll be in the bathroom."

Maybe I am a first impressions kind of guy and if you fuck it up within the first five seconds you might as well just pack up and go home. But only after you've bought a round of drinks and told me I was funny. Seriously, I don't dislike everyone. Just most people. I enjoy meeting a new group of fans (did I say fans? I meant friends) so they can spend the evening fawning over me while I narrate ridiculous and obscene airplane stories. I live for that. Who doesn't? Well introverts probably don't but thankfully, my pendulum swings off the extrovert chart. If I dig deep enough I can muster up enough fakeness with people I don't find amusing to get through a short introduction, but it's difficult. I usually have to spend the next day in bed recovering. It's a price I am willing to pay.

Is that a defense? Sounds like a crock of bullshit to me. Wow! I really am a dick. But wait, there's more. I only struggle getting along with people if they are assholes to me, or they talk a lot of shit that makes me roll my eyes and wish I was losing consciousness in the cargo hold of the airplane. You know it's bad when you'd rather have no oxygen than listen to people talk.

That entire three day trip was an odd turn of events for me. Granted, I did not like Carol, and for good fucking reason, but she didn't like me first. That was a struggle. I was fine with me not liking her but the second she showed signs of resentment towards me—I fell apart. Did my five second first impression turn her off like a plate of liver and onions? What could I have done differently? If Amber hadn't laid it out for me in black and white I might have spent the entire trip wrecking my brain about what I did. Why didn't she like me? Was it because I asked to see her flight attendant manual? Damn, if that was the case, I can only imagine how she treated her OB/GYN on pap smear day.

For years I worried about what people thought of me, while running around judging and disliking everyone I met. You can burn up a lot of energy worrying about why people like or dislike you. It's tiresome. It's unnecessary. To think of what I might have accomplished in my life if I didn't give a fuck what others thought of me. I could have gone to medical school and became a world-renowned proctologist. Who wouldn't want to spend the day fingering middle-aged manholes all day? That's a normal Saturday night for most of my friends. If I didn't care about what others thought of me maybe, just maybe, I could have lost my virginity at a decent age. Nobody should be a virgin at 28 years old. Nobody.

Does it really matter what people think? Does it matter if persons A and B hate you but persons C and D think you are amazing? I learned a valuable life lesson watching *RuPaul's Drag Race*, the lesson being: it's none of your business what other people think of you. If someone doesn't like you, that's their problem, not yours. Can we get RuPaul to tour the country presenting that message to our youth? It should be the motto of every elementary school in the world. Think of the confidence and self-esteem kids would have with that message pumped into their ears. It did me wonders and I am an old fart.

RuPaul's advice came in handy a few months later on another flight when I found myself caught in the middle of two flight attendants and their verbal altercation on the airplane.

Keegan, Wendy, and I were working an easy four day transcontinental trip. I say easy because on the second night there was a San Francisco layover which allowed me to sleep in my own bed. That's always a treat. Our trip included only three legs: Cleveland to Dallas, with a short overnight layover; Dallas to San Francisco, with a 24 hour layover; and finally the red eye flight back to Cleveland.

Keegan was the lead flight attendant and from the beginning complained about working this position. He was so adamant about not working the front of the airplane that he texted me the day our schedules came out requesting I swap positions with him.

My text read: "No."

A few hours later, as if his cell phone died and he never received my response, he sent me a position swap request from our airline scheduling software. He obviously doesn't know me. The only position swap I'll entertain will revolve around gay sex in a bed, not on an airplane. Well, unless the gay sex happens on the airplane and then I guess I'd accept. Who wouldn't? Everyone wants to have sex on the airplane. I declined his non-gay sex position swap request. Two days later, I received another one. It was apparent that Keegan was more aggressive than a bisexual threesome about this position swap.

Again, I declined.

Without trying to sound like a total bitch, I sent him another text message reminding him that if I wanted to work the front of the airplane on this trip, I would have bid for it myself. Unfortunately, the message emphasized how big of a bitch I actually am. Oops. Some messages just come across how they come across. I was the senior flight attendant on this trip and even though I had plenty of weight, I didn't want to push it around. He finally got the message.

What can I say about Keegan and Wendy? They were friends on Facebook and possibly liked each other's photos on Instagram. Whether or not they were friends outside of work, I have no idea. I doubt it, but that's just my theory. In my opinion, Wendy wasn't the type to socialize in public with the likes of Keegan. For all intents and purposes, let's say they were only Facebook friends. Which I define as not being friends at all. Just because you click that little friend icon with someone on social media does not mean you are friends. I don't care what Mark Zuckerberg tells you. There's a word for that, it's called acquaintance. The online Google definition (trust me, I looked it up) for acquaintance is: *a person one knows slightly, but who is not a close friend.*

And that's if you have physically met the person. If you have never laid eyes on your Facebook "friend" then that's an entirely different word. That word is stranger. You can't argue black and white print, especially when it's delivered by Google. That's equivalent to receiving a message from L. Ron Hubbard if you happen to be a Scientologist.

During the hours we spent at 38,000 feet, Keegan provided Wendy and I with a pointless Christian sermon. It went on for hours, just like the headache his voice gave me. Keegan was a big gay Christian. How big? Picture Big Gay Al from *South Park* big, but skinnier and with a higher pitch voice. Keegan definitely had gay voice. It was so awful he made an 11 year-old girl sound like she smoked two packs of Camels a day. Not only was he a big gay Christian, he hated being gay. As you can imagine, I couldn't relate to him at all. He was a gay-bashing Christian who spent countless hours of his life bashing his own lifestyle. I might as well been working a trip with Ted Haggard. At least Ted got dick. All Keegan got were calluses on his right hand.

Listening to Keegan would frighten gay teens into suicide. Thankfully, we were flying to Dallas and as we all know, there are more steers in Texas than queers. His entire dialogue was focused on God, Jesus, being gay, and Christians. He was relentless. Flying with Keegan should require a pair of earbuds and a roofie pill to block out all his evangelizing. I felt violated. It was as if my ears were being raped by the Holy Ghost. Preaching was his favorite mid-flight past time, "Gay people are such whores. They are sluts," he looked up from the book he was reading while the three of us sat in the back galley. I ignored him but he continued, "Jesus still loves us though. But why are all gay people whores?"

I looked at him to watch his facial expression, "I blew a Hispanic Jesus once. It was hot. He talked about his girlfriend while I sucked his dick in a seedy motel."

Keegan glared at me like he witnessed a school shooting, so naturally I continued, "Oh to be young again."

He slammed his book shut, "Joe! That's just terrible."

I didn't think it was all that bad. "No. It was actually quite good."

That was enough for him. He stood up, lifted up the silver snack bin he was using as a chair, placed it back in the holder and stared at me, waiting for an apology. It would be a long wait.

Keegan was the worst kind of gay and the worst kind of Christian. Two behaviors that should never find themselves in a marriage. He spent hours discussing his internal battle with religion and being a gay man while trolling Grindr for the cutest guys 10 feet away. I was embarrassed for him. What was he going to do? Find the guy with the biggest dick but not exercise his demon? (And by demon I mean dick.) As big of an atheist as I am, I found myself thanking baby Jesus that we were working a four to five hour flight and not on our way to Sydney.

Throughout the entire trip he obsessively read a book written by some God fearing gay man. I couldn't begin to remember who the author was or the title of the book. To be honest, I didn't care. All I remember was that it was written by some gay Christian guy who spent an abundant amount of time arguing Bible scriptures to relieve gay men of their religious guilt. I am not in favor of censorship or book burning, but this garbage that Keegan was reading belonged doused with lighter fluid and set ablaze inside a tin drum under some overpass in Los Angeles. Keeping the homeless warm was about all this book was good for.

You may think I am a barbarian—and you are right. Actually, I felt bad for Keegan and his struggles. He walked around reminding me of someone carrying the weight of the world on his bony shoulders. Or at least the weight of a large wooden crucifix. His scars ran deep and spilled over with years of religious bullshit. In Keegan's defense, he never admitted to any of that but I saw right through him like a pair of nude mesh panties. Being a 40 year old gay man, and a recovering Catholic, I pick up self loathing quickly. Talk about having low self esteem. His conversations tended to be so heavy I was afraid we'd have to remove the liquor cart from the flight because of weight restrictions.

Even with his aversion towards being gay, and the holy roller mumbo jumbo he spewed out like acid rain, the three of us seemed to work well together. How was that possible? It's simple, I am a master at being a fake son of a bitch. That's an *hijo de puta* for you Spanish readers. Pulling off the fake card is a gift from the Universe. Or God. Or Xenu. It doesn't matter who you choose, just go with whoever you thank after a fantastic orgasm. The second Keegan was out of earshot and on his way to the front of the airplane, I'd shake my head at Wendy, "That boy is fucked up."

As the lead flight attendant, Keegan was responsible for being the executive decision maker in the airplane cabin. If you want to be nitpicky, then yes, the captain is the main man—or woman—in charge, but for this story we'll just say that the lead flight attendant is in charge of the cabin, which, technically, we are. That makes sense because the lead flight attendant receives more pay and as we all know, mo money equals mo problems. If you don't believe me just ask The Notorious B.I.G. Oh wait, never mind.

Let's just say when the luggage hits the overhead bins, I start looking around for the flight attendant in charge. If there's stress to be had during a flight, it belongs on the shoulders of the person making the most money. Correct? When I am standing in the middle of the airplane during boarding and someone throws their bag down and demands, "Excuse me, Stewardess... Help me with my bag!"

The first thing I do is look around to make sure that this rude passenger is talking to me. How do I know? They could be traveling with someone named Stewardess. Trust me, if there is someone walking around with the name Schartzmugel, then Stewardess doesn't seem like such a far stretch. After confirming that they are speaking directly to me, the second thing I do is respond ruder, "Hold on. Let me get the lead flight attendant." Usually the asshole's bag gets checked.

That's where Keegan failed. He refused to make a decision or answer a question to save his life, or more importantly, mine. Whether he refused or just didn't have the balls remains a mystery. Whenever Wendy or I asked him the simplest questions he froze up. No matter how elementary the question was, he never had an answer.

A normal conversation with Keegan went something like this, "Keegan, two passengers are fucking in the back lavatory."

"What do you think we should do?" His voice cracked into the interphone.

"I'm not the lead flight attendant. You make the decision."

"See. I hate this position!" He'd hang up the interphone while I immediately went back to eavesdropping with my ear to the lavatory door waiting for the two passengers to climax.

Here's a confession, I made that entire dialogue up. That was a typical conversation with Keegan but I've never had two passengers fucking in the lavatory. I wish I had. I am not that lucky. I've never even had to yell at a passenger for giving a handjob in the last row of the airplane. I figured adding airplane sex in the middle of this story might help me prove my point. Alright, I really just wanted to talk about airplane lavatory sex because GODDAMN IT—it never happens on my flights.

I am all for collaboration on my flights. Teamwork is essential to guarantee a successful flight. Without some form of solidarity on the airplane you can go from synergy to synerg-no in a matter of minutes. You don't have to be a flight attendant to understand that. It's the same in the office environment. Nobody wants to share a cubicle with someone who depends on you to make all the decision. With Keegan it was simple, he was free to call on me when it came to the important outcomes: questioning the removal of a passenger, a life threatening medical, or an irate passenger. Not mulling over what time to start coffee service. Make the decision and pass it along.

Even with Keegan's indecisive behavior, our trip was still workable. Wendy and I managed by rolling our eyes enough behind his back to give ourselves migraines. Have you ever rolled your eyes enough to give yourself a headache? Don't. It really happens. Fighting back the tears from a headache while serving fat passengers cups of sugar water made it easier to deal with him. I can't explain it. Rolling our eyes at him made us laugh which helped with tolerating his behavior. It's just too bad I didn't pack enough Advil to fill a plastic tub.

It all fell apart when we arrived at San Francisco International Airport to work the red eye back to Cleveland. As planned, I spent the night at home. I met them at the airport for report time and nothing seemed out of the ordinary when I walked up to the gate. Wendy waved over at me as she sat on the large white sleek window ledge overlooking our airplane parked at the gate. Keegan stood behind the counter flipping through the flight manifest.

"Good evening, Mr. Keegan," I greeted him placing my luggage against the wall, "how was your layover?"

"It was fine," Keegan answered. Wendy was too far away to hear the question "The gate agent said there is a technician on the airplane working on a seat at row 19."

I sighed, "Are we delayed?" That's a rolling question in the airline industry. There are two things we can always count on—uniform non-compliance and delays.

Before Keegan responded, our two pilots walked up behind me and the captain questioned, "Delayed? Why are we delayed?" He was tall and lanky with no facial hair and big lips. That's all I remember about him. I remember less about the first officer. He made no attempts at communicating with us, and I couldn't begin to dig down deep enough to remember his appearance. Short with a God-like complex and small dick? That pretty much sums up most pilots, or at least the pilots I dislike who refuse to show me an ounce of respect.

The gate agent piped in, "No. We are not delayed. We just have a technician on the airplane fixing one of the seats," she was getting defensive before we responded, "We need to board this flight and get it out on time."

By now, Wendy had made her way over to the gate and joined the five of us huddled around in a circle working out what time to board. "Are we already having drama?" she asked. I smiled at her while sipping on the coffee I picked up on the way to the airport.

Nobody verbally answered her. Keegan was having tunnel vision, "What time should we start boarding? Should we start on time?" He asked out loud to anyone who wanted to answer. A few more decibels higher and dogs living in the next town over could have responded.

Before any of us had a chance to reply the captain answered, "We will board the front of the airplane first and then after row 19 is fixed, we will start boarding the rear of the airplane. Is that good for everyone?"

Easy enough, right? We all agreed unanimously, grabbed the handles of our luggage, and filed down the jetbridge. The gate agent yelled out one last time before closing the oversized gate door, "I'll start sending them down in five minutes."

We ignored her like we always do.

I immediately saw the technician kneeling down at row 19 as I started down the aisle. When I approached him, and his overexposed butt crack, I noticed the seat he was attempting to fix, 19D, was reclined all the way into the seat directly behind it. That wouldn't fly (pun intended) especially with a full flight. All one hundred and forty seats had a passenger eagerly awaiting it and I doubted the person sitting in 20D wanted some stranger staring up their nose for five hours.

After the three of us completed our security checks, in what seemed like record time, we started boarding the airplane. My only indication was when I looked up the aisle towards the front of the airplane and saw people lined up like cattle. There was no heads-up from Keegan but that was normal. He'd probably just call to the back of the airplane and say, "We are boarding. Is it alright with you that I call you and tell you?"

Instantly, the front of the aircraft began to fill up with passengers and they spilled down the aisle. Exactly like they weren't suppose to. Wendy become irate, "What the hell is he doing up there? They are already at row 19."

I stopped counting the liquor cart and looked up the aisle to see passengers piling up behind the technician. The look on their faces mirrored the look on Wendy's face. Even with arriving at the gate on time, and having our airplane awaiting us, we started boarding a few minutes late. Not a big deal to the flight attendants and pilots, but when it comes to airline passengers, it's like punching them directly in their genitals with a sledge hammer; or so they act. In our normal everyday existence, a few minutes is nothing. Think of all the minutes we waste in our lives; sitting at red lights, waiting for our cappuccinos at Starbucks, biding time until our sexual partner climaxes. It's endless. I literally just wasted a few minutes writing that line about waiting a few minutes. It's that easy to waste minutes. When it comes to airline passengers a few minutes is no different than a few hours. They are like my cats, they have no concept of time. These people could board the airplane five minutes late but arrive at their destination 20 minutes early and still not be happy. Then, to add insult to injury, the airline will send out their friendly little satisfaction survey which gives the passengers the chance to bitch about boarding late while completely forgetting they arrived to their destination early. People wonder why airline employees are such bitches.

I picked up the interphone and called the front of the airplane. Keegan answered on the second ding, "Hi. This is Keegan."

"Hey. It's Joe." The airline makes us answer the interphone like that but seriously, who the fuck else would it be? A passenger? The Virgin Mary? Only in Keegan's dreams. Responding on the interphone like that when 10 flight attendants are working makes sense. On an airplane with three flight attendants, it's just foolish. I continued, "We need to stop boarding. These people are piling up back here and the technician's ass is hanging out into the aisle."

He was flustered, "What do you want me to do? They keep coming down the jet bridge."

I snapped, "Just have them wait on the jet bridge!" I looked at Wendy. There was steam coming off her arms, "Have the captain go up to tell them to stop boarding."

The interphone went dead.

I went back to counting the liquor cart. Once I was finished I slide it back into place and glanced back up to the front of the airplane. Keegan was planted in the front galley talking with the captain while passengers continued to pass him. What the fuck was he doing? Planning an early morning pilot blow job session once we landed in Cleveland? I was almost jealous. What really pissed me off was when he finally made eye contact with me and simply threw his hands up in the air signaling his defeat. My dislike for Keegan was certified platinum from that point on.

Once Buttcrack (aka the technician) finished fixing the broken seat he pushed his way passed all the passengers fighting his way to the front of the airplane. From that instant, the tidal wave of people that flooded the entire back half of the airplane was overwhelming. Most of them went straight to the lavatory, which is never a surprise. Why use the restroom in the airport when you can wait until you are on the airplane and use tiny lavatories? Makes perfect fucking sense. Boarding continued but Wendy and I were irritated with the way Keegan managed the entire process.

She was vocal about her dislike for him, "I know he's got problems and troubles in life, but damn, that's no excuse for being a terrible flight attendant."

I agreed while leaning against the back galley smiling at passengers as they walked down the aisle. The interphone rang. Before I could speak, Keegan jumped right in, "Joe. There's an older lady up here who almost fell coming onto the airplane. She can't even make it to her seat in row 14. What should we do?"

I looked at Wendy and rolled my eyes. That reminded me to take some Advil before we departed, "Is she drunk?"

"I can't tell. Can you come up here and talk to her?"

"Sure. I'll be right there." I hung up the interphone and addressed Wendy who was staring at me, "Some lady almost fell up there and he wants me to talk to her."

"You mean he wants you to handle his shit." she said bursting into laughter.

I smirked and stepped into the aisle pushing my way upstream from the crowd of passengers fidgeting with their bags and trying to get to their seats.

The little white haired lady was seated in 1D clutching her purse like she stole it. Boarding had slowed down and there were no passengers walking on the airplane. I stepped into the front galley and approached Keegan. "What do you want me to say to her?"

"I don't know. Whatever you'd like."

I guess slapping his smug face was out of the question. But if I did, I could probably go home for the night. No. I needed my job. I approached him another way, "Let me rephrase that, what have you said to her already?"

He looked down at her with disregard, "Nothing."

Perfect. I had no problem assisting him and offering up my advice to help but like always he brought nothing to the table. He was setting himself up to take no responsibility for the outcome.

If looks could kill, his lifeless body would have fallen over into the flight deck. I turned from him and bent down to face the passenger, "Good Evening. How are you?"

She didn't make eye contact and looked forward without turning her head towards me. I tried again, "Hello. Are you alright?"

"Yes," she whispered.

This was like having a conversation with my grandmother after she was hospitalized for falling and breaking her hip. "Are you on any medication?"

"No."

"Have you been waiting a while at the airport?"

She finally looked over at me, "Yes." I politely peeled her boarding pass out of her veiny hand to address her by name.

I turned and looked up at Keegan who stood there chewing on his fingernails. I wanted to punch him in his balls but I continued questioning the passenger, "Ethel, how many drinks have you had?"

"Four."

"Four?" I questioned. She didn't respond.

Four drinks? That's even a lot for me and I am a heavyset guy. Grandma was probably 95 lbs fully dressed so it was no surprise she almost fell while walking onto the airplane. It was a shock she actually spoke. I stood up and looked at Keegan, "Did she come down the jet bridge in a wheelchair?"

He muttered, "I don't know," while continuing to snack on his hangnails.

This dude didn't know much of anything on this trip. I whispered to him, "I think she's had too much to drink. She should probably come off the flight." I bent down to ask her a few more questions but before I could get another word out, the gate agent stepped onto the airplane with our final paperwork. Boarding had concluded and the gate agent was ready to close the airplane door. Unbeknownst to her, we were dealing with what appeared to be a drunk old lady in 1D. I smiled at Ethel even though she wasn't looking at me. She was now rummaging through her purse, most likely looking for the piece of shit she placed in there yesterday. Ethel was saving that hard turd for a rainy day, and sadly, I created a storm. If she did have a piece of dried shit in her bag, she'd probably fling it at me the first chance she got. My hope was for it to hit Keegan instead. Listen, I know old ladies and they love to shove everything in their purses; including a firm piece of dooky. I straightened myself out and walked towards the airplane door away from the passenger and motioned for the gate agent to step out onto the jet bridge with me. There was no doubt in my mind that Ethel was as deaf as my sports obsessed grandfather but I wasn't taking any chances, especially if her hearing aid was turned up. Keegan followed.

If Keegan had taken a break from chewing on his fingers long enough to step up to the plate and handle the situation, my outlook on him might have been different. He was, after all, the lead flight attendant. To my surprise, he initiated the conversation once we were all on the jet bridge. Sadly, it was to throw me into the airplane engine. "Joe talked to the lady in 1D and she's drunk. She's suppose to be in row 14, or something, I don't really remember. He wants her to come off the flight." He blurted out flailing his hands around like he was swatting away invisible flies.

"Wait a minute, " I aggressively put my hand up in Keegan's face. If I had been an inch closer he might have taken care of the hangnail on my right thumb. "Please don't speak for me." He cowered down. I looked at the gate agent and gave her the quick and full rundown on the conversation with Ethel.

Not wanting to delay the flight the gate agent responded, "Well if she's drunk we'll take her off the flight."

Keegan's eyes bulged out of his head. "I just want to clarify," he said looking at the gate agent and then over to me, "you're the one making the decision to remove her from the flight, right?"

She paused for a moment as she walked past us back onto the airplane, "Yeah. Sure. I don't care, we just gotta get this flight out."

Once Ethel was off the flight, and the main airplane door was closed, I armed and cross checked my doors and took a deep breath. That always helps me to stay mindful of my attitude and my reaction to people. If I don't do this I usually fly off the handle and start yelling. It's a fact that I do not meditate enough, which results in not enough deep breathing, and a lot of flying off the handle.

My attitude improved rather quickly. I had barely unfastened my seatbelt when we hit the 10,000 feet chime and Wendy came racing into the back galley. With the clank of my seat belt against the jumpseat she yelled out, "He's an asshole," and flopped into the jumpseat across from mine.

This should be interesting. I turned on the galley lights enough to see what we were doing but not bright enough to disturb the last row of passengers. "What happened? We've been in the air for five minutes."

"We got into it up there!" Her body language was set on destroy. I wouldn't have messed with her even if I was carrying a gun. She stood and placed both hands on the galley counter while continuing to unload her frustrations, "He was yelling at me in front of the passengers in row one. Can you believe that shit?" She grabbed her plastic water bottle from inside the metal bin and started drinking. I waited. "And then he asked me if I thought he was a bad flight attendant."

"What did you say?" I asked, glued to my jumpseat.

She let out an angry laugh, "I said yes."

"You said yes?" That gave me the power to stand up and get to work. Before that I felt drained from the entire boarding process, but this scene woke me right up. This was some ABC daytime drama kinda shit and I didn't want to miss any of it. This is the kind of excitement that keeps bitches awake working a red-eye flight. I started pulling plastic cups out of the bin and placing them on the counter, "I can't believe you said yes. You've fucked him up for years now."

"I really don't care. Joe, he's terrible. You know that. He can't make a decision and won't take responsibility. I'm done dealing with his crazy-ass nonsense."

I loved Wendy and not because she was absolutely right. Keegan made me nervous. He probably made everyone he worked with nervous. You never want to work with a flight attendant who makes you nervous. And I don't mean nervous like he'd steal your laptop from inside your laptop bag while you were in the lavatory or rape you in your hotel room on a layover, but nervous like standing in the galley crying and praying to Jesus while the airplane sunk to the bottom of Lake Erie. That kind of nervous. Not the nervous you want to deal with when working on an airplane. Working with competent individuals—who are not afraid to make important, quick decisions—are the only flight attendants you want to work with. You'd think that was the only type of people the airlines hired but as you can see, in the case of Keegan and so many more, some nuts fall through the cracks.

With Wendy hunkering down in the back of the airplane and Keegan shuffling around up front, I was positive we could manage through our five hour flight without her pulling out the rest of his hair. To be sure, I asked her if she'd be able to work with him without killing him. She gave me a cool, "Sure. I don't really give a fuck about him anymore."

That was all fine and dandy but I'd need something a little more solid to go on before feeling comfortable. My main concern was that if there was an emergency situation on the airplane, would they be able to work together as a team? "Are you guys going to be okay if we have an emergency? That's all I care about."

"Oh yeah. I'm cool with him as long as it's work related. But he better not come back here acting like everything is normal because it ain't."

That was fine with me. Being friends or even liking the person you are working with is not a requirement as a flight attendant. Like I've said before: I barely like anyone I work with. As a minimum requirement, you need to set aside your differences during an emergency situation and work together for the safety of everyone on the airplane. My gut instinct told me that Wendy was telling me the truth. She wasn't going to lose her job over someone like Keegan. That was a fact. I hated the idea of getting involved but my parental instincts kicked in. After our service was completed and most of the passengers were asleep, I made my way to the front of the aircraft to talk with Keegan. As I approached the front galley I noticed he was slouched down in his jumpseat reading his book. Was he crying? Jesus Christ, I hoped not.

"You alright?" I pulled down the jump seat and sat beside him.

"I am fine, Joe. I have no problems with her. She verbally attacked me and told me I was a horrible flight attendant. What am I supposed to do?"

"Well, yelling at each other in front of passengers is probably not the best thing to do."

"I'm sorry about that." There was an awkward pause. I debated whether to get up and stand in the galley but he continued, "Do you think I'm a bad flight attendant?"

Motherfucker! Why did he have to go and ask me such a loaded question? I went from innocent bystander to finding myself in the hot seat. A seat so fucking hot the hairs on my ass were starting to smoke like bacon. This altercation had nothing to do with me but here I was smack dab in the middle like the participant in an unwanted threesome. Which is any threesome you participate in when you really just want to fuck the hot person in the relationship but they came as a bundle. It's like only wanting basic cable but those greedy assholes make you get HBO too. I deserved this for sticking my nose in their business. If there was ever a next time, I'd find myself taking a break in the lavatory while they beat each other down with fire extinguishers. I wanted to be truthful so I prepared myself for the backlash that came with telling him the truth. Could he handle the truth? I doubted it. He was no Tom Cruise in *A Few Good Men.*

If there's one thing I've learned is that when faced with a circumstance like this, it's important to choose your words wisely. I took a long deep breath promising myself to start meditating the moment we landed, "Do I think you are a bad flight attendant? No. Do I think you shouldn't work the lead flight attendant position? Yes."

Holy shit. Where did that come from? An answer like that deserves the Nobel Peace Prize. If not that then at least a standing ovation. I hate boosting my already overinflated ego but I am what you'd call a talented motherfucker. He stared at me without saying a word. Even with such a fantastic response I had no idea what to expect. Keegan was emotionally unstable and that's a lot coming from a guy like me. I've been known to cry while listening to Lionel Richie.

I was confident in my response. It was award worthy and truthful. I've worked with hundreds of flight attendants and as shocking as it may sound, he wasn't the worst. He was far from the best. Alright, he was pretty fucking bad but the longer he stayed silent the more I prepared for the eruption.

There was no outburst so I continued, "I think you need more confidence making decisions. What are you afraid of?"

Another pause and then he answered, "I don't want to get in trouble."

"From?"

"The airline. They'll fire me if I make the wrong decision."

It took him long enough, but his fears finally came out after I peeled his emotions back like the skin on an onion. Or a big fat uncut Mexican dick, whichever you prefer. I'll go with the latter. All I know is that they can both bring you to tears.

We've all been there, right? Not being face-to-face with an uncut Mexican dick—that only happens to the lucky few—but having fear about management waiting for you to make one mistake so they can terminate you. I was the same way. I worried myself drunk frightened that I'd make a mistake and lose my job. Forget to bring a bottle of water to a passenger? Terminated. Call in sick with Ebola? Terminated. Accidently ask a lesbian passenger, "What would you like to drink, sir?" You guessed it, terminated. If that's not bad enough, then you find yourself added to a anti-lesbian email group that you didn't want to join because-you actually love lesbians-but are easily confused by their Justin Bieber haircuts. That's how fearful I was about airline big brother watching over me. After spending years on the Standards Advisory Team I woke up one morning while on a Tampa layover and stopped giving a damn. I made a commitment to myself to always do my job to the best of my ability. I also decided never to waste one more second of my valuable time worrying about being terminated. Especially when it came to being a flight attendant. Let's be real: I serve nuts and sodas, I don't work at NASA figuring out how to get people to Mars.

I had to break it down in a fluffy way. I knew exactly what to say. "This is what I do, " I said, trying to relax him, "I always make the best decision with the information that I have at that exact moment. I may find out later that it wasn't the best thing to do but at least I followed through on it. Does that make sense?"

He nodded, "Yes, it does. Will she talk to me? I still don't even know why she is so upset with me.

"Let me go back and ask her. I also need to make sure that if there's an emergency you guys can work together."

"Joe," he was obviously offended, "of course. I do my job. I'm not a bad flight attendant."

I took my time collecting trash through the airplane. I wasted as much time as possible walking through the airplane figuring out what to say to Wendy. Most of the passengers were asleep so I took the occasional empty plastic cup and spent the rest of the time crotch shopping all the guys.

Wendy was perusing her magazine when I walked into the back galley. When I stepped into view she closed her copy of Glamour and asked, "What's he got to say?"

Stuffing the almost empty garbage bag in the trash bin I delicately answered, "He doesn't think he's a bad flight attendant and he'd like to talk to you."

Without making eye contact she reached into her bag, pulled out another magazine, and with a bitter tone responded, "I have nothing to say to him. He's crazy and when we land I'm deleting him off Facebook."

I bowed my head and sat down in the jumpseat. My duties as inflight mediator were over. Why did I even care about these two? I disliked Keegan and I only met Wendy a few days prior. There was also the possibility of never seeing the two of them again. If they could keep from verbally attacking each other until the end of this flight, I'd consider it a victory.

While I sat there in my jumpseat I thought of the time I flew with Carol and Amber. I remembered struggling with why Carol disliked me so much but Amber didn't spend a waking second trying to bring us together. Amber handled our situation matter-of-factly by walking up to the front galley and simply stating, "She just doesn't like you," That was it. No drama. No further questions. No answers. Sometimes people like you, and sometimes they don't.

INFLIGHT BOYFRIENDS

The first time I heard the term inflight boyfriend, or IFB, was on the television horror reality show *Fly Girls,* which aired on The CW for eight episodes in 2010. I don't know if you could call it a true horror show, but it was gruesome to watch, gave me nightmares, and sent me to the urgent care for a penicillin shot each time one of these flight attendants looked at a male passenger. A better title might have been, *American Horror Story: Fly Girls*. If they had slapped that title on it and put it on FX, it might still be on the air. At least with that information viewers could prepare themselves for the mid-air collision disaster taking place each episode. Who wouldn't want to watch Jessica Lange taking it up the ass from a group of drunk and horny businessmen in Palm Springs on a short 10 hour layover?

I do not speak from experience. I never hook up with anyone unless I have at least 15 hours to recover. I'm no Jessica Lange.

You are probably blind from watching *Fly Girls* and someone is reading this to you. I feel your pain; watching the entire season of *Fly Girls* stole four hours of our lives that we will never get back. That's if you managed to get through the entire short season. If you did, I am sorry for you. In all honestly, reading this book will probably steal more time than that. My apologies. *Fly Girls* should have been aborted quicker than a teenage pregnancy. I imagine the cast was not only terminated from the television show but had their wings ripped off their designer uniforms and were shamed into selling their bodies on Hollywood Blvd—better yet, making super roast beef sandwiches at Arby's. Either made me happy.

There was never an episode that didn't start with them boarding the airplane, standing in the aisle—may I add not helping ugly passengers with bags—and working the male businessmen like sharks to chum in the ocean, "Hey Britney. Did you see 3A?"

"Yes. I did," adjusting her silicon tits, "He is totally my IFB for this flight."

"No way," pursing her collagen injected lips, "I saw him first. He's mine."

They'd giggle, get phone numbers, go to hot tub parties on layovers, push up their tits every two minutes, and catch the worst case of vaginal herpes before they even departed the gate. Terrible flight attendants with a go get 'em attitude. These fly girls acted like whores who carried around Zithromax in their overnight tote bag instead of face wash. Why bother washing your face when you spend your entire layover face down in a pillow?

The show was so fake that I wanted to find each one of these flight attendants and the executive producers, and repeatedly run over them with the airport tug. I was anti-fly girls the moment I watched the first episode and found out they were all on reserve, based in San Francisco, had a high end crash pad in Los Angeles, and were all hot. Where were the fat girls? A flight attendant reality show without at least one fat girl is preposterous. It's like Paula Deen baking sugar cookies without using the n-word. It's not realistic. My airline could produce a television show on The Food Network called *Fat Fly Girls* and it would be a hit.

The promo for the pilot episode of *Fat Fly Girls*:

On this week's episode of Fat Fly Girls: Holly stumbles through LAX hungover from her layover the night before, bulging out of her unflattering uniform, and destroying a Double Double from In & Out that she picked up before she got to the airport. Will she wipe off that cheese hanging from her double double chin before the first passenger boards? Watch and see this Friday night at 10:00 p.m.

I get upset when it comes to false reality. I am way more interested in a television show about *real* flight attendants. I want to see their true struggles and how they cope. I'm evil like that. There's nothing better than watching a full grown adult crying to their parents while broke on reserve, having their luggage stolen off the airplane mid-pairing, or trying to cram as many minis in their panties while walking past security trying not to sound like a box of empty wine bottles being carried down a flight of stairs. That takes skill. Only flight attendants with over 10 years of seniority can walk off an airplane with more liquor than they sold on a Las Vegas out and back. That's my kind of real life drama. I want blood. I want tears. I want to watch a pretty blond flight attendant get her ass beat by the wife of the pilot who just finished landing his private jet in her lady hangar. That's television.

Once on a Cleveland to Seattle flight, I worked with a flight attendant named Cloris. As friendly as Cloris was, she carried around a sour look on her face that resembled an angry mugshot. I call this—mugshot face. Cloris wasn't outright ugly but any leather handbag looks attractive with the right accessories. We will just say that she wasn't winning any beauty contests. Although, rumor has it she won Miss Baltimore DMV in 1987 but I never investigated that claim any further. Cloris' mugshot face resembled an unloved girlfriend on too much crack who got busted for her boyfriend's drug smuggling. Think of Whitney Houston but much whiter, wilder hair, and without the voice of an angel. Cloris' voice was more like sandpaper-sandpaper that smoked two packs a day. That kind of mugshot face and voice can make a fellow flight attendant call in fatigue from fear. Once you got over the mugshot, Cloris was entertaining. She was also a bit older than me and cursed a lot. That helped me see past her unpleasant features and loved her the moment we met in the crew lounge and she blasted out, "Why the fuck is our flight delayed?"

Cloris was crass, loud, and reminded me of Irene. I wanted to share that information with her but refrained for fear of her ass raping me with the airplane emergency flashlight. Cloris was a New Yorker and their first instinct is to slam things into your asshole. It's true. I have fucked a few New Yorkers and after those experiences, let's just say that I never felt comfortable again bending over to tie my shoe in Greenwich Village. The airplane emergency flashlight is housed underneath our jump seats, and although I don't mind sitting above that thick piece of plastic, I am certainly not prepared to have it enter me in a violent manner, especially right before a Seattle transcon. The only thing I like to put inside me before a transcon is coffee, not a big black flashlight. If you've never seen an airplane flashlight, they are big. Baby arm big. Black guy from Kenya big. If inserted into your rectum you'd walk with a cane for months, possibly years. Talk about explaining that on-the-job injury to your flight attendant supervisor. I don't even like asking her for a pen.

Gay male and straight female flight attendants cater to the hot guys on their flights. It's just in our nature. Especially mine because I don't get along with ugly people. Before you scream about being offended and want to verbally attack me on the airport shuttle bus, let me explain. It's not that I don't get along with ugly people, I just have nothing in common with an ugly person. How the hell am I expected to strike up a conversation with one? "How are you today, sir? Have you ever thought about having that mole removed? You know, like Madonna."

I agree that focusing our attention on all the attractive passengers on a flight makes us sound like a bunch of fly girls but there is a huge difference: most of our interactions with hot passengers don't end with us on our knees in the Ft. Lauderdale Hilton parking lot. We aren't going to ignore you if you're unattractive, but you shouldn't expect unlimited free drinks and extra nuts if you have missing teeth, a bad hair piece, or smell like vinegar.

I hate when passengers smell like vinegar.

Straight male flight attendants (there are more than you think) are just as bad. *To Catch A Predator* could do an entire episode on straight male flight attendants when a hot female passenger walks onto the airplane. Being of age isn't a concern for these guys when it comes to flirting. A few years ago, I worked a flight from Chicago to Santo Domingo with this straight guy who refused to talk about anything but his inflight girlfriends. His name was Pablo and he actually refrained from using the term inflight girlfriends and just called them, "Pablo's bitches." It was romantic in a dirty pimp sort of way. He led me to believe he had enough bitches to star in a Snoop Dogg video. I felt bad for these girls because I doubt he paid well. On our way to Santo Domingo, we stood in the front galley discussing his "bitches" while I tried holding down my lunch. His behavior was appalling. Whenever a female passenger walked up to use the lavatory, which happened often, he completely ignored me and stalked the passenger like a hungry lion hunts a gazelle. He'd sniff the air like a bomb sniffing dog whenever a female passenger walked by. I figured he was smelling their vaginas, and because he was Puerto Rican-it made sense. Straight Puerto Rican men have the ability to smell the police, when their landlord is walking up the stairs to collect the rent check, and vaginas. If I had to guess, it's a gift from God; probably more of an apology for making them so fucking lazy. I deduced that he could not only tell which female passengers were menstruating but which ones were ovulating so he knew who to stay away from.

"Damn Joe! She's hot. You want to give her my number?

Looking embarrassed for him, "Uh. She's 14 years old. I had to move her out of the exit row."

"Really? But she's hot, bro."

"I will ignore that and pretend you are having some sort of Puerto Rican stroke." I walked off with a trash bag to collect service items from passengers. You know it's bad when you'd rather pick up half eaten apples, snot rags, and cups of ice than listen to some creepy Puerto Rican pedophile.

Cloris and I made our way to the gate area to find out why our airplane was running late. We hadn't met the other flight attendant so we assumed she'd show up at the gate. I expected her to be late and she did not disappointed.

I had known Cloris for 15 minutes, and because she was an older New Yorker—and obviously Jewish because she convinced the barista to give her a free espresso pump in her latte—I decided to keep my gay vibe to a minimum. Cloris figured out I was gay within the first five minutes of us meeting. That was fine, but I normally tend to set my gay flame low when meeting new pilots and flight attendants. The only time I ignore that clause is when I want certain people to stay as far away from me as possible. If you want to see a 60 year old straight male pilot hanging off the bumper of the hotel shuttle, just sit next to him and say, "You smell sexy. What kind of cologne is that, Brut?" It's like spraying a homosexual skunk all over the van. Homosexuality propels dick pilots as far away as humanly possible. Some of them would rather fly the airplane with a remote control from a KKK meeting than sit in the flight deck knowing there is a homosexual onboard.

I meshed well with the crew I was working with, but I still decided to keep my gay mannerisms low key so not to scorch their eyebrows during the first day of a four day trip. I'm no Judy Garland but I have been known to queen out and vogue at the gate when my flight has been cancelled and I've been released from duty. I had four days for them to meet the real Joe and ease into my crazy. I felt happy knowing that even though my flame was lower than normal, if we decided to toast marshmallows in the hotel lobby I could be of service.

The entire crew was standing by the gate when the airplane finally arrived and passengers started deplaning. Airline passengers are completely clueless of the airline process. They could be standing at the gate for hours and the moment the airplane pulls up to the gate they will run up and ask the gate agent, "Are we ready to board?"

I'll never understand it. An older lady did exactly that and Cloris became irritated. "These assholes don't pay attention," she whispered to me from the side of the counter, "They haven't even fucking deplaned yet. Does she think that people just vanish out of their fucking seats?"

I smiled, "Maybe she thinks this is her own private jet."

"She better fucking think again."

"I hope she's in your section." I couldn't help but egg her on even though I knew I was taking a chance of landing in Seattle with a flashlight up my ass.

"Hey Joe," she smirked, "Fuck off."

Things changed rather quickly after the clueless old lady walked away from the counter and a young attractive man ran up to the gate needing assistance. He was sweating and out of breath which made him even sexier. I didn't have enough time to collect my thoughts before Mrs. Robinson—a.k.a. Cloris, was on him like a river leach. "How may I help you?"

The gate agent and I looked at each other while the passenger answered in a soothing voice that made my pubic hair uncurl, "I was wondering if this flight serves meals?"

He ran from the security line for that? To ask about an airline meal? If he got that sweaty and worked up over airline food, then someone was getting fucked if there was turbulence over the Rocky Mountains. The look on Cloris' face gave her away: she was definitely rooting for some rough turbulence with a side order of bareback. The thought made me shiver. She whipped her hair back, and at her age that was cause for a 911 call "What's your name?

He smiled, "Gage. I'm in 1F,"

"Oh wonderful. You're in my section," I heard her nipples harden, "We don't serve hot food but there is a restaurant right there and you can bring *anything* you want on the flight."

I wondered if anything included: rubbers, lube, geritol, and a box of matzo ball mix to gag her with.

After we boarded and conducted our security checks, Gage was one of the first passengers on the airplane. He couldn't have been over 25 years old and appeared perfectly capable of stowing his own bag, but Cloris wasn't having any of that. This was her inflight boyfriend and she tossed his bag around like she wanted him to toss her vagina around. She was perspiring and exerting so much energy I was afraid we'd need to get her a wheelchair when we landed in Seattle. While conducting service she talked to him at every possible opportunity and ignored the other passengers in her section. I can't say she ignored them, but she made it a point to let everyone know that Gage came first, which at the tender age of 25 was not going to be an issue.

Halfway during the flight I walked up to the front galley to make sure Cloris hadn't gone into cardiac arrest, or worse—experienced a vaginal prolapse mid-flight. Seriously, how much excitement can a vagina that's been hanging around since the Eisenhower administration handle before it collapses on itself? Definity not a question that I needed answered. I also didn't want the responsibility of scooping up her aging vagina off the galley floor with a safety information card while the thirsty passenger in 9C rang his call bell for another Sprite. Just in case, and because I have never been faced with pushing a woman's vagina back inside her, I stopped at the overhead bin where my luggage was and grabbed my flight attendant manual. Whether or not there was a bullet point in the manual under the medical tab for such an emergency was a bridge I'd cross when the time came. Luckily, I never had to cross any bridges. What I did find was Cloris hovering over Gage like a helicopter bringing him things that he wasn't asking for and didn't need. I patiently waited for her in the galley and eventually she broke away from Gage and walked over to me.

"Cloris, he's one man—not a Jewish family of five going on vacation to Orlando. He really doesn't need 17 cans of Sprite and 24 bags of nuts."

Laughing it off she reminded me of the obvious, "He's so hot. If I had the chance I'd take him into the lav and fuck his brains out."

I threw coffee up in my mouth.

As disgusting as it was to hear her raspy vocal chords spew such nonsense, I couldn't help but laugh and feel the same way. Gage was a stud, and without even trying he made my sphincter dance the Macarena. No music needed. He had jet black hair, a chiseled face with a five o'clock shadow, and when he took time away from writing in his journal he flipped his hair to the side, gazed out of the window, licked his lips, and smiled. His teeth were so white and perfect I just knew he gargled with straight Clorox and spit right before he started foaming at the mouth. If he was a spitter I'd have to teach him what all Catholic priests teach their altar boys: only good boys who swallow go to heaven. Gage flipped his hair like he was on the red carpet with millions of his fans swooning over him. In reality, the only people drooling over him were me and Cloris and we couldn't have cared less about his hair. This was an all-eyes-on-bulge situation. Unless he was hiding Trader Joe's sausage links down his pants, he was happy to be on the flight.

When I am bored on a flight (which is most of the time unless someone is dying or we are moments away from crashing) I play this game where I like to walk down the aisle checking seat belts. I will admit I am not checking for anything but hard cocks and bulges. It's the truth. I am not embarrassed or ashamed by this confession. We all do it. Well, I can't speak for everyone but I can speak for the cock hungry flight attendants. It's like masturbating. I am sure there will be a few prudish flight attendants who never admit to checking male passengers bulges but they do it. Most passengers may feel violated by this revelation but welcome to our world. We feel just as violated the moment you step into our galley and decide to yoga pose your fat ass in our Au Bon Pain salad.

Gage spent much of his time deep in thought. He chewed on the end of his pencil, stared out the window, and then wrote something down. I tried eavesdropping but he was very good at closing the notebook after jotting down a note. Maybe he was writing his number down to give me when he walked off the airplane? A total cock slap in Cloris' face. The way this was going I'd end up getting his number but need maintenance to replace all the emergency flashlights on the airplane.

The more I watched him the more I sensed something wasn't right. Like I've said before, I have the worst gaydar in the world. Helen Keller had better gaydar than I do and anal sex is part of my daily regimen. I am dead serious. Anal sex is my One A Day vitamin. Actually, at my age it's more like One A Year, but who's counting? The ability to pick out another gay guy goes beyond my reach and unless he's in full drag—or trying to stuff me like a Christmas turkey—I am oblivious to his homosexuality. Liza Minnelli married a gay man and her gaydar is finer tuned than mine. I am either completely thrown off or blind to most advances by gay men. I believe most straight guys are gay, and when I do meet gay guys—unless they just wrapped up a production of Cats—I think they are straight. I've never been able to master my gaydar, which makes sense because I've had way more sex with heterosexual men.

I sat in my jump seat while Cloris was in the front lavatory. She gave me explicit directions, "Don't look at my man." The moment she locked the lavatory door I decided to keep at least one eye on him at all times. He knew I was watching him because whenever he looked up I'd turn my head fast. When we did make eye contact, I smiled and he refused to respond. That made me angry. I started having a five hour crush on him and daydreaming that he was my inflight boyfriend. I was no better than Cloris. I was no better than a whorish fly girl. I imagined roasting peanuts on the coffee pot hot plate for him, and using all the maxi pads in the lavatory to stitch together a perfect pair of couture slippers telling him, "Don't worry about getting your feet wet with all the piss on the floor, your slippers will soak it up." I sensed there was more queer coming off Gage than from the members of a gay marching band wrapped in rainbow flags, but that was just my inner desire. My gaydar was never accurate. He'd walk off the airplane and I'd never know if he was gay, straight. or transgender. The fact that he didn't smile back made me lean towards transgender.

Cloris and I took our seats during our final descent into Seattle and the wetter his lips got, the hotter and moister she got. I was afraid she was going to combust and all I could think was, "Where the hell is that Halon fire extinguisher?" Oh right, it's under my seat. She was hotter than the most intense girl scout campfire which made me instantly crave s'mores. It was in that instant that I smelt something odd. The faint aroma of mothballs and Earl Grey tea surrounded me so I asked, "Are you British?"

"No. Why?" She responded but continued looking at Gage.

"Just curious." I realized that Pablo wasn't the only one who smelt a simmering vagina. Had he passed that along to me so many years ago while we stood in the galley talking about his "bitches?" More importantly—was I now Puerto Rican? If so, I'd fill out the paperwork for my food stamps and cancel my car insurance the moment I got to the hotel.

"Oh my god! He is so hot. I love everything about him," she started fanning herself with her PA book, "I'm sweating so fucking bad."

I gave up worrying about her raping me with an emergency flashlight. Obviously, she'd be taking all the flightlights with her to the hotel and spend the night shooting morse code into her uterus. I had enough of this foolishness. As the airplane touched down I snapped, "Calm down. You're a fucking mess. I can smell your uterus burning all the way over here."

She laughed out loud, "Do you think he can? I hope so."

AIRLINE PASSENGER INSANITY

Flight attendants don't have the luxury of picking the passengers who travel on their flights. If we did, each seat would be occupied by someone sexy instead of asshole kids, crazy people, the elderly, or anyone requiring a wheelchair. Did I lose you at wheelchair? I apologize. There's nothing wrong with someone dependant on a wheelchair, I just don't want them on my flight. It's simply too much work. Does that make me sound like a total raging bastard? I apologize, again. I'd honestly settle for passengers who actually read their boarding passes, say please and thank you, and take their anxiety medication before they arrive at the airport. If it's the fast-acting kind, they can even take it at the gate before they walk down the jet bridge. I don't care.

Lunatics come in all shapes, sizes, colors, and religions. Even if a flight attendant makes eye contact with each passenger boarding the flight (good flight attendants always try to do that) crazy often slips by unnoticed. Not every wacky person looks like Crazy Eyes from *Orange Is the New Black*. A trip to the airport turns the calmest human being into a menace to society; a ticking time bomb waiting to explode at 38,000 feet—and always right before beverage service. Drama regularly happens once the flight attendants bring out the beverage cart. And why not? The most opportune time to start a riot on the airplane is when it's humanly impossible for the flight attendant to get away from an attacker. I probably shouldn't have said that. Forget that last sentence. I'm serious.

An airline passenger's true insanity comes to a head when they arrive at the airport. If you don't believe me just go to your local airport, find a seat, and watch the madness. Have you ever sat at the gate area and watched people swarm around waiting to board a flight? It's thrilling. The biggest problem are large families on vacation, in particular parents with their three children, carrying car seats, luggage, personal items, and diaper bags trying to go on a family vacation to Disney World. It stresses me out just thinking about it, and I don't even have to take out my liquids or remove my shoes. I've probably watched more marriages fall apart working one flight to Orlando than Dr. Phil has seen in his television career. Why do they do this to themselves? They're just asking for a horrible travel experience marked by so many failed expectations. No three year-old remembers meeting Mickey Mouse. At that age they barely remember not to shit themselves.

Human beings and chaotic airports are an emotionally toxic combination. If you've ever spent any amount of time at the airport you completely understand. My job would be easier if airports were empty. An empty airport sounds so attractive. No children yelling. No long lines for coffee. No wheelchairs running over your sore achy toes. There I go again with the fucking wheelchairs. Hopefully nobody from the ADA is reading this book. I realize a fully functioning abandoned airport is not possible but I'm taking a moment to daydream. Think about it: a deserted airport. Sounds lovely, right?

I've encountered countless stories and experiences throughout my years as a flight attendant; some my own and some shared with me on the jumpseat during long red-eye flights across the country. The idea of remembering them all is overwhelming. This book would be over 1,000 pages and there are enough ridiculous books that large (I'm talking to you, Bible). What I've retained in my memory are the experiences that I've laughed about and retold to friends over the years. The same stories that I am sharing in this book.

Like the flight I worked out of Jacksonville one morning when it was so fucking early my coffee hadn't kicked in yet. I was in the front galley preparing oatmeal for breakfast. Nothing glamorous. I wish I carried eggs and bacon around in my tote bag, but I've been known to forget to pack underwear so there's no way I'd remember scrambled eggs. We finished beverage service quickly (passengers are rarely thirsty that early in the morning) so I took the opportunity to scarf down my breakfast between call bells and questions regarding when we'd be landing and what body of water we were flying over. It's usually Lake Idontgiveafuck. The precise location of this lake is lost to me but I am certain it was named by the Native Americans.

I quietly hid in the front galley from the judgemental eyes of the passengers in the first few rows. Seems like a shady move but it's necessary. The second a flight attendant contemplates eating food, or stealing a moment for a drink of water to stay hydrated, a passenger undoubtedly requires service. It never fucking fails. It's as if they huddled together at the gate area prior to boarding to work out their game plan.

Skinny old lady in 1A: "Mildred, we need you to keep your eye on the fat bald one with glasses. The moment he attempts to drink or eat anything I need you... Mildred? Pay attention and put your croissant away. Like I was saying, when the fat bald one tries to eat, you ring that call bell."

Mildred: "What if I don't need anything?"

1A: "Doesn't matter. Your job is to ring that call bell. And Bob..."

Bob: "Yeah. Right here."

1A, "Every time he sits down you need to get up and use the bathroom. And stretch in the galley. That's extremely important. You can't stretch enough."

I began stirring my oatmeal when I heard a strange clipping sound coming from the other side of the bulkhead. The bulkhead is what separates the galley from the rest of the airplane. Snap! Crack! Pop! Sounded like someone was deep into a box of Rice Krispies. I slowly peaked around the bulkhead to see a very beautiful dark-haired women in 1E attacking her feet with toenail clippers that resembled pruning shears. How did she get that weapon through security? Not the clippers but those sharp dagger demon nails. Those toenails belonged in the National History Museum attached to a life-sized Neanderthal mannequin, not on the feet of a passenger on my flight. This lady had the thickest toenails I'd ever seen on another human being. Each time she clipped one it pinged into the air like a rocket. She was a toenail ninja and I was afraid she'd put someone's eye out, or even worse, get one of those talons in my oatmeal. If I had crunched down on anything other than my spoon she would have gotten a face full of Quaker Oats. Her discolored nail clippings flew around like confetti—great if it was New Year's Eve—but it was the middle of September and there were no balls dropping on this flight.

On a flight to an island in the Caribbean, a male passenger, probably in his early thirties, waited patiently in the back galley to use the lavatory. For reasons unknown to anyone with a functioning brain, he pulled out his dick and began pissing on the galley floor.

The flight attendant working yelled, "What are you doing?"

"I have to pee and I can't hold it," he answered calmly,

The quick thinking flight attendant pulled out the trash bin so the passenger could finish relieving himself. Anything works better than the galley floor. A full grown adult on a commercial airline yanks his dick out and pisses on the floor and thinks nothing of it. Are you kidding me? Unbelievable.

But it gets worse. I suppose urinating on the galley floor doesn't seem so bad when you compare it to the drunk guy who woke up on a red-eye flight, had to piss, and started drowning a little girl sitting next to him with urine. When the girl's father awoke from what sounded like someone treading water in the seat next to him he began screaming profanities at the urinator. That didn't make a difference. The urinator continued spraying her down like she was engulfed in flames. Splash. Tinkle. Splash. The father witnessed his daughter's first golden shower. I guarantee that dad is still in therapy. Maybe the drunk passenger was dreaming that he was a fireman? We will never know.

The bottom line is that people are fucking crazy. I struggle with them each time I approach an individual on the airplane and they leer at me like they're fighting back the urge to kick me in the head rather than place their personal carry-on item under the seat in front of them. There was a time I blamed the TSA fully for making airline passengers so obnoxious at the airport. That's until I became a flight attendant and interacted with these people on a daily basis. I'm not saying the TSA's security theatre doesn't play a considerable role in making people's lives miserable-take your shoes off, throw away your bottle of water, take off your jacket, pull out your laptop, discard your tube of toothpaste, steal your iPad-but now that I understand the airline industry, I've concluded that most of the blame falls on these crazy passengers.

There's another trigger that turns a normally laid-back person into an unmanageable mess when it comes to air travel: our mood-altering friend, alcohol. Don't act like you don't know who I'm talking about. Alcohol has been a good friend of mine since I was 16 years old. We have a love-hate relationship. Actually, now that I am older it's more of a love-hangover relationship. Alcohol is the gift that keeps on giving once the airplane has departed from the airport. What makes most people dance, sing, and have fun at their local Irish pub has more of a dark approach on people once they are intoxicated on the airplane.

One evening on a flight out of Portland, Oregon I had to remove an intoxicated passenger from the flight after she stumbled onto the airplane. She fell over her suitcase and slurred her words so badly she barely used the left side of her face. I immediately checked the manifest to confirm that Mary Jo Buttafuocco hadn't boarded. Listen, I don't mess with New Yorkers who survive a bullet to the fucking head. No way. That's just asking for trouble. My idea of living dangerously is accidently undercooking pork, not going head to head with Superman's long lost Aunt.

It wasn't Mary Jo, which bummed me out. It was, however, some cunty bitch who thought she was above the word of the flight attendant. After watching her collapse into her window seat, I decided she needed to sober up inside the airport, not inside the airplane after departure. To say she was enraged sounds childish. She made an angry caged tiger look like a hungry kitten. The first thing she did was threaten me with a lawsuit. Drunk people always want to threaten you with a lawsuit. I don't get it. They are drunk, you are sober. From my experience, it's a safe bet to say that the sober individual is in the right. Why am I even trying to rationalize the thought process of a drunk person? That's like attempting to understand a toddler throwing themselves on the ground during a temper tantrum because you didn't put the correct number of ice cubes in their sippy cup. It makes no fucking sense.

The drunk Portland lady dropped threats on me like ice in a hailstorm. She was hell-bent on tracking me down and ending my career. I stood in the aisle with my arms folded, watching security handle her like an oversized bag that needed to be checked. She slung insults my way that fell to the floor without harming me or my nicely pressed uniform. I have no memory of these insults. It's probably a good thing. No need to remember negative comments delivered by a drunk person. I have enough of those from Irene.

What I do remember her saying was, "I know the owner of this airline. Do you know him?" She looked over at me while security tended to her, "I will have your job. My husband will be calling him tonight."

My facial expressions vanished. I stood as still as stone. I figured by ignoring her I'd keep my cool and not lash out, which was the only thing I wanted to do. I refused to respond which infuriated her "Do you know who I am?" she asked.

I fought back the urge to scream, "I don't give a fuck who you are. You could be the Princess of Portland and I wouldn't give a flying fuck." I pushed that thought so far down I almost shit myself.

With airport security looming over her she had no choice but to leave. After 10 minutes of her continuous, "Do you know who I am?" and, "I will have your job for this," the security guards convinced her to either walk off the airplane or be carried out. Without another word, she stood up at her window seat and slammed the top of her head into the overhead bin. My decision to have her removed was instantly validated. That bitch was too sloshed to fly on an airplane for a five hour flight. I've learned dealing with drunk passengers is easier on the ground so security can escort them off the airplane. Once the airplane departs the only alternative to handling a disorderly drunk passenger is to divert the airplane, which is what happened during a regularly scheduled non-stop flight from Seattle, Washington to Dallas, Texas.

At one point in my flight attendant career I was given the position of conducting flight attendant checkrides. If you think that was an easy job, you are correct. It was significantly easier than lifting heavy bags, serving Diet Cokes, and dealing with asshole passengers. I am thoroughly aware that a high percentage of flight attendants fall into the asshole category, but I'd rather deal with an argumentative flight attendant any day than a self-absorbed airplane passenger. My favorite part of the job was that I got paid to fly around the country without having to wear my uniform. There I was, an average Joe, in my khaki pants and button down shirt, occupying a passenger's seat while evaluating other flight attendants to be sure they were in compliance with airline policies and procedures. It was heaven. Sure, I was deemed a traitor by a few of my peers but that had no effect on my decision to take on this responsibility. The harsh words and dreadful looks rolled off my back. I never blamed my coworkers for being abrasive towards me when I'd surprise them with a checkride. I'd hate that shit too. Part of the flight attendant culture is an us-against-them point of view. It doesn't matter whether you are a ground operations employee, a pilot, a gate agent, or a flight attendant supervisor—if you are not an active flight attendant—then you aren't with us. It's odd and childish but that's the way we come out of training. Us against everyone else.

After ending a fantastic full day of sightseeing in Seattle, I masturbated—What? I got needs— took a quick nap, showered, shaved, and hopped on the hotel shuttle van to the airport. Earlier in the week I emailed Doug, the flight attendant I'd be evaluating, letting him know to expect me in Seattle. No need for any surprises when I arrived at the gate. Sometimes I sent an email; sometimes I did not. It all depended on who I'd be completing the checkride on. Actually, there's no reason to dance around the subject, it really depended on where the flight attendant was based. This was a Miami crew which instantly brought my threat level from code orange to code red. Senior flight attendants can sometimes be super bitches and Miami was full of them. Many of the senior flight attendants at my airline are based in Miami. It's a fact you don't want to fuck with these individuals. They're ruthless and give off a tremendous amount of attitude. Enough to make reserve flight attendants cry just by looking at them. Even their supervisors are scared shitless. If one of these senior mamas happened to be in the crew lounge, you'd find most of the supervisors hiding under their desks. Think I'm joking? I'm not. I'm as serious as a red-eye boner. On their knees and under their desk. That's really not saying much though, most of the Miami flight attendant supervisor's spend their Friday and Saturday nights on their knees in the Twist parking lot. (For you straight readers, that's a gay bar in Miami Beach.) I guess they just look at it as practice for their work week. I wouldn't know. I've never been on my knees in a parking lot. I save all my knee work for the bathroom stalls inside the bar. I hate gravel.

These senior Miami bitches are crustier than the last slice of bread in the loaf. A select few would rather spit in your face than take the time to look at you. It's true. I promise you there are flight attendants from my airline reading this book on the jumpseat and laughing because they know I am talking about them. They won't even hide it. They'll happily agree and add, "He's talking about me, I just know it."

If they could bitch slap me in the face and not get terminated they would; especially when I walked up and greeted them with a friendly, "Hi, I'm Joe and I'm here to do your checkride." Because I knew that I always carried extra tissue in my pocket for the unexpected bloody nose. Well, that and the unexpected quick jerk session on a long airport layover.

When I arrived at the gate I was perkier than a set of teenage tits. Rested and ready to get to Dallas, I was eager to meet Doug and the other two flight attendants working the flight.

Doug's warmth wrapped around the gate area, "Hi Joe. Thanks for that email. I really appreciate the heads up." My smile was large enough that everyone waiting to board the flight knew I'd never had my wisdom teeth removed. He didn't have to say anything else, he basically had me at, "Hi. Joe."

Doug wasn't bad on the eyes either. Unless he generated a decompression or poisoned a passenger with expired coffee creamer, he already passed his evaluation with a rainbow of colors. Now that I think about it, all three of them were pleasant and friendly. I had never encountered that from Miami based flight attendants before. Was it a trick? A ploy to get on my good side so they'd have the chance to distract me, roofie me, and then report me to my supervisor for falling asleep on the job? Talk about being paranoid. I'd either have to stay alert during this evaluation or stop watching James Bond movies. Who am I kidding? I'd stay alert.

Our flight was booked with only 70 passengers. Simple. A great flight to complete a checkride. Enough time to talk with the flight attendants, answer all their questions, and still get all my work done before we landed in Dallas. After I introduced myself to the pilots I obtained my seat assignment from the gate agent and followed the crew to the airplane. Doug was working the mid cabin position so I happily took a seat in the empty exit row.

Stopping at row 14, I placed my bag in the overhead bin and told Doug I'd join him in the back of the airplane for the first part of the evaluation. Time went by quickly during this process. With my checklist in hand I followed him up and down the aisle watching while he completed his security checks and answered all the questions I tossed his way. He did well. I'd ask a question and then swiftly check off the coordinating box on the checklist. The position was easy enough that a lobotomy patient with permanent brain damage would ace the job.

Within minutes the passengers started to board and Doug took his place in the middle of the airplane while I quickly returned to my seat. I spread out my paperwork and laptop computer on the empty two seats marking my territory. It's like a cat marking a new piece of furniture. We've all done this when rewarded with an an entire row to ourselves.

Once airborne, I sat in my seat trying to stay undetected and keep my eyes open. My day exploring the Space Needle, Pike Place Market, and the first ever Starbucks was catching up with me. I simply wanted to land in Dallas and catch a day nap before my flight back to Cleveland. To be honest, I didn't give two shits about this checkride or any other checkride for that matter. I rarely did. But it had to be done, so on went my game face and I pushed through it. And I hate tooting my own horn but I had an unbelievable game face. I used it often. It should come as no surprise that it was also the face I used to deliver a heavy passenger their fifth bag of nuts. It was needed. I could never let a flight attendant know that I'd rather receive a prostate exam by The Hulk than spend one more second watching them pour a Sprite Zero.

I say that as if having The Hulk's finger in your ass was a bad thing. Not for many. Probably only bad for an Airbus captain. They seem to hate everything. Did you notice I didn't say first officer? You'd have to fight them off with an oxygen generator while they fought to get to the front of the line.

When we reached cruising altitude, and the seat belt sign came off, most of the 70 passengers stretched out in their rows to sleep. Damn them. Jealousy had me green with envy. Or was that the gumbo I had for lunch at Pike Place Market? No worries, I'd figure that out soon enough. I went from sleepy to exhausted in the 15 minutes it took for us to reach 38,000 feet. I surmised the barista gave me decaf instead of blonde roast. The benefits of being a Starbucks Gold Member mean nothing when you are about to fall asleep on the job. With my tray table down I dove deep into the checkride paperwork. The faster it was done the quicker I'd get back to the book nestled into my tote bag. While conducting checkrides, if we had downtime— which we always did—we were never allowed to watch television or listen to music. Basically, no earbuds in our ears. Understood. But the rules said nothing about reading a book. So that's what I always aimed for. That was my goal, to get the work done quickly so I could sit back and read my book while getting paid. Not much different than when I'm working as a flight attendant.

After a few minutes of jotting down notes on Doug, I felt the passenger sitting behind me fiddling with the back of my seat. It wasn't constant but it was noticeable. He'd grab the top of my seat and give it a strong tug backwards. What the fuck was he doing? And why the fuck was he sitting behind me? There were rows and rows of empty seats on this airplane and this dude had to sit directly behind me? I shrugged it off hoping he'd stop once situated. I didn't look back. I had no idea what he looked like. As employees of the airline, we are discouraged from confronting passengers on the airplane when we fly standby. We take our seats, shut up, and enjoy flying for free. It's really not a bad deal. The only time I struggle with that is when I am surrounded by screaming children and I can't tell them to shut the fuck up. That's painful. Even though I wasn't flying standby, I considered this to fall within the same category.

Like clockwork, the flight attendants all stepped into the aisle to start beverage service. With most passengers stretching out to take full advantage of their own row, many had fallen asleep before the flight attendants glided down the aisle like ghosts collecting drink orders. I was the first row in Doug's section. He politely stopped and greeted me, "Hello sir. May I get you something to drink?"

He was cute, "No, I'm good. I've got my own bottle of water."

Doug passed to the next row after confirming the person across from me was asleep. As soon as he was out of view, I flipped my paperwork over and went right back to checking off boxes under the service section of the checklist. I barely marked off two boxes before my ears picked up on some unfriendly banter coming from Doug and the passenger behind me. He stood firmly in the aisle and I heard him say, "Sir, I'm sorry but we charge for alcohol and headphones."

"That's bullshit. Since when?" The passenger's condescending tone instantly struck a nerve and I wasn't even the one interacting with him. I felt bad for Doug. I tried recalling any features of this guy's face but nothing surfaced. Any memory of what he looked like was lost among the distractions of conducting the evaluation.

"We've always charged for those items." Doug kept his cool. I already began noting his professionalism while managing this passenger. It was obvious this guy had been drinking well before he arrived at the airport. Doug continued, "May I get you something to drink?"

He sharply responded, "Just give me a Budweiser." Then without any reason added, "Don't be such a pussy."

At that point I found myself straining my neck to see behind my seat. It was time to put a face with this disrespectful voice. I didn't know who to expect. I sat there twisting in an extremely uncomfortable position. Honestly, I am not flexible. I can barely step out of the shower without needing two Vicodin. I blame it on my age. I was almost at the point of needing a chiropractor to get me back in alignment when Doug addressed me from above, "Can you help me with this?" He asked so the passenger heard his request and then bent down to whisper in my right ear, "He smells like a bottle of booze."

There went being incognito for the flight. As much as I didn't want to get involved, leaving Doug alone to deal with this asshole was out of the question.

"Sure." I placed my paperwork in the seat next to me and locked the tray table in place. I stood up and spun around to face the passenger seated behind me.

It was dark throughout the entire airplane so it was hard to make out his facial features. As I moved in closer his brightly lit television screen immediately gave away all his nooks, crannies, and wrinkles. He wore a dingy Dallas Cowboys baseball cap, a dark colored t-shirt, and jean shorts frayed at the bottom. I looked his ass up and down. His face was withdrawn and he had no facial hair to hide his double chin. That's chubby boy etiquette 101: always have facial hair to hide that unwanted neck skin. He looked exhausted. I'm guessing at some point he'd been dragged through a muddy swamp and left out on the river bank to dry in the sun. The best Hollywood coke addict couldn't keep up with the lines on this guys face. If humans were aged by lines—like rings around a tree—I'd guess this guy wrestled velociraptors during the late Cretaceous Period.

I bent down on one knee while he stared at me. With enough charisma to charm a snake I muttered, "Is everything alright here?"

"Who the hell are you?"

This dude was a real sweetheart. His mother must have been proud. "I'm a flight attendant at this airline. I'm doing a checkride on your flight attendant." I stated again, "Is everything alright here?" The stench of whiskey escaped his lips and caught me by surprise. Homeboy could have benefited from some Listerine UltraClean. I'd have failed a breathalyzer test from being that close to him.

"I don't care who you are," he pointed at Doug who was now standing behind me, "I'm talking to this guy."

Continuing to smile on bended knee, "I understand that, but now you are talking to me. You're raising your voice and alarming other passengers."

He looked around to see a few passengers sitting up to see what all the commotion was about. That soothed his mood for a brief second, "Listen, I just want a drink. There's no problem."

You know that instant when you can physically sense an oncoming confrontation? It happens to me often. It's a rising heat that begins at the base of your neck and progresses until it encompasses your ears. Your heart rate elevates just enough for you to realize that you are not on a treadmill at the gym but interacting with some dickhead who's got you all flustered. I guess I have way too many confrontations.

"Well, sir," I braced for his aggressive impact, "we won't be serving you any alcohol on this flight." Deep breath, "But we'll gladly get you some water." He started to grimace, which added more lines to his face. "You have the entire row to yourself. You should try and get some rest."

"I don't need any goddamn rest. I need a drink." My words fanned his flame. He looked around to catch the eye of a male passenger a few rows over, "Can you believe this bullshit? Telling me I can't have a drink." The other passenger quickly stuck his head back down behind his seat avoiding any showdown.

I touched Doug's arm and nodded for him to follow me to the back of the airplane. Erwin, one of the other flight attendants, was already on the interphone with the captain. The moment I stepped into the galley Erwin handed me the interphone.

Captain Reed asked, "What's going on?"

I briefed him on the passenger situation. I added that Doug and I were encouraging the guy to chill the fuck out and take a nap but it was going nowhere and that he was escalating the situation by raising his voice and attempting to get other passengers involved. Captain Reed suggested we move the passenger to another section of the airplane, where there were fewer passengers, and to follow up with him when we were done.

I hung up the interphone and looked up the aisle into the dark airplane, "He wants us to move the guy and see how that goes."

Erwin frowned, "That's not gonna help."

I shrugged my shoulders, "I know. Let's just move him to the back and see if he'll quiet down."

Doug and Erwin followed me to the seat leaving Stacy, the third flight attendant, in the back galley. Doug stood above me like a mountain lion preparing to pounce on a jogger while I knelt back down beside row 15. Now that I look back, I realize I was too close to this passenger. I put myself in grave danger by removing any safety barrier between me and that crazy fuck. He could have easily spit on me, or worse, done some major damage to my beautiful baby face. But I wasn't thinking about myself at the time.

Completely stupid move. It's not like the airline rewards you for getting a few teeth knocked out. The Selfless Flight Attendant Award should be handed out to all flight attendants who put themselves in harm's way for the betterment of the entire flight. Actually, that sounds more like the Dumb Ass Flight Attendant Award. Being an award whore, I'll take any award that has my name on it. Or even one that's left blank and comes with a sharpie. I'm not picky. Awards aside, I simply wanted this guy to shut the fuck up and go to sleep. If I had an industrial-sized Xanax I'd have forced it down his scratchy throat. I tried making eye contact with him but he was locked on Doug. That wasn't going to affect Doug at all. Doug was super gay and threw so much shade it took a hell of a lot more than a few dirty looks from a homeless looking guy to take him down.

"Sir, what is your name?" I asked while my two flight attendant bodyguards surrounded me.

He broke his gaze and looked at me, "Why do you want my name?"

"So that I know what to call you when we are talking to each other."

He muttered, "Melvin."

"Alright. Melvin, please grab your belongings and come with us," I got to my feet and looked at Edwin who stood in his practiced Mr. T stance ready for action.

"I'm comfortable right here. Where's my drink?"

This wasn't going to be easy.

"Melvin, why don't you come back here where it's more comfortable and then we will discuss your drink."

Surprisingly, he stood up and shuffled behind me and Doug. Edwin took up the rear making sure Melvin didn't sprint to the front of the airplane. Or try anything else stupid. Melvin dragged his feet slowly to irritate us, and as I pointed to the aisle seat in row 24, he flopped into the seat and threw his bag against the airplane window.

"There. Are you happy?"

I didn't bend down on one knee. That reminded me too much of a marriage proposal and I didn't want to think of marrying this trash bag. It was time to discuss the rules of air travel and alcohol with Melvin. I expected it to end badly.

Drinking alcohol before or during a flight can be tricky for some passengers. The air inside the airplane is dry. Add to that the diuretic effects of alcohol and you've got a passenger who becomes dehydrated, which increases their intoxication. Being dehydrated on the airplane is a serious matter. Most passengers drink when they fly so it occurs all too often. I am not saying you shouldn't enjoy an alcoholic beverage on your flight, just be responsible so I don't have to stop everything I am doing to help your drunk ass out. Eating dinner and drinking water will help the situation. Having alcoholic drinks on a flight is a luxury we have all indulged in one time or another. I love drinking bloody mary's while I'm flying. Not while I am working the flight, but traveling for leisure. I can practically hear some of you dialing the number to every airline ready to report me while flipping over to the next page. Traitors. And to think I was going to buy each and every last one of you a free cocktail the next time you were on one of my flights. Just for buying my book. I was keeping that a secret but you fucked that chance up.

Now that I think about it, an early morning bloody mary might make for a better day of dealing with neurotic people. What do you think? Someone write to the FAA and request that for me.

Because your flight attendants are responsible for the safety and wellbeing of every passenger on the flight, we have the right to stop serving alcohol anytime we feel a passenger has had enough to drink. The last thing I want is someone getting intoxicated on my flight, driving away from the airport, and killing a family of five on their way to Universal Studios. We keep track of exactly how much alcohol every passenger has on the airplane. We communicate a lot in the galley and behind the scenes regarding passengers who are drinking alcohol on the flight. And you thought we were just back there reading magazines and ignoring your call lights. Well we do that too, but we also watch you bitches like hawks. Not only are we responsible for the alcohol we sell on the airplane, we are also responsible for the alcohol the passengers bring onto the airplane. I know, it's babysitting in the air. Flight attendants should receive honorary degrees in Early Childhood Education for dealing with you people. At some airlines (check with your airline before you fly), the rule is that if you bring your own minis, small bottles of wine, or cans of beer in your carry-on bag you are allowed to drink them, but you must inform the flight attendant what you have, and for legal reasons they have to dispense it to you.

That didn't matter for Melvin because he was cut off from any alcohol no matter if he brought it or not. He'd be refused an alcohol swab for fear he'd suck it dry.

Stacy handed me a pair of plastic headphones and I stretched my arm out to Melvin, "Here's a pair of free headphones so you can watch tv." I held them out for him to grab. Getting him to settle down and watch television seemed like the easiest solution. He played around with his seatbelt and clicked it into place.

"I'd rather have my drink. Where's my drink?"

"Melvin. We won't be able to serve you anymore alcohol tonight," my palms started sweating, "so please take the headphones and get some rest."

"This is fucking *bullshit*. I wanna speak to the captain about this." He raised his voice again, "Where's the captain?"

"He's flying the airplane. Melvin, I need you to keep your voice down and get some rest. That's your only option right now." I pointed for Doug to follow me to the back galley while Edwin stood guard over Melvin.

Doug called the flight deck to brief the pilots on Melvin. I stood in the aisle between the two lavatories while Doug spoke to Captain Reed. I overheard Melvin yelling at Edwin. Edwin didn't flinch. He stood there with his arms folded looking at Melvin with a look of discontent. Why wouldn't this guy just shut up and go to sleep? Fucking with Edwin was not the smartest move. If Melvin was pleased with himself by bullying Gay Doug and Gay Joe, he had met his match with Straight Edwin.

Doug hung up the interphone and looked at me perplexed. He whispered to me and Stacy that Captain

Reed wanted us to calm the passenger down and if that didn't work he'd make the decision to divert the flight.

Calm the passenger down? What the fuck did he think we were doing? Prepping him for a midnight parade down the aisle? I silently wished not to divert. Extending our night longer than planned made going to bed seem unreachable. And think about all that fucking paperwork. You might not know this, but the main reason flight attendants encourage their passengers to behave is so we don't have to fill out paperwork. The airline demands we fill out reports for everything. If the flight diverts. If an engine falls off. If the captain drops a stink bomb in the toilet of the front lavatory and the airplane goes out of service. It's not simple paperwork either. It makes getting approved for a home loan feel like sending a tweet.

The four of us needed to settle Melvin down. That was the prime objective. With each minute that passed his voice became more boisterous. He wasn't talking to anyone in particular just yelling out for anyone who listened. Edwin, Doug, and I focused on him while Stacy took care of any call lights or passenger requests.

From the back galley I heard him barking at Edwin, "Hey. Hey. I need to speak to him. Get me the captain!"

Edwin continued standing there with his arms folded, "Dude. Settle down. You're acting crazy for no reason. Just chill."

"Don't tell me to chill. I want the captain. You can't treat me like this."

I stepped back into the aisle and walked the few steps up to row 24 and sat on the armrest across from his seat. I pleaded, "Melvin. I'm begging you. Please just lay down and get some sleep. If you continue this behavior we are going to divert the flight."

"Are you threatening me? You can't threaten me. I have rights."

It was a surprise he never attempted to get up and charge at us. I guess that was something to be happy about but this was still annoying as hell. My temper was seeping out of my pores, "It's not a threat; it's a fact. If you don't keep your voice down we're gonna divert this flight and have the authorities meet the airplane."

He was relentless, "Then divert the plane. I really don't care. I want to talk to the captain and tell him how you are treating me."

Edwin followed me as I made my way to the back galley. I was beyond furious. Melvin being noncompliant was hitting every last one of my nerves. A few passengers in the middle of the airplane started ringing their call bells out of curiosity. Stacy passed us in the aisle to answer call bells and comfort passengers. The flight being half empty helped but his voice began echoing throughout the airplane.

Edwin stepped into the galley, "I'm going to punch this fucker in the face."

I couldn't agree more but we weren't going to do that. "Just stay back here and let me and Doug deal with this guy. Call the captain and let him know what's going on."

After downing a bottle of water and composing myself I stepped back into the aisle to approach Melvin. He was twisting in his seat and feverishly waving his hands trying to catch the attention of anyone that looked his way. Stacy refused to walk past his row so she waited until Doug and I were blocking him before she slide by and back into the galley.

"Melvin," I sighed deeply, "I need you to keep your voice down. We can't have you acting like this tonight. Do you understand?"

When he responded, small splatters of saliva flew out between the space between his two front teeth, "Why are you treating me like this? I didn't do anything. I just want a drink. You can't treat me like this."

"We just want you to settle down and get some rest." Doug calmly stated.

Melvin turned to Doug, "This is all your fault. I want to speak to the captain. Bring me to the captain."

"That's not going to happen." I stepped in, "We're giving you one last chance to settle down or we are going to divert this flight."

After a slight pause it seemed our words had finally broken through his ornery disposition. Nope. Not even close. He sarcastically asked, "What if I said I was gonna take down this airplane?"

That set off the emergency brake in my head. I looked at the floor to process what he had said. And to take a few deep breaths to calm myself down before I physically attacked him. He sat there waiting for my reaction. It was hard not to give him one. I turned to my left to catch Doug's expression but he was already walking towards the back galley. He stopped and began talking to Edwin who was back on the interphone with the captain.

If Melvin wanted an emotional response to his threat he'd be waiting a while. Without saying a word, I swiftly proceeded to the back galley with the rest of the crew.

Edwin handed me the interphone as I approached and then he walked back into the aisle to keep an eye on Melvin.

I briefed the captain on the tactics we used to settle down the passenger and that our attempts were unsuccessful. I ended it by saying he threatened to take down the airplane.

"That's all I need to hear. This is a level two disturbance and we will be diverting. Let me speak to one of the working flight attendants." I handed the interphone to Doug and took a step back to settle my nerves. My fight response kicked in and I'll be honest, I wanted to beat the shit out of Melvin. I wanted to stand on his neck until he wasn't yelling anymore.

Edwin walked to the back galley with a sheet of paper and snapped me out of my daydream, "He just threw this on the floor. It's a note to the captain."

Doug took the handwritten note and read verbatim to the captain:

> Dear Captain,
>
> I am a good person. I didn't do anything wrong. Your flight attendants have verbally abused me and threatened me. All I want is a drink and they won't give me one. I am a professional and I refuse to be treated like this. I have never been treated like this in my entire life. I will have all of your jobs.
>
> Melvin Shadwick

Doug hung up the interphone without saying another word, "Oh, he's pissed."

307

I snapped a picture of the note with my cell phone. I figured it might come in handy one day. Within seconds of handing the note back to Doug, Captain Reed came over the PA in an aggressive but informative voice, "Ladies and Gentlemen. It seems that there is a passenger on our flight this evening who refuses to cooperate with our flight attendants. This has led us to make the decision to divert to Denver to allow the authorities to handle this situation. We apologize for any inconvenience this has caused but safety is our number one priority here. Thank you. Flight attendants please prepare for landing."

We heard the landing gear drop and looked at each with astonishment. The airplane descended fast which meant we were minutes from landing in Denver. Edwin started cleaning up the back galley while Stacy made her way to the front of the airplane to close up her galley. Doug walked up a few rows and asked a muscular gentlemen traveling alone to sit in the row across from Melvin to keep an eye on him. I stopped to make sure Melvin's seatbelt was fastened.

He looked confused. His aggression and anger subsided. Now he looked like he was about to be grounded, "Listen man, I won't say anything else for the rest of the flight."

"Too late, Mel. We're landing," I stepped out of the way to allow our muscular passenger access to his seat across from Melvin. The big beefy guy looked happy to assist. We reminded him to simply watch that Melvin didn't get up once we landed, not to crush his ribcage just for the fun of it. Although I figured that might be enjoyable for everyone, everyone except Melvin.

Once we landed and blocked in at the gate everything happened in a flash. The bright airplane lights illuminated, the door opened, the FBI boarded, and swept down the aisle rushing up to Melvin like he had explosives attached to his chest. Nobody moved a muscle. The tension so intense I was afraid to fart. The passengers sat like statues until the FBI agents passed their row and then they spun around to catch a glimpse of the live action unfolding. Nothing was audible from my seat but actions speak louder than words. Stretching my neck to watch, I witnessed four FBI agents physically remove Melvin from his seat and march him down the aisle and off the airplane in less than two minutes.

I guess we really were preparing him for a parade down the aisle.

After Melvin deplaned a few more FBI agents came onboard to debrief with the crew on what exactly occurred between Seattle and Denver. The entire event took less than an hour and when Stacy finally closed the airplane door in Denver-sans Melvin-the passengers erupted in applause. No one complained or expressed frustration for the diversion. The passengers who didn't immediately fall back to sleep commended the flight attendants on a job well done.

After we reached cruising altitude, I finished Doug's evaluation and invited him to sit down next to me and review what I had written.

How can you give a flight attendant anything less than a stellar review after dealing with a passenger like that? You don't. Doug received a perfect score. As I closed up his folder and placed it in my laptop bag, I reminded him to fill out an incident report once he was back in Miami.

He frowned, "I hate filling out incident reports."

I zipped up my laptop bag and stuffed it under the seat and smiled, "Don't we all."

KIDS ARE ASSHOLES

Kids are assholes. I could end the chapter with those three words and move on to the next, but I feel the pressure to explain myself and provide a solid example of why I feel this way. While I'm at it, I might as well confess that I fully endorse abortions. I think abortions should be provided free to mothers well passed the child's birth. I'm thinking up until they know their alphabet.

As a child, I was personally touched by an abortion. Irene had an abortion when I was two years old. Once I found out what an abortion was and how a simple vacuum hose impacted my life, I became ecstatic. You might say it was a surprise gift I didn't have to wait until Christmas to open. And honestly, I would have hated sharing my toys with a sibling. Thankfully for me and you (the reader), she murdered my baby sister instead. I was simply the lucky fetus. I know for a fact the idea of terminating my life crossed her mind while I resided in her uterus. Whenever I did something childlike and stupid-like spilling milk on the counter or forgetting to flush the toilet-she'd retell the story about how when she worked for a grocery store she'd spend her lunch breaks smoking cigarettes and slamming heavy boxes of canned food against her pregnant belly. I doubt she was just checking to see if I'd answer. No worries. This solidifies how stubborn I truly am. I refused to allow her—or a few cases of canned fruit— the power to keep me from writing this book.

All jokes aside, when I became an adult I felt bad for Irene. I guarantee she regretted telling me about her abortion. And that she continued trying to kill me when I was the size of a lemon. Who tells their 10 year old son they had an unborn baby ripped from their womb? And that it was a little girl? And that it was the biggest mistake of their life? And that if she had her way she'd have had two abortions under her belt? Once I comprehended what that meant I figured she worked for a therapist who planned on having me on a sofa from the age of 10 until I was placed in a nursing home. Even though I pitied her, I managed to use the abortion against her whenever the chance presented itself.

"Joe. I hope you are brushing your teeth and getting ready for bed."

"Yeah. I'm all done. You know who isn't brushing their teeth and getting ready for bed? My baby sister. Why? Because you killed her."

It makes sense why strangers stopped her in the grocery store and told her I resembled Damien Thorn from *The Omen*. Not only did I look like the Antichrist, I made jokes about dead fetuses.

No doubt you think I am a heathen for this confession. I probably am. Who jokes about abortions? Damien the Omen does, that's who. And anyone who's had their little soft fontanelles repeatedly bashed in by cans of fruit cocktail. I may jest about abortions but at least I've never had one. That's got to be a testament to my character, right?

Is it better to joke about an abortion or have one? I knew someone in high school who had so many abortions she had a Planned Parenthood Club Card. Apparently, she thought having a dilation and curettage (D&C) after an abortion was easier than carrying condoms around in her purse. Who fucking knows… I'll never understand teachers.

My hope for more abortions doesn't vanish once I step onto the airplane-it intensifies. When I hear a toddler on an airplane screaming like a pterodactyl I wonder why its parents didn't go the abort route. It must be easier than raising them and dealing with dirty diapers. It's definitely cheaper. How much is an abortion? $500? That's way easier on your wallet then paying for college. Can't afford the abortion costs? No problem—DIY. An at home abortion can't be that difficult. Maybe a little messy but nothing that some Clorox and Brawny can't clean up.

My flight attendant manual explains step by step how to deliver a baby but there isn't a word in there about how to abort a fetus (I'm pretty smart so I could figure it out). Completing a successful mid flight abortion is probably easier than getting most passengers to put their carry-on bags under the seat in front of them. What does one need for an abortion at 38,000 feet? Hot water, a wire hanger (sorry Joan Crawford, but sometimes ya need one), a few on board blankets, and a few shots of vodka. The vodka being for me. I need as much alcohol as I can get before I get close to a swollen vagina. Even though I have never been faced with the task of performing an abortion on a flight, I am prepared. I am an abortion flight attendant Boy Scout. I even carry a wire hanger in my tote bag in case I need to perform an emergency abortion on a flight.

"Hi. May I get you something to drink?"

"I'll have water. I'm pregnant."

"Oh you are…" Looking around to be sure nobody is listening, "Want to meet me in row 30? I've got a rusty hanger with your name on it."

I have gotten way off track. Let me start over.

Kids are assholes. It is a fact. I am sure at one point in your life you have agreed that the kid sitting next to you was a complete asshole. Maybe it was at the grocery store, or Toys R Us, but most definitely on the airplane. Passengers become so furious over screaming kids on their flights they'd probably slip money into my apron pocket if I actually did conduct abortions in the back galley. What a great way to make tip money for the van drivers.

That's the last of the abortion talk. I promise to speak to my therapist about all this at my next appointment.

As surprising as this may sound I do not hate children. I do not love them, either. Let's just say I like kids enough not to drop them into a pit filled with hungry Catholic priests. However, dangling them upside down and naked over the edge for a few hours sounds entertaining. I love watching priests foam at the mouth.

On a late summer afternoon a few years ago, I found myself commuting from JFK to Orlando on a crowded and chaotic flight. What am I saying? I've already established that all Orlando flights are crowded and chaotic. The only place you will find more chaos is on a Martin Luther King Blvd after a shooting. With all the luggage, strollers, and families surrounding the gate in Orlando, I couldn't help but fear that I'd be sitting on the jump seat the entire way home.

After waiting for what seemed like an hour, the gate agent called my name to the gate. I think she called my name. She could have been yelling out the lunch specials from the airport Panda Express. She was Asian so I honestly don't know. When I approached the counter she handed me a boarding pass for seat 3F. This pleasantly surprised me because it was a window seat located in the front of the airplane. She scanned my boarding pass and I swiftly made my way down the jet bridge and onto the airplane.

I introduced myself to the flight attendant, took my perfect window seat, and started settling in for the flight. This was smoother than I expected. After I pushed my tote bag under the seat in front of me I looked up to notice a guy walking onto the airplane. He was young, handsome, and dressed in a dark blue polo and tight fitting jeans. He wore the kind of jeans that lay everything out for you like Google Maps. The best part was he stopped at my row. This Orlando flight was getting better by the second and now I had entertainment to occupy my time. Much better entertainment than my laptop and the article I was writing for my blog. He reached down to pick up his bag and hoisted it over his head with one quick swoop. Big dick. Big muscles. Slim waist. I hit the nonrev jackpot. Just as I started fantasizing about causing so much commotion that security might greet us when we landed, he looked at me, smiled, and said, "We're sorry."

What was he sorry for? The fact that he had a shirt on. And who's we? Was he talking about the snake that he smuggled through security in his jeans? I hope he named it because if not, I did. Anaconda and I would be sexting pals by the end of the flight.

"Hi," I smiled, "Sorry about what?"

No sooner did the words escape my lips did his mini-me dart from around the corner and propel himself onto the middle seat. It startled me to the point that I yelled out and almost slapped the kid. I went from semi-hard to flaccid quicker than elbow macaroni in hot boiling water.

"Sit still, Jacob. Let daddy put your stuff away," he softly said to his son who, if I had to guess, was around three years old. Why was this happening on my perfect flight? I'm no stranger to being cockblocked, but never has it been by someone whose balls hadn't dropped yet. The possibility of the handsome father sitting in the middle seat and leaving Jacob to fend for himself on the aisle was a long shot but I refused to give up hope. I silently prayed for the solo father to buckle the little fucker into the aisle seat and sandwich himself between us.

That did not happen. First Reeta and now Jacob... I hate airplanes with a middle seat. Once the hot dad finished moving their bags around in the overhead bin he sat down in the aisle seat and began pulling toys out of another bag. Within seconds Jacob began jumping up and down on the seat like Tom Cruise. Someone needed to tell this asshole that this was an airplane and not a sofa at Harpo Studios. Did I look like Oprah? Nobody answer that. While he assaulted his seat like a Scientologist attacks an apostate he continued crying, "I want window."

I ignored him like I do the homeless in New York City. Was he howling at me or his father? I hoped it wasn't at me. The only way I was moving out of this window seat was if it was down the emergency slide. Jacob was here to test my patience. It was obvious. Unfortunately for him, I'd exhausted all my patience during the van ride on the Van Wyck heading to JFK. This was the first time I ever wished that every passenger on the airplane was a raging Christian and that the rapture sucked them all up into the abyss. Or heaven. Wherever. It doesn't matter as long as they were all off my flight. Well, except the pilots. Someone needed to fly me to safety. But who am I kidding? Pilots may be dogs but they aren't going to heaven.

While passengers continued down the aisle I stared out the window wishing Jacob gone. If only he was small enough to be forced back into his mother's womb; I'd gladly be first in line to start pushing. With his father paying no attention to him, he slipped his sneakers off and threw them on the floor. Thud. Thud. The kid was fast. Not as fast as a Las Vegas hooker picking up a John on a 38 minute flight, but pretty damn close. I didn't trust him or his pathetic father. The burning sexual desire I had for him was lost due to his bad parenting skills, and the outline in his jeans—that would make Ron Jeremy jealous—didn't seem to matter anymore. He had the brain of a goldfish. The mastermind and brains behind the entire operation belonged to a three year old. I kept my left eye on him and his father and my right out the window. Without looking away from his cell phone, the dad immediately picked up the shoes and handed them back to Jacob.

"Put your shoes back on. Please be a good boy for daddy." He said while staring at his phone. The shoes were back on the floor before he finished the sentence.

I had to hand it to this kid; he had his dad wrapped around his peanut butter sticky fingers. Jacob needed medication, something strong, like Propofol. If I had a moment alone with him I would have crushed up one of my Vicodin tablets and sprinkled it into his sippy cup. I'm glad I didn't, I'd surely be popping them like tic tacs before the flight was over. Jacob was a F4 tornado that could easily sweep us all off to Oz. One look at him and The Wicked Witch of the West would have doused herself in water just to escape. I turned my head looking over at him and noticed cracker crumbs all over the place. Not just the floor but his seat and the edge of my seat. The sad part was he hadn't eaten. He hadn't put anything in his mouth except for his nasty brat fingers. Do kids just exfoliate crumbs from their dirty little bodies?

It didn't stop with the crumbs and the screaming. His dad was pulling out every toy from their magical tote bag all while staring at his cell phone. After pulling out a few coloring books, alphabet blocks, and a G.I. Joe figure, a red stuffed lobster was yanked out and placed on the seat.

When he saw the lobster his breathing increased. So did his bouncing. Snotty mucus flew out of his nose and landed on the already stained carpet. Was that a toy orgasm? Not the same toy orgasm that I'm used to, but close enough. He orgasmed over a red fucking lobster. Are you kidding me? And I witnessed the entire thing at my seat. Well, better me than Jared Fogle. Jacob grabbed the red lobster and decided it was time to involve me in his chaotic life. Like him being on the same airplane next to me wasn't enough. With his little fat arm he flailed that red fucking lobster around his head and in front of my television interrupting my *Will & Grace* marathon on TBS. The two of them must have thought I enjoyed sitting in my comfortable airplane seat, with my earbuds packed into my ears, staring at the television with no desire to actually watch the program on the screen in front of me. I imagined turning to the two of them and blurting out, "I'd much rather watch your kid play airplane with his fake dirty lobster doll than watch Karen Walker mix amphetamines with a gin martini and insult Grace's small tits."

I really needed that martini.

Just to be clear, all this shit occurred before we took off.

After take off the altitude made his crazy intensify. On his back, with his feet against the tray table, he kicked and stomped the seat in front of him like the Tazmanian Devil. I patiently waited for the passenger seated directly in front of him to confront the dad about his kid's behavior, but of course he stayed silent. People never speak up when there's good cause. I had damn good cause to say something but I was flying standby, which meant I couldn't indulge in any confrontations with other passengers. Jacob thrashed around like a seizure patient. I didn't know whether to hold his tongue down with a spoon or just shove that fucking lobster down his throat.

Father of the Year barely said anything. When he did speak all he said was, "Honey, don't do that." That's it. That's all he managed to say throughout most of the flight. He could have recorded those exact words, left the recorder on the aisle seat, and disappeared. Where's the parenting in that? Other than those four words, he remained stationary like he was recovering from spinal surgery. I fought the urge to lean forward, tap his shoulder, and tell him to man up and control his child. Why are parents afraid to beat their kids in public? There's nothing wrong with threatening and beating the shit out of your kids if they're acting like assholes. Don't want to beat them in public? Fine. Forget doing it in public. Take them by the arm, go into the airplane lavatory, and don't come out until they are begging for forgiveness. Personally, I'm all about threatening. If I had kids, they'd think their father was Tony Soprano. A little discipline helps these asshole kids not grow up into asshole adults. We have enough asshole adults. Members of the KKK. The entire Westboro Baptist Church congregation. Donald Trump supporters. Trust me, we have enough assholes to last us until we colonize Mars. We don't need any more. As a child, if I even glanced at Irene cross-eyed while at the grocery store, she dropped whatever she was doing, dragged me to the car, and spanked my ass until you could fry an egg on it.

This little rugrat thrashed around the seat for the entire two hour flight. How he didn't run out of energy—or just die—was a mystery. Why wasn't the father more alert to his child's needs? Jacob required more attention than a brand new puppy. No wonder his mother was nowhere to be found. I'd have abandoned the two of them too. If Jacob continued with that behavior he'd soon find himself motherless, fatherless, and selling his ass for crack in West Hollywood. He was a psycho who frightened the likes of Norman Bates. I will admit that I know nothing about raising a child. What I do know is that I had a real life Chucky doll occupying the seat next to me.

As our flight approached Orlando to land, he was literally hanging all over me trying to look out the window. The thought never crossed my mind to switch seats with him. Obviously the nice thing to do. Unfortunately, I'm not that nice. I watched television wishing him to sit down and stop kicking my leg. After the kind of assault my left leg had endured I'd need a wheelchair to take me off the flight. He walloped against me like I was filled with candy and this was his birthday party.

"I want window! I want wiiiiiinnnnn-ddddddooooooooooow!"

I closed the shade. Fuck you, Jacob. If I can't have peace and quiet you can't have the window. You can't even look out and see the clouds. Dick.

I looked over at the father at least 10 times throughout the flight and he never made eye contact with me. Not once. I thought about nudging my left elbow into Jacob's throat to calm him down but I'd no doubt press too hard. I am sure of it. That kid deserved to be locked up in a basement until his 18th birthday. After all these years I finally sympathized with the mother from *Flowers In The Attic*. It should have been called *Assholes In The Attic*. As I sat there wishing for him to hurry up and become an adult, or even better—just fall the fuck asleep—I had a memory of working a trip with an incredible flight attendant.

I was scheduled for a three day trip and had the pleasure of working with Regal, a fantastic woman who always laughed at my jokes. Even the not-so-funny ones. I've learned when a person laughs at your jokes, they're a keeper. You make them your friend. Or your spouse. That answers the age old question of why ugly, fat comedians have drop dead gorgeous wives-it's all about the laughter. Regal reiterated how wonderful and fabulous I was each time she saw me. That made me like her even more.

The two of us had been flying all day. We were exhausted and counting down the minutes until our flight from Nashville to Orlando landed. It was an Orlando flight so it was jam-packed with kids. So many it seemed that parents were bringing them on the airplane as carry-on luggage. Our trip occurred on a smaller airplane with no third flight attendant. In the middle of beverage service, I walked down the aisle with two bottles of wine for a passenger in my section when I became distracted by a female voice projecting over the back of her seat to the row behind her. Her voice echoed the sound of someone who had just finished off a carton of Camel cigarettes; I immediately questioned why she was on an Orlando flight and not on her way to West Palm Beach. There had to be a breathing treatment awaiting her in Boca. I stopped at the row to see what the fuss was about. I am nosey, and on my airplane I am the only bitch who yells. With a disgusted look on her face and a hairdo that most likely cost $4.99 at Supercuts, Bertha turned around in her seat and verbally attacked the male passenger traveling with his wife and small child.

"Can you please do something about your kid?"

"What do you mean?" The father in the middle seat questioned regarding his daughter who sat directly behind her.

Bertha yelled, "She's been kicking my seat since we took off. Do something about it."

I monitored their conversation, I decided not to get involved unless the confrontation escalated. From past experiences, I know there's nothing worse than sitting in front of a child who spends hours kicking the back of your seat, but even this lady was out of line. From where I stood, the little girl's legs were inches away from reaching the seat.

He calmly said, "I had no idea. You could ask me in a nicer tone."

"This is my nice tone!" She answered abruptly and turned back to the book she was reading.

I made eye contact with the father and smiled; he did not. His anger wasn't directed at me, that I knew for sure, but I sensed he wanted to wrap his hands around Bertha's throat until she stopped breathing. To be honest—she had it coming. I continued tending to my passengers for the rest of the flight while keeping a close eye on Bertha, making sure she wasn't gagging on her copy of *The Shack* each time I walked by.

After we landed and blocked in at the gate, I stood in the front galley thanking everyone as they walked off the airplane. The father made his way up the aisle with his wife and daughter and I thanked him. He smirked. They walked off the airplane and onto the jet bridge just as the ground operations employee brought up their stroller. While the wife took the bags and continued up the jet bridge into the terminal, the father tended to his daughter and her stroller. Bertha walked passed me but I rejected her eye contact making it look like something caught my attention in the middle of the airplane. She looked like a Shar Pei and was bigger than I first thought. When she stepped onto the jet bridge it went down a good three inches. I laughed.

One thing about Bertha was she didn't know when to leave well enough alone. Fat, stupid, and dined on kibble. That's Nashville for you. She waddled right up to the father as he bent over strapping his daughter into her stroller, "You need to learn how to discipline your child,"

He continued fidgeting, ignoring her comment. It seemed as if he was taking the high road. Not what I would have done, but kudos to him for not being vulgar and crass like me.

Not so much. Apparently, he was my long lost twin.

He snapped up from his position and unleashed on her, "Mind your fucking business, bitch!" His voice roared through the jet bridge and right into his daughter's ears. Definitely poor parenting but I'm excited thinking about her busting out the word *fuck* on her first day of kindergarten.

Bertha stood there in shock. Actually, it might have been a brain bleed from her head exploding. I am not a doctor so I do not know. Just to be safe I grabbed for the AED but then turned back to the scene and said fuck it. My fear was she'd go into cardiac arrest and fall over, bringing the entire jet bridge crashing to the ground-another reason to dislike Bertha. The dad grabbed the stroller handles and pushed his kid up the jet bridge ending the conversation. Bertha didn't respond. She had no words. He sucked the alphabet right out of her meaty esophagus. As Regal and I collected our bags and walked off the airplane we had to jump over her jaw. She still hadn't picked it up. It was a fat jaw.

The next morning was a repeat of the night before. Regal and I boarded so many asshole kids you'd think we were heading to Sudan to marry them off. Anarchy at 38,000 feet. Rambunctious children and their overstressed parents up in the aisle before we even started beverage service. Rocking their annoying brats and breastfeeding in my galley while I attempted to pour the old lady in 2B some decaf coffee. Out of control. Regal came to the front of the airplane to grab something and I took it as an invite to bitch about all the kids on the flight.

"There are only 100 seats on the airplane so how could there be 1,000 kids?"

Regal placed her hand on my shoulder and encouraged me to take a deep breath. She shared, "I was flying with my mother a few months ago and I thought I was prepared bringing my son with us. I was wrong. We brought everything on the flight. Toys, books, crayons, food…"

"Sleeping pills?"

"No," she thought for a moment, "but that's a great idea." Smiling she continued, "We brought everything else. He wouldn't sit still or stop crying. I was up in the back galley asking for juice, milk, anything to shut him up. He was a lunatic."

"Really? You couldn't control him."

"He was like a different kid. I was so embarrassed. He didn't stop crying until we landed."

I thought about that for a minute. If a trained flight attendant was unable to manage her own child on a two hour flight, how could we expect a novice airline passenger to do it? Was that asking too much? Then I remembered Bertha. She was tough on that father and all he was doing was taking care of his kid and keeping her quiet on the flight, which he did with great success. I stand by my belief that the little girl's legs were too short to kick Bertha's seat. Bertha was just a cranky mean bitch. I did not want to be a Bertha. Even Bertha doesn't want to be a Bertha.

That memory was lost until I found myself sitting next to Jacob on the flight to Orlando contemplating whether to smother him with his red lobster or let him live to see elementary school. I held a grudge against Jacob for simply breathing. But let's face it: he's a kid and even though kids are assholes, I'm an adult and needed to act the part. I shifted my anger and frustration from Jacob's bad behavior to how his father must be feeling. Would I ignore my child if he was an asshole? No. I'd beat the hell out of him. But Jacob's father felt the best way to handle him was to ignore him. Not the way I'd do things, but who am I to judge? Another reason why I don't have children and the universe gave me a dick instead of a uterus.

Everything became crystal clear: I couldn't be a Bertha to this dad or his son. I felt bad for the father and instantly wanted his big dick again. I may have ADHD.

While these thoughts played out in my head, Jacob continued carrying on like an asshole. No question about it. He was practically in my lap trying to open the window shade while his father played some random game on his iPhone. After I finally came to terms with Jacob, and stopped daydreaming about his demise, I carefully nudged him back into his seat. Why wasn't his seatbelt on?

Removing my earbuds I waved over to the dad and caught his attention. "He should really be wearing his seat belt."

He peeled his eyes off the iPhone and looked over at me flustered like I was employed by Child Protective Services, "Oh... right. He must have unbuckled it." He nestled the cell phone between his thighs and under his huge bulging ball sac and pushed Jacob down in his seat, "Enough young man. You've been harassing this guy the entire flight."

Oh. So he was aware of the hell his seed had put me through for the past two hours. Interesting.

"I want window. Daddy, now!"

"No. Sit there and behave."

During their back and forth argument Jacob tossed his stuffed red lobster in the air and it landed in the row in front of us. Without hesitation, the passenger—who had endured Jacob kicking and pushing on his seat throughout the entire flight—tossed it right back. He was done with Jacob, too.

While Jacob and his dad wrestled to get the seat belt fastened I became caught in the crossfire. "Do you have any kids?" He asked me as he finally pinned Jacob down by the throat (I knew that's how it was done) and fastened his seat belt. He was sweating. That made him even hotter.

I laughed, "No sir."

"You are smarter than I am."

No six words were ever truer.

THE STRANGE
ARTICHOKE LADY

On a crisp San Francisco morning in the middle of August, Matt dropped me off at the airport to catch an early flight to Omaha, Nebraska. Before I go any further I know exactly what you are thinking: Why the fuck visit Omaha? And on purpose? I've asked myself that same question. Was it the rich culture? The love of a great Richard Marx's song? (If you don't know the song "Hazard" from 1992, you are dead to me.) The hopes of obtaining a low interest rate loan from Warren Buffett?

A lube optional bareback cornhole party? Not exactly, but pretty damn close. What brought me to Omaha was a friend's wedding. A gay wedding. A gay wedding taking place across the state line in Iowa. Let that sentence sink in for a few seconds. Go ahead. Take your time. Still confused? A Democrat might explain it as two loving and consenting adults—who just happen to live in the midwest—experiencing the joy of matrimony. A Republican might explain it as a two-homosexual-cornholing-dudes-burning-in-hell wedding. That pretty much clears it up on both sides of the argument. But let's get to the big question, the one we are all asking, or at least the one I asked when I received the invitation in the mail. Was it legal for two homosexuals to get married in Iowa?[2] It's so far-fetched I checked Wikipedia to make sure gay marriage was legal before I started looking up flights. To my surprise, it's as legal as buying marijuana in Denver. That was a relief. I had accidently thrown away their wedding gift receipt.

Let me correct myself before I get gay bashed walking out of a hotel one day by another gay. Many like calling it same-sex marriage. An even better term is simply, marriage. No need to add anything to it. But for the sake of this story, I'll refer to it as same-sex marriage. Like I was saying, same-sex marriage in the Midwest? How the fuck did that happen? A better question might be, how had the world— or at least that region of the United States—not collapse into the depths of hell?

According to many radical Christians, Jesus is super-duper fucking pissed-off about marriage equality. Apparently, he's so upset that he will be returning to Earth at any minute. Any fucking minute! You might think that's UPS knocking at your front door with your Amazon package but nope… it's gonna be Jesus Christ. If you were raised Catholic like I was, you've been hearing that shit since the first time you were forced to admit to your sins.

"Jesus is coming! Jesus is coming!" He's been coming for so long I think the correct term is edging. "Jesus is edging! Jesus is edging!" Sounds way more accurate. My grandmother bleached her sheets in preparation of Jesus coming. She was one of them crazy Catholics. I find it

---

[2] As of June 26, 2015, same-sex marriage was legalized in the entire United States. Take that, bigots!

better to wash your sheets *after* someone came, not before. Shows you how much I know about preparing for the rapture. According to my grandmother, the only thing that stood between her and a ticket to heaven was a set of crusty sheets.

Humanity has gone through quite a few gruesome events in our history. The Holocaust. Donald Trump running for President of the United States. The time I shit myself at a gay bar after a night of hot wings, beer, and shots of Jägermeister. None of those atrocities matter to the crazy Christians. Well, unless a crazy gay Christian cleaned up the disaster I left behind in the restroom stall. What if it was Keegan? That would explain a lot.

The only event these so-called Christians focus on, when it comes to Jesus, is same-sex marriage. According to them, same-sex marriage has pissed off Jesus enough to bring him back to Earth triggering Armageddon. Can that be right? Not the six million Jews exterminated by the Nazis? Nope. Not bad enough. It's same-sex marriage that has infuriated Jesus enough to throw up his hands and call foul on the people of Earth.

I need to hurry up and move to Mars.

But what if Jesus Christ has already returned? What if he's masking his identity for fear of being turned into a human scarecrow again? I'd hide for sure. How many holes can one person take in their hands before they're forced to work as a sous chef draining vegetables? If you don't think it's possible he's already returned, just take a look at psycho David Koresh. Remember him? From Wacko, Texas. I misspelled that on purpose. Waco. Wacko. What's the difference? He even looked like Jesus. Not Middle Eastern

Jesus but long-haired whitey Jesus. The Jesus my grandmother cleaned her sheets for.

In all honesty, Mr. Koresh—aka Texas Jesus—never claimed to be Jesus Christ. What he claimed was to be the final prophet. And that he was the son of God. I don't know about you but if it walks and talks like the son of God-it's probably just some crazy person. Along with the gazillion Christians in the United States, the FBI did not give a fuck. Prophet Schmophet. What did the FBI do to him? Kaboom! Set him and his followers ablaze. Scorched them to the ground like they were at Burning Man. *Prophet on Fire*. If only Alicia Keys was around to record such a hit I'd have run to Peaches for that CD. Poor David. Poor Jesus. I can't imagine what's worse: crisping up like a charred marshmallow or hanging in the hot sun for a few days? All I'm saying is that if I was the Lord & Savior and returned to this fucked up planet, I'd be hiding out working in the shoe department at Lord & Taylor in case I slipped up.

Jesus Christ: "Don't hesitate young man. You should purchase these shoes."

Customer: "Do you really think so?"

JC: "Yes. For I am your Lord & Savior."

Customer: "What?"

JC: "Um. Yes you should. For I work at Lord & Taylor."

But back to same-sex marriage. How many evangelical Christians do you think we lost when Iowa declared it was unconstitutional to deny two loving adults the opportunity to marry? Did these righteous individuals crumble in the streets dying of heart attacks as hundreds of gays skipped down the streets of Des Moines, Iowa with rainbow glitter flying out of their asses? If not dead in the streets then certainly barricaded in their basements waiting for the mall to close so Jesus could wrap up his shift and save them.

Now that that's off my chest I can move forward with the scene that developed during the second leg of my flight from San Francisco to Omaha, the Denver to Omaha leg. Flying free on another airline is fantastic, but traveling standby often leaves you-or specifically me-with a shitty seat. Or a shitty boarding pass number depending on the airline I'm flying. When I fly on airlines with open seating it's always a disappointment. I am thrilled to get on the flight but know that my ass will be in a middle seat. Sandwiched between two strangers who I'll never want to see again. It's inevitable.

When I grab my boarding pass from the gate agent and read it out loud I feel like an elderly lady calling bingo numbers in a church basement, "C59. I'm the last to walk on the airplane. Bingo!"

I boarded the flight and instantly started scanning the rows while walking down the aisle. Carefully looking at each empty middle seat—that's all that was left—I tried determining who I'd want to crawl over in case the airplane became engulfed in flames. There wasn't a single person worthy of spending the next four hours fighting over an armrest with or having to straddle each time I had to get up use the lavatory. I reached the second to last available middle seat and decided it was time to man up and deal with the consequences. The seat was nestled between a large white woman and a fit black lady. The hefty white woman was seated in the aisle so I concluded I'd die attempting to climb over her thighs in the event we landed in pieces on the runway. "Man up, Joe," I kept telling myself, "Man the fuck up! You can't always have the perfect seat on the perfect flight. Remember, you didn't even pay for this fucking ticket."

A reality check can do wonders in that type of situation.

Looking crisp and professional in my flight attendant uniform, I made eye contact with the white lady on the aisle, smiled, and placed my luggage in the overhead bin.

"Excuse me, is anyone sitting between you?" I asked closing the overhead bin.

"It's empty." She answered moving her copy of *Dear John* by Nicholas Sparks, a Bible, and an overstuffed Burger King bag from the seat. The smell of her french fries would be the death of me. So would her Bible if she started preaching. "You know what," she said out loud, "let me give you the aisle seat and I will sit by Loretta." She pushed up the armrest, unbuckled her seat belt, and shimmied her ham cheeks over into the middle seat. As she pushed Loretta up against the window, Loretta pursed up her lips and gave me a look as if to say, "Bitch! You white fuckers won't let a black woman have nothing!"

"Thank you very much." I waited for her to get all the way into the middle seat when I realized she was already as far over as she was going to get. No way was her ass fitting on just one seat; that reminded me of attempting to stuff Shamu into a fish bowl. Hopefully, Loretta had some butter or Crisco in her carry-on (you know, in case she wanted to fry up some chicken in the galley mid flight) but the way she stared me down, I lost all hope for buttermilk chicken.

I knew any possible friendship with Loretta was over the moment her left arm became disabled and crushed by the weight of her caucasian friend. She hadn't even had the opportunity to fall in love with me like most black women do.

"Lord in heaven, this thingamajig ain't working," my seatmate stated while attempting to pull the armrest down after it became stuck on one of her belly rolls.

I smiled, "It's alright. This will be fine."

Before I had time to secure my seat belt she looked over, "My name is Sandy. As you probably guessed, this is Loretta. We work together. It's been a long time. How many years has it been, Loretta?"

Loretta bitterly answered, "It's been a long time. "

Sandy continued, "That's true. It's been a long time. We've been in Denver for work." I looked over at Loretta and smiled. She gave me so much shade I thought the sun went down.

"Nice to meet you ladies. My name is Joe." I pulled out my cell phone to text Matt informing him I made the flight. I will be polite to anyone who is polite to me but I wasn't looking to make a new friend, especially with Sandy. Loretta maybe, but that's because I still had my heart set on some Southern fried foods from the back galley.

Sandy immediately invaded my space. She leaned over and watched every word I typed into my cell phone. My first reaction was to type, "the bag is onboard and activated," but no need to involve the FBI on a silly prank just to scare the french fries out of Sandy. Now that I remember back, maybe she wasn't invading my space as much as just sitting in her seat and leaking out into any additional open space.

Sandy hounded me like a timeshare salesman the moment I slide my cell phone back into my front pocket. "What airline do you work for? Are you a pilot?"

"No. I'm a flight attendant."

"That's nice. A male flight attendant. I didn't realize there were male flight attendants." What the hell did that mean? If I didn't know better I would have sworn Loretta was smirking. The flight attendants hadn't yet begun their safety demonstration and I was ready to spend the next few hours sitting in the lavatory.

"Why are you going to Omaha? Are you from Omaha?"

"I'm going to a wedding in Iowa." I patiently waited for her to ask about the bride and groom so I'd have the chance to end our conversation as fast as it started. I figured by spilling the details of the wedding and the fact about the participants honeymooning for a week in Sodom, she'd spend the rest of the flight with her head in the Burger King bag reciting Leviticus 20:13. For you heathens, that's the kill-the-gays part of the bible.

No luck. Sandy wasn't interested in the wedding, she was just interested in interviewing me, "Where do you live?"

"I live in California."

"I've never been to California. Do you need a ride from the airport?"

Was she serious? I feared the invitation included a ride from inside her trunk. "No. I have a friend picking me up." At that point I stopped looking at her. I focused on the big breasted flight attendant trying to fit the life vest over her helmet hairdo.

Once the safety demonstration was done, the flight attendant made her way down the aisle. As she approached the row I pulled out my crew ID attempting to introduce myself, but she continued on without saying a word. Did she even see me? I couldn't decide if it was her Texas-sized tits that kept her from making eye contact with me or just her Texas-sized bitchy attitude but I barely got a nod as she paraded by me with a painted on smile.

I had hoped Sandy lost interest in me, but who was I kidding? "She didn't seem to notice you're here."

Pulling a book out of my tote bag I placed it in the seatback pocket, "Yeah. I should have brought chocolates."

Sandy snapped her head around while stuffing a fistfull of french fries in her mouth. The aroma from the crispy french fries made my stomach roar. She questioned, "You pay them in chocolate? I need your job."

If I had chocolates I'd toss them at her to shut her up so I could read my book in peace. Loretta hadn't made eye contact with me since our initial interaction and now I could understand why she wanted an empty seat between the two of them. I wanted to look over at her and remind her that my presence had saved her from hours of nonsense conversation but I didn't want to ignite another discussion with Sandy.

During the first 20 minutes of the flight Sandy was silent while attacking every morsel of food in her Burger King bag. The lull was luxurious and I greeted it like a long lost mute friend. I dove into the pages of my book and welcomed the only sound emanating from our row: the sound of Sandy gnawing her food like she had just been rescued from a deserted island. At one point, it reminded me of two cats feverishly licking each other clean. Her lips smacked together like two lesbians going at it in a Subaru. Although the moaning over her food annoyed the fuck out of me, anything was better than being interrogated by her relentless questions. Sadly, I wasn't off the hook. Far from it. She took her oversized tongue, licked the last of the Hershey's Sundae Pie off her plastic white spork, and went right back to me.

Turning her entire body to the left, "Joe, are you married?"

Hiding inside the cover of my book wasn't an option. This is the one reason I hate flying in uniform. Whenever a pilot or flight attendant wears their uniform in public they are representing the airline that provides them with a weekly paycheck. It's the curse of flying for free. The position I put myself in so I can carry on a large bottle of face wash without having to check a bag. It doesn't matter if said pilot or flight attendant is at the grocery store, on the bus, or-in the case of my Omaha flight-sitting next to someone who wishes they were Katie Couric. We are the face of the airline and I am sure my employer frowned upon me telling Sandy to choke on a french fry.

"Yes." I didn't take my eyes of my book. I am accustomed to behavior like that because it frequently happens to me when I am sitting on the jumpseat working with someone I either have nothing in common with or just don't like. There is no better way to annoy me than attempting meaningless conversation when I am not giving off any vibes that I want to talk. If my face is deep in a book without making eye contact with you, I probably don't want to spend the next four days hearing about your pet bird and gay husband.

"That's wonderful. I'm married too; so is Loretta." Loretta looked over giving me a half-I don't give a damn what you people are talking about-smile and went right back to her crossword puzzle. Loretta had all the power in the world to save me from this conversation but she still hated me for being the catalyst to our Sandy disaster. The bitch held a grudge. I didn't blame her. It was my fault. Taking the seat between the two older ladies in the row behind us might have been the better choice, but I wanted to avoid the possibility of performing mouth-to-mouth on two stiff corpses somewhere over Nebraska. I figured sitting here made life easier. I took a gamble. I'm glad I don't play the lottery. When I looked back and saw the two older ladies sound asleep, I regretted my decision. Sure, they were most likely dead, but at least they wouldn't have talked my fucking ear off. I'd have managed sitting between their stiff corpses until one of them started to smell.

I gave up all hope of reading my book. Sandy was an emotional terrorist who hijacked my personal space. As I prepared to conjure up some fake pleasantry, Sandy's attention focused on another passenger sitting across from us. She began waving her hands in all directions and settled on a handkerchief wave. When her left hand breezed over my book I looked up to see her fluttering about in her seat trying to grab the attention of the gentlemen across the aisle from me.

"Excuse me, Bill? Bill is that you? Hello. Bill!" She jumped up and down and Loretta looked back over at me.

Any imagined friendliness that I felt from Loretta was officially gone. Especially after she dropped her pen due to Sandy's eruptive behavior. It bounced off her knee and onto the floor never to be seen again.

The passenger next to me ignored Sandy for as long as possible. A challenging task if I do say so myself. He finally sneered over the newspaper he had crinkled in his hand and turned his head to face us. I wanted to inform him that I had no idea who she was, and to welcome him into my living nightmare, but from his facial expression I gathered he didn't care. When he made eye contact with her it, was an open invitation for her to invade his personal space with her existence. I put my book down. This interaction looked too good to pass up.

"Bill? Bill!" She was yelling directly into my ear like her lips were a bullhorn. "It's me, Sandy. How are you?" I looked over at Bill to watch his reaction.

Bill paused, looked at me, then to her, and coolly answered, "I don't know you." It happened that quick. Done. He went directly back to reading his newspaper. I smiled and went back to my book. If I had balls the size of Bill's my conversations with Sandy could have ended before the airplane door closed.

Sandy shrugged her shoulders, leaned towards me even further, and whispered, "He looked like Bill. If you knew Bill you'd think he looked like Bill, too." She turned over to Loretta, "Do you know Bill from the fourth floor?"

"He got fired three months ago." Loretta responded and closed her eyes again. She might have been praying for the airplane to go down. I know I thought about it a few times.

My hopes of her bumping into someone else she knew and leaving me alone were crushed.

"What airline do you work for?"

When I told her she looked up to the ceiling in deep thought. "I've never heard of that airline. Is it new?"

Now she had my attention. "Really? You've never heard of us? I didn't know that was possible." Surprised and bewildered by her ignorance I sat there staring at her. We locked eyes which creeped me out. Only because she still looked hungry. I might understand if I was dressed in regular clothes but I had sat next to her for the past hour with the name of my airline blasted all over my flight attendant wings. Could she read? I didn't care. If she didn't know about my airline then she'd never be a passenger on one of my flights. That made me smile.

"I guess I don't get out much. I'm just a good Nebraskan girl. Born and raised," she put her hands up towards the ceiling, "thank you very much. I live for my husband, my beautiful kids, Jesus, and chocolate pie."

"Honey," I closed my book and placed it in the seat back pocket, "we all live for chocolate pie."

She laughed, "You are funny. You must make your wife laugh all the time."

The pilot's voice broke up our conversation informing everyone that we were 20 minutes from landing at Eppley Airfield in Omaha. Perfect timing. Sandy took that as a trigger to put away her belongings; I took it as a desire to find out more about this quirky person. I spent the entire flight fighting off her questions, and against my better judgement, I was about to unleash on her what she had done to me, "Have you heard of California Air?"

"Nope."

"Just Jet Airlines?"

"No," she smiled.

Loretta looked over, "Oh come on girl, you never heard of Just Jet Airlines? I've even heard of them."

I was getting annoyed, "Quality Airways?"

She looked at me like I was speaking a weird language created in the far off land of California.

"Nope. I guess I don't know much. I just found out what an artichoke was. You gotta eat the meat off the leaf." She shook her head and grimaced, "Some people even make a dip. Have you ever had an artichoke?

Nodding my head slowly, "Yes."

"Strangest thing, right? I've never seen anything so strange."

"I have Sandy. I have."

OPERATION: TOMATO ASS

I always go that extra mile when providing customer service. Working in the customer service industry, whether you flip burgers, pour coffee, or fly people all over the country, it's imperative you carry around a tattooed smile. At all times. As if your life depends on it. To simply be nice and helpful doesn't cut it anymore. In my industry, the traveling public are over-the-top demanding. People have lost their minds when it comes to their expectations. These airline passengers believe they have the right to be rude, critical, and disrespectful to their flight attendant all while expecting us to be gracious, even if the airplane is plummeting thousands of feet into the ocean. Thankfully, I have not experienced plummeting thousands of feet into the ocean. If I had, I'd be smiling the entire way down.

The customer service gene is scientifically impossible to find, but I was born with it; kinda like Maybelline. What is the customer service gene? It's the gene that gives one human being the ability to handle another human being—in a customer service setting—without literally beating the shit out of them. Losing one's cool is a sure sign the individual who presents themselves as a born customer service person is a fraud. Don't get me wrong, my buttons are pushed harder than an obese person through the terminal in a wheelchair, but I was born with the tools to look away, smile, and handle the situation without losing my composure.

On a San Diego to Las Vegas flight I was walking through the aisle with my flashy white smile, working the customer service dance that has made me very popular with the ladies. I wish it made me popular with the gentlemen but I will take attention wherever I can get it. My customer service dance includes taking drink orders, smiling, flirting, and making passengers feel like they are in first class even when they are seated in the back of the airplane.

I promise you if I was driving that bus, Rosa Parks wouldn't have said shit.

I approached this wiry white haired lady in 5C and before I could speak she said, "Can I ask you something?

"Sure. What can I help you with?"

"Is it true that we are only allowed two drinks per flight?"

That was an odd question. I quickly surmised that at one time in her life she had been cut off during a flight for abusing alcohol, and most likely the flight attendants.

I politely responded, "You can have more than two drinks," she immediately smiled, "but how many drinks you have, and when you are cut off, is up to me. "

She accepted that response and nodded, "Fair enough. I'd like two Heineken and bring them out at the same time."

When I got to 6C, who I'd learn right away was an apparent friend of the Heineken lady, it became obvious these two ladies were on a mission to enjoy themselves on this short flight. I grinned, "May I get you something to drink?"

When she smirked, her meaty cheeks bulged up into large fleshy round balls. "I'd like a water and a bloody mary," she pointed up to 5C, "You can put her drinks on my tab, too."

The passenger in 5C turned around, "Thank you, Desiree. That is so sweet."

I piped in, "Ooooooh. Are you ladies out to have some fun this weekend?"

Desiree's cheeks perked up again, "Yes we are. We got a three night deal at the Imperial Palace on the strip and it came with two free buffet tickets. I hear the hotel is super great."

Poor thing. I didn't have the heart to tell her that the Imperial Palace should have been condemned in the mid-1990's. When I finished taking drink orders, I quickly brought out the two Heinekens and bloody mary to Desiree and her traveling companion.

When I can—but sometimes it's impossible—I serve the passengers who paid for their drinks first. Yes, I understand that everyone on the airplane paid a lot of money for their airplane tickets but when you are shelling out an extra $5.00 for each drink, you deserve to get that drink fast. I will break it down further for you. When passengers pay for alcoholic drinks, and they usually order more than one, that's revenue for the airline. Revenue for the airline means job security for me. It might also mean extra crash in the pocket of your flight attendant. Some flight attendants are paid bonuses for their onboard sales. If they don't sell anything during the flight, they don't make any extra money. No extra money makes most flight attendants unhappy. So if you see your flight attendants bringing out alcoholic drinks before your free Coke, it's because they want these passengers to get nice and buzzed, order more drinks, maybe pass out a generous tip, and help the airline bank the cash so they get a nice bump in their profit sharing the following year.

After delivering the alcoholic drinks to these two ladies I walked back to the front galley and started pouring Sprites, Diet Cokes, and whatever else the first few rows in my section ordered. A few minutes went by before I overheard a slight commotion in the cabin. I leaned sideways from my workspace to look down the aisle to check it out. Shit always happens on a short flight when everyone in your section orders a drink. It never fails.

I was under attack! Runners in Spain have a better chance escaping a herd of bulls than I'd have escaping what was heading my way. Desiree galloped up the aisle towards me with a crazed look hanging off her jowl. The cup of ice in my hand dropped onto the counter and I braced myself for impact. What happened to her? Did she shart and blow out her tent-sized panties? Did she mistake her earbuds for tic tacs? Was she on fire? All these thoughts coursed through my brain as she raced full speed down the aisle. Perhaps she was on fire. I couldn't see any smoke coming off her fleshy body but that didn't comfort me. She was moving at stampede speed. If I did see flames, I'd be trampled over before I could do anything about it. And let me remind you, row five is not that far from the galley. This all happened within mere seconds.

My first instinct was to reach for the Halon fire extinguisher and hose the bitch down. Stop her dead in her tracks. But with the mass of flesh hanging from her hips, the foam in that little red can stood no chance. Hitting her in the head might have worked but I simply wasn't fast enough. She was on me faster than a closeted male Republican on a dick. When she finally came to a full stop in front of my jumpseat I realized she was not on fire.

Relief. "What's wrong?" I calmly asked as she pushed me aside and took up most of my galley space. She continued jumping up and down spitting out words that made no sense. After a few seconds of this erratic behavior, she pointed at her jeans and I finally understood what was causing Desiree to hop up and down like she was an extra in the show *Stomp* on Broadway. On her left pant leg, wrapped around her hefty thigh, was the largest red stain I'd ever seen. At first glance, it appeared as if her monthly visitor paid a surprise visit. A visit she—nor I—was prepared for.

My imagination went wild. "What is that?"

Breathing heavy she declared, "It's tomato juice."

Awareness swept over me. Tomato juice? That was nothing. Then my mind started wandering with ridiculous ideas. Like it always does. What if another passenger smuggled a skunk on board the airplane? What if we were innocently flying to Las Vegas ignorant to the fact that Pepe Le Pew was hiding under a seat awaiting the perfect opportunity to squeeze his anal glands all over one of the passengers? And he found that person in Desiree. Not the jackpot you want to win. What if (there are a lot of what ifs in this wandering) after she mixed her vodka and spicy tomato juice, Pepe jumped onto her lap, and sprayed her down like a male cat marking his territory? And, like pouring condiments on her second Double-Double In & Out burger, she instinctively doused herself with tomato juice and ran from the scene?

I had to find that skunk before we ran out of tomato juice. As I turned and started down the aisle she squealed, "I spilled my bloody mary all over myself. Goddamn it! These are three hundred dollar jeans."

I spun back around and knew for a fact she was not sporting $300 jeans. How did I know this? Because they don't sell $300 jeans at Walmart. I awkwardly squeezed around her towards the lavatory, opened the door, and nodded for her to enter and take care of her business. I wanted to toss her in myself but throwing out my back was not my idea of a good flight.

As I've hinted already, Miss Desiree was thick in the hips. She was also thick in the thighs, ass, arms, stomach. tits, legs, and neck. I wouldn't put it past her to be sporting a pair of Fred Flintstone feet inside her brown flats. I wondered if those flats were $300, too? She reminded me of a slab of bacon you'd find in Paula Deen's kitchen. I didn't care how plump she was, or that she'd bulge out of the small lavatory like sausage trying to escape its prison casing, I simply wanted her out of my galley.

I was not rude. I was stern. What do you expect? She dripped tomato juice all over the galley floor like a broken water pipe. How many cans of spicy tomato juice did I hand her? One can? Ten cans? I completely forgot but from the mess it seemed the latter. Where was all the tomato juice coming from? I forced approximately 20 wet sanitary napkins into her hand and told her to use those along with the paper towels in the lavatory to soak up the juice cascading down her robust leg.

I figured she'd close the goddamn door to clean herself. Even if being stuffed in the lavatory cut off her circulation, she could at least attempt at some level of privacy. I turned around, concluding my job was done. I had provided the napkins, the lavatory, and a smile. As I went back to filling up cups with ice, I never gave it another thought that she'd at least try closing the lavatory door. If not close it completely, then halfway. Aim at maintaining some of her dignity. Nope. The fucking lavatory door was wide open. How did I know? Because she continued complaining about her jeans over my shoulder. Now that I think about it, she did the right thing. Deciding not to cram her entire body in the lavatory was for the best. Actually, it was physically impossible. If she succeeded we'd have made an emergency landing so a technician could grease her up to get her ass out. Butter also comes in handy in these sticky situations. Did I already mention Paula Deen?

With my back facing her, my blood pressure elevated when I considered that she might actually take her jeans off. I was well prepared to call the pilots and have security awaiting us at the gate when we landed if that happened. I am trained for all types of terrorist activity and going down without a fight was not an option. I was dealing with a level 10 disturbance. Technically, airline disturbance levels only go up three levels but after considering her weight and how fast she moved-I took no chances. Peeking over my right shoulder, acting like I was too busy to know what was happening, I witnessed her butterball ass protruding out the lavatory door while she endlessly wiped off the tomato juice from her jeans, hoping it beaded up and rolled off like RainX.

I stayed focused on preparing drinks for my passengers. Her ordeal was not my problem. I grabbed the full tray of drinks and started down the aisle when she stuck her head out of the lavatory and aggressively asked me, "Can you please take care of my backside?"

"Umm, What? Your what? When? How? What? Oh no-I, umm, I don't feel comfortable doing that." I coughed out with a smile but almost gagged on the hummus and pita bread I had for lunch. It wasn't digested enough for me to handle cleaning her backside.

"Please," she said, practically in tears, "I just need you to wipe me off on the backside."

That may have been the sentence ejected from her plump full lips but my little brain heard something different. Something completely different. Perhaps the roar of the airplane engines played a factor in what I'd processed but my brain translated her request into, "I can't reach around with these two ham hocks hanging from my arms so could you please take a dozen sanitary napkins and wipe the tomato juice out of the crack of my big fat ass." That's what I heard. Loud and clear. As if she took the megaphone, placed it against my ear, pushed the button, and unleashed hell on me in my own galley.

Desiree had no average ass. Her one ass was easily two of my own asses. When she referenced her $300 jeans she was literally referring to the labor and the material cost that was put into making them.

"Don't you have someone that can help you?" I looked at the flight deck door hoping they could hear me, "I really don't feel comfortable doing that."

Screaming for assistance from the other flight attendants would get me nowhere because they were in the back of the airplane conducting their service, oblivious to my Desiree dilemma in the front galley. Those bastards. I thought about picking up the interphone and pleading assistance from anyone. An air marshal? A grandmother knitting her infant grandson a new baby blanket? A knitting needle to the neck sounded appropriate. Losing copious amounts of blood and going unconscious seemed inviting when faced with her ass.

"Come on. I need your help! These are the only jeans I have for my entire trip," She demanded while standing midway between the lavatory and the galley. "Pleeeeeeeeeeeeeease. I can't stand here all day."

If Desiree had her way I'd be washing her jeans by hand in the lavatory sink while she stood behind me sipping on another bloody mary shouting commands that I had not been trained for, "Hey! Make sure you really scrub the crotch area because I don't want dogs sniffing my kitty cat. My kitty cat purrs, it doesn't hiss. Watch it, don't scrub SO hard you'll take the blue off them."

It became hard to hide my irritation with her. It had been a mere 40 minutes since she stepped onto my airplane. And changed the course of my life. Time meant nothing to someone like Desiree, whose sole purpose was to make me her bitch. In what seemed like a short period of time, she found herself bent over and spread eagle in the front lavatory begging me to wipe her fucking ass. Wipe her ass! What do I know about wiping ass? Actually, I know a lot about ass wiping from my days as a nurse but never did I imagine having to do it on the airplane. I had to draw the line and I drew it between my hand and her ass.

What did I even know about Desiree? She was chubby. That was obvious, but so am I. Can't fault her for failing out of Nutrisystem. Have you seen their food? She liked vodka. That alone might con me into wiping her ass. But she wore imaginary $300 jeans. Imaginary jeans that were way too tight. An outright no-no. On a positive note, she made it easy for me to reference Paula Deen twice in a brief period of time. Make that three times. Having a great source for joke material was another way to get me down between her legs... Wait a minute! NO! No fucking way! What was I thinking? Those few points did not substantiate me wiping her ass from front to back until it was spotless. I may be bald but I am no Mr. Clean. Granted, I've touched men way more intimately in the past without knowing their names, but this was different. I was sober. And I was standing in an airplane in front of over 145 passengers who I knew by now had foregone whatever they had been doing at their seats and focused all their attention on the freak show in the front galley.

With the tray of drinks still in my hand, I swiftly thought of a way to deter the situation away from me cleaning her pants, "Can your friend in 5C come up and help?" I was hopeful her friend had downed both beers and was up for anything. I'd offer her a free six pack if she was game. Desperation arrived. I honestly didn't know what to do, "Is there anyone on the flight that can help you?" There had to be someone else that was man-or woman-enough to tackle this operation. A boyfriend? Daughter? Neighbor? Long lost cousin? The guy in 1C? Anyone else but me. I might as well been talking to my jumpseat because her attention was centered on nothing but the stain that was painted across her thigh. And me wiping it clean.

Then it fucking happened. And I wasn't prepared. Desiree gave me the most tragic look I'd ever seen on another full-grown adult. Like she had just found out Walmart raised their jean prices. My customer service gene went into overdrive and I lost all will power. I knew what I had to do. It was dangerous—no doubt about that—and I'd probably never make it out alive but goddamnit, Desiree needed her backside taken care of and I was the only person around capable of getting the job done.

The entire situation reminded me of going scuba diving without ever taking a lesson. "Alright. Hold still for a moment." I placed my full tray back onto the galley counter and grabbed some napkins from inside the galley bin. Without knowing if, or when I would resurface for air, I took a long deep breath and started Operation: Tomato Ass.

There was no way the three of us-me, her, and her ass-were fitting in the lavatory at the same time. I solemnly placed my pride, my crew ID, and my last will and testament on the counter. At least Matt would know what to do with my body when the airline flew my hollowed out carcass home. Even though there'd be nothing left of my body after this scene. Disintegrating into a cloud of dust was the fastest way to go. The chances of that were slim; my luck ran out when Desiree boarded the flight. Hopefully, if my eyes weren't blown out of their sockets they could be donated to someone in need. That momentarily soothed the pain.

Having this unfold in front of everyone on the airplane was soul-crushing. Desiree's head, tits, and stomach were stuffed in the lavatory while her ass, hips, and legs were in my galley. Grasping onto the handful of paper napkins as if my life was ending, I bent down on my right knee, and grabbed one of the galley carts for support. The instant my knee touched the discolored galley floor, the airplane began gyrating from side to side. Off balance from kneeling, the strain forced me forward towards her girth and then back against the galley cart. What the fuck? Hitting turbulence while your head is mere inches from the entrance to Lucifer's summer home was not the way I wanted to go. Turbulence, light or not, was no laughing matter when face-to-face with an ass like that. At any moment I was prepared to taste tomato juice jeans. If I was lucky there might be a hint of vodka left behind to give me a slight buzz. The aggressive pressure only lasted a few seconds before the pilots leveled off the airplane. Bless them. I'm not a religious man but being down on one knee staring at more denim than the hardest working Chinese child laborer has ever seen led me to my first one-way conversation with Jesus Christ.

Hi Jesus.

It's Joseph. No, not your dad. One of the gay guys from Florida. Yeah, that one. Yes, the one who likes Vicodin, wine, and anal. To be honest, that doesn't narrow it down too much. You got it. That's me. Can we get back to my issue for a moment? Are you paying attention? Jesus Christ! Huh?

No, it's just an expression but I see that got your attention. Listen, I did not see this coming when I woke up this morning but I am about to die by the hands of this passenger's ass. Please take care of my husband, my friends, and my cats. That's all I ask.

P.S. If she does fart, please let me go fast. Don't make me linger on for days like you did behind that rock. See you in a few minutes.

Sincerely,
Flight Attendant Joe

I moved the paper napkins towards her ass crack and began to wipe.

Using a long, up and down stroking motion seemed smarter because focusing on one single area made me want to cry. Looking down from above, the stain appeared localized to just her ass, but once eye level it became clear the mess spread faster than chlamydia at an airline pilot summit. That tomato spill was more challenging than cleaning up after the Exxon Valdez. The galley lights were set on bright but sadly provided me with little to no light as I was defeated by the shadow of her meaty physique. I leaned in further and continued holding my breath, frightened that a slight tickle might release her anal pressure blowing my contacts out onto the dirty galley floor.

I wiped at the ferocious tomato stain for what seemed like hours. Truthfully, only a few minutes had passed, but in my defense time stands still when faced with that type of predicament. Just as I'd given up on life, and prepared to give St. Peter a good ol' high five, she held onto the door frame, let out an animalistic trumpet sound—reminding me of a Hippopotamus taking a shit—and popped the top half of her body out of the lavatory. Astonished the lavatory door didn't break off with her as she emerged, I glared up at her towering over me. She peered down and nodded acknowledging my professional housekeeping skills. I snapped back into a standing position with the once dry paper napkins now covered in red liquid as if I helped clean up a murder scene. In the trash bin they went. I took a few more off the counter and dried off the sweat beads encircling my head. She smirked as if receiving a happy ending after an amazing massage. I felt used, abused, and most importantly, violated by a woman. My first instinct was to curl up in a corner, hold my knees up to my face, and let out all the tomato juice tears that had welled up in my eyes.

But I still had a job to do.

Desiree stepped away from the lavatory and closed the door, "Thank you, Joe. I'm sure my jeans are ruined but if you give me a free bloody mary, that should make up for it."

Really? A $5.00 bloody mary would replace her $300 jeans? An argument began to brew up inside me but I let it pass. She sucked all the strength out of me. Her and her fucking tomato jeans. I visited hell, came back, and only managed to hand out two drinks.

My customer service gene took over and I smiled warm enough to melt a fucking iceberg. Reaching into the liquor cart I pulled out a vodka mini and gave it to her, "You deserve it. I hope your jeans survive this fiasco." My bullshitting skills are so on par I could run for president. I filled a cup with ice and handed her another can of tomato juice, "Now don't spill this one. We are about to land and I haven't even handed any other drinks out."

"You are the best. I'm writing in a letter for you." She took her drink and waddled back to 5C.

As quickly as it all started-it was over. I guzzled down three cups of water, mopped the second round of sweat off my bald head, and went into the lavatory to wash my hands with scalding hot water before getting back to work.

Stepping around the galley corner to restart my beverage service I almost slammed into an attractive male passenger heading towards the galley. He politely excused himself and made his way into the lavatory and closed the door. My heart started to race. Was this the reward for my run in with Desiree's ass? I leaned my ear towards the lavatory door and patiently waited for his cries for help. What did he need cleaned off his sexy jeans? If I was lucky it would smell like bleach and taste salty. I paused for a moment, with a full tray of drinks in my hand, waiting for him to open the door. Many different scenarios ran through my mind of how we'd both fit in the lavatory, close the door, and lock it. I'd make it work. The ability to breathe came second to being locked tightly in an airplane lavatory with a stud.

The door never opened. It was apparent he hadn't spilled anything on his jeans and if he needed help, my name wouldn't be yelled out. I stopped at row one and started handing out beverages. The first row of passengers were polite and understood the catastrophe that I endured. While handing a Sprite to the lady in 1C, I scanned the glowing faces of the passengers awaiting their drinks and I made eye contact with Desiree.

Her Cheshire Cat grin confirmed it's always the person's ass that you don't want to wipe that you end up wiping.

And she never wrote in a compliment letter!

Smoking Shenanigans

Even though I've lived my entire life without smoking a cigarette I'm sure my lungs are blacker than a Jamaican runner in the Summer Olympics. My parents' addiction to nicotine left me spending most of my childhood living in what could only be described as a dirty chimney. No Mary Poppins. No Supercalifragilisticexpialidocious. No singing and dancing. Just tar and the prospect of cancer. I wasn't the only victim of their cancer-causing smoke. Irene's chihuahua, Chiquita, never had a chance. She required continuous oxygen before her second birthday. The hum of her concentrator was louder than her bark. Have you ever tried walking a miniscule dog who's attached to the tubing of an oxygen concentrator? It's not fun. It also cockblocks you receiving any park head from random married guys.

Alright, she wasn't actually put on oxygen, but she should have been. She wheezed like my grandfather when he napped in his recliner. At least I escaped daily to high school for a breather. Chiquita was a prisoner to their cigarette smoke. I'd walk into the house after school, covering my mouth like a resident of Kabul, while Irene lit up a cigarette at the dining room table asking, "Can you take Chiquita out for some fresh air? She needs to go out."

"You bet your ass she does."

"Excuse me?" She'd say looking up from her cross-word puzzle book.

"Nothing." When I opened the door Chiquita bolted out of the house like her asshole was on fire. Poor dog. I despised Chiquita, but if I hadn't loathed her presence in our house, I'd have felt sorry for her little lungs. They were small Oreo cookies stuffed with chocolate filling. As much as Irene loved that dog, she put her health at risk the moment she picked her up from the breeder. When I say she loved that dog, she loved that fucking dog. Her love for Chiquita left the Cinderella role wide open for me. I had an ugly step-Chihuahua that received more love and better healthcare than I did. When I coughed, Irene demanded I cover my mouth and sent me off to school. When Chiquita coughed, she received filet mignon for dinner.

Months away from needing a new voice box, Chiquita finally died of emphysema in 1987. It was a tragic end for a dog who I assume prayed daily to be crushed underneath a snow tire. Irene did not take it well; she cried ashes for weeks. It was as if Elvis Presley died all over again. To be perfectly clear, my heart did not weep for Chiquita's death. I relished in her absence. While Irene double-fingered her cigarettes to relieve the stress of losing her beloved dog, I celebrated with a rare filet mignon. My parents' cigarette smoke torture lasted my entire youth. On good days I'd be able to breathe, but on bad days it was like living in Pompeii right after the eruption.

The first guy I ever dated was a smoker. Caught up in the excitement of my first love—and that he peeled my shrimp at dinner—I looked past the fact that he spent more time on the patio with a cigarette in his mouth than he did in the bedroom with my dick in it. A year and a half of playing second fiddle to a pack of Kools will only last so long. Don't even get me started when it came to kissing that motherfucker. Kissing him reminded me of what tonguing gutter trash from *Les Misérables* resembled. Resuscitating a decomposed cat carcass tasted better than placing my lips on his. Not that I ever placed my lips on a dead cat, but you understand the image I am trying to relay. Listen, if I have to scrape my tongue across teeth that are yellow and gritty, I'll just deepthroat a fucking stick of butter. After him, I promised myself never to date another smoker. I'd fuck them but I wouldn't marry them, which follows the same guidelines I set for guys with small dicks.

In 1988, when I was 16 years old, Irene and I traveled from Orlando, Florida to Hartford, Connecticut to visit family and friends. I'd never flown, and the excitement of flying on an airplane had me counting down the months and days in advance. The countdown started at 185 days, and each morning after breakfast I'd scratch out the current date on the typewritten piece of paper that was taped to my bedroom closet door. I imagined that's how girls prepared for their first period; a taped countdown on their closet door with the hopes to wake up a woman. I just wanted to go on vacation.

Irene booked our seats together in the back of the airplane. I didn't understand what that meant until 45 minutes into the flight and I thought the airplane was going down. "Mom! Did an engine explode? Why is there so much smoke?"

"This is the smoking section," she replied pulling out a Winston 100 and grabbing her lighter, "I can't go two hours without a fucking cigarette."

"Are you trying to kill me?" I questioned sitting up to witness all the smoke billowing from each seat in our section. It had to be the most intense cloud of smoke I had ever experienced in my entire life. Only the citizens of Auschwitz had seen this much smoke in the air at one time.

Claustrophobia set in. The fuselage walls began closing in on me. I had to get up. Squeezing passed the guy sitting next to me, I finally broke free into the aisle. The thick fog of smoke disoriented me, but I managed to find my footing and started toward the back of the airplane. Finding the lavatory was my main objective. I didn't have to pee, I simply needed a break from the gas slowly suffocating me.

When I reached the back galley I peeked through the dark gold curtain to see something out of the *Twilight Zone*. Two of the flight attendants were standing up in the galley wearing surgical masks and preparing food. Surgical masks? On an airplane? Something told me that they weren't performing open heart surgery on the beef tips we were having for dinner. Another female flight attendant had an oxygen bottle tucked between her legs attached by a tube to the plastic mask, which she sucked on like she was about to blast off into outer space. Their muffled conversations made me want to strap myself down, open the airplane door to let in fresh air, and possibly suck out the entire back half of the airplane-including Irene.

I will always remember that flight as the worst two hours of my life, and I've sat through *Three Men and a Baby*.

Worried the flight attendants might choke to death in the back galley, when I got back to my seat I looked over at Irene, "Mom? Those poor flight attendants have to deal with this smoke all the time."

"That's what they get paid to do," she answered taking another puff off her cigarette. Then after a moment she added, "They signed up for this job."

"I think they signed up to hand out soda and nuts, not live the rest of their lives in an iron lung."

"Why are you such a smart ass?"

That was my initial education on flight attendant seniority. The junior reserve flight attendants worked in the back of the airplane leaving the senior mamas up front. Seniority was more than just getting a better schedule and service position, it was living an extra decade without going through chemotherapy. These poor flight attendants started their day smelling like Dior and left smelling like Marlboro.

My disgust for cigarette smoke has lasted my entire life. When smoking bans took place in bars and restaurants I rejoiced happier than when my STD screens come back negative. The afternoon I graduated from flight attendant training I made it known to anyone who listened that at no time, under any fucking circumstances, would I tolerate a passenger smoking on my flight. Never! I'd nip that shit in the butt the moment a passenger walked on my airplane. Yes, *my* airplane. If I'm working on it, it belongs to me. Cigarettes in your front shirt pocket displayed like a trophy? Not on this flight. Hide them cancer sticks for the entire flight. No need for you to even think about lightening up. While seated on my jumpseat, I'd create these elaborate stories of how I'd react to a passenger smoking on my flight. These scenarios usually started with me walking down the aisle, smacking my plastic handcuffs in my hand, making even the two packs a day smokers cringe in their seat. It's hard to smoke a cigarette when you are hogtied and handcuffed on the floor in the front galley. I'd add that to my safety demonstration just so passengers understood that I had a zero tolerance policy for smoking shenanigans on my flight.

My first run-in with a passenger smoking on one of my flights did not turn out as dramatic as I had imagined. Madison and I were flying from Minneapolis to Atlanta. She was a doll: statuesque, blond, cute, perky, and taught me how to put my cell phone in a plastic cup and listen to music in the galley while preparing for service. Best trick ever. Who knew a plastic cup could project a Madonna song all the way up to row 20? Not this guy. Madison was the lead flight attendant while I held down the back of the airplane. Delays, mechanicals, and short overnights made me want to kill everyone who requested a wheelchair for when we landed in Atlanta. We had just completed service and I was in the back galley—jamming out to Jennifer Lopez—when I noticed a Hispanic male making his way to the back galley. I turned down my music and smiled as he approached me. He stood in the galley with a blank stare obviously looking for the airplane lavatory. Why do passengers make using the bathroom such a project on the airplane? It's either a swinging door that you pull open or a bi-fold door that you push and slide aside. It's that simple. Most passengers stumble around the lavatory door like they are drunk college girls trying to enter their dorm room.

"Bathroom?" He asked pointing towards the coffee maker.

"No. That's a coffee maker. The lavatory is right there," I pointed at the door, "it's open."

He looked over but didn't move. I refused to open the door for him. He was a full grown adult and at some point you have to let nature take over and hope for the best. A minute later he moved over to the door but still had no luck opening it.

"It's a door. Turn the handle and open it."

With the same hesitation I have when it comes to shaving my balls, he slowly twisted the door handle and entered the lavatory. The door wasn't closing so I pushed it shut with my foot. Something told me that this guy's massive shit could take down a Cessna 182 on a sunny day over Pompano Beach. Being trapped in the galley while his impressive shit Kraken emerged was not an option. I evacuated the area walking up the aisle to visit with Madison.

Madison and I stood in the front galley bitching about our brutal trip while an array of passengers made their way to the back galley to use the lavatory. To be honest, I lost track of who had gone back there. Men. Women. Children. Puppies. I couldn't have cared less. My mind was filled with thoughts of landing in Atlanta, riding the van to the hotel, taking a scalding hot shower, burning my uniform, jerking off, and then passing out with a smile across my face.

After the crowd cleared away I started back down the aisle towards the back galley. It didn't take long for the smell to assault me, it hit my face like a ton of dicks; a passenger had been smoking.

I have this weird sense of smell. It's a power sense gifted to me by the universe. Probably because I am blind as a bat and deaf from too many years listening to my Walkman at full volume. There's no medical confirmation on this diagnosis, and it's plain conjecture on my part, but I have a nose as powerful as a blind person, which makes me believe I was Helen Keller's dog in a past life. My nose can smell odors that other people in the room cannot. It is a blessing for sniffing out fires and freshly baked chocolate chip cookies, but a curse when seated four rows from a shitty diaper.

At 38,000 feet, in a metal tube with recirculated air, you know the difference between roasted nuts and cigarette smoke. I sprinted to the back galley to catch the perpetrator. Man, woman, or punk-ass teenager, I didn't care-someone was getting put in a headlock. My heart raced and I felt my blood pumping in my temples. Where were my handcuffs? I couldn't remember where I'd put them, but I'd have Madison grab hers once my knee was in this terrorist's back. The back lavatory was unoccupied. I opened the lavatory door and the stench washed over me and my eyes began to water.

I quickly stepped into the lavatory and opened up the trash receptacle bin to search for the cigarette butt. The crucial detail when catching a passenger smoking on your airplane is finding the cigarette butt. Did the smoker throw it in the trash can? Did they flush it? Is there going to be a fire onboard the airplane? There's nothing worse than burning up on your way to Atlanta because some asshat decided to smoke a cigarette on a three hour flight.

The missing cigarette butt caused my neck to turn a dark shade of red. I was ready to fuck someone up. You can always tell how angry I am by how red my neck gets. It turns pink for passengers who haven't fastened their seat belt after I've asked them five times in a row, crimson for anyone who orders coffee on a 30-minute express flight, and scarlet for fuckers who decide to smoke on my airplane.

This was a scarlet moment.

I stormed up the aisle to the front of the airplane. Before Madison had a chance to look up from her magazine, I turned the airplane cabin lights on bright and grabbed the interphone to make an announcement. It went something like this, "Ladies and Gentlemen. Sorry for this interruption but we have a problem!" One hundred heads popped up in unison, "I want you all to know that one of your fellow passengers has endangered each and everyone of us on this flight. One of you was smoking in the back lavatory. I need to know who it was." While I scanned the crowd making eye contact with each passenger, Madison tried fitting herself into one of the service bins. Filled with enough rage to challenge the Westboro Baptist Church, I transitioned from happy-go -lucky Joe into a split personality that Sybil would avoid. Sybil had nothing on Outraged Joe. Outraged Joe didn't give a fuck. He was saving lives by making an unprofessional scene on the airplane. What was the airline going to do? Fire him? Me. You know what I mean.

Addressing the entire airplane I continued, "I need to find out who was smoking. If I don't, we'll have security waiting for us when we land in Atlanta!" I slammed the interphone down onto the receiver and started marching down the aisle like it was D-Day. Madison followed behind me to show her support, but mostly for fear of what I'd do if left alone.

As I advanced down the aisle, scanning the faces of the tense passengers in their seats, it didn't take me long to sniff out the lady in 17A and her male travel companion in 17B. I zoned out. Madison stood behind me while I leaned in hovering over 17B, "Excuse me?" I stared at the two of them. Both of them ignored me which increased my shade of red. Waving my hands in front of their faces, the guy in 17B finally broke concentration and looked up at me. I calmly asked, "Were any of you smoking in the lavatory?"

"No," he answered. One simple word and then he abruptly turned back towards his regularly scheduled programing. Did he think he had a choice in this interaction? We all know the answer to that-even if he was oblivious to it at the time. I was delivering an emergency broadcast alert directly at their faces.

Super pissed, and my neck hitting Merlot status, I stuttered out, "Uh. Hello! Are you sure? Cause from where I'm standing it smells like a dirty ashtray in your row."

He looked back up at me, "I already told you we weren't smoking."

The female passenger in 17A had yet to make eye contact with me. My Stevie Wonder senses alerted me that this bitch was the firestarter I was looking for. If I squinted just right I could see the haze of cancer hovering around her. Dragging her out of the seat and into the aisle to sniff her breath seemed to be the logical thing to do. I let that idea pass without a second thought. I may be reckless but

I'm not stupid. An action like that would end my flight attendant career.

"Listen," I directed my anger towards 17A, "I know you were smoking in the lavatory. It's obvious. You guys smell like you just walked out of a bar." I could have left that insult out but it was too late. My mouth had been working without the help of my brain since I picked up the interphone, "I just need to know where the cigarette butt is."

"I told you. We weren't smoking."

"Alright. Be that way. We'll have security waiting for you when we land." I regained my posture and walked towards the back of the airplane.

Madison followed behind me and put her hand on my shoulder, "Are you ok? Maybe you should listen to some Madonna."

I shut off the airplane cabin lights, "No. I'm not ok!" I slipped my hands into plastic clear gloves and moved towards the lavatory door. The tight gloves made a rubber band snapping sound as I secured them around my wrist. I wished it was the sound of my hand gliding across 17A and 17B smug faces. "Who the fuck smokes on an airplane?" I opened the lavatory door, pulled out the trash bin, and sifted through dirty snot rags and a bloody used tampon trying to track down the ticking smoking time bomb.

"Wow. That's strong." Madison stated as she held the door open for me so I wouldn't be stuck in the lavatory with the odor.

After five minutes of intense searching, the cigarette butt was nowhere to be found. My next move was to call the flight deck and report the incident to the pilots.

Pushing all my emotions into the lavatory I focused on delivering nothing but facts and data. Anyone in the airline industry will tell you that when completing incident reports or reporting disturbances to the flight deck, you should never allow your personal feelings to get in the way. Only give pilots and management the facts and data. They only want the facts and data. Simple enough, right? Sometimes. It sounds all fine and dandy written down on the pages of the flight attendant manual, and recited in your head while waiting for the pilots to pick up the interphone, but delivering facts and data can be challenging when you're enraged with a blood pressure of 210/135 because some asshole was smoking in the lavatory. I did my best, "Captain, the passenger in 17A was smoking in the aft lavatory."

He asked, "Did you actually catch them smoking?"

Did that matter? I continued reminding myself about the facts and data but my emotions were gradually decompressing, "I didn't physically catch her smoking in the lavatory but the smell is so strong at their row that unless they bathe with cigarette smoke-scented soap it was one of them."

He sighed, "Well if you didn't actually witness them I don't know if there's much we can do. I'll still call ahead for security to meet the flight."

"I guess that's fine. Thanks." My dissatisfaction was evident but I was positive that once airport security walked on the airplane and smelled what these two fuckers were cooking they'd both be handcuffed and carted off to jail. And they'd sit there trying to afford bail. I expected bail to be set at $10,000,000 for smoking on an airplane. Possibly even more.

While picking up trash during our final descent into Atlanta, I strutted passed 17A giving her the most unpleasant expression my facial muscles could create. Instead of looking angry and intimidating, I resembled a pug trying to take a shit after a week of constipation. That didn't bother me; that's how I normally look during fits of rage. I spent a few extra seconds at their row fiddling with the trash bag to get their attention but they refused to acknowledge me. Frustrated, but feeling confident that I'd win the war, I finished collecting trash from the rest of the passengers, cleaned up my work galley, and strapped myself into the jump seat.

During takeoff and landing our flight attendant duties include a 30-second review. A 30-second review is an FAA requirement to keep emergency information fresh in our minds for the off chance our airplane breaks in half during landing. Knowing which side of the airplane we are seated on, how many passengers are on the airplane, and where our disabled passengers are seated seems to be crucial to surviving an airplane crash. I don't know about you but all I care about is where I am seated and whether we've crashed on the ground or in the water. That alone determines whether I'm even going to attempt to get out. None of that mattered while we were landing. I was fixated and preoccupied with 17A. Trying to recite which side of the airplane I was seated on didn't seem as important as obsessing about this whore who smoked on my flight. My 30-second review turned into a five minute fantasy of these two fucknuts being carted off the airplane by security.

We landed safely in Atlanta. Once we came to a complete stop at the gate, I got out of my jumpseat before the captain turned off the seat belt sign. I disarmed my two airplane doors and paced back and forth in the galley like a hungry tiger.

A male passenger approached me with his young child, "Can she use the bathroom? She can't hold it."

Insane and practically foaming at the mouth I aggressively responded, "No sir. This lavatory is evidence regarding the passenger who was smoking on the airplane." None of that was true. Pure and utter bullshit but I believed every word that came out of my mouth. It's funny how you can make up nonsense and believe it in a moment of hysteria. I had personally gone through the entire lavatory with my own gloved hands and came up empty handed. Even with that reality, I firmly believed the airplane would be taken out of service while security never rested until the cigarette butt was located and destroyed.

While passengers took their sweet ass time deplaning, I craned my neck down the aisle watching 17A and 17B collect their belongings and exit the airplane. The moment they disappeared I called Madison on the interphone, "What's going on?"

"They are talking to security right now. I will talk to you in a few," she hung up. I patiently waited until the last passenger walked off the airplane and had to fight back the urge to get on the interphone and threaten everyone's lives for moving so goddamn slow. I ran to the front of the airplane and looked out onto the jet bridge to find one last passenger being transported up the jet bridge in a wheelchair. Where were my criminals and the police?

Madison and I feverishly cleaned the airplane, grabbed our bags, and without saying a word sprinted up the jet bridge to the gate area. I envisioned the two assholes being handcuffed and shipped off to a maximum state penitentiary. As we stepped out into the gate area I was shocked to find nothing happening. No security. No police. No criminals. No Anderson Cooper covering this breaking story. My questions directed towards the gate agent went unanswered as she refused to discuss the outcome with me.

Madison stepped up beside me pulling her luggage, "Joe. The van is waiting on us. Let it go."

I lowered my head in defeat. I had indeed lost the war. As we passed a large group of passengers waiting to board a flight to Nashville, I noticed the smokers standing in line at the gate next to it being issued seats for an Orlando flight. I was baffled that security let them off the hook allowing them to board another flight within 10 minutes of being busted for smoking. My hopes for justice were squashed in the blink of an eye. I've never looked at airport security the same after that incident.

As irrationally as I reacted to that female passenger smoking on my Atlanta flight, the next time I encountered a passenger smoking (I know, twice in one career?) I handled it with more grace and class. Well, as much grace and class as someone like me can conjure up.

On a flight from Boston to Albuquerque, I was working with Abigail and Keegan, and we had the unfortunate luck of having a smoker on the flight who lost the battle of not lighting up for a five hour transcontinental flight. I always enjoyed working with Abigail. Her infectious laugh gave me life which made me spend most of my free time in her galley. It was better than being hijacked in the back galley while Keegan continued crying about being single and Jesus hating him for craving a big fat dick rather than a deep dish vagina.

"I don't know why I am single," he'd say the moment we were alone in the galley, "why can't I find a man who loves me and is a Christian?" His complaints and preaching were on a continuous loop from the last time I flew with him. I remembered it all too well. The four day trip where his friendship-if that's what you call it-with Wendy came to a crashing hault. The shame he carried around for being gay was nauseating.

That's the reason I spent so much time with Abigail in her galley. I wasn't paid enough to listen to Keegan cry for hours about being single and Jesus not loving him twice in one lifetime. My time was too valuable. The first trip we worked together I swallowed down his shame like a shot of tequila, but I had learned my lesson now. He could save all that drama for someone who had never worked with him before. Let a stranger have all the fun.

While Abigail and I stood up in the front galley talking about how much we loved and missed our cats, the interphone rang. Of course it was Keegan. We looked at each other, and then at the interphone, waiting for the bravest person to pick up the call. Neither one of us flinched as the ding from the phone echoed through the airplane. A few tense seconds passed and Abigail still hadn't reached for the interphone. Goddamnit. I buckled under the pressure and reached for the interphone. I'm so weak when it comes to my job, "This is Joe. What's up?"

His squeaky voice reminded me of an Orca whale, "I think someone was smoking in the lav."

For a quick moment I forgot I actually disliked flying with Keegan. I had a new enemy and whoever that person was they were smoking on the airplane. When the words, "smoking in the lav," finishing processing in my brain I didn't even respond, I hung up on him. I sputtered out incomprehensible words towards Abigail's direction and raced through the airplane as if it were already on fire. Flashbacks of my Atlanta outburst and unprofessionalism replayed in my mind. My emotions were faced with a difficult decision: act like a raging lunatic again or calm the fuck down and handle the situation like someone who's been trained to handle emergencies on the airplane. I knew what I had to do. As I passed the last row and entered the galley I was in full control of my anger, which surprised me because I am never in control of my feelings.

Keegan leaned on the jumpseat with his hands against his head staring at me as I stepped into the galley. He lacked the amount of excitement I had regarding a passenger smoking on the flight. That was no surprise, a dried mop gave out more energy than Keegan. I placed my hands on my hips and simply asked, "Did you see who it was?

"It was 15F," he answered, "I watched her walk out of the lav."

"Did you look for the cigarette butt?"

"No."

"Did you talk to her?"

"No."

Fucking Keegan. When was I going to put him on my avoid to fly with list? Working the entire trip with a toddler seemed easier. My hopes of him learning valuable lessons on how to handle passenger situations from our last trip were squashed. It was obvious that he didn't learn a fucking thing. Keegan was destined to always be a worthless flight attendant. He probably needed direction on how to take a shit and wipe his own ass. I'd stay far away from assisting in that, but if he did have a vagina-which I can't confirm he didn't-I'd suggest back to front just to make him suffer.

I opened the lavatory door and pulled out the garbage can to search for the cigarette butt. While I donned gloves and picked through the trash bin, Keegan stood there brain dead. I made a mental note to ask our recruiting department if our airline had a habit of hiring people who had undergone a lobotomy.

"Damn. It's not in here." I put the trash bin back under the sink and closed the lavatory door, "Do you want to go talk to her?"

"I don't know what to say. I'm not good at this kind of stuff," he said nervously chewing on his hangnails. How he had any left from our last trip I'll never know.

"But you found it. It's like finding a fire. Are you gonna walk away from a fire in the overhead bin because you don't know how to use the fire extinguisher?"

"I've never dealt with a passenger who smoked on a flight."

Jesus Henry Christ! This kid was a nightmare. "Follow me and learn something."

The two of us walked up the aisle towards 15F. I looked back to make sure Keegan was trailing me because his body language screamed that he wanted to hide in the galley. But I refused to let him off the hook that easy. We stopped at row 15 and the female passenger in 15F had just finished covering herself up with a heavy black jacket and leaned her head against the window to take a nap. She wanted us to believe she had already fallen asleep but that shit wasn't going to fly. Not today. I may not be ancient like some of the old hags I work with, but I also wasn't born a week ago. I know a con when I see one. Smiling, I leaned in over the two other passengers in the row, put my hand on my chest, breathed deep through my teeth, and let out a long drawn out, "Hiiiiiiiiiii." She immediately opened her eyes and acted confused like I had disturbed her sleep. I had zero patience for this shit, "Can you come to the back of the airplane with us?"

Without waiting for her to reply, I motioned for Keegan to follow me and we swiftly made our way to the back galley. Once there, we turned around to greet 15F as she made her way towards us but to our surprise she had caught up and was already standing between the two lavatories. She smelled like a jazz lounge and her face was more weathered than New Orleans after Hurricane Katrina.

I opened the lavatory door and pointed inside, "Did you use this lavatory?"

With a Scandinavian accent she answered, "Yes."

Truly unexpected. I expected to go straight for the jugular after hearing her lies but she told the truth. When I expect someone to lie and they come out with the truth it's hard for me to recover. I looked at Keegan who continued snacking on his hang nails like they were string cheese.

"Did you smoke in the lavatory?"

With a deadpan expression, "Yes." She looked over at Keegan and added, "I only took two puffs."

Surprised by her honestly, I almost gave her a free pass. Would it have been so terrible for me to tap her lightly on the hands and send her back to her seat? Without an extra Diet Coke, of course. Was that something that I could live with? Letting a smoker off scot-free? Fuck no! What in gay hell was I thinking? I prepared to unleash my verbal beat down but paused for a moment before I spoke. Handling this incident differently than the last time was important to me.

Apparently, it wasn't that important. It should come as no shock that I lost my cool the moment I opened my lips. I came at her like a pimp collecting his money, "You endangered all of our lives on this airplane because you couldn't wait another two hours to have a cigarette." At first she didn't respond. She just stared at me the way Irene did the night I caught her pissing in her dresser drawer after drinking a case of Budweiser and taking too many hits off her bong.

"I only took two puffs," 15F stated in a very calm and quiet voice. She looked to Keegan for reassurance but he didn't offer any. The only thing he had to offer anyone was a pile of chewed up dead skin.

I actually felt bad for her but I stood my ground, "I understand that, but you can't smoke on an airplane. I don't care how many puffs you took. Two puffs. Twenty puffs. This is a no puff zone! Where is the cigarette butt?"

She looked back towards her seat, "I put it out. It is in my bag."

While she watched, I opened the lavatory door one more time, pulled out the trash bin, and started pushing soiled tissues around making it look like I was checking for fire embers. She needed to know this was some serious shit and I wasn't just talking to her because I was bored on a long ass flight.

When I felt confident she understood the seriousness of smoking on an airplane, I placed the trash bin back into the lavatory and Keegan walked her back to 15F to confirm that she had the cigarette butt. I stayed surprisingly calm over the entire situation and felt empowered when I called the flight deck to tell the captain the situation. "This is Joe. 15F was smoking in the lavatory and she confessed to it. Can we have security meet the flight?"

"Did you find the cigarette butt?"

"Yes. She put it out and saved it for later."

When we arrived at the gate she was greeted by the police. Who knows what happened to her but, hopefully, she was fined $10,000 by the FAA or deported back to Stockholm to spend the rest of her life in prison trying to keep her tits out of another woman's mouth. The interesting part about this lady was her composure during the entire interaction. Most passengers become agitated by simply asking them how they take their coffee, but 15F didn't even flinch after being accused of smoking in the lavatory.

I'm guessing this wasn't her first time lighting up at 38,000 feet.

Airlines in the United States banned smoking on airplanes in 1998, but some passengers still think nothing will happen to them if they decide to light up in the lavatory. Perhaps they believe the little cigarette light with the line across it is for the person sitting in the other seat. We tell passengers that all flights are non-smoking, and even have signs all over the airplane, but passengers still ignore us. How can we get passengers to follow the rules? We can't. We can only report them to security if we catch them smoking. My job would rock if flight attendants had the authority to carry around a can of pepper spray. A few squirts of pepper spray to the eyes, handcuff their hands behind their back, and-just for being stupid and endangering the lives of everyone on the airplane-a quick taser to the genitals.

Well, maybe that's going too far.

No Hustler For You!

Managing unstable passengers keeps me on the edge of my jumpseat more than running out of alcohol on a Las Vegas flight. Taking a job working inside an airtight metal tube full of strangers with nowhere to escape should make every flight attendant question their sanity. In the event a schizophrenic passenger forgets to take their medicine, the most we can do is hide in the lavatory, which can actually be unlocked from the outside. On most flights, I sit on my jumpseat looking out over the sea of passengers wondering who is going to lose their shit before we land. Who's a pedophile? Who's cheating? Who likes fisting? Who swallowed an eight ball before leaving for the airport and will barricade themselves in the lavatory trying to fish it out of the toilet? It doesn't matter because once the airplane has departed, a flight attendant who comes in contact with a crazy passenger is held hostage by their insanity.

The key to squashing these outbursts at cruising altitude is to be observant. Watch passengers like a hawk watches a bunny scurry across an open field. Catch the fuckers before the airplane door closes. That's the pivotal point in securing a drama free flight. Catch them fuckers first.

On a flight from Cleveland to Dallas I was working with Abigail and Keegan. Again! When I saw their names on my pairing I assumed they were buddy bidding with me without my consent. Not cool. Buddy bidding is when one flight attendant requests to fly trips with another flight attendant. Abigail I didn't mind so much, but I had reached my breaking point with Keegan. An important factor in buddy bidding is that the requesting flight attendant be junior to their bidding partner because senior flight attendants' schedules are created first. If a junior flight attendant requests to fly a trip with me and there happens to be an open position, they will get to experience my awesomeness. Sounds great, right? It is if you enjoy working with the requesting flight attendant. If you don't then you are stuck with both insane passengers and a crazed flight attendant who thinks the worst thing about his life is that Jesus hates him for butt sex.

My first task after we finished this pairing was to file a complaint with the human resource department and ask for a full investigation on why the hell I was being awarded so many trips with these two. It was getting to the point where I could write a book on Abigail and Keegan titled *Abigail Laughs and Keegan Cries About Religion and Cock*.

The three of us were starting our first of three flights for the day. I am not a lazy complainer but working three flights in one day can be exhausting. Mind melting. I enjoy taking it easy. I am more of a one, or maximum two-flights-a-day kind of flight attendant. If my job is to stay fresh, polite, and happy while serving ungrateful passengers bags of nuts, then the least the airline can do is not work me to death. Especially if they want the passengers to come back.

Is that too much to ask? On this trip I was the senior flight attendant and I was awarded the back galley position. As the lead flight attendant, Abigail (thankfully it wasn't Keegan) worked in the front, and self-hating Keegan was holding down the mid-cabin position.

During boarding, a scruffy, mangy-looking twenty-something young man walked on the airplane. I watched him shuffle down the aisle and take his seat in row 19. From 15 feet away it was obvious this guy had yet to meet a bar of soap that he liked. Once all the passengers had boarded, Abigail made her pre-departure announcement that the airplane door was closing momentarily. That was my signal to do a final cabin safety check in my section. I straightened my tie in the lavatory mirror and slowly walked the aisle with my hands tucked behind my back, ensuring everyone had their cell phones and electronics turned off, bags carefully placed under the seat in front of them, and seat belts fastened.

I strolled passed the dirty slimeball in 19D and stopped in my tracks after noticing he had ripped the cover off a *Hustler* magazine and somehow attached it to the seatback so it covered his television screen. I paused for a moment. I took a step back, confirmed it actually was the cover of a porno magazine, leaned into his personal space, and pointed at the magazine cover, "Sir, I need you to take that down for me."

Looking up he asked, "Why?"

His dirty pores and unbrushed teeth were mere inches from the front cover of a *Hustler* magazine and he had the audacity to question me. I snapped like a turtle and leaned my weight on the back of his seat, "This is inappropriate material and some of our other passengers may become offended. Please take it down."

"Why?" He looked me directly in the eyes, "I bought this magazine in the airport. There's nothing showing on the cover."

That was a true statement. There was no sign of nipples, ass, or bush; the only lips on the front cover were smeared with red lipstick and plastered across the slutty model's face.

"I understand, but I need you to put it away," I replied while I continued standing over him trying not to speak loudly. It was my duty to get the message across, but I didn't want to embarrass this douchebag in front of other passengers. Why I wanted to protect him from humiliation was beyond me. I figured that was how to handle the situation even though his deliberate defiance was starting to work my last nerve.

We stared at each other for a few seconds and then he turned his head toward the lady sitting next to him, completely ignoring me, and mumbled something under his breath. I couldn't make out what he said, but if I had to guess he probably wanted me to take a tree trunk, stuff it up my ass, and spin around on it. Who did he think I was? Keegan on a Reno layover?

Mr. Asshole was not playing nice. I hate when a passenger goes out of their way to make my day a living hell. I refused to say another word. I turned and walked up to the front of the airplane to give Abigail and Keegan a quick rundown on the situation. I also figured that by stepping away for a few minutes he might do the right thing and remove the porno cover.

I still have faith in humanity. I honestly don't know why.

As I approached the front galley there was no hiding my anger. I folded my arms as I positioned myself between Abigail and Keegan, "The guy in 19D put the cover of a porno magazine in front of his television. It's *Hustler.*" I said *Hustler* like I was disappointed it wasn't *Dirty Power Tops and The Bottoms Who Love Them.* Is that even a magazine? If it's not, it really should be. At least if it was a gay magazine I could have confiscated it and used it at the hotel on my layover.

Abigail asked, "Who? What seat is he in?"

"19D. He's the grungy looking dude with that nasty homeless-looking backpack."

She frowned, "He's weird. I should have known something was up with him. He stopped up here when he walked on the airplane and said, 'It's the cockpit. Why do they call it a *COCK*pit?' He emphasised the word cock." She whispered the word cock each time to protect the ladies' ears seated in the front row.

Keegan turned his bobble head around and screeched, "Well he can't have that. What makes him think he can have that? He can't have that on the flight. Who does he think he is?"

"Settle down, Keegan. I have it under control. If he doesn't put it away we'll remove him from the flight." They both shook their heads in agreement. I spun around, smiled at the lady seated in the front row, and strolled down the aisle to the scene of the porno crime. In all honestly, my nerves were on edge. With each row I passed my anxiety rose until I felt my heart violently pumping. The perfect opportunity to pop a few Xanax if I'd had a prescription. I reminded myself to contact my doctor the moment I landed to ask why I wasn't on Xanax.

Why was I afraid of this passenger? Something made me extremely uneasy about him. Confronting people everyday is what I do and I am damn good at it. Great actually. I could tell people that I have a bachelor's degree in confrontation—scratch that, a master's. I love confrontation. It's like fuel that keeps me warm on winter nights, but here I was, nervous about dealing with this low life passenger who wanted to argue with me about a porno magazine he had out in public for everyone to see.

When I walked up to row 19, I was relieved to see he removed the magazine cover. Excellent. I'd jot that down as a win for Joe. But he feverishly was attempting to stuff another sheet from the magazine into the crevices of the television monitor to block the screen. I smiled, "Are you trying to shut off your television? Here let me show…" I was in mid sentence—holding my breath while I leaned over him to power down his television screen—when I noticed the *Hustler* magazine open, on his tray table, to the most inappropriate section of the magazine. There for everyone and baby Jesus to see, including the female minor seated across from him, were enough fake tits to make a plastic surgeon uncomfortable. If the tittie show wasn't enough, a legally blind person could make out each picture of the cover girl stuffed with cock and balls. Out of the corner of my eye, I noticed the two older Mexican ladies seated next to him in 19E and by the window in 19F. The last time I'd seen fear like that on a Mexican's face was when the INS knocked on my neighbor's door and carted him and his entire family off to Tijuana. I swear I had nothing to do with it. All I will say is that Jorge might think twice before making empty offers to share his haul of fresh crabs from the sea and then act like he never offered them up in the first place.

Magda and Marisa (or as I like to refer to them as M&M, the spicy Mexican chocolate kind) were shaking so violently in the seats next to 19D that they were burning off the empanadas they inhaled at the gate before boarding the airplane. It's a scientific fact (I really don't know if this is true) that Mexicans don't leave the house without empanadas. They'd forget their seven children at home before they'd forget a meat pie. Puerto Ricans do the same with Goya Adobo Seasoning, whites with anything gluten-free, and blacks with fried chicken.

Magda prayed, holding her rosary so tight I was afraid she'd give herself stigmata. I'd have to get this bitch off the flight before we closed the main airplane door. Wrestling with stigMagda mid-flight because she deemed herself a miracle and could walk out on the wing at 38,000 feet was out of the question. I didn't give a fuck if she had stigmata on her hands, feet, or tits—the only miracle that was happening on this airplane was that I wouldn't kill someone before departure. If I was ever going to pray, it was at that moment, so I looked up at the overhead bin to compose myself. Jesus Christ give me strength, or better yet, stigMagda Ortiz put down that goddamn rosary.

With Magda destroying her rosary beads and Marisa crying real tears (not the fake ones that people do when they want an upgraded seat), it was obvious that M&M were about to start chanting some voodoo curse. Did I have to remind them it was only a porno magazine on the tray table and not real passengers spread eagle fucking? There was no denying 19D needed to quickly put away his pornographic material but it was not cause for crying in your empanada.

I took my hand and flipped the front cover over to close the magazine, "Sir! What did I say? You're gonna have to put that away." Placing my right hand on the back of his seat and my left on the seat in front of him, I decided it was time to intimidate. "You can't have that type of material in view of other passengers." I did not lower my voice. If the police were boarding the airplane soon—which I anticipated to be true—I'd need as many witnesses as possible.

"Man, why you gotta be like that? I ain't done nothing wrong." He looked around trying to catch the attention of other passengers hoping they agreed. Nobody within earshot responded. The only feedback he got was from a few people who shot daggers at him and the occasional tear from 19E. The father of the little blond girl in 19C switched seats with her which placed him across the aisle from the dirt bag. I was the only obstacle standing in the way of him beating the fuck out of 19D. Nothing fazed porno guy. He refused to cooperate, "I bought this in the airport and I can read whatever I want on this plane. Go away."

Anyone with a watch and 20/20 vision could count the vein in my neck pulsating. I had to correct him, "No sir, you *DO NOT* have the right to look at, display, or read inappropriate material on this airplane. We will not tolerate this type of behavior." I always love ending an unfriendly confrontation on the airplane with that line. Basically it's your last chance to set yourself straight before I yank you out of your seat by your *Hustler* magazine and toss you off the airplane.

He wasn't going to let this end. He took out a black sharpie from his jacket pocket, opened up the magazine, ripped off a strip and started writing my name down from my uniform wings, "Joe, is it? You won't tolerate this behavior. Really? Ok, we'll see about that when I contact the airline." It took him his entire rant to spell out J-O-E across a blond hairy labia. It took all my energy not to laugh in his face. I'd never before had my name written out so angrily across a picture of a vagina. I guess I can check that off my bucket list.

What was this guy thinking? A letter to my airline complaining that I refused to let him read his filthy magazine in public for everyone in coach to see? I envisioned something like this being written across the orgy scene on page 32:

> Dear Airline,
>
> My mom paid good money for me to fly from Cleveland to Dallas to attend my child support hearing. I hate to fly unless I'm high or drunk. I can't do that because of your stupid rules so I used my last $20 to buy a Dr. Pepper, a bag of Doritos, and a *Hustler*. I figured the Dr. Pepper would satisfy my thirst because I can't drink before the hearing and the *Hustler* would put a smile on my face and a lump in my shorts for the three hour flight. And the Doritos are because you people don't sell food. This faggot flight attendant Joe decided that he

didn't want to see my magazine and embarrassed me in front of the young lady seated across from me. She was hot. I liked her until her dad switched seats with her. Why is everyone a dick at this airline? I think she was at least 17 years old. Maybe even a sweet 16. How dare Joe do that? I bought this magazine at the airport and the chick at the counter said I could read it on the airplane. I figure she knows what she's talking about because she WORKS AT THE AIRPORT and she should know if she is selling the magazines, right? That queer ass faggot Joe don't sell magazines. He don't even like pussy. How's he supposed to know what my magazine is about? He don't know shit. I'd like him fired and I would like a full refund so that I can get caught up on my child support payments.

Thanks.

D. Bagg

My concern wasn't that he wanted to write a letter about me, or our interaction, but that he blatantly refused to put the fucking magazine away. If he continued like that, I'd be stuck waiting for security to drag him and his *Hustler* off the airplane. I couldn't understand why he was arguing with me. A sane person would put the magazine away. I'd put it away. I have no problem with porn; I watch porn all the time. I'm actually shocked I took a break from watching porn to write this book. It's perfectly understandable to look at porno magazines but they don't belong on an airplane. Maybe in the lavatory during a red-eye flight, but not in row 19 before coffee service. This guy was more disruptive than members of NAMBLA at an elementary school bake sale.

I passed the point of irritation and quickly moved onto beat down mode. I took a few deep breaths and envisioned stuffing the magazine down his throat if he continued disobeying my direct orders. The passengers within four rows were watching my every single move and M&M had each removed a small white bottle etched with a cross on the front. If either one of those zealots sprayed me with holy water I'd have to report an on-the-job injury. "Sir, I really need you to put the magazine away. Now!"

"I can do whatever I want. You're just the flight attendant" He responded loudly and flipped open the magazine. There was no getting through to this guy, and to be honest—fuck nonsense like that. I get paid to jump out of burning airplanes, not deal with passengers who have no common sense. That's not true. As of right now, while writing this book, my score is zero jumping out of burning airplanes and 3.543 dealing with passengers with no common sense. 19D was being a total douchebag and I refused to let him get away with this behavior. Without saying another word I lifted my hand off his seat back and walked to the front of the airplane, passed Abigail and Keegan, and straight into the flight deck to speak with the captain.

I informed both pilots, "Hey guys, 19D has a porno magazine and refuses to put it away." The captain and first officer turned and looked at me at the same time. I continued, "We need to remove him from the flight."

The captain without missing a beat asked, "What kind of magazine is it? Is it a good one?"

Really? Is this what I had to deal with. I wanted to tell him it was *Dirty Power Tops and The Bottoms Who Love Them* (I am obsessed with that title) just to watch his hair turn whiter, his face crawl into the back of his head, and his body turn to dust like the Nazi guy in Indiana Jones when he drank from the wrong chalice.

"It's a *Hustler.*"

"Oh. That's nasty," he wrinkled up his nose in disgust, "You tell him that if he doesn't put the magazine away he's coming off the flight."

I didn't have the heart to tell him that Keegan, Abigail, and I had already made the decision to pull 19D off the flight and that this conversation was simply my way of being polite and giving him an update on the situation. The passenger was coming off the flight or the three of us were; no confusion about that.

Another trip down the aisle to greet my new favorite person in row 19 and I noticed the magazine was not on the tray table, the television, or in his lap. I was also pleased his cock had not made an appearance and that M&M hadn't turned him into a ferret. Kneeling down next to him I asked, "Sir, are you going to keep that magazine out of sight for the entire flight?"

He refused to let up, "I don't understand what the problem is. I can read whatever I want whenever I want. This is America."

"Alright sir. I'm done." For the final time I spun around and headed full force to the front of the airplane. As I approached the front galley I noticed the airplane door was closed. "Why is the door closed?" I asked Abigail.

"The gate agent said we had to close on time."

I became angrier, "Well looks like we need to open it up because that passenger needs to come off the flight." I walked into the flight deck again and informed the captain to contact the gate agents and let them know we had to reopen the door.

Once the airplane door was reopened the gate agent stood on the jet bridge with a puzzled look on his face, "What's going on?

I gave him the lowdown as quickly as possible, "The guy in 19D doesn't want to put his *Hustler* magazine away and I am done fighting with him about it. He needs to come off." Not two seconds after I finished my sentence, 19D appeared at the front of the airplane standing between me and Keegan in the front galley.

"You can't tell me what to do, bro." His face was flushed and he had either been crying or M&M splashed him with holy water. I couldn't tell. He continued, "I have rights."

I barely wanted to make eye contact with him. If I were out in the real world, or at the Adult Emporium, and not in my uniform, I would have beat the fuck out of him right where he stood. Smug looking prick. My heart still races thinking about how disgusting and inappropriate he was in front of the other passengers, that little girl and her father, my Mexican M&Ms, and of course in front of me. He needed his ass kicked and I wanted to do it. I've never been one to win a fight but he was small and scrawny. With any luck I'd only walk away with a few scratches, a *Hustler* magazine, and a case of scabies. I smiled at the gate agent and then looked at 19D, "Sir, the gate agent is here to talk to you. Have a nice day."

I walked to the back of the airplane and tried to cool down. Watching from the back galley he stood next to Keegan waving his hands around and pointing at the gate agent and then down the aisle towards me. I was too far to hear what he was bitching about, and honestly, at that exact moment I didn't give ten shits. A few seconds later he stormed down the aisle, opened the overhead bin at row 19, grabbed his dirty bookbag, and proceeded to deplane the aircraft.

Like nothing happened, Abigail announced over the PA, "Flight attendants please prepare for departure and cross check your doors."

It was over as quickly as it started.

After we finished the safety demonstration the three of us had a quick debrief in the back galley to update me on what happened after I walked away from the front galley. Abigail practically giggled the entire thing out, "The gate agent didn't even have a chance to tell him to leave. He left on his own."

A little surprised I responded, "What? Are you kidding? He chose a slut magazine over a flight he paid hundreds of dollars for? That's insane. I get upset when I miss the free bus ride from the train to the airport."

"Apparently," she continued, "He told the gate agent he'd take the next flight because you were mean to him. What a kook."

"Well, good. This is the only flight to Dallas today so he can sit in the airport until tomorrow jerking off to his fucking magazine." I sat down in my jumpseat and strapped myself in while they stood over me, "This is going to be a long ass day, and if this is how it's starting, I'm going to need more coffee."

After we landed that evening I took a moment to look up the flight attendants working the next day's flight and I was pleased to find out it was my friend Evan. I texted him immediately and gave him the passenger's name and told him to be on the lookout for him.

Evan text response was typical: *"Was he hot?"*

I responded: *"Not the point."*

That next afternoon Evan texted me back: *"He wasn't on the flight. The gate agent said he cancelled his reservation."*

All that because of a *Hustler* magazine? Incredible. I couldn't help but wonder what airline he considered flying to Dallas. What airline allows a passenger to read a dirty smut magazine while young girls and frightened Mexican ladies shake in fear?

Not an airline with me on the payroll, that's for sure.

BAD THINGS HAPPEN
WHEN YOU FLY STANDBY

The only reason I become a flight attendant was to travel. Not just to travel—anyone with a good paying job or alimony can do that—but to travel for free. If anyone believes for one second that we sign up as flight attendants to simply pass out cups of sugar water to fat people who can barely fit in their seats, they are mistaken. Flying for free is the only reason I put up with the rudeness flung at me on any given flight. Now, some might share with you that they took this job for the flexible work schedule, or to move out of their overbearing parents house, but what we didn't sign up for was the abysmal paycheck. If a flight attendant ever tells you they accepted a position as an air servant for the excellent pay, they are full of shit. The day I hear a flight attendant make that statement I will bitch slap them with a first class amenities kit. I am not kidding. Our pay isn't horrible, but no airline can compensate a flight attendant enough for flying around all day passing out drinks waiting for the day when the captain—who makes all the money—calls the back galley to announce that the airplane will miss landing at JFK by 15 miles. I don't fucking think so. No amount of money can cover that kind of therapy.

The reason most of us slave away at 38,000 feet is because of our itch for adventure. An itch only scratched by free airfare. Think of it as having psoriasis and free airfare is the calamine lotion. If the idea of never having to fork over another red cent for an airline ticket is intoxicating, the act is addictive. It's like being dependant on Vicodin and having your doctor husband write you endless prescriptions. (Side note: How fucking amazing would that be?)

Unless you are in the airline industry—or addicted to Vicodin—you have no idea what I am talking about. Explaining this to my non-airline friends gives me a migraine. Kind of like explaining to creationists that dinosaurs did not roam the Earth 6,000 years ago spending their afternoons playing in the Garden of Eden with Cain and Abel. In all honesty, I am at a loss for words on the subject matter of dinosaurs and children being best friends. Do they not show Jurassic Park at the Creation Museum? Conversations like that make me want to slice off my own fucking ears.

On one of my first trips as a flight attendant I met my friend Sam for a late breakfast during an overnight layover in Richmond, Virginia. For the civilized world, that's brunch. In Richmond, it's breakfast—even when scarfing down mimosas and eggs midday. My guess is Virginia restaurants don't support brunch because it sounds too gay. Virginia doesn't like the gays—or anything remotely gay— including the words: cock, deep, moist, penetration, and my all time favorite, brunch. Virginia is for lovers as long as it's not butt-sex lovers. This paragraph has most likely pissed off the entire state of Virginia. You're welcome, America.

As much as I enjoyed chatting with Sam, there was one big problem: he was ugly. Nice enough, but ugly. We are no longer friends, and I'd love to say that it was because he wronged me or did something terrible, but it's because of his looks. What? I do my best to refrain from consorting with ugly people. Everyone does that, right? Or so I thought. Apparently, I'm wrong. My own husband says I am a horrible human being for thinking this way. I completely disagree. I'll smile and politely remind him that I don't kill ugly people (I'm not barbaric) I simply befriend them for short periods of time. I am not wishing them into an ugly concentration camp where they can all live and work together. How terrible. Or perfect? Do we know if one exists?

Back to Sam. How ugly was he? So ugly his mother hated inviting him over for Thanksgiving dinner because he'd scare everyone out of the house, leaving her to sit across from him while he dismembered the turkey with his bare hands—while it was still alive. As single and ugly as he was, and trust me on that, the only thing on his mind at brunch (fuck you, Virginia) was talking about female flight attendants and whether I knew any single ones. I didn't give an explosive diarrhea about single female flight attendants. I wanted to talk about my fabulous flight benefits and not his desperate attempt to date anything with a vagina. It seems that when you are ugly and straight, any pussy will do.

Sam barely grasped what I was saying, "What do you mean you fly for free?"

"I fly anywhere my airline flies for free. I don't pay anything."

"You don't pay to fly?"

"Are you listening to me?" I wanted to slap him because I knew he was thinking about flight attendant's private parts, "I just said I fly for free."

"Where?"

"Sam, are you fucking stoned? I said any city my airline flies too."

"That's cool," he said sipping his coffee.

"That's your response? What the fuck? I just told you I have the most amazing benefit in the world and you say, 'That's cool.'" I refused to accept his reply. That reaction was only fitting if I told him I received 15% off purchases over $50 at Kohl's, not that I fly for free. I had to prove my point by making this as grandiose as possible so he'd fully understand. Without losing momentum I quickly added, "Actually, I fly on all the domestic airlines for free." His head practically exploded on the wall.

"Get the fuck out of here?" He splattered coffee on the table, "Holy shit! Now I really need some single flight attendant digits."

The freedom to fly all over the country without paying for airfare makes me as happy as Ed McMahon crawling out of his grave, knocking on my front door, and announcing on national television that I have won the Publishers Clearing House Sweepstakes. The ability to walk up to an airline ticket counter and ask for a free empty seat is mind-blowing. I am a superhero with the ability to fly free. I'm kind of like Superman, but more like Wonder Women because I am gay and the idea of soaring around in an invisible jet sounds better than picking bugs out of my teeth while flying faster than a speeding bullet. Even though I fly for free on standby, and there has to be an open seat available, I pinch myself each and every time a gate agent hands me a boarding pass without me ever having to touch my wallet.

Could I afford to travel as much if it wasn't for free? Hell no. I am a flight attendant. A majority of my money goes towards important things: wine, clothes, therapy, my cell phone bill... more wine. I have flown from Washington Dulles to Honolulu, Anchorage to Seattle, and Boston to Los Angeles for free on airlines that I don't even work for. Focusing on my benefits keeps me sane—and out of jail—when dealing with asshole passengers. It's healthier than swishing their ice cubes around in my mouth and spitting them into a cup before pouring in a can of Sprite. I simply remind myself that I am a flight attendant and I fly for free.

Each airline has their own specific agreements with other participating airlines allowing flight attendants and pilots to travel on their flights for free. It's called a reciprocal cabin agreement. Reciprocal cabin agreements make it possible for commuting crews to get to their reporting bases to start work. I basically use it to go on vacation and make my friends jealous. Most airline crews wouldn't be in this industry without reciprocal cabin agreements. Not all airlines fly to every destination on the map. If a flight attendant lives and commutes from BumfuckIdaho Airport and the airline they work for doesn't fly there, they have to rely on another airline for transportation. That's why this benefit is so amazing. It's way more exciting than a discount at Kohl's.

Reciprocal cabin agreements don't just cover domestic travel. They allow us to purchase discounted standby tickets on other airlines for international travel as well. If I told you exactly how little these tickets cost, you'd run right out and marry a flight attendant. I'm serious. You'd marry them even if they were obese and had a face full of acne. International standby tickets may not be completely free, but flying internationally as a flight attendant is exciting. If free domestic air travel is the cake then discounted international travel is the frosting—and who doesn't love some international frosting spread across their lips?

With all this positivity about flying for free you should know there's a little negativity lurking in the shadows. Don't worry, I know exactly where to find it because it haunts me every fucking time I step foot in an airport. Hold on because I am about to do a 180 on your ass. Seriously, you may get whiplash so grab something bolted to the ground and don't let go. I'll admit, I've spent plenty of time putting the joys of flying for free high up on a shiny white pedestal one might find at Crate & Barrel. And it really does belong up there. For the most part, it's amazing. It's fantastic. It's orgasmic. But it's time to give that pedestal a swift kick and throw some reality into the mix. While I love the free part, it's the standby part that turns me into a raging lunatic. Uncontrollable. Crazied. Psychotic. Those are words that describe my behavior when I actually get on the flight. When I fly standby for international flights I become a complete and utter irrational schizoid. Strip me down, hose me off, lock me up, and throw away the key. As much as I love flying for free, I am horrible at the uncertainty of standby travel.

The first time I traveled internationally on standby was in 2008. It was a New York City departure for a quick hop across the pond to Paris with Evan. Total cost: $77 roundtrip. The shock of the price kept me up tossing and turning for a few nights. Who pays under $100 for a flight to Paris? Do I even need to answer that? The ticket confirmation email vibrated my cell phone jolting me out of my crash pad bunk bed at 1 a.m. I laid there dumb-founded thinking there was an error. Evan was on a trip so I couldn't ask him. I decided to send him a text the following morning. There had to be a mistake. Right?

Wrong. The price was legit. Soon I'd be traveling on a wide-body airplane on my way to learn just how much the French hate Americans. That lesson came within my first few hours after arriving in Paris. The French don't hate Americans, we are just assholes. Great. Not only have I pissed off Virginia but now I can add the other 49 states as well. What can I say, I like making everyone feel equal. Back to Paris, there's nothing more embarrassing than listening to some redneck chick with a double chin from North Carolina yell in English while standing in line at a beautifully decorated fromagerie, "How much is this cheese? *CHEESE!* How much? Why doesn't anyone speak English in this godforsaken country?"

I've learned that anything which brings us joy often comes with a heavy price. A late night concert which leaves you dead tired in the morning. Having a record breaking financial year but then forking over half of it to Uncle Sam. Flying for free with the chance you might not obtain a seat on the airplane. That last one kicks me in the sac. Hard. With a sledgehammer.

Many flight attendants and pilots have no problem flying standby. Honestly, I don't know how they do it. Is there some secret online course they've taken preparing them for the drama of flying standby? If that's the case then why the fuck haven't I heard of it? Even when the last seat is given away to another standby passenger, these magical individuals handle themselves with the grace and ease of a wrongly crowned Miss Universe.

I act like Kanye West on stage at the MTV Music Awards.

When you find yourself stressing, panicking, or freaking out over the thought of not knowing if you will make the flight, I hate to tell you but flying standby may not be for you. It's not for me, but sadly I keep going back. Why? Because it's free, and I love free.

To save my sanity, and my job, I created a list of six rules to follow when managing my anxiety while traveling standby. They are as follows:

1. Calm the fuck down! Nobody has died (yet).

2. Always bring treats for the flight attendants so that if you do get a seat, it might be in first class.

3. Have as many backup plans as possible. Have a plan A, B and C. There are 26 letters in the alphabet. If you are smart, you will have a plan for them all.

4. Try not to swear, scream, stomp your feet, throw your luggage, do shots of tequila, or smack annoying children while standing at the ticket counter.

5. Take deep breaths and remember that everything works out in the end.

6. Refrain from hovering at the gate area. Also avoid sweating, talking to oneself, and pacing back and forth so you don't give the impression that you are about to blow yourself up if you don't get on the flight.

Number six is must. If there's one rule you implant into your brain make sure it's number six. Don't be an amatuer and forget that important detail the way I did traveling internationally back in 2010. Don't get me wrong, I didn't intend on blowing up the airport, but the way I was sweating and pacing around the gate area you'd have thought I had more dynamite strapped to me than an Al-Qaeda housewife.

Evan and I were embarking on an elaborate vacation that took us to Madrid, Barcelona, and—unbeknownst to us at the time—a quick overnight stop in Helsinki. It was our annual we-are-flight-attendants-and-fly-for-free vacation, which we took to celebrate our fabulous lives as flight attendants. Yay for discounted airfare, boo for flying standby. This trip was mine to plan. Actually, I planned all the trips because I'm a control freak. Evan never griped about my freakish desire to control everything. His only request was that we ventured out of the United States. I immediately chose Madrid and Barcelona. When I called him to confirm our itinerary he was giddier than a post-op male-to-female transexual getting her first set of tits. I eagerly tapped away at my laptop on long layovers and on my days off searching for hostels and airlines with open flights from JFK to Madrid. Within a few hours of planning I learned that all flights out of Barcelona back to the states were completely full on the date we scheduled our return.

This triggered my full blown panic attack before we even packed our bags.

Sitting on my sofa with sheets of paper spread out everywhere I urgently texted Evan: *"Queen. What are we gonna to do? All flights are full leaving BCN and I don't want to get stuck in Spain."*

He instantly texted me back: *"Relax. Everything will be fine. Okkkkkkkurtt! Just think of another way home."*

Evan never panics when he travels. This makes me hate him. Alright, I don't really hate him—he's one of my best friends—but it makes me want to hate him which works for me. How he maintains his composure in the stickiest of standby dilemmas is a mystery to me. He's so fucking calm. If every airline on the planet seized their operations and he was left trapped inside a mud hut in South Sudan he'd smoothly say, "Girl, let me just fix my hair, find a hut with a strong WiFi signal, and we'll jet out of here in a few."

He'd be rich if he found a way to bottle up this attitude into travel-size containers and sell it on Amazon. First, I'd buy stock in the product. Second, I'd purchase a 10 year supply and dab that shit behind my ears, under my pits, and anywhere else I could reach.

I was challenged not to fall apart planning this trip. Unfortunately, I'm Jenga being played by drunk people when it comes to flying standby. My record for losing my shit during our annual trips wasn't a solid one. Paris comes to mind. You remember Paris, right? The $77 round trip to Paris. This memory still breaks me out in hives. Evan and I stopped for a caffeine boost while strolling down the Champs-Elysees. The weather was fantastic, matching our moods. While he stood in line to place our cappuccino orders, I ducked into the restroom to relieve myself. After I finished draining my bladder, I bent over to flush the toilet and—*kerplunk*—my brand new camera slipped out of my jacket pocket into the toilet. With no time to think I reached down and fished it out of my own urine. The screen was dead and it refused to turn on. I started to cry. Not for the fact that I had dropped a not-so expensive camera into the toilet but because I had fucked up, again. Matt had bought me this camera specifically to bring on my trip to Paris because I had lost our more expensive camera the month prior. Losing two cameras in two months is beyond irresponsible. People in Saudi Arabia are executed for less.

Walking out of the restroom with my pissy hands grasping my pissy broken camera I broke down while Evan stood in front of me double fisting cappuccinos. "I dropped my camera in the toilet. It's fucking ruined," I was weeping, "I can't believe this happened. All my pictures are lost."

He stood there leaning from foot to foot and then erupted into laughter, "Girl. It's a camera. No big deal. All you gotta do is pull out the sim card and your pictures will be saved."

Nothing helped. His rationale advice lost to my hysteria. "No. You don't understand. Matt bought me this camera after I lost the other one last month."

This sent him into another fit of laughter, "That's right. You lost that camera at JFK last month." He couldn't stop laughing as we walked up the hill towards Montmartre.

In that moment I realized hating him might not be as difficult as I had earlier anticipated.

Lucky for me, I had put Paris behind me and learned valuable travel lessons from that stressful experience. I continued telling myself that while I planned our Spain adventure. After several hours researching flight options from Barcelona to JFK, it was clear that we wouldn't be coming home that way. As I was about to throw my hands up in defeat and cancel the entire trip, a flicker of hope came across my laptop screen when I randomly pulled Finland out of my ass. Seriously, pulled it right out from between my buttcheeks and slapped it down on the table. *Splat!* Now if you're wondering how I came up with Finland, I couldn't even begin to tell you. Like I said, buttcheeks. What I can tell you is that it was a genius plan and nothing like it has come out—or gone in—my ass ever since.

The plan was set. After three days of sightseeing in Madrid we'd hop over to Barcelona for an additional three days, zip up to Helsinki for a 24 hour visit, and head home on a wide open flight aboard an Airbus 340. Wide open. Two words that I love hearing when flying standby, not when performing anal sex as the top. The Helsinki answer was a gift from the standby Gods. Evan and I were touched by the Gods. Sounds dirty when you first think about it but, in retrospect, it's better than being touched by your creepy uncle. Agreed?

Once we arrived in Spain, our trip started out as one of the best travel experiences of my entire life. Nothing seemed to go wrong. For starters, all the standby flights we had chosen had ample seating to accommodate us throughout our entire trip; I made sure of this before we left JFK. I confirmed with the airlines obsessively and to the point that Evan eventually told me to stop calling them because they had enough nutty passengers to deal with. He was right. Once we wrapped up our time in Madrid we were off to Barcelona. While checking into our Barcelona hostel the front desk clerk informed us that they had no double beds available. The scene got extremely tense. Sirens alarmed in my head but seconds before sweat started cascading down my face the owner appeared inviting us to stay in a private apartment only a few blocks away. We didn't even have to blow him, which is always a plus. Well, it was for me. I think Evan was disappointed. I even went out of my way to guarantee no camera drama by keeping it deep inside my front jeans pocket at all times. That camera was never out of sight or off my person. My outlook on flying standby began turning around, which was important because if I planned on spending my life traveling as a flight attendant, I had better get my shit together.

Unfortunately, not all the electronics I traveled with on this trip were as closely guarded as my camera. For our last night in Barcelona, we set out to have dinner along the chaotic boulevard of Las Ramblas. Tourists flock to Las Ramblas for the sights, smells, and party atmosphere. Most people seem to relish in the disorder. Not me. Strolling toward our restaurant, among the thousands of tourists overcrowding the city streets, my guard was up high in an imaginary watch tower ready to shoot at any menace headed our way.

The main threat in Barcelona were the infamous gypsies patrolling the dark alleys and bustling streets. They were everywhere. Dirty. Asking for money. Asking for food. Asking for anything and everything. It was hard to ignore them but like any good American, I did my best. As beautiful as Barcelona was, my impression was that these nomads owned the city. They were as much a part of Barcelona as the architecture, paella, and football. I commented to Evan, "There are so many gypsies here. It makes me nervous."

He walked beside me sweeping my overt fears into the gutter, "Don't worry. We've been here for three days. Has anything happened?

"No."

"Exactly," he continued, "I've traveled all over the world. There's nothing to be scared of. Girl, you're scared of everything."

In agreement I nodded, "You are right. Why do I do this to myself?"

He laughed out loud, "Cause you're crazy. Remember that time we were in Paris and I yelled at you not to get too close to that parked van with no windows? You thought you were getting kidnapped."

That made us both laugh. I could always count on Evan to pull me out of my silly overreactions. I stopped for a moment and looked around, "I think this is the restaurant from the other night." I walked over to the menu stapled to an old chipped paint easel, "I can't tell. They all look the same."

Spinning on his heels, "Yeah. This is the place. Let's see if they remember you from when you were drunk and put on a dead shrimp puppet show."

He was also good at reminding me of how crazy I get after too many beers. "I hope not. I just want to try the black paella."

Evan flung his nose in the air, "Nasty."

The middle-aged balding server hurriedly ushered us to our seats a few tables back from the busy crowds walking along the street. Still in the middle of all the commotion but not as much foot traffic. The perfect people watching table. We instantly noticed our dining neighbors to my left. A mother, father, and their gay son. We didn't need to see his membership card for confirmation. His gayness was brighter than the full moon lighting up the evening sky. His brilliance engulfed both our tables to the point that if there was a power outage, I'd still be able to read the menu on the table.

"Look at that queen," Evan whispered, "She's out with mommy and daddy on vacation."

I chuckled and grabbed my cell phone and snapped a stealth photo of the family triangle next to us, "She's so gay. She makes us look butch." Again, we both screamed with laughter allowing everyone in the restaurant to know we were present and accounted for. The gay looked over and made eye contact but he wasn't laughing. Did he hear us? Most likely. Gays tend to have supersonic hearing. Probably from all the years of having to eavesdrop on bullies talking shit about us in high school.

The waiter approached with two glasses of water and took our orders. As I handed the oversized menu back to him I focused my attention on Evan, "This has been a fun trip," I raised my glass of water in the air, "Cheers to a great trip."

He lifted his and smiled, "Cheers, queen. We always have the best times."

"We sure do. I can't wait to get to Helsinki and see what it's like."

Evan answered but he was distracted by the crowd of soccer players causing a scene in front of the restaurant, "I'm sure it will be nice. Look at that guy," he licked his lips, 'Helllller Mr. Soccer Man. Can I play with your balls?" We both howled and he continued, "I wouldn't mind him scoring a goal in my butt."

"Well you can't score anything because we are sharing an apartment."

"She's a cockblocker. My bestie is a cockblocker."

After taking another sip of the tepid water, I placed the glass down and noticed a grungy stranger walking up to our table. I looked away but felt him standing there awkwardly staring at us. He didn't say a word. All three of us experienced a moment of silence while the rest of the world chattered on. I did my best to avoid eye contact but my curiosity got the best of me. Our eyes connected and I watched as he studied us for a few beats and then thrust a piece of paper a few inches from my face. Evan completely ignored the man which left me to deal with the haggard looking homeless guy shaking a white sheet of paper at me.

Focusing my eyes on the paper, I noticed it read: Por Favor. Dame dinero. Gracias.

I turned my head away but responded to his request, "Lo siento. No tengo dinero."

That wasn't enough for this guy. Like I said, these gypsies run Barcelona. Without budging an inch, he continued to lift the paper up and down in front of me while pointing at it. When I didn't respond he dropped the paper on our table.

There were at least a dozen other people seated in all directions around us. Why was he fucking with me? What about the other gay guy at the next table? I silently asked myself these questions while the gypsy focused his attention on making me as uncomfortable as possibly. Finally I snapped, "No, no tengo dinero. Adios!" My aggression worked. He picked up his piece of paper and as quickly as he appeared he vanished. Gone.

"See," Evan turned to me, "You know how to handle these people. They are harmless."

I agreed. I felt self-assured handling the situation. I needed that boost of confidence and now that I had tasted it, nothing could stop me. It was so simple. Why was I afraid of these gypsies? You just had to be firm and to the point with them or they'd take advantage of you. The same is true when flying on an airplane full of Puerto Ricans and Dominicans. Show any sign of weakness and you'll have footprints on your back. And a dick in your ass… but only if you're lucky.

Within seconds of my gypsy encounter our waiter arrived with our entrees. The smell of the meal made the past few minutes a faint and forgotten memory. He set our heated plates down in front of us and politely asked, "Algo mas?"

We both smiled letting him know we were all set. He nodded and disappeared to the next table. The black paella instantly put me in a trance. The collection of shrimp, mussels, and fish married with a heaping pile of squid ink rice made me reach for my cell phone to take a picture.

"Matt will never believe I ate this," my left hand swept over the table to grab my cell phone but there was nothing there except air and table cloth. No cell phone. Evan had already taken a bite of his food, unaware of the tension building up in my veins. My eyes moved from the paella to where my cell phone had been moments ago. It was gone.

"Oh my god. Where's my phone?" I demanded, which alerted Evan. I frantically moved the few napkins out of the way on the table assuming my cell phone was under one of them.

"What's going on? Where's your phone?" Evan asked putting his fork down. He picked up a few napkins on his side but found nothing.

I desperately lifted my plate of food and sat it back down. Then I lifted the tablecloth and searched between it and the table. Pushing my chair out I looked under the table for any sign of my iPhone. I had not placed it in any of these locations but when you are about to have a nervous breakdown thinking rationally does not come easy. I stood up violently, pushing the stainless steel chair backwards enough so that when it hit the concrete the noise caught the attention of a few patrons. "My phone is gone. Fuck! Where did my phone go?" I patted down my shorts. When I didn't feel anything I reached into the pockets to double check. My cell phone was thin but it wasn't that fucking thin.

"Maybe you misplaced it. It didn't get up and walk away," he looked around at people gawking at me, "you just took a picture."

I barely heard him, "Holy shit. It was that gypsy. He took my phone." With that revelation I took off running. I kicked my chair to the side as I bolted out of the restaurant into the busy street. I ran a few yards before stopping from the congestion of people along the street. Blood pumped vigorously through my heart leaving my insides feeling like a 9.0 earthquake had struck. It was only a matter of time before the tsunami of emotions hit.

Even though I stopped running, my breathing continued at lightening speed. I can only imagine it was my body attempting to make me hyperventilate before the night was over. Placing my hands on my hips, I looked to my left and right, feeling the pulse in my neck grow stronger with each breath. A river of people flowed passed me, ignorant to my predicament. Their jovial conversations and laughter angering me with each moment that past. I hated them all. I hated Barcelona. I hated myself for leaving my phone on the table and for not placing it safely in my pocket. And goddamn it—I hated those gypsies. Standing on my tip toes I attempted to scan the crowd but then lowered myself back down. Who was I looking for? All I remembered was a dirty guy wearing a worn baseball cap, dark colored clothes, and sporting zero facial hair. Was that the sketch I'd give to the police? I'd get blank stares because that description fit half the people on the street. What if I included the white piece of paper? Any information helps, right? They'd surely know who had my cell phone at that point. Then it hit me. I was fucked. Who was I kidding? Would the Policia Municipal even care about my stolen cell phone? My incident report would be haphazardly jotted down while the chiseled jawed, muscular officers spent the next few hours laughing about the faggot gringo who left his belongings out on an open table in Barcelona for thieves to confiscate.

I really hated Barcelona.

My adrenal glands were spent. Every drop of adrenaline stored in my body was used up on that one stressor. At least that's what I believed. Adrenal glands are constantly producing adrenaline. Enough that a normal person may react to many emergencies thrown their way at once without losing the fight response. That's normal people. I am far from normal. There was no doubt in my mind that my body didn't have enough left to help me jump out of the way of a runaway truck.

When I got back to the table, Evan was updating the waiter on the situation. He offered to package up our food and informed us we did not have to pay the bill. I had no interest in eating after chasing ghosts along Las Ramblas. I lost my cell phone, my appetite, and the will to enjoy the rest of our vacation.

"I can't believe this fucking happened. I took a picture of that queen at the next table and sat the phone down right here," I smacked the table. "I bet you he took it when he put that piece of paper down on the table. Probably scooped it up and ran off. I can't fucking believe it."

Evan let me vent. He stared at me and took in all my frustration and hatred for the situation. I appreciated that. No joking. No laughing. And let's not forget, no cell phone.

On our walk back to the apartment we each carried our takeout boxes, souvenirs of a fucked up last night in Spain. I tossed the white styrofoam container into the first trashcan we came across. "I want to go home. What am I going to do without a cell phone? I can't even call Matt."

"You can use mine. We have one flight to Helsinki with a quick 24 hour layover tomorrow and then we'll be on our way home," he paused, "I'm sorry about your phone."

"Thank you. I'm never leaving home again."

He looked over at me, "Don't say that. Bad things happen. It's how you react to it that matters. You can get another cell phone. Once you come to terms with this you won't feel so bad. I promise."

I didn't want to hear it. While he rambled on with words of wisdom, I focused on my stolen cell phone. I lost it in a strange country and it was probably already on the black market in Morocco being manually fingered by some homeless monster who hadn't used soap or cut his fingernails since the 1990's.

Being violated by Barcelona was not part of my plan, and nothing Evan said or did snapped me out of my misery. As we climbed the stairs to our apartment I was hit with a frightful thought, "Oh my god!" I looked over at Evan, "I have dirty pictures and a jerk off video on my cell phone."

Evan laughed, "Girl. You're gonna be famous."

The next morning Evan did his best to joke and snap me out of my funk, but as quickly as he'd make me smile I'd revert back to my miserable state. I am not ashamed to admit that I acted like a big fucking baby. A daycare full of toddlers in shitty diapers handled themselves better than me. I wanted to stomp my feet and scream at everything and anything that passed my way. I only refrained from doing that because of Evan, I didn't want him to have me committed in Spain. If you think being robbed and having your personal information available for strangers is terrible, I guarantee being locked up in a psych ward in Barcelona made losing a phone feel like misplacing a pen, albeit an expensive one.

Like most people these days, I have an unhealthy attachment to my smartphone. It's not just an electronic device that I carry around with me everywhere I go, it's a part of me. It's an electronic limb, a limb that was severed from my body by a dirty gypsy. I took baby steps but the phantom pain was excruciating. How people manage after losing a limb is beyond me. They are the strongest individuals on the planet. I am a weak bitch. The agony was so bad I had to fight back the urge to throw myself into the Mediterranean Sea after my phone was amputated from my life.

"Do you need to call Matt?" Evan asked during our early morning cab ride to the airport.

"No. I'm good. I told him everything he needs to know last night."

"Are you sure you don't want to file a police report before we leave?"

I looked out the window, "Fuck it. That phone has already seen more border crossings than I have. I just wanna get out of here."

I barely said two words on the flight from Barcelona to Helsinki. Thankfully, we were seated a few rows apart from each other. No need to be seated next to my chatty friend when all I wanted to do was be a recluse and cope with the pain.

By the time our flight landed I had experienced all five stages of grief. My mind processed thoughts and emotions quicker than items purchased in the express checkout line at Target. First came denial, "This can't be happening to me." Then anger, "I will fucking end that asshole if I ever find him." Followed by bargaining, "I swear I'll never leave the United States again if I find my phone," and depression, "Please let this airplane hit a mountain. I can't live through this."

After the full three hour flight I was able to walk up to Evan at the Helsinki Airport and share with him my acceptance of the situation. He was off the airplane first and all smiles as I approached him, "How you feeling? Any better?"

I finally smiled, "Yes. It's just a phone. Worse things could have happened. I'll just get another one when I get home."

He erupted with enough joy for both of us, "Yes! That's the way to look at it. Alright. Let's get out of this airport and see what Helsinki has to offer."

We arrived in Helsinki on a Sunday night. Here's a note to jot down in your travel journal for that fine New England-like Scandinavian city: don't bother visiting on a Sunday. Either the city had been overrun with vampires who sucked the entire population dry, or nobody leaves their home on a Sunday. I wouldn't even say the streets were dead. More like abandoned. Forever. I checked the map to make sure we hadn't landed in Chernobyl—we were in fact in Helsinki.

The two of us checked into our hostel, took showers, and headed out onto the quiet streets before the sun finally disappeared for the evening. Occassionaly, my emotions snuck up and tapped me on the shoulder reminding me that even though I had accepted what happened in Barcelona, I was still miserable as fuck about it. We walked down cobblestone streets, hit a few gay bars, and read signs that probably only meant something on a planet 120 million light years away. A planet without vowels.

The next morning I barely waited for Evan to get dressed before pushing him out the front door. He wasn't happy about it, "What's up with you? The flight isn't leaving for four hours."

"I know but I don't want to take any chances. This is our only way home today."

"Chill out, queen. Damn."

I ignored him and focused on one thing and one thing only, getting the fuck home.

We arrived early at the Helsinki Airport hastily making our way through security to check in with the gate agent. Evan trailed a few feet behind me but my tunnel vision prevented me from looking back. The moment we cleared security my entire body screamed to be home. I was one flight away from being in New York City and another flight away from my husband and cats in Orlando. I could almost feel the humidity building up around me.

No other passengers were waiting in line as we walked up to the counter and greeted the elderly blond gate agent. I arrived first and placed my crew ID on the counter, "Hi. We are listed standby on this flight to JFK. Can you check us in?"

Without looking up she took my ID and began entering information into her computer. I glanced over at Evan who had finally caught up and was leaning against the counter. He smiled which made me relax. Things were looking up. I hadn't forgotten about my cell phone drama, but now that I was finally checking in for the flight home I was able to find peace with what happened. After the ticket agent finished with my ID she placed it onto the counter and snatched up Evan's. He looked at her and asked, "How does the flight look?"

The name bar on her blouse confirmed her name was Olga. After a few seconds of typing, she handed Evan back his crew ID and happily answered in a thick Finnish accent, "The JFK flight is full. You probably won't get on, but you can still wait."

A bald eagle could have flown into my mouth. I stood there thinking to myself, "Close your mouth, Joe. Yes, you are in shock, but don't embarrass yourself. You did a fine enough job of that in Spain."

The two of us had nothing more to say but we didn't move. Honestly, I couldn't have moved even if I tried. I'd have pissed myself right there at the counter if my bladder was full. The utter shock of hearing we might not make the flight left me frozen solid. Evan was the first to move away but I stood there waiting for her to admit her mistake and reassure us there were enough seats on this airplane for all the standby passengers in Helsinki, whether they were going to JFK or not.

"Are you sure? I just checked the other day and there were many seats open." I whimpered out.

Olga spoke as if she were behind the food line prep station at a crowded IKEA explaining they had just ran out of lingonberry sauce. "Yes. I am sure there were," she responded with a hint of annoyance, "but today there are no seats."

Something was terribly off about this information. I knew for a fact there were enough open seats on the flight. I triple checked before we left the states. I'll admit that was a week prior but how many fucking people need to purchase last minute tickets from Helsinki to JFK? She had to be lying. I convinced myself of it while we faced off at the gate. I also convinced myself that Olga was nothing but a dirty Hitler-loving Nazi who wanted nothing more than to slap a pink triangle on my forehead and send me to the wood-burning ovens to make pizzas for her and her other Nazi airport friends. How did this bitch escape the Nuremberg Trials? That's what I wanted to know.

"What should we do?" I desperately tried making eye contact with her but she was obviously done addressing me, "This is the only flight back to the states."

She continued tapping away at her Nazi computer, "Wait until we call your name." Before I could respond she turned and walked down the jet bridge closing the door behind her.

Defeated, I stepped away from the counter and made my way over to Evan who was perched on his rollerboard eating almonds one at a time as cool as a cucumber; a cucumber that I wanted to slam up Olga's swastika.

"Look at the sexy guy over there," he pointed with an almond between his fingers, "I'd have him for breakfast, lunch, and dinner. I wonder if he needs a husband?"

"I can't believe we might not make it on this flight. Can this fucking trip get any worse?" I paced in front of him like a caged zoo animal, "What the fuck are we going to do? I don't want to get stuck here tonight. What are we—"

"Chill out, queen." he interrupted looking away from his future ex-husband, "You do this every time we travel. Maybe if we get stuck here we can find those two Russian guys who wanted to take us back to their hotel last night. They were cute."

"They wanted to cut us up and dispose of our bodies."

"You are so negative," he stood up from his suitcase and wiping crumbs off his dress pants, "I'm going to the restroom. Watch my stuff."

"I'm just freaking out."

"I know girl, you always freak out. If you keep sweating and pacing like that, acting all crazy around the counter, they ain't never gonna let us on this A340. They're gonna think you converted over to Al-Qaeda."

He was right; with my wide eyes and sweaty neck, I looked crazier than Ted Cruz caught on camera at a gay pride parade. While he went to the restroom I leaned my suitcase against the wall, sat down, and counted to ten. One. Two. Three… When that didn't work, I started over again. After seven goes at that I could have simply counted to 70 the first time around.

When Evan sauntered back to me sitting on my suitcase he carefully looked me over making sure I wasn't about to explode. "You doing okay?"

"Yeah. Just waiting for them to call our names."

"They will. At least you're not pacing in front of the counter. That's a relief." He looked around, "Where did my husband go?"

"He already boarded."

"Oh. Maybe I'll get to sit next to him on the flight."

As Olga announced the standby passenger's names who were granted passage onto the airplane, each time I didn't hear her accented voice announce, "Evan or Joe," my blood pressure went up a few points.

"Elisa Kivela," 125/89

"Frans Lampo," 144/94

"Jana Keto," 165/113

Was she ever going to call our names? My faith wore thin as I watched her put down the intercom phone and step away from the podium. My heart sank. Actually, it almost quit functioning. If it were up to me, it would have stopped beating. Thankfully, my body knows how to survive better than I do. There were only a handful of people left scattered around the gate area. Though we were in a busy airport, it was eerily quiet within 20 feet of our gate.

Evan maintained his composure but I watched as he frowned the moment Olga stepped away from the counter. I assumed he thought that hint of disappointment escaped me but I saw it. I saw it loud and fucking clear. I stood up. Who sits in a heated situation like this? I needed to pace. I needed to move. I needed to fucking sweat. Who cares if the gate agents thought I had a bomb strapped to my chest. What good does it do me if I'm not on the airplane to detonate it?

While staring down at the floor, pacing behind Evan, I noticed someone walking towards us. It was Olga. Sweet amazing Olga. I instantly forgave her cuntish ways. If there had been a fish market in that airport I would have purchased her the biggest perch she could fit into her big

Finnish mouth. Holding two pieces of paper in her hand, and without a word, she handed the last two boarding passes to us. The last two fucking seats. I had never been so happy in my entire life. My blood pressure went from near heart attack level to spa day level.

We thanked Olga but got no response in return. She simply walked back behind the counter and continued working at the computer. I didn't care. She could have kicked me in the balls with her high heels and I'd still have bought her a fish. Olga was my Willie Wonka and she had presented us with two golden tickets. Tickets to escape a country that uses the words—haju häpy ja vittu—to express the terms "fuck you" and "smell cunt" interchangeably.

Grabbing the handle of my suitcase, I followed Evan down the jet bridge and onto the brand new A340. My happiness overpowered me and I refused to stop smiling. Who gave a fuck about a stolen iPhone? I was on my way home where a brand new cell phone waited for me at the store.

I took my aisle seat, fastened my seatbelt, and sighed so deeply the man sitting next to me looked over, "Happy to be going home?"

"You bet your ass I am."

WITH LOVE
FROM MOTHER RUSSIA

Flight attendants generally refrain from waking sleeping passengers while conducting beverage and food service. It's rude. It's inappropriate. It's downright mean. But sometimes shit happens. Have you ever tried pushing a cart down a narrow aisle while passengers bulge out of their seats? It's nearly impossible. If I do happen to accidentally wake a passenger while they're trying to catch a short nap on the flight I usually brace for impact. Once these sleepyheads are fully awake they tend to viciously attack. It takes all my energy not to throw a cup of ice in their lap to chill them the fuck out. Nobody wants their face chewed off when asking a stranger how they take their coffee.

During my early years as a flight attendant, I cared little about who I disturbed on the flight. It meant nothing for me to randomly wake up sleeping passengers simply out of boredom. My mentality was if I can't sleep, neither can you. Total bitch move, right? I frequently bumped into passenger's legs or kicked their feet, especially if their legs protruded into the aisle. The first time I tripped over a passenger's shoes and landed in an empty aisle seat, I started stomping my way down the aisle instead of shuffling my feet. Shuffling your feet only works for people wading around in the ocean attempting to avoid a stingray, not on an airplane. When I work a red-eye flight and a passenger has their size 13 shoe in the aisle, their ass gets stomped on. Flight attendants can't risk injury because passengers are too cheap to pay for a business class seat to stretch out their long ass legs.

It's not all bad. Flying during the day seems to be easier for passengers when it comes to keeping their feet and legs where they belong, which is out of the aisle. Nighttime flying brings out the selfishness in most passengers, which makes no sense because they usually paid less for their tickets. If I've learned anything about the airline industry, it's that people who paid the least amount for their tickets expect the most—which includes not only their seating area but the aisle adjacent to them. That's why I tend to avoid working in the back of the airplane where the poor people congregate. You know who I'm talking about. The redneck dude who's normally sneaking a cigarette on a Greyhound bus lavatory. He gets his cousin to buy him a ticket on your flight from Wichita to New Orleans and you spend two hours tripping over his feet because he thinks he owns the entire fucking airplane.

That's why I simply wake the fuckers up, "Oh I'm sorry, sir," crushing their dirty feet under my work shoes, "you might want to put your bare feet back under the seat in front of you before you lose a toe."

As fun as that sounds—and believe me when I say it was—I stopped that practice long ago, but not for reasons you'd expect. It had nothing to do with being nice and not finding joy in crushing the bare feet of inconsiderate assholes. That made flying red-eyes entertaining. It's that an awake passenger is a passenger who will constantly ask for something. People who sleep don't ask for shit because they are asleep. Ever wonder why your flight attendants ask you to close the window shade when you are about to fly cross country on a red-eye flight? It's purely for selfish reasons. If the shade is closed you will sleep throughout the flight and not wake up asking for juice when the sun rises over the East Coast. It took me a few months to figure out that if I tip-toed through the airplane like Santa Claus on Christmas Eve, the passengers would sleep until the airplane touched down in our final destination.

Now when I wake up a passenger it's for a damn good reason, like reminding them to fasten their seat belt, asking them for their phone number, or if they are male—which they always are—offer them a first class blow job to relieve the midnight pressure building up between their legs. I'm serious, this is no laughing matter. As the flight attendant it is my job—scratch that, my duty—to check for explosive devices and I hate to say it but the guy in 4C looks like he's ready to blow. In all honestly. I've never sucked a dick on the airplane. What do you think I am, a whore? Don't answer that. Even though a piece of man flesh has never touched my lips on the airplane I still like to put the offer out there on the tray table. Right next to their bag of salty nuts.

The tricky part about beverage service is knowing exactly who wants to be woken up and who doesn't. Some do. Some don't. How the fuck am I supposed to know the difference? It's like playing airline Russian roulette with thirsty people and their combative emotions. There has to be an easy way around this dilemma.

Wait a minute... I think I've got it. An excellent idea just entered my mind as I typed away at my laptop. I hope nobody else has thought of it or I will feel pretty fucking stupid. What if the airlines attached a perforated coupon to a passenger's ticket? Hear me out before you abandon the idea. One side could read—WAKE ME—and the other side could say—DON'T FUCKING BOTHER ME. Or something like that. You get where I am going with this. Before the airplane takes off, the passenger rips off the coupon and attaches it to their seat. Where they attach it on the seat I have no idea. Like I said, this idea just came to me and I haven't thought it all the way through yet. Just bear with me. When the flight attendants come around for service, they read the side of the card that's facing up and know exactly what type of service the passenger expects. Crafty thinking, right? You're welcome. I've probably just changed the entire airline industry while writing this book and sitting on the sofa in my underwear.

I doubt my brilliant idea will ever be implemented. For one, most airlines keep passengers' tickets after they are scanned at the gate. And two, as simple as my resolution sounds, people would still fuck it up. Part of being an airline passenger is not knowing how to do the simplest tasks on the airplane.

But have no fear, I believe I have the answers. Whether you fall asleep or not, ordering a beverage should not be the hardest part of your travel experience. It should be the easiest. To assist with this, I have created a few quick tips to help anyone when they order a beverage on a flight. No matter your travel background, once you incorporate these into your travel toolbox your entire life will change. Mark my words. And you thought all flight attendants were bitches.

1. Stay awake so the flight attendant can take your drink order. Sounds easy, but probably the hardest thing for an airline passenger. There's nothing worse than walking passed a sleeping passenger only to get verbally abused later because you skipped over them.

2. Stay awake after you place your order so you can receive your drink. Some flight attendants will simply walk the drink back to the galley if you are sleeping and you'll never even know they attempted giving it to you. You'll believe they completely forgot about you. After you wake up you'll ring your call bell and act all bitchy when it's you who fucked up in the first place by falling asleep.

3. Put your tray table down so that if you do manage to stay awake to give your order, but then pass out before it's delivered, the flight attendant can place your drink on the tray table and it will be there for you to enjoy when you wake up. Sure, it will be watered down and taste like nothing, but at least you were served.

4. Read your menu card. If you can read this book, you can read the selection of drinks on your flight.

5. Take out your earbuds or headphones when the cart arrives at your row. When you see the flight attendant with the beverage cart, you know what time it is. It's service time. So why play deaf, dumb, and blind forcing them to ask you three times what you'd like to drink? It's like you've never seen an airline cart before... Oh!?! What's this? A boxy metal contraption? I wonder what's inside, hookers?

6. Order for your children. Period. The flight attendant has 48 other passengers to serve while you sit there wasting time convincing your toddler to order apple juice instead of Sprite.

7. When it comes to ice for your drink, let us know what you want. With ice? Without ice? Two cubes? A half a cube? I don't give a fuck but I'm not a mind reader. Just tell me so I don't pour you a Diet Coke and then have you sneer up and say, "I didn't want ice."

8. Listen when the flight attendant talks to you. It's called mindfulness and makes dealing with other human beings much easier. If the flight attendant asks you, "May I get you something to drink?" Try not responding with, "Do you have a spoon?" The last time I checked there was no spoon service on the flight. Pay attention!

9. Ask for the entire can. Some airlines give the full can of soda automatically but some airlines do not. You only get a cup, usually a cup filled to the brim with ice and only two sips of soft drink. If you know you are going to be thirsty five seconds later, ask for the full can. Your flight attendant doesn't care, but what we do hate is when you suck that sugar water down in one sip and start demanding more before I've even handed out drinks to the last row.

10. Alcohol is not served on every flight. Some flights are too short to serve alcohol. If it takes you longer to check the mail than it does to get to your destination on your flight, there's a good chance they don't serve alcohol. Ask the flight attendant when you board the airplane. If they won't be offering alcohol on the flight, don't be a dick about it. If they do offer alcohol, still don't be a dick.

That helpful list might have come in handy on one particular flight from Los Angeles to Miami. After completing my beverage service, I made my way down the aisle collecting trash like I always did. You can never go through the airplane enough times collecting trash. It seems like passengers bring their trash from home just to throw it away on the airplane.

"Hi. Do you have any trash?"

"Oh yes, here," handing over a plastic cup, some coffee grounds in a plastic baggie, and four egg shells.

"Egg shells? Why do you have eggshells and coffee grounds?"

"Trash pick up is on Thursdays at my house. Figured this was easier."

At least it feels that ridiculous. As I walked through the airplane picking up plastic cups one right after another, a passenger standing behind me aggressively tapped me on the shoulder. I instantly felt hot breath on my neck. My first thought was, "Dad? Is that you?" but realized if it was indeed my father, the smell of Aqua Net and cigarettes would have given him away.

With my signature fake smile I turned cheerfully asking, "May I help you?"

I stood face to face with the guy in 14C. In a rough, disturbingly loud Russian accent he yelled while pointing at my face incensed, "You! You didn't wake me to ask me what I wanted to drink. Why did you not wake me?" He sprayed me with enough saliva to keep me hydrated for a few weeks—helpful if I found myself stranded in Death Valley—not flying in a controlled environment at 40,000 feet. I don't want to sound prudish but I refuse having another man's spit all over me while I'm on the airplane unless I'm on my knees in the flight deck. Sorry, but I have standards and they don't include drunk passengers. Working pilots, yes. Drunk passengers, no. When the Russian asshole opened his mouth and flashed his yellow stained teeth I immediately smelled the gritty streets of Moscow on his breath.

14C was what I'd assumed to be a typical, middle aged Russian male. He could have easily been cast as the lead villain in a James Bond movie flying a helicopter over an erupting volcano while pushing his henchmen out one at a time to their fiery deaths; or something dramatic like that. He had the look nailed to the point that I quietly questioned if he had a team of stylists along with him. Flowing salt and pepper hair, thick gray beard, rosey red alcoholic cheeks, raspy vocal chords, and fingers thick enough to be cast into dildos for female midgets. Luckily for the rest of us, there were no little people with hungry vaginas on the flight.

I continued smiling while my patience wore thin. "Sir, I don't wake sleeping passengers. What can I bring you?"

"You wake me up! I need vodka. Vodka! Do you hear me?" We were flying over Phoenix and with the volume of his voice I assumed the entire city below heard him. "Beer! Anything. What do you have?" His anger and rudeness didn't bother me as much as the dirty looks he projected my way. As if I personally destroyed Chernobyl. Sure, my farts smelled toxic but not even one of my chemical warfare fart bombs could take down an entire city—maybe cause a delay at the Moscow Airport—but not burn the skin off newborn babies. He must have known I farted at the front of the airplane before I started collecting trash. But how?

It didn't matter. When I farted in the front galley I instantly knew the lady in 2C was keen on my mishap when she pinched her nose asking, "Do I smell something burning?

"Burning?" I responded, "I don't smell anything. Do you have any trash?"

"It smells like burnt matches and death. Like burning flesh."

"I don't know what you're talking about," I had to distract her before she caused a scene, "let me get you a glass of red wine and some extra napkins to cover your nose. I'll be right back." I lived through my sexuality being outed to my entire high school class in 1990, but I was damn sure not going to have this white haired Republican calling me and my stinky ass out on a flight to Miami.

While Mr. KGB towered over me enraged about his absent drink, I noticed the whites of his eyes getting redder with each angry breath. On second thought, maybe it was alcohol poisoning. I tried focusing on the task at hand: managing this grim breathed son of a bitch who was practically foaming at the mouth and ready to scratch my eyes out. Great. I had a slightly intoxicated, foul breathed Russian werewolf on my flight.

Our aggression bubbled over while standing in the aisle. Neither of us budged. His crimson eyes sent my nerves into overdrive but I didn't back down. There's not much worse than being eye assaulted by a Russian while flying over your own country. Totally tolerable in another country but not on your own home turf. Here I was, flying over the United States of America, the land of the free and home of the brave, being verbally attacked by a Russian. Acting out the movie *Red Dawn* was not part of the plan for this trip, but here we were rapidly heading in that direction. I blamed him for Patrick Swayze's death, the cancer that killed him, and for ruining any chance of a sequel to *To Wong Foo, Thanks for Everything, Julie Newmar*. I also blamed him for Jennifer Grey's career-ruining nose job.

Taking a few quick breaths I forced my anger aside, "Sir. What is your name?" My hand shook so uncontrollably that the plastic white garbage bag sounded like leaves rustling in the breeze. That must be what it sounds like when Michael J. Fox takes out the trash.

"Ivan Mudak. I need vodka."

"Yes. I know you do Mr. Mudak. I will be right back. Return to your seat and I will be there to take your order."

I needed a quick 60 seconds to cool down and get him back into his seat. Ivan caused quite a scene in the middle of the airplane and with his broken English and thick accent, I was afraid a few of the gang members seated in his area might get involved and beat the shit out of him. Although I love when straight roughnecks come to my rescue, and the idea of Ivan's face crushed under a steel toe boot was appealing, I didn't want World War III breaking out on my flight. There was no doubt in my mind that Ivan held me personally responsible for the fall of the USSR. I couldn't handle another cold war on my shoulders.

I gave up collecting trash and stormed to the back of the airplane, passing a number of passengers holding up trash. I refused to make eye contact. The mere thought of interacting with any paying passengers put me on the verge of: a) screaming at the top of my lungs or b) punching someone in the throat. If any passengers had tossed their empty cans or egg shells at me, I would have probably made them eat it.

Stepping into the back galley, the flight attendant I was working with looked up from her *People* magazine ready to attack, "Jesus Christ, Joe. I thought you were a passenger."

"I'm so angry right now, Felicia," throwing the garbage bag on the floor I didn't give her time to respond. "Calm down, Joe. Calm the fuck down." I find talking to myself in third person always makes me feel better. And saying the word fuck. These two behaviors give the impression that I'm a complete lunatic, and if you mess with me, your face is bound to look like Rihanna's after movie night with Chris Brown.

"What happened?"

I briefed her on my interaction with Ivan. She offered to handle the situation but I declined. I relish in the prospect of confrontation, and although this was a challenging one—honestly, I should have taken her up on the offer to help—I had to deal with this asshole myself. I came up with a game plan, knowing that if I waited any length of time he'd march to the back galley to continue our battle. Getting back out into the aisle was my top priority. The idea of being pinned against the galley counter with his breath burning the beard off my chin was about as appealing as sitting down to a meal of liver and onions. I'd kill him with kindness, and if that didn't work, I'd manage the motherfucker right into a set of plastic handcuffs. The entire fiasco had me thinking about a fantasy that sits quietly in a corner of my mind, one that's been there since finishing flight attendant training. Normally, I saved that fantasy for passengers caught smoking on my flight, but in a rare occasion like this, it worked perfectly. It is the fantasy where a passenger steps so far over the line that I am authorized to beat the shit out them badly enough that their family wouldn't recognize them in baggage claim.

The way things were going, if Ivan refused to back down when I approached him again—he'd be the one fulfilling my fantasy on our way to Miami. I envisioned him increasingly becoming more agitated the longer I made him wait for his drink. In a final fit of rage he'd snap and we'd find ourselves boxing like angry kangaroos in the middle of the airplane. I'd announce to the gang members—who were up and ready to stab us both—to sit the fuck down while the seat belt sign was illuminated as I repeatedly smashed the side of Ivan's head against his aisle seat. Finally, to prove I was the alpha male, I'd drag him face down across the vomit-stained airplane carpet and then make his Russian bride my bitch until we landed. The idea of having his wife complete my second beverage service and pick up trash while I sat comfortably in her seat watching *The Real Housewives of Atlanta* was hotter than if I bent her over the armrest and made her scream for more vodka.

Now, before anyone calls the police or reports me to the FAA, it's only a fantasy. Flight attendants are not authorized to literally beat the shit out of a passenger. We have the authority to handcuff and safely secure them in a seat until the authorities arrive to cart them off to jail. That's all. But for a minute, just think about how wonderful that fantasy plays out. Sounds fun, right?

After another set of deep cleansing breaths, I picked up the trash bag, put it into the trash bin, and made my way up the aisle to 14C. I turned facing him and bent down on one knee staring directly into his bloodshot eyes. After another deep breath I began, "Ivan, this is the United States of America," I reminded him in case he had forgotten, "we don't act like that on an airplane. What may I get you to drink?" The heat protruding from his mouth dried my lips. Goddamn his breath was atrocious. In all my years I had never smelled anything so putrid. Did Colgate come out with new shit-flavored toothpastes? Colgate Advanced Shitening? Colgate Sensitive Shit? Colgate UltraShit with Peroxide? Colgate Blast of Shit? That was the only explanation: Ivan brushed his teeth with shit. When he spoke, my contacts went fuzzy forcing me to shake my head to get them to refocus.

"Vodka. Beer. Vodka." He continued barking at me, "What kind of beer do you have?"

My initial response was to pull out my own Tourette's card and bark back, "Dick. Prick. Fuck you!" But he didn't have Tourette's. He was just as asshole.

"Ivan, do you speak English?"

"Da. Da." He looked over at his wife who clearly wanted to crawl into the seatback pocket, "Of course I do. What kind of question is that?"

"Do you understand that I will not tolerate you yelling at me on my airplane?"

We stared at each other like two pugs who didn't like the smell of each other's bungholes. I refused to back down. I had Mr. KGB by his baby balls and with each rancid breath he shot my way, I squeezed those peaches tighter. A few more moments and I might have reached the pit but he eventually looked up, "Da."

Finally, I was getting somewhere with this creep. My pleasant flight attendant tone returned and I began listing the beers available on our flight for him. He blurted out, "Heineken. Bring me Heineken. What kind of vodka do you have?"

"Absolut."

"That's shit vodka," he responded pushing me to break character and bust out laughing. Informing him that our "shit vodka" went perfectly with his shit breath was something I could only do if I planned on terminating my employment once we landed. "That's fine," he stated, "Bring me one."

"What mixer do you want for the vodka?"

He snapped, "Nothing!" That worried me.

A few minutes later I delivered him a Heineken, a vodka mini, a cup of ice, and set them all down on the tray table on top of a napkin and walked away. Any further conversations with Ivan would only occur if we were faced with an emergency evacuation, and I made no promises even to fulfill that obligation.

I walked up the aisle to the front of the airplane and entered the lavatory to fix my tie and splash water on my face. My collar was soaked after working up a sweat putting out the vodka volcano that erupted in the middle of the airplane. I needed to cool off. After painting on another fake smile I started back down the aisle collecting trash. When I reached Ivan's row he dropped his empty Heineken can and vodka mini bottle into the trash bag. Let me explain why my eyes were forcing their way out of my skull while this happened: Ivan basically drank a full can of beer and downed a vodka mini within the same time frame it takes a normal human being to enjoy a sip of water. My first reaction was to get on the interphone and request assistance at row 14. There had to be an Alcoholic Anonymous sponsor on the flight who'd be able to help me out in this emergency. My mind raced with attempts to remember at least one of the 12 steps. I concentrated while looking down into the garbage bag. *Think! Goddamn it, Joe, think!* The idea of God came to mind. Did one of the steps have something to do with bending over while intoxicated and allowing God to ass rape you without a condom? Was my memory playing tricks on me? Something about giving it up to God? I lost it. I had no fucking clue. All the drunk friends that have come in and out of my life and not one of them had gone through AA. I guess that's why they were my friends. I refused to be friends with people who are afraid of alcohol. An ass raping by God? Yes. A classic Manhattan cocktail? No. Without making eye contact, I smiled and continued walking down the aisle collecting empty cans and hoping it was the last time Ivan and I interacted.

Thirty minutes later I was walking through the cabin collecting trash... again. After turning down Felicia's assistance in managing Ivan, I was slightly surprised that she made zero effort to lift a finger to help out with any other tasks. She must have concluded that due to her being the senior flight attendant on the trip it liberated her from picking up trash. Whore! I reminded myself that if we crashed off the coast of Florida and I found her holding onto the raft's mooring line, pleading for help, I'd cut it—

by mistake of course—and wish her the best. "Bye Felicia. Ride your fucking *People* magazine back to Tampa."

Ivan gave me heart palpitations. It wasn't a full blown panic attack, but just enough chest pain to make me question if we were allowed to use the AED on ourselves when dealing with mentally challenged Russians. My stress might have been eliminated if Felicia completed at least one trash pick up during the flight, but I knew that was asking too much. I'd have more luck being the pivot man in a flight deck circle jerk than expecting her to get off her ass. I accepted my destiny as solo trash collector on the flight. That was fine. She'd get hers if we crashed in the water. I officially marked her off as shark bait.

Making eye contact with Ivan made the hairs on my arm stand on end. I attempted to look at each person and simply skip over his scowl but he grabbed my attention, "May I have another Heineken?" Surprisingly, his tone was pleasant and not the Mt. Ivan eruption I lived through from earlier in the flight.

It seemed as if destiny brought me to this exact moment in time. A time where I'd find myself on a flight with an aggressive Russian who tested my patience and the ability to manage my emotions without getting terminated. A few months before meeting Ivan, I occupied the jumpseat next to Natasha, a Russian-born flight attendant at my airline. I have forgotten our final destination but I do remember questioning her about the personality of Russians. I referred to them as "her people" which she did not appreciate. Let's just say I was pleased she'd taken her prescribed dose of Xanax that night or I'd have been peeling my cheekbone off the airplane door.

She shared with me in the dimly-lit front galley that Russians are usually angry and drinking. She added that when Russians aren't angry and drinking, they are enjoying their other two pastimes: being angry and drinking. She said, "Russians rarely apologize for anything. Why should we apologize?" She felt strongly about this, "If your flight is delayed why should I apologize? It's not my fault. I understand you are not happy that your flight is delayed but it has nothing to do with me."

I tried helping her understand, "Yeah, but we work for the airline so we represent the airline. You are simply apologizing that the passenger is in the situation they are in. Not that it was your fault the flight was actually delayed."

Natasha didn't agree, "No. I don't apologize. That's stupid. Not many Russians apologize."

Point taken. Russians don't apologize. They also get snippy when you disagree with the reasons they give for not apologizing.

"Russians love to fight," she continued while I drank down her cultural knowledge like a White Russian, "It's in our blood. We fight to dominate the situation. How you react determines the outcome."

But even before my talk with Natasha, and my run-in with Ivan, I knew exactly how abusive people of this culture were toward flight attendants. Based in JFK, I spent months at my crash pad in Kew Gardens listening to flight attendants complaining about flights to Moscow—that is, when they actually did work the flights. More often than not they called in sick just to get out of their Moscow trips. From my eight months in that crash pad I witnessed enough sick calls to wonder how airlines actually staffed these fucking flights.

My mind refused to understand it. I'd have given up my best toenail to fly internationally and spend the night in Moscow. Walking the curious streets of Moscow sounded thrilling compared to overnights in Buffalo. People don't travel to Buffalo to experience a different culture, they go there to die in blizzards. Listen, if I'm required by my employer to spend the night in a city with a temperature that drops below -10 degrees, I'd rather be in an exciting city on the other side of the planet.

One flight attendant expressed how he truly felt about Moscow one night while we sat on the sofa watching a 2008 Presidential debate, "Those flights are the worst," he dialed a number into his cell phone, "They're a bunch of rude assholes and completely empty the liquor cart."

"The entire cart? Stop lying," I questioned while placing my *How To Visit Buffalo and Not Kill Yourself* guide on the side table.

"It's true," he whispered while on hold with Crew Scheduling, "They start with vodka and work all the way down to the Malibu rum." He put his finger up in the air to start the show, "Hello. Yes. This is Troy Smith," he paused to cough and then shot me a thumbs up, "My employee number is 4458 and I need to call in sick for my Moscow trip tonight."

I placed Ivan's second Heineken on his tray table and he pointed his finger up to alert me, "Wait. I have something for you."

My anti-terrorist training kicked into high gear. As I prepared to pick up the beer and crack it over his massive skull, he reached into his pocket and produced a thick wad of cash. American dollars. Greenbacks. Fresh and crisp like a Vlasic dill pickle. He licked his thick dildo fingers—I almost threw up on the toddler sitting across from him—and starting flipping through his money. I felt like a prostitute. One who hated having a stranger's salami stored in her meat pantry but then acts like it never happened once she's collected enough cash for a weekend trip to Cozumel. That exact kind of prostitute.

Without saying a word, or making eye contact, he pulled out $20 and flicked it at me as if I was one of his bothersome mistresses. I stood there motionless. The thought of slapping it out of his hand and asking, "What kind of flight attendant do you think I am?" crossed my mind but I hadn't had someone pay me off since I was 11 years old and caught Irene growing marijuana in my grandparent's backyard.

Ivan sat there fanning himself with the $20 like his air vent was broken. I glanced over at his wife. She looked at me solemnly, making me realize I should take the money and forgive his inexcusable behavior. The boulder-sized diamond on her wedding finger told me that this lady knew all too well about being paid off. I figured he either pissed her off quite often or pushed for anal way more than she agreed on her wedding night. Letting him off the hook that easy made my brain hurt. And don't judge me, but I was curious to see if he'd offer up an anal option. Listen, even if you don't want something, it's always nice to have choices. You never know what sounds good until you have options. Just ask those greedy bisexuals.

I instinctively declined his tip but he insisted, "You take money. Take it."

"That's ok. You don't have to tip me."

He looked at me and winked, "I don't have to but I want to."

I snatched the $20 out of his hand faster than he expected. He instinctively pulled his hand back but not before that crisp $20 was safely in my front apron pocket. The wink threw me off. Although I thought about the anal option for a brief second, when he winked at me I realized that if I didn't keep moving I'd be forced into a game of Russian anal in the back lavatory. That's a bullet I was not prepared to take.

As I walked away with more money than when I started the flight, I couldn't help but feel pleased at how everything turned out. The right thing would have been for him to apologize and for me to hand him back his money, but that's not how the situation played out. Who cares about doing the right thing when you're managing assholes at 38,000 feet? I have no qualms with passengers paying me for their inappropriate behavior and Ivan was a bad boy.

Stepping into the back galley, I sat down on the empty jumpseat. Felicia continued reading the same *People* magazine she pulled out after we originally finished beverage service. I sneered at her but she didn't notice. I couldn't wait to watch her drown in the ocean. After being rescued, I'd whimper out to the airline that I did my best to save her but she refused to let go of that fucking magazine.

After a few seconds she looked over, "How's your Russian? Has he calmed down?"

My initial instinct was to blurt out about the tip and share my new found wealth with her and the other flight attendant working in the front of the airplane. Normally, if we are lucky enough to receive a generous tip, the flight attendant will do something nice for the crew. Purchase cups of coffee in the morning, buy a round of drinks at the hotel bar, or pick up the hotel van tip for the entire crew— pilots included. But I wasn't sharing a fucking red cent with the bitch. Can you blame me? She refused to pull her eyeballs away from the inside of that magazine throughout the entire flight so I assumed it was only fair that I refused to pull out any cash from my apron. I zipped my mouth up tighter than an overweight flight attendant strapped to a jumpseat. I never felt guilty because I earned that tip. 'Hard to Handle Ivan' was truly a handful. A Russian handful who refused to verbally apologize for being a demanding asshole and who's only way of atoning for his sins was to pay me off.

Fine by me. If every verbally abusive passenger handed me $20, I'd only need to work two trips per month.

BLOW JOB CONFESSIONS

When I was 20 years old I sucked off a Puerto Rican guy named Jesús. I did it just to check off the name Jesús on my cock-sucking resume. What can I say? We are taught to strive towards our goals, and one of mine was to experience Jesus juice directly from the source. I figured if it was good enough for underage boys waking up in Michael Jackson's bed, it was good enough for me.

Sucking Jesús was stressful. He was 18 and smelled like McDonald's french fries and Adobo. Not necessarily a bad combination but definitely not on my favorite's list. There was that and the fact that each time I went down on him his pager vibrated with messages from his girlfriend, Lupita. That shit was annoying. Nobody wants to work that hard and not have full attention on themselves. I wasn't making arroz con pollo, I was sucking his dick.

Jesús and I hooked up twice. Twice was enough. It felt like each time I had his dick in my mouth, Lupita was standing over me questioning him about her next prenatal appointment. Did I forget to mention she was pregnant? Eighteen, pregnant, and with a baby daddy who liked playing hide the chorizo in Joe's throat—one of my favorite games, I might add.

Our solo hookup almost didn't happen. It was 1992 and I was employed as a swing manager for McDonald's. I was also a virgin. Twenty years old and I had yet to meet a cock other than my own. I knew I liked cock but hadn't experienced inviting one into my mouth. I had the same reality with a kiwi. You know you're going to like it even before you try it. Jesús and I worked the late shift along with an older Puerto Rican guy named Sergio, the guy who instigated the hook up.

On boring nights while Jesús, Sergio, and I wore the drive-thru headphones, they talked dirty to me with comments like, "Joe, tu mama la penga?" Or even nastier remarks like, "Fag boy likes the uncut dick." Truly a human resource department's worst nightmare. And here you thought McDonald's employees were simply sharing into their headsets how you wanted your Quarter Pounder cooked. I tried playing off my disgust from their crude comments, but I finally gave in accepting the fact that they were right—I wanted cock. And if I got two for the price of one I'd consider that better than a Kmart blue light special. Why not just throw myself in head first, right? Anyone could suck one dick, but two dicks at the same time? That's impressive. If there were a dick sucking hole punch card, I'd be that much closer to a free blow job.

Once I played along with their inappropriate broken English conversations, Sergio set the game in motion. Remember *The Game of Life*? Where you'd spin a wheel and move spaces to start a career? Start college? This was kinda-almost-slightly the same type of game except I called it *The Puerto Rican Game of Life*; where you flipped a pastele in the air to see who's dick you sucked first. Don't quote me, but

I believe that version is the highest selling game in Puerto Rico.

Obviously, Sergio concocted bisexual rendezvous in the past. He manipulated our ears with filth to the point Jesús and I were heavily panting while handing Chicken McNuggets out the drive-thru window. The plan initiated and the three of us decided to meet at McDonald's at 2 a.m. Once there, we'd drive to Sergio's apartment while his wife, Isabella, was out of town at a church group mission.

Thank you, Jesús. And the little baby Jesus.

I arrived at 1:55 a.m. and found Jesús already parked behind the restaurant in his beat up car. His car barely functioned but I could have cared less. My mouth was about to be stuffed like a Puerto Rican Big Mac. I pulled up alongside his car singing, *"Two all beef pengas, special sauce, and some cheese..."* You get the rest. It was about to go down. Correction: I was about to go down.

We sat on the hood of my car waiting for Sergio to arrive. We barely spoke. The fear bubbling off us was apparent. Finally at 2:30 a.m., Sergio called Jesús informing him that Isabella had come home early and the mission was cancelled. I was upset. Jesús was upset. I guarantee his dick was even more upset.

My mouth was devastated.

"What can we do, Joe?" Jesús asked standing beside my car while I stared at the bulge in his pants. He was 18 years old so I assumed even the thought of unzipping his pants made him excited. And he was Puerto Rican. With Puerto Rican men there is no such thing as straight. They all tend to end up bisexual by the end of the night. Asking a

Puerto Rican guy if he wants his dick sucked is like asking a fat guy if he wants another piece of pie. The answer is always yes. It doesn't matter who delivers the slice.

"I really wanted to suck some dick tonight." I responded without looking at his face. I was dickmatized by his button up jeans, which I was certain held back more skin than a fat lady's stomach after bypass surgery.

He grabbed his crotch and smiled. That's all the confirmation I needed. I took the restaurant keys out of my pocket and we walked up to the side door and entered the McDonald's. Who needed Sergio? Sure, I was hoping for two cocks but this wasn't the time nor place to be nitpicky. When you are zero cocks and counting, you take the one you have available. I shut off the alarm inside the restaurant; I was terrified. Going to prison wasn't as frightening as me losing my $6.10 per hour job as a shift manager. What about Irene? And my grandparents? What if the first cock I sucked ended up being in prison? I couldn't worry about any of that. I had to pop my blow job cherry before I got carted off to prison, and here it was, in the same place I packaged up Happy Meals for children.

Without saying a word we walked behind the counter, through the grill area, and into the back storage room. I opened the walk-in freezer and immediately closed it. What was I thinking? Nobody wants to receive a blow job in a freezer. Eskimos might, but definitely not Puerto Ricans. While I searched for the ideal blow job location, Jesús stood there with his hands in his pockets letting me do all the work. If I ever questioned him being Puerto Rican, I didn't anymore. Puerto Ricans refuse to work even when they are about to receive head.

I slide a tall bin to the side and found the perfect spot. As if Mary Magdalene herself led me there—from one Jesus hoe to another—I threw him down onto the semi mopped greasy floor and had my way with him. He didn't stop me, nor did he care. There I was, a manager performing oral sex on one of my employees. Manager of the year? Not quite. Would an unprofessional act like that haunt me for the rest of my life? Who fucking cared. I was in the storage room at McDonald's sucking dick under a week's supply of Big Mac buns. I'm not lying. While readjusting my position, I pushed my hair out from my eyes, looked up, and saw a sleeve of buns hanging over my head. At least if I got hungry I'd have something to snack on; it took Jesús forever to get off the cross.

If I'm confessing about blow jobs, there's really no reason to stop now. No need for me to be shy. It should come as no shock that I am prone to sucking dick at work. I can't help it. I clock in and then I cock in. It's all in a day's work. The second time I fellated a coworker was while I was employed as a nurse. Yes, pick your jaws up off the floor, I performed oral sex while inside the hospital working an overnight shift. Jesus Christ! I really am the devil. You might think with my own shot of Jesus juice I'd have turned out different—but sadly, it doesn't work that way.

In 1998 I worked at a medium-sized hospital in Central Florida. One evening, right before I was about to report off, the nurse manager asked me to work a double shift in the Skilled Nursing Unit (SNU). That unit sucked. I hated it. Not because the work was hard but because the low census left me bored out of my fucking mind. Nights on the SNU unit left you searching for something—or someone—to occupy your time. Someone like Diego.

The night I met Diego, the SNU unit was quieter than normal. On really slow nights I'd quickly finish my assessments, hand out medications, and be done. It was that simple. Nothing more, nothing less. It was the rehabilitation unit, not ICU. But that night I was scheduled for a late night admission. While I sat at the nursing station with my legs up on the desk reading a book, I heard the wheels of a stretcher coming down the hall. Standing up to greet Diego and the other orderly, I watched them turn the corner with my new patient. An elderly lady with a bad attitude and a hip replacement. Two things that go together like pilots and alimony.

Diego handed me the patient's paperwork, grinned awkwardly, and led the stretcher down the hallway to the appropriate room. Grabbing an empty chart folder, I started putting together the patient's chart. There was no need for me to rush in while the patient care technician took vital signs, got the patient situated, and completed an inventory of her belongings. After they transferred the patient to the bed, Diego and his coworker pushed the stretcher passed the station again but I didn't pay them any attention. Sitting back down, I started writing in the chart when I heard breathing above me. I looked up jumping, "Oh my God. You scared me."

"I sorry. I am Diego. What's up?"

We hired Neanderthals? I had no idea. I wanted to grab a dictionary and slap him across the head with it but I don't believe that's the fastest way to learn the English language. He never met an English verb he liked, or understood, that was for sure.

"I am doing well. I'm Joe. How are you?"

"Good. Good. Listen," he smiled and I noticed some teeth were missing, "I have question." He looked around to make sure nobody was near. "Want to do movie?"

Do movie? What the fuck did that mean? Was he asking me to go to the movies? How incredibly uncomfortable, especially with the gold wedding band shining from his finger.

"On a date? Are you asking me out on a date?" I laughed at him. He looked absolutely ridiculous standing there with his pock-marked face and wearing a blue surgical cap. His acne was so bad that if NASA lost all communication with the Space Shuttle, the astronauts could have easily mistaken Diego's face for the runway during an emergency landing.

"Si. Si. Movie?" He smiled again and I looked away. I was working a 16 hour shift and the last thing I needed was his smile imprinted on my memory until the wee hours of the morning.

I smiled and put the patient's chart under my arm. Fifteen minutes must have passed since the hip replacement arrived, and even if it hadn't, she needed me more than Diego. "I don't think that's a good idea, Diego, but thank you. I have to get back to work." Walking around the nurse's station, I headed towards the hip's room never looking back. How long he stood there was anyone's guess. Thirty seconds? Five minutes? Who knows. Most likely he walked away defeated in tears. I can't guarantee it, but I am

JOE THOMAS

most certainly positive he cried. I'd bet that old lady's recovered hip—he cried.

He also refused to give up. Three years I had worked in that hospital without ever seeing his face, and now, each time a new patient was brought up to my floor, it was by him and his gap-toothed smile. One night he brought me chocolates, another night a Coke. Soon we were chatting every single night although I barely understood half the words that came out of his mouth. Our late night interactions distracted me from my indifference towards him. Diego was not pretty. He wasn't handsome, either. He'd have a hard time paying a prostitute for sex, but here he was bringing me treats, hitting on me, and with a wife and kids at home. I soaked it up. But why? What island magic did he sprinkle onto my late night chocolate treats? Was it some Voodoo hocus pocus that gay white men have no control over? The answer had to be hiding in his baggy light blue scrubs. The idea of a monster cock living between his legs intrigued me. Seconds after that thought entered my mind, I promised myself he'd be slapping me silly with it in no time.

During a random Diego encounter outside a patient's room, he asked me for the 100th time to go out on a date and I finally agreed. He dropped to the floor. That's the truth. He literally fell to the ground in shock. Exactly like the black lady did when she realized her husband wasn't numb from the waist down. I don't blame her. I'd fall to the ground, too. Even at 70 years old bitches need the dick.

"You go with me to movie?"

"Yes. I will." I started towards another patient's room, "now I have to get back to work."

452

"Wait. I have plan. You call me at home. Tell wife you are hospital. You need me." He looked around nervously again and pulled a wrinkled napkin from his pocket with his home phone number scribbled on it. He shook with fear. I expected he thought his wife hung out in the dirty linen can sitting next to the nursing station. "You understand?"

I took the number and stuffed it into my front scrub pocket. "Yeah. That's fine." I answered losing interest. I had no idea a simple movie date included a conversation with his wife. A wife who probably spoke less English than him. I'd be lying over the phone to some stranger who wouldn't understanding a thing I was saying. That eased my guilt a little. I excused myself, remembering that I had to give an enema to an old man. That's always a reality check.

When I spoke to his wife the conversation went well. She answered, "Hola."

My nerves were shot but I went along with the plan, "Hi. This is Ben from the hospital. We are short staffed tonight and will need Diego to come into the hospital as soon as possible."

"Hello Joe. Is me, Diego."

Apparently she handed him the phone the moment I said, "This is Ben." I had no idea my home-wrecking lie took only three words. I placed the call from the hospital parking lot and within 10 minutes he was pulling up next to my Kia Sportage and sitting in my passenger seat.

"Hi. That was eas—"

His tongue was down my throat before I restarted my car. Did I expect that? Possibly, but is anyone truly prepared for a tongue slapping while attempting to start a car? I struggled getting the car in drive. He paid for our movie tickets but we sucked face for the entire two hours. He whispered things into my ear but hell if I understood. Some words were in English. Some in Spanish. And some I'm pretty sure weren't real words at all. When I dropped him off at his car, the front of his jeans were wet, and not from spilled popcorn butter. Diego created his own butter and spent the entire car ride persuading me to taste it. The entire experience had gone too far. Slightly flattered and highly grossed out, I declined. Two emotions I had no idea went together.

At work the next night he came up to the nursing station without a patient. "I think I love you."

"You don't love me, Diego. You have a wife."

"I no want you to move to Seattle." His accent butchered the name of the city, "You stay. Be with me."

"You have three kids and a wife. I can't be with you." I left out the ugly part. No need kicking a homely man when he's down.

"I be with you and my wife."

I laughed out loud, "Diego, I don't think we should talk anymore. You are married and I am moving to Seattle. This is a bad idea."

Seemed solid, right? I let him know the deal. Our date was bad. The fact he was married was bad. It would never work. It was over. I instantly missed my late night chocolate and Coke treats but ending this emotional affair was the only answer.

He started shifting from one foot to another. He removed his surgical cap and scratched his matted hair. I waited a second and continued, "Diego, are you listening to me? Do you understand what I'm saying?"

Next thing I knew I was on my knees in a conference room with my mouth stuffed fuller than an altar boy at the Vatican. After we were done—which didn't take long—I was barely able to function for the rest of the night. Did that happen? What was I thinking? Not the fact that I sucked a coworker's dick, *again*, but that it was an ugly person's dick. Was I so desperate for dick that I'd take any dick? What was next? Homeless dick? Transgender dick? Random guy in the back of Walmart dick?

After that dickscapade, I had a few nights off to think about what I had done. My pager went off with Diego's number but I never replied. He called my house a few times, which reminded me never to give out my home phone number again. When the phone rang, I'd refuse to budge from my bedroom. On one occasion Irene opened my door, "There's some Puerto Rican guy on the phone who barely speaks any fucking English?"

"It's probably work. Tell them I'm not here."

"I don't think so, Joe. This is the third time he's called." She left my room and closed the door.

While working my shifts I avoided him at every turn. If I heard a stretcher coming down the hall, I'd hide in a patient's room until I knew he was gone. Sometimes I'd hide in an empty room, or in a bathroom, afraid he'd come searching for me. A few times I feared being stabbed to death by a handful of syringes.

I'm not trying to brag, but my blowjobs might cause someone to kill a bitch.

Eventually Diego got the hint and we lost touch, even though we worked in the same hospital. My guess was he found himself another white guy to get him off. Most likely

Ryan from the sleep lab; he looked like the biggest cocksucker at the hospital.

Managing to stay blowjob free at work was quite a challenge. I figured I licked that problem—licked it good. But I was wrong. Eventually, I fell off the wagon and landed head first onto a dick. Don't worry, my mouth was wide open. Thank goodness, too. I firmly believe that's what kept me from poking an eye out. It all started after reporting in Cleveland for an easy-looking four day trip. Those tend to be fun if you're working with a good crew. If not, you find yourself spending 96 hours with shitty coworkers you'd wish were lost forever in the airport.

After spending a few minutes in the crew lounge, I quickly realized this trip sucked. It hadn't even begun but the word *sucked* flashed in all caps in my mind. *SUCKED! SUCKED! SUCKED!* Now that I think about it, possibly a little foreshadowing on my part?

Was it too late to call in sick? I felt sick. Was it the oatmeal I shoved down my throat before leaving Evan's house? No. It had to be Lori, the lead flight attendant. We met right away in the lounge and she instantly rubbed me the wrong way. Lori's dirty blond hair was secured in a ponytail while she pranced around acting like a high school cheerleader. Sadly, Lori looked more like she was closer to pushing 70 than pushing a set of pom poms. Seventy years old and still searching for a decent night cream. She had more wrinkles than an angry Shar Pei. All she needed was a full can of spray starch and a hot iron. Problem solved.

I agree that I don't get along with many people. I don't deny it. It's part of who I am but I try giving strangers the benefit of the doubt. Until I catch them lying to me during our first encounter, then I'm done. Seriously, you might as well just go home.

In a high pitched annoying voice she asked, "How long have you been here?"

"Almost five years." I answered while pulling out my required flight attendant items.

"Oh. Me too."

Interesting. Lori was unfamiliar to me. I'm notorious for not knowing many flight attendants in my base but generally you know the people in your seniority bracket. Or you've at least heard of them. I didn't know her at all and trust me, you only had to meet Lori once to remember her. "Cool. So what class were you in?"

She told me and I made a face. I'm no mathematician but even I know when something doesn't add up. I answered, "That doesn't make sense. That's only three years."

"Five years. Three years. Is there really a difference?" She responded staring into a pocket mirror applying a dark red lipstick.

What the fuck? Did I hear that right? Yes, bitch. There's a big fucking difference. That's like walking around telling people you have an 800 credit score when you are barely pushing 500.

It got terribly worse once we got onto the airplane. Every time Lori spoke, I cringed like I did when my grandmother sent me off on Sunday mornings to confess my sins to Father Long. Father Long loved my sins. In all honestly, I think he just loved boys on their knees.

"Do you know James Johnson?" She asked while I checked the exit row for safety information cards, "He's my boyfriend."

"I don't know him," I answered then moved to the back galley to complete my security checks. I turned around and she was right behind me. Fuck. Because I'm a nice guy I continued questioning, "Does he work here?"

"Yes. He's one of us. He's on reserve in JFK. You'll meet him tomorrow morning during our sit."

I let her talk but in all honestly, I didn't give a damn about her or her boyfriend. There was nothing about her that interested me. Our trip had barely started and I couldn't wait for it to be over. I spent six days in a car, driving cross-country with my cat screaming in my ear for hours and that seemed more peaceful than hanging out with this leather bag for four days.

The first day of our trip went quickly, which was fine by me. I literally threw myself off the shuttle and into the lobby of our layover hotel in Charlotte, North Carolina. No offense to my North Carolina readers but I never feel welcome in Charlotte, especially as a gay man. Usually when I am in that part of the country I spend most of my time hiding under the bed listening for the burning of torches, or Billy Graham supporters yelling, "That cocksucker is over here. He's in room 3543."

After collecting our room keys, the captain politely asked. "Are you gonna meet us down here for dinner?"

I declined and told him that I had to run to the store, call my husband (I whispered that part just in case Billy Graham was listening), and go to bed. Our van time the next morning was 4:15 a.m. and I needed my rest. I was exhausted from listening to Lori talk about her boyfriend all day.

The next morning the four of us met in the hotel lobby. 4:15 a.m. is a horrific time to be dressed and standing in a deserted hotel lobby waiting for the shuttle. It's the worst van time when working with people you don't like. Hell, I don't enjoy seeing another human being that early even if I do like them. My feelings towards the captain and first officer were indifferent but the two of them seemed to be cheering for Team Lori and not Team Joe. That kept me clear from any serious conversations with the two of them.

They chatted like best friends during the ride to the airport while I bounced around with my head against the glass window. "Dinner was fantastic last night. You should have joined us, Joe," she cheerfully stated while we all stepped into the airport.

"That's nice. I was tired. But thanks for the invitation." All lies. They could have chipped in and bought me a three-course meal and I'd have still been hiding under my bed waiting for Billy Graham to break in and cart me off to conversion camp.

Our first flight from Charlotte to JFK was uneventful. In JFK, we had an hour and a half sit before departing for Detroit. I was not looking forward to a 20-hour layover with these three but I had plans to keep myself preoccupied. Once we got to the gate and all the passengers deplaned, the four of us left the airplane to get breakfast. It was only 7:30 a.m. and I had yet to get any caffeine in my bloodstream. How I kept from killing the three of them on the hotel shuttle will always be a mystery to me.

Lori, Captain Brian, and First Office Connor stuck together like crazy glue. Actually, any glue became crazy once you added Lori to it. As we stepped out of the jet bridge and into the gate area, we were greeted by her boyfriend. What can I say about James? Enthusiastic. Flashy. Colorful. Flamboyant. You get what I'm hinting at here, right? James made queens voguing at a Madonna concert look tame.

I smiled, introduced myself, shook his hand, and walked away to the left while the four of them veered to the right of the airport. A toddler had a stronger handshake than this guy. Was his wrist broken? Let's hope so because no adult straight man's wrist should be that limp. The idea of keeping them company during our airport sit never crossed my mind. Being far away from them made me happy. Hiding my displeasure was impractical. Since meeting her, my face had become a Lori hostility billboard. After purchasing myself a cup of coffee, I sat down by the gate area tapping away at my iPad. A few moments later Connor approached me, "Hey. I'm going down to the airplane. You staying up here?"

"Yeah. I'm trying to post something on my blog and I can't get on this fucking internet."

He stood in front of me with the plastic container housing his breakfast, "Alright. Well take down my number. If you need me to come up and open the door, just text me."

Grabbing my phone I typed in his number, "Okay, got it." and went back to my iPad. I was so adamant about getting the article posted that breakfast slipped my mind. I had no luck. I gave up on trying to log onto the internet when I noticed the three of them were back on the airplane and the gate agent glared at me like I was delaying the entire flight.

While waiting for the hotel van in Detroit, Brian looked over at me, "Are you gonna hang out with us today or hide in your room like last night?"

I laughed. "I don't think catching up on sleep means I was hiding in my room." I left out the part about Billy Graham and my distaste for Lori. "I'll hang today. I've got some stuff to do downtown but we can meet up later."

I lied. I refused to hang out with them the night before because I didn't want to hang out with Lori. Her voice sent chills down my spine and I had to stop myself from punching her in the throat. But after spending a few hours that morning with Brian and Connor, I realized they were nice and if they made the effort to be nice to me, the right thing to do was throw them a bone.

After collecting our keys, we got onto the elevator and got off at our respective floors. Brian and Lori stepped off on the second floor and Connor and I rode the elevator to the third. We walked beside each other until I stopped at 304, "Ok. I'll talk to you later."

He kept walking and didn't look back, "Alright. I'll text you when we get downtown."

I made it downtown by 11:30 a.m. After spending a few hours walking around, exploring, and taking pictures, I still hadn't heard from Connor. I'd survive if he forgot to text me. Missing an afternoon listening to Lori talk about her boyfriend might save me an extra 45 seconds at the end of my life. She was that soul crushing.

I stopped in a mall to take a bathroom break. When it comes to shitting I have a three minute window. Once the countdown begins there are only two options: get on a toilet or get a new pair of underwear. I found the restroom, got comfortable on the toilet, and just as I was about to unleash the fury—my phone vibrated.

It was a text from Connor: *"Hey Joe. It's Connor. We just got downtown. Where u at?"*

I couldn't tell him I was in the middle of yelling at Jesus for allowing something that disgusting to come out of my body so I simply just typed: *"At the mall. Tell me where you are. I'll be there soon."*

After my bathroom escapade I walked about a mile until I met up with Brian and Connor at an Irish pub. They were both sitting outside and had just ordered beers. "Hey guys. Where's Lori?" I asked pulling out a chair next to Brian and having a seat across from Connor.

"She's shopping," Connor answered while Brian tapped away at his cell phone. A sexy brunette waitress walked up to our table with a pen and pad in hand ready to write down our orders. Brian could barely pull himself away from his cell phone. I'd learn later that him and his wife were leaving for New Zealand the day after our trip was over and he was finalizing plans. Lucky him. When my time came, I ordered a double gin and tonic and started talking to Connor about my day out in the city.

Thirty minutes past before Lori showed up. It was a calm 30 minutes. The best 30 minutes of the entire trip. Her walking up to the outside seating area reminded me of the tornado that transported Dorothy to Oz. If only Lori got carried off somewhere else. Kansas City perhaps?

Kansas City sounded perfect. I'd be so fucking lucky. Both her hands held onto large shopping bags, and with a flip of her wrist she tossed them across the table and pulled out a chair.

"Oh my God. It's chilly out here. Are you guys cold?" She asked while putting down her bags and placing them on the ground between her and Connor. My inner voice screamed to get up and leave. Gulp down my drink, throw some money on the table, and hightail my ass out. But I stayed. The pilots had grown on me and I hated missing a fun opportunity because of some obnoxious female troll.

"I'm fine." I answered looking across at Connor. Sadly, the guys were all too quick to please Lori.

"It's alright," Brian looked up from his cell phone, "but if you want to go inside we'll go inside." At the end of his sentence the waitress walked over with an additional menu and Brian asked, "Can we move inside? It's getting cold out here."

"I don't think it's cold," I reinforced my opinion while collecting my utensils and gin and tonic. I followed behind them into the bar with a slight attitude. I continued acting like a spoiled brat. My desires never matter when there's a vagina in the mix. The bitch with the vagina always gets what she wants. The fag with the dick plays second fiddle. Vag beats dick all the time.

During the next hour the four of us sat in a booth talking about everything under the sun. From past vacations and Auckland to Lori's eye appointment and boyfriend. We were in dire need of a conversation reboot. Connor saved the mood by moving the discussion away from Lori's medical problems and towards something way more entertaining: Urban Dictionary.

Taking a sip of his drink and placing the glass down he randomly asked, "Do you guys know what a donkey punch is?"

Buzzed from my second drink, I bit on his joke setup, "No. What's that?"

Leaning against the wall he smiled a cocky college boy grin, "It's when you're fucking a girl in the ass and right when you're about to cum, you punch her in the back of the head so she tightens up on you."

Brian shook his head. I laughed out loud. Lori picked her lips up off the table.

"That's just pure disgust." She said putting her hand to her face, "Boys are disgusting."

For a brief moment Connor and I made eye contact and I liked him a lot more than I did at the beginning of the trip. It was my turn, "Alright. What about a Dirty Sanchez?"

"Dude. That's an easy one. You gotta come up with something harder than that at this table," Connor laughed out while taking a sip of his drink. We were all getting wasted. Well, technically not all of us. Connor, Brian, and I were drinking while Lori enjoyed a glass of water with lime. Water with lime and a splash of judgement.

"What's that? A dirty who?" She asked looking at me and then Brian. She had given up on Connor.

Hoping she'd ask I eagerly broke it down for her, "Dirty Sanchez. It's when you have shit on your dick and rub it across the girl's upper lip."

Connor laughed spilling his drink on the front of his shirt, "That's some funny shit, Joe. You're gonna give her a heart attack." He was right. From the look on her face she'd need the AED before our report time the next morning.

"She asked. I told." I grabbed my cell phone off the table, "Alright guys. This has been a lot fun but I gotta do laundry at the hotel and get ready for bed."

"You gonna take the hotel shuttle back with us?" Brian asked, "It'll be here in about 20 minutes."

It was a brisk late afternoon and I wanted to enjoy it. I also wanted to walk back alone to take the edge off my buzz. And I had had enough of Lori. "I'm good. See you guys later." Walking away from the table I looked back, "Don't stay out too late."

Back at the hotel, I grabbed all my dirty laundry and headed down to the first floor laundry room. I'm always prepared to do laundry. When packing for a multiday trip I never forget laundry soap pods, dryer sheets, and enough quarters to finish two loads. During periods when I'm working multiple trips in a row, there's no way to get out of doing laundry. Because of my transcon commute, I always schedule myself back-to-back trips. After wrapping up my four day trip with Lori, I had a three day awaiting me.

The hotel laundry room was around the corner from the front desk lobby and I was disappointed to find that the washing machine was out of service. Not good. I left my bag of clothes on the washing machine and walked to the front desk to inquire about when the machine would be fixed. With no underwear and white t-shirts for the next day, I started to panic. When I turned the corner into the lobby I noticed my three coworkers standing at the front desk.

I had nowhere to hide. All three of their heads turned at the same time. Brian yelled out, "Joe! Come have a drink with us. Come on."

I started laughing as I walked up to them, "You guys are a mess. I have to do my laundry." Then I looked at the young woman working behind the counter, "The washing machine is broken and I need to do laundry."

"We know," she picked up the phone and started dialing, "The maintenance man is on his way now to fix it. Should be about 30 minutes, but I'll call him again."

"See Joe," Connor stated, "Come have a drink with us."

How could I turn that down? Especially with his big puppy dog eyes and the memories from our college humor rant at the bar. Being a sucker for a good looking straight guy, I surrendered, "Alright. Let me bring my clothes upstairs and I'll be right down."

The hotel bar at the end of the main front lobby made it easy to keep track of the maintenance man. Walking into the bar I noticed the three of them sitting at a round table in the corner. From the look of things, Brian and Connor were preparing Lori for the starring role in their pilot bukkake. That bitch. Another reason for me to hate her. My first instinct was to do a 180 and go back to my room, but just as the door closed behind me, Connor looked over, smiled, and kicked the stool across from him out so I could sit down. There was no way out of this now.

Mid conversation with Lori, Brian stopped talking and looked over at me, "I have a bar tab running. Go get yourself a drink."

Never one to turn down a free drink, I ordered a double gin and tonic and returned to their conversation. It was mostly about work, which is common when working flight crews hang out on layovers. We spend more time bitching about the airline industry than any other topic. It's boring. And the easiest way to ruin a double gin and tonic buzz. Needing to change the topic of discussion quickly, I decided to make the conversation about something I love to talk about: me and my flight attendant blog.

"What's it about?" Brian asked.

"Airline shit. And I like trying to make people laugh. I think I'm funny."

"You know who's funny? My boyfriend. He makes me laugh all the time," Lori added. Her eyes were glossed over. Somewhere between the downtown bar and the hotel bar she swapped out her glass of water for a mixed drink. Apparently, a strong one. Another drink like that and she'd land on her ass with a thud.

Was she really testing me? I released venom like a cobra, "Really? He didn't seem that funny when I met him." I ended my sentence and finished my drink in one final gulp.

As I placed my empty glass on the table, the front desk clerk pushed open the door and said, "The washing machine is fixed. It's all yours."

"Thank you. Alright guys, it's been real but I got shit to do. Don't drink too much." I stepped away from the table and pushed in the stool.

"Don't be a slam clicker, Joe. Come back and have one more." Connor insisted.

"You bitches don't give up," I said. Everyone laughed but Lori, "Okay, I'll be right back."

Keeping my promise I returned after starting my laundry and proceeded to enjoy a few more drinks. Two intensely strong gin and tonics to be exact. Connor picked up the tab on these drinks. When the timer went off alerting me my clothes were ready for the dryer, I excused myself but hurried back. Officially drunk and over the hump of holding anything back—I let Lori have it.

I started with her boyfriend, "I think your boyfriend's gay. Totally gay. He's gayer than me."

"He's not gay. Why would you say that?" Steam began to rise off her upper lip.

"Because he's gay. I bet he takes it up the ass."

She frowned and pushed her glass aside, "I really don't think you're being nice. Why are you saying that?"

I'd hit a nerve. "I'm only speaking the truth." I put one hand in the air, the other on my drink, and pursed my lips. That's my go-to gesture when destroying someone's happiness. It let's you know I stand by my statements. It's the exclamation mark at the end of my verbal assault. But I hadn't finished, not yet. While Lori's mind raced for a response I glanced at Connor who was thoroughly enjoying my attack on her. He ate it up like a bag of rainbow Skittles. That encouraged me to push on, "He probably wants you to strap on a dildo and tear his hole up. Have you torn up his hole?"

Brian and Connor were literally hunched over in hysterics. They could barely speak which added fire to my flame. When a group of people laugh at my jokes, I take it to the next level. A hint of comedic advice: always take it to the next level or you will lose the people around you. Nothing's worse than losing your momentum when telling inappropriate stories to strangers. Possibly getting called into the human resource manager's office might be worse, but if the jokes are great, who gives a fuck?

When my glass was empty, another one magically appeared thanks to Connor. He placed it on the table in front of me while I continued destroying Lori, "I can tell you wanna fuck. It's written all over your face. You probably want all three of us to gang bang you, right?"

"No. I definitely don't want that." Her pleasantries were officially over. She also stopped drinking. Who could blame her? I'd have left the party if I was on the receiving end of my commentary. But I did not care. I lost count of how many drinks I had and this was payback for lying to me at the beginning of the trip. And for introducing me to her gay boyfriend.

My barrage of inappropriate comments continued spewing across the table at her, "I think you do. I think you want to be spit roasted by these two pilots. One in the front and one in the back. Sound good?"

Lori shot daggers at me. Sharp ones. Fucking Miracle Blades. The same knife that allows you to cut a metal pipe, carve out a heart, and julienned it before devouring it. That knife. She was angry. Reporting me to human resources was well within her right. I expected one of her stipulations to ending my flight attendant career included a front row seat to witness management ripping the wings off my uniform and tossing them in the trash.

Without warning, Connor punched me full force in the left knee, "You're fucking hilarious, Joe. Holy shit. Dude! I haven't laughed this hard in a long time."

"Connor. If you punch me like that again I'll call human resources on your ass. I got them on speed dial."

Another round of laughter by everyone but Lori. At that point she was done. Completely over me. The only way she'd laugh at me now was if I slipped on the floor and busted out a few teeth. All four of us became quiet for a few moments while collecting our thoughts. An odd silence. Brian finished his beer and placed the glass down, "Well guys. It's six-thirty and we have an early show tomorrow. I think I'm done."

We all agreed in unison. It was time for me to go anyway. The alarm on my phone went off 20 minutes prior alerting me that my clothes were done. It was time to go to bed. My mouth had caused enough trouble for one layover. Brian and Connor closed out their tabs while I stood by the door next to Lori. She hated me and refused to speak to me. Who could blame her? I let it slide off my back.

Brian, Lori, and I headed through the front lobby towards the elevator while Connor took an immediate right outside the bar pushing through the glass doors leading out onto the patio. I had no time to worry about where he was going. Right before the three of us reached the elevator I said goodnight to them—Lori ignored me—and turned making my way down the hall. Following the tacky hotel carpet, I turned again positioning me about 10 feet from the laundry room doorway. Just before reaching the laundry room, a door opened at the end of the hallway and in walked Connor. An odd short cut but it appeared he was heading towards the stairs.

He failed to notice me so I yelled, "Stop loitering in the hall."

Turning to make eye contact, he proceeded to pull down his pants, present me his full moon, and then as quickly as it happened yank his shorts back up and disappear into the stairwell.

The shock of what happened stopped me in my tracks. If the maid had been vacuuming, my eyeballs would have been lost forever. My mind was in full spin cycle as I stepped into the laundry room. What straight guy moons a gay guy in a hotel hallway? Had this ever happened before? What was going on? Was I having a stroke? I grabbed the dryer and leaned forward taking a few deep breaths.

"It's most likely the alcohol." I said to myself while throwing my clean clothes into the bag and riding the elevator up to the third floor.

Entering my room I reiterated the words out loud, "It's just the alcohol." I felt better. And grateful it was in fact, not a stroke. Dumping my clothes out onto the bed, I began folding each item but as I stood there staring at my colorful Target underwear—his beautiful white ass kept popping up in my mind. Any attempt at shaking these thoughts from my head were useless.

Underwear. Ass. Socks. Ass. White t-shirt. White Ass.

What was I supposed to do? Was he sending me an invitation? How fucking stupid did I have to be to not pick up on it? He practically handed his ass over to me on a silver plate. A silver plate! I've never even had Thanksgiving dinner served to me on a silver plate. I felt the urge to fish for more information and find out his motives. While pacing back and forth in front of the bed I thought, "What would Evan do?" Knowing exactly what Evan would do I picked up my cell phone and shot Connor a text.

I was glad I had his number. My fingers shook as I typed: *"Yo. That was fun. I hate when the night has to end so early."*

Within seconds he replied: *"Yeah man. That was fun. You r fuckin hilarious."*

While folding clothes, I went back and forth from my socks to my cell phone. After a few minutes of normal guy banter, I decided to bring up sex. If there's one thing I know about straight dudes, they love talking about sex. Sports. Drinking. Tits. Fucking, That's about it. And usually in that order. I responded: *"Lori wants to fuck. She'd fuck both of you. You could totally fuck her tonight."*

Taking the bait he typed back: *"Lololol. I'd fuck her. I'm a whore."*

The conversation was beyond juicy: *"Then get you some. She wants it."*

He didn't respond. Not wanting the conversation to end, I came back with another comment. A point blank one. A 'get some dick before bed or go home' kinda text: *"You might not wanna moon a gay guy in the hall."*

A follow up quickly appeared: *"I don't know why I did that. If I was gay I'd be a top."*

Our conversation was beyond hot. I was sexting with a pilot and it wasn't even my birthday. I expected him to pass out within minutes leaving me to reread the text messages while jerking off. For some reason, I felt the desire to counter with: *"I'm not gonna go there about you being gay."*

Without skipping a beat, my cell phone vibrated delivering a message I never saw coming: *"Why? Do you wanna hook up or something?"* The response came quickly enough leaving me to believe he had already typed out the words waiting for the perfect time to hit send. He found it.

Dead. Did I just die? Maybe the roof collapsed and I was in my afterlife. An afterlife which included a hot straight pilot making the moves on me via text message. All this while folding laundry on a layover and with a number of alcoholic beverages. I'd hoped my afterlife excluded doing laundry for eternity but if it included pilot cock, I'd be happy.

Staring at my cell phone for a few seconds seemed reasonable. More like a few minutes because words had escaped me. How was I supposed to respond? Honestly, the smart thing would have been to put my cell phone down, shut off my light, and go to bed. But I am a human being and human beings make stupid mistakes.

Or in this case, a smart mistake that checks off the pilot box on my cock-sucking resume: *"Sure. I'll suck your dick."* Simple and easy. As if I was asking him to get me a cup of coffee.

"Dude I'm fuckin nervous. I've never done this before,"

I replied with sweaty hands: *"We aren't getting married. If you want your dick sucked just let me know."*

A few minutes went by before he answered: *"I have to make a call and then I will get back to you. Hang tight."*

I became quite nervous. What the fuck was I thinking? My heart thrashed around inside my chest ready to burst out of me like the creature from *Alien*. If Connor was nervous about this being his first time with a guy, I was equally nervous for allowing it to go this far. At any moment I could have texted him back and stopped this entire conversation but the excitement had me second guessing my moral judgement. Moral judgement? What's that? Those two words buzzed around my head the entire hour I hadn't heard back from him.

Have you heard of the ventromedial prefrontal cortex? No? Neither did I until researching it for this book. The ventromedial prefrontal cortex is a portion of our frontal lobe. It is the section of the brain that assists us in making moral decisions, even when we know right from wrong—like being faced with the moral dilemma of sucking a straight pilot's dick or aborting the mission before suck off. Such a difficult predicament, and one I was left on my own to solve. It seemed that the entire frontal lobe portion of my brain was inoperative. Broken or missing, I couldn't tell, but impossible to fix on such short notice. It must have snuck out for a late night stroll and got jumped in some dark alley in Detroit. I'd be sure to slap flyers alongside the highway on the way to the airport.

They'd read something like:

> Dear Citizens of Detroit,
>
> I've completely lost my fucking mind. And my morals! If you find a lonely moral compass in the gutter, please return it to the lost and found department in baggage claim at the airport.
>
> Sincerely,
> Flight Attendant Joe

But now that I think about, maybe it abandoned me that night in 1998 when I was sucking dick for Jesus while tucked away inside a McDonald's stock room. Holy shit! What if I never had morals to begin with? Was that possible? It couldn't be. I'm a good person. I've never robbed a bank, murdered someone for their wallet, or pushed an old lady down to get to the front line. There had to be another explanation. Maybe my frontal lobe battery had simply died and needed to be recharged? A good night sleep would fix that up. Right?

Around 8p.m., I concluded Connor either fell asleep or came to his senses. At least one of our frontal lobes worked. I shut off the lights and crawled into bed. Flipping through the television channels, I realized it was for the best. Sucking pilot dick on a layover was a really bad idea. A really, *really* bad idea. I promised myself after the hospital suckathon that I'd never allow myself to become dickmatized at work again. Especially while being a flight attendant. Who did I think I was? A twenty-something female with big tits and no brains? Not me. My moral compass simply pointed south towards one of their crotches.

When my cell phone vibrated I almost shit the bed. I picked it up so fast it wobbled around in my hand and fell to the floor. It was a text from Evan: *"Hey quizeeeeen. You up?"*

I ended the conversation quickly telling him it was late and I had an early report. I placed the cell phone back on the bedside table when it vibrated again. Figuring it was Evan, I waited a moment before checking the message.

Connor came through loud and clear: *"You still up for it? What r u doing?"*

What was I supposed to do? I could play it off like I had fallen asleep. The right thing to do was easy enough but that's not what I did. My brain screamed, *"Do the stupid thing. Do it!"* That's what happens when your frontal lobe is all fucked up. Judge as you'd like, but we have all made stupid decisions; thought with our sexual mind instead of our rational mind. I answered: *"I'm up. Watching tv."*

"I'm scared. What if this opens Pandora's Box?"

That should have been my cue to evacuate the airplane. Abandon ship. Sadly, I hung on for dear life. If he was questioning his sexuality, did I really want to be the one helping him out? And by out, I meant of the closet. A huge benefit of being a flight attendant was having fun on layovers, not ruining lives. Was all this happening for a reason? What if he was gay? Would his fiancé rather know he was gay now or after they were married? Was I actually helping her out by offering up my services? Yes, of course. My moral compass was back. Resting awhile must have restarted it. As a firm believer in things happening for a reason, it became clear my task was to help him out of the closet or to realize he was straight. Either way, dick was involved.

However it went, I was helping. Doing a good deed. Giving back to the community. It's amazing how we can trick ourselves into believing our bad decisions are for the betterment of others. After the last sliver of my morality faded, I continued with the conversation: *"We aren't getting married. I'm sucking your dick. Don't be dramatic."*

"Lol. u always hit on your pilots like this?"

What the what? If memory served me right, he was the one who brought up the topic of hooking up. And the fucker mooned me in the hallway. Total pilot move. Blame everyone else. Was that how the story would go down in the history books? All my fault? Hell no. Saving the text messages to prove my innocence was imperative. Did I say innocent? Alright, I was far from innocent, but this was a joint venture, not a solo job.

And just to set the record straight, those scandalous text messages were deleted years ago.

I started getting annoyed: *"Listen man, you brought it up. You coming over?"*

"I don't know. All this sounds really hot. I've just never done this before."

His indecisiveness dragged on longer than a stuttering flight attendant trying to read the safety demonstration. This back and forth dick sucking ping pong talk had become exhausting. He either wanted it or he didn't. Calling him made perfect sense but that seemed too real. Conversing via text message kept our entire conversation in a fantasy haze. We continued texting: *"It's up to you. Let me know."*

"Should I come there or you come here?"

There's nothing worse than an unsure pilot: *"Come to 304."*

He responded one final time, *"On my way."*

I flung myself out of bed and turned on one of the lamps. Skipping around the room like a prom date about to lose her virginity, I ran over to the door and propped it open with the safety latch so he could walk right in. No need knocking. Alerting any flight crews of our soon-to-be devious act was unthinkable, but more for him than me. Can you imagine having to sit in the flight deck somewhere over Lake Erie trying to explain to your captain why you were sneaking into a male flight attendant's hotel room? We'd surely be found hours later at the bottom of the lake. My heart raced like a fat guy waiting for Five Guys. And I only had one hot guy coming over. If he was nervous about opening Pandora's Box, I was wrecked about opening Joe's Mouth. It took him about three minutes to rush down the hallway and enter my room.

"Hey." He closed the door making a beeline towards the bed.

I shut off the lamp allowing the television to shine throughout the room. "You want me to turn off the tv?"

"No. It's cool." He sat on the bed and looked around the room.

He looked gorgeous. Much sexier than when we hung out at the bar. Sporting a white tank top, basketball shorts, and wire-rimmed glasses he almost had me melting into the carpet. The poor housekeeper. What a mess that would be to clean up.

"You want to watch porn? I have my laptop," I had no clue what to say, "I can find you some straight porn to watch. Do you need it?" Interacting with him reminded me of how frightened I was the first time I placed a penis in my mouth. All my experiences and I still found myself shaking in my boxers. Why was I not cooler about this scenario? I should have been. As cool as the cucumber I was about to meet. We sat in silence for a few seconds. My mind raced. What do you offer a straight pilot besides the blow job? Vodka? A *Hustler* magazine? First class meal? I had leftover chicken salad in my small refrigerator but that was my lunch the next day. Completely off limits. I'll suck your dick, but I won't starve myself. I have limitations.

"I don't need porn. I'm good."

I moved over to the bed. "Can you believe this? I can't believe you're gonna let me suck your dick."

"Please stop talking before you freak me out."

"Sure. Sorry." Oops. Leave it to me to scare off the straight dick before it made an appearance. Connor laid down the number one rule, stop talking and start sucking. Now, I may be rusty on my Catholicism but I do believe that's the commandment that comes right before, "Thou shalt not commit adultery." Those weren't his exact words but I read between the lines. A bunch of uncomfortable lines. The entire situation was fucking awkward. I felt awkward, and he had to feel equally awkward. That's what I thought until he leaned back against the pillows and I noticed he wasn't feeling awkward at all. He was hot! And harder than lava rock.

"Can I touch you here?" I asked before rubbing his inner thigh.

"Yeah. Do what you want." He lifted his shirt to show off his slightly hairy chest. His body was perfect. I gazed upon him like a pilot God sent directly to me from Crew Scheduling. "But I want to warn you. I'm not gay so I probably won't cum. Don't be offended."

I stared at him with my hands up his basketball shorts. Was that a dare? A dare to make sure he got off? Challenge accepted. I promised myself the only thing coming between me and his unborn babies was my airport report time. Limitation number two, I refuse to be late for dick.

How do you even call Crew Scheduling for that? I imagine something like, "Hi. This is Joe. Listen, I'm running late. I got this massive dick in front of me that I'm trying to suck and things aren't going so well. In fact, things are backed up worse than runway 13R at JFK during rush hour. If you could just delay the flight until I get there, I'd appreciate it. Oh yeah, before I forget, the first officer will be late too. Thanks."

When I finally completed the daunting task of Connor's fellatio—and trust me, it was more strenuous than a Jillian Michaels kettlebell workout—he looked down at me, "Thanks. At least I'm not gay."

I wiped my chin, "That's all you've got to say? Was it at least good?"

"Yeah. It was good," he pulled his shirt down, "but I had to think of my fiancé the entire time."

Did I have the right to be insulted? Even if I didn't, I was. Here I still had my finger on the trigger of his joystick and he felt the need to inform me he thought of his fiancé the entire time. I moved from between his legs so he could stand and pull his basketball shorts up. We didn't talk as I walked him to the door and opened it up.

"You aren't going to act all weird tomorrow, are you?" I asked standing to the side to let him out.

He smiled, "No worries, Joe, I'm a professional." And with that he was gone. I closed the door, brushed my teeth, and went to bed. I relieved the pressure built up in my groin. I really had to, there was no way out of it. My balls were cobalt blue.

After shutting off the television I recapped the entire night in my head. When the fantasy finished playing out, I'd rewind and hit play. I'd be lucky to get one hour of sleep that night. From the moment he casually gave me his cell phone number at the gate in JFK to me locking the door behind him, I deduced this operation was planned. What else could it have been? The entire situation played out like a scripted airline porn. A pretty fucking hot one if you ask me. Drifting off to sleep I had one final thought... Connor either lied about never having his dick sucked by a guy before or he simply used me to figure out his own sexuality.

Whatever the case, I wasn't angry. I helped him out and I helped his fiancé out. My good deed was complete.

The next morning all four of us met in the hotel lobby to catch our van to the airport. Connor avoided me like I was wearing a t-shirt that read: Guess Who I Sucked Off Last Night? When I greeted him he nodded walking passed me like a stranger.

Professional my hot fucking mouth!

The van ride was controlled by Lori and Brian. It was still early so Connor and I were able to disappear into the leather seats unnoticed. It worked out well because we were both obviously exhausted and not in a social mood. Plus, he sat in his seat stiffer than his cock from the night before. We might as well have had the word GUILTY tattooed across our faces. Even the van driver picked up on it. Truthfully, I don't know if he did, but that's what feeling guilty does to you. Makes you think everyone knows the horrific things you have done when in reality nobody does. Except for the guilty party, which in this case, included me and Mr. Stiffypants.

We had two easy flights that day but when we got to Jacksonville, Lori called in sick for back pain. That's the excuse she gave me but I'm thinking it was to report me to management for verbally attacking her at the hotel bar the night before. Let's face it, I said some inappropriate shit. I deserved to get reported and probably terminated. My blame fell on the gin and tonics but that took me only so far. As Brian, Connor, and I waited for a replacement flight attendant, I decided to simply enjoy my last few days as a flight attendant. At least I got to check off the pilot dick-sucking box. Always think positively.

After the new flight attendant arrived, we boarded and took off for Indianapolis. We were on day three of four and still had one more overnight in Indianapolis. During our flight, the pilots needed a lavatory break. I let the other flight attendant go into the flight deck while I stood guard at the galley. Brian came out first and then after returning to the flight deck, Connor came out. After he used the lavatory he spent a few minutes stretching in the front galley. I figured that was my time to strike up a conversation hoping he meant what he said about being professional, "How you feeling? You doing alright?"

"Yeah. I'm good. I've got a sore throat. Started the other day."

A sore throat? I couldn't believe it. He was sick and let me suck his dick? Was he kidding me? Everyone knows the penis is a spigot of germs. How dare he? I looked at him and made a disgusting face, "Oh great. Now you tell me you're sick. Lovely."

He smirked and disappeared back into the flight deck. We barely spoke for the rest of the trip. And I was fine with it. When we finally landed in Cleveland on our last day he picked up the interphone and called the back galley,

"Hey, Joe. It was great flying with you. You are a funny guy."

"Thanks. You too."

We never spoke again. And in case you were wondering—because I know you are—nothing like that has ever happened again on a layover.

When I got to Evan's apartment that night I briefed him on my entire trip. The good. The bad. The ugly. The blowjob. Actually, I left the blowjob out. I'd wait for the perfect time to recant that story. Once we were deep into our second bottle of red wine I coolly added, "Guess what else happened on the trip?"

"What?" Evan answered sipping on his glass of wine while tapping something into his cell phone.

"I blew the first officer in Detroit the other night."

He gay gasped loud enough to pull the paint of the walls, "You did WHAT?"

I went into full storytelling mode and left out no detail. Evan is no stranger to my stories and this was a fresh new juicy one that kept him on the edge of his seat. When I finished, I took a sip of wine and waited for his reaction.

"Oh my god! I'm totally jealous. That shit never happens to me," he chugged his glass of wine, "You have the best stories."

I finished the last of my wine, grabbed his glass, and stood up from the sofa to go refill them in the kitchen, "I know, right? Maybe one day I'll write a book."

The End

Acknowledgements

There are so many people I need to thank for making this book a reality. I'm sure I will forget a few so let me just go on record and say THANK YOU to the entire planet. That pretty much covers it.

First off, I'd like to thank Jesus. I'm kidding. Did you really think I was being serious?

To my amazing husband Matt, thank you for reading and giving me constructive feedback on my book. You are my rock. You drive me absolutely crazy sometimes but I love you from here all the way to that Bibimbap restaurant on the corner. You have supported my desire to be creative throughout our entire marriage. Well, except for that time I wanted to start a concierge business in Orlando. Good call on that one.

To my brother from another mother, Mike. Even though you didn't make an appearance in this book, I promise we will have an entire chapter together in my second book. Actually, this acknowledgement is your official appearance in my book so I guess I'm off the hook. That was easy. Don't hold any of this against me when you write my biography after I'm dead.

I couldn't write an acknowledgment without a shout out to my Trick Daddy. Meeting you—and nicknaming you—has been one of the highlights of my flight attendant career. I appreciate the patience you've shown while attempting to explain how airplanes work. I still don't get it. Remember that time I asked you to read a portion of the book on a deadhead flight? You laughed and told me I was ridiculous. Now, let's hope that ridiculousness makes me enough money to buy you a boat.

David, you have been here with me since the beginning of my flight attendant career. The crash pad. The highs. The lows. The laughs. The drunken escapades. The memories we share from our travels have inspired me in so many ways. I can never repay you. And thanks for never leaving my ass behind in a foreign country.

Adam, you are hands down my favorite captain of all time. Let me go on record and state to the entire Earth population that you are not the pilot in that last chapter. I'm not saying I wouldn't, but frankly, your wife scares the fuck out of me. Thank you for your Instagram support, all the airplane pictures you've sent me for my blog posts, and for our daily inappropriate conversations. Those conversations have inspired me to be even more over the top.

My manager, Garon. When I was 100% sure I knew the path I wanted to take you'd come along and redirect traffic. My book and I needed that. Let's hope we sell the shit out of this crap so you don't fire me.

Russ & Sharon for loving me like their own son. That's one of the greatest gifts I've ever received. Remember the first time we met at the barbecue place in Orlando? I bet you didn't expect me to stick around this long.

The hottest, most sensual, perky-boobed, comic on the planet. I am not talking about myself, I am talking to you Laura Jean. From the moment I met you in that dark nasty flight attendant crew lounge, I have questioned my homosexuality. I'd literally throw myself on the bisexual fence for you. If I was on stage, all I'd need is you in the

JOE THOMAS

audience. That's the type of balcony person you have become, but you'd still have to pay for a ticket—Daddy's got bills.

Tyson, my book might have sunk faster than the Titanic if you didn't pull me aside and tell me to rethink my title.

To Irene for not aborting me.

Tim P. for providing me the internal imagery for my book cover. That's all it took for you to be in my book. That and all the amazing cat cards you mail me.

Ryan Lopez for bringing my book cover vision to life. It is amazing! I am so glad your sister's, husband's, brother's, boyfriend saw my ad on Instagram.

To Robby for always making me laugh and helping me out with airplane lingo when I needed it.

Ryan, thank you for responding to my late night JFK questions via Facebook and for that one time you parked my arriving airplane at the gate closest to the Starbucks. That's impressive!

Sara, thank you for reading an advance copy of the book, giving me your feedback, and not deleting me off Facebook. Actually, let me check. Be right back. Okay, we are still good.

To Renee, you literally saved my book from looking like a 5th grader wrote it. Hopefully I have learned something about commas. I doubt it. That's why I have you. Editor extraordinaire. (Side note: she edited this acknowledgement and I had a comma error. *FUCK!*)

To Madonna Ciccone for being my one and only deity since I was 11 years old. I'm expressing myself because of you.

To comedians like Kathy Griffin, Joan Rivers, Chelsea Handler, Kristen Wiig, Louis CK, Chris Rock, Sarah Silverman, Tina Fey, Amy Poehler, and countless others— thank you for not giving a fuck, allowing people like me the strength to say whatever the hell we want.

Last, but certainly not least, to all the characters in this book who I have interacted with throughout the years. I appreciate you all. All of you. Seriously. The good, the bad, the people I hated then, and the people I still hate now.

About This
So Called Author

Joe Thomas is a flight attendant and the creator of the barely successful blog *Flight Attendant Joe*. He resides in the San Francisco Bay Area with his husband Matt and his two amazing and loving cats, Tucker and Harvey.

Made in the USA
San Bernardino, CA
07 November 2017